3. 7. 07

# The Origins of Co

To Jeremy

# The Origins of Complex Language

*An Inquiry into the Evolutionary Beginnings of Sentences, Syllables, and Truth*

ANDREW CARSTAIRS-McCARTHY

OXFORD
UNIVERSITY PRESS

*This book has been printed digitally and produced in a standard specification*
*in order to ensure its continuing availability*

# OXFORD
UNIVERSITY PRESS

Great Clarendon Street, Oxford OX2 6DP

Oxford University Press is a department of the University of Oxford.
It furthers the University's objective of excellence in research, scholarship,
and education by publishing worldwide in

Oxford New York

Auckland Cape Town Dar es Salaam Hong Kong Karachi
Kuala Lumpur Madrid Melbourne Mexico City Nairobi
New Delhi Shanghai Taipei Toronto
With offices in
Argentina Austria Brazil Chile Czech Republic France Greece
Guatemala Hungary Italy Japan South Korea Poland Portugal
Singapore Switzerland Thailand Turkey Ukraine Vietnam

Oxford is a registered trade mark of Oxford University Press
in the UK and in certain other countries

Published in the United States
by Oxford University Press Inc., New York

ISBN 978-0-19-823821-8

# Preface

Until the early 1990s, my work in linguistics centred mainly on the theory of inflectional morphology. This is a somewhat esoteric area within what, to many outsiders, seems a rather esoteric discipline. It may seem a far cry from there to the origin of language – a topic which is the reverse of esoteric, in that every thinking person has surely at one time or another speculated about how humans acquired a characteristic that differentiates us so spectacularly from all other animals. Yet there is a link between my research in these two areas.

Spoken language involves a partnership between sound and meaning. In most people's eyes, however, it is not an equal partnership. Meaning is the senior partner, we tend to feel, in that spoken words exist in order to express meanings. Yet my work on inflectional morphology led me to wonder whether, in some real sense, things may be the other way round: meanings exist in order to provide something for spoken words to express. Stated so baldly and crudely, this idea sounds bizarre, even ludicrous. Yet the more I thought about it and explored its implications, the more it seemed to me that this idea leads us to a satisfying picture of how and why humans have acquired the kind of language that we have. This book is the outcome of that exploration.

A second impetus for my work on language evolution dates from further back: my undergraduate training in philosophy. It often seemed to me then that philosophical discussion of language could profit from a more serious effort to disentangle those aspects of language that are somehow essential (and therefore of interest to the philosopher) from those that are accidental or parochial (and therefore presumably do not deserve philosophical attention). Serious thought about language evolution requires that one consider alternative directions in which language might conceivably have evolved. Thinking about such alternatives led me to the startling conclusion that even so apparently fundamental a distinction as that between sentences and noun phrases is not essential but accidental. This, in turn, rekindled my undergraduate unease about many philosophers' linguistic assumptions. The overlap which thus developed between my recent linguistic concerns and my earlier philosophical ones has helped to make the writing of this book particularly satisfying.

The book would not have been written without help from many quarters. Colleagues in the Cognitive Science Discussion Group at the University of Canterbury allowed me to air ideas on various occasions over several years, and I am grateful for their comments, particularly those of Jack Copeland, Kate Kearns, and Diane Proudfoot. The New Zealand Government's Marsden Fund gave me a grant that enabled me to attend the International Conference on the Evolution of Language in Edinburgh in 1996; I am grateful to Jim Hurford and the other organizers of that conference for allowing me to speak there. The Marsden grant also enabled me to visit Leslie Aiello and her colleagues in the Department of Anthropology at University College London for a month in 1996. They encouraged me to think that my ideas were compatible with the anthropological evidence on human evolution – which is not to say that they necessarily agree with anything I say. Apart from Leslie, I would like to thank the following people, at UCL and elsewhere, whom I talked to during that visit: Michael Ashby, Richard Hudson, Rita Manzini, Geoffrey Miller, Alan Montefiore, Camilla Power, Simon Strickland, Volker Sommer, Elizabeth Whitcombe, and Deirdre Wilson.

For discussion, criticism, or advice at various times I would like to thank Bill Abler, David Armstrong, Mark Aronoff, Elizabeth Bates, Derek Bickerton, Robert Bull, Catherine Callaghan, Lyle Campbell, Iain Davidson, Daniel Dennett, Evguenia Dovbysh, Michael Dukes, Myrna Gopnik, Jim Hurford, Ray Jackendoff, Robert Jackson, Bill Labov, Peter MacNeilage, Gary Marcus, David Nash, Daniel Nettle, Fritz Newmeyer, Johanna Nichols, Steve Pinker, Geoffrey Sampson, Andy Spencer, Stephen Stich, Peter Strawson, John Taylor, Peter Trudgill, Bruce Waldman, and Robert Worden. I would also like to thank the people who responded to a query that I posted on the Linguist List about sign language: Franz Dotter, Nancy Frishberg, Clare Galloway, Dawn MacLaughlin, Carol Neidle, Des Power, and Bencie Woll.

John Davey, my editor at OUP, has been a tremendous source of advice and encouragement. I would also like to thank Michael Studdert-Kennedy and two other anonymous referees who supplied detailed comments on the whole manuscript.

None of these people is responsible for my mistakes, or should be assumed to share my opinions.

I would like to express my appreciation to the staff of the University of Canterbury Library. Nearly everything I needed that was not in the Library was supplied promptly through interloan. Without their efficiency, writing a book with such an interdisciplinary scope as this would have been far harder.

Finally, I would like to express my thanks to my partner, Jeremy. Without his constant support and enthusiasm, this long project would have taken even longer.

A. C.-M.

*July 1998*

# Contents

# List of Figures and Tables

## Figures

## Tables

# Abbreviations

ASL     American Sign Language
BSL     British Sign Language
CS      conceptual structure
EIC     Early Immediate Constituents
MRI     magnetic resonance imaging
NP      noun phrase
PET     positron emission tomography
POT     parieto-occipito-temporal junction
SRS     secondary representational system
UG      Universal Grammar

# 1 Introduction

## 1.1. The Puzzle: What was Rudimentary Language Like?

It is not hard to imagine the world before human language existed. All we need to do is visualize the world as it is, but with human beings and all their works expunged. For the sake of verisimilitude, we may include in the picture a selection of animals that became extinct only after humans had arrived, such as mammoths, sabre-tooths, and dodos. We may also tentatively include some of our hominid ancestors themselves,[1] walking upright but still ape-like and still, *ex hypothesi*, languageless: that is, vocalizing in roughly the way that chimpanzees or gibbons do, perhaps, but not producing utterances composed of words. It is also not hard to leap forward mentally two million years or so from then and visualize a world soon after the appearance of people speaking an unequivocally modern sort of language. The people we conjure up will probably be cave-dwelling hunters and gatherers, but also sophisticated creative artists of the kind who produced the famous cave paintings at Lascaux and elsewhere in southern France more than 25,000 years ago.

More of a puzzle, however, is visualizing what people were like at a period about halfway between those two points. What was it like to have more language than modern apes, but still not as much as modern humans? Which aspects of language came early and which came late? For example, did those ancestors at the halfway point already have something like modern grammar and syntax while their vocal apparatus was still unable to produce the whole range of modern speech sounds, or did things happen the other way round? And what about the size of their vocabulary? This intermediate period in human evolution has a special fascination just because it is so difficult to picture. There is something eerie in imagining creatures (our own ancestors, in fact) who were like us in that

---

[1] I use the term 'hominid' to mean any primate of the genus *Australopithecus* or the genus *Homo*. Some primatologists and anthropologists now use 'hominid' to include primates of the genus *Pan* (i.e. chimpanzees), distinguishing the non-chimpanzee hominids as 'hominines'. I retain the older usage simply because it is better established. No theoretical claim is intended.

they could use words to talk to each other, yet unlike us in that their mode of talk was somehow rudimentary or embryonic. But what evidence could we possibly find to show how language evolved?

This last question underlies the reluctance of most modern linguists to concern themselves at all with language evolution. Speculations about language origin seem to be just that—speculations, with no prospect of being either confirmed or falsified. Various language-origin theories of the eighteenth and nineteenth centuries are remembered because of their quaint nicknames, such as the 'bow-wow', 'ding-dong', and 'yo-he-ho' theories (Barber 1972); but they are remembered only to be dismissed with amused condescension. Most modern linguists believe that the Linguistic Society of Paris was sensible in 1866 to ban all papers on this supposedly intractable topic.

The Paris decision may have been sensible at a time when there was no immediate prospect of discovering relevant empirical evidence. But it has never inhibited anthropologists, psychologists, and neurologists from thinking and writing about language evolution. Increasingly, some linguists too are coming to see this topic as once again researchable; and the fact of my writing this book shows that I agree with them.

## 1.2.    The Importance of the 'Outsider's' Perspective

The proposal about language evolution that I will put forward in this book is novel in two respects. First, it draws on evidence from two areas which at first sight have little to do with each other—namely, the physiology of the vocal tract and the process of vocabulary acquisition in early childhood. Secondly, its persuasiveness will depend largely on the reader becoming convinced that certain aspects of contemporary human language that may at first sight seem natural or inevitable are in fact quite odd, and demand explanation.

I do not offer my proposal as a complete account of every aspect of language evolution. Rather, it is intended as an explanation for some aspects of language that other evolutionary accounts leave unexplained or else try to explain in ways that I find unconvincing. When discussing other accounts in Chapters 4 and 6, I will thus not be trying to supply an encyclopaedic summary of contemporary views, but will rather be focusing on whether or not they render my proposal superfluous by explaining the same facts better. My conclusion will be that none of them does. Some of these accounts conflict with mine, and I will suggest reasons why mine is better or at least no worse. Others are independent of or complementary to mine, dealing with distinct aspects of language evolution.

The second novelty that I claim for my approach calls for more comment straightaway. All researchers on human language up to now and into the foreseeable future have a characteristic in common: they are native speakers of some human language. That is so obvious that the reader may wonder what could be the point of mentioning it. The point is that our position with respect to human language is in an important respect different from that of an animal ethologist with respect to birdsong or primate communication, and different too from the position with respect to human language of a hypothetical linguist from Mars. This special position has advantages but also disadvantages. One advantage is that we enjoy a kind of knowledge from our own experience that is denied to the animal ethologist or the Martian. One disadvantage, however, is that our intimate familiarity with our subject matter may blind us to what is strange about it. A central theme of this book will be that one characteristic of human language that deserves to be considered strange is the universality of the syntactic distinction between sentences and noun phrases (NPs);[2] and I will claim as a merit of my perspective the fact that it supplies a reason for it. The structure of the argument with regard to the sentence/NP distinction is thus rather unusual. In most areas of science the fact that some phenomenon needs explaining is agreed among researchers in the field concerned, although they may disagree over which of several possible explanations is best. But my argument concerning the sentence/NP distinction must start one stage further back: I must persuade the reader that it really does need explaining before offering my own explanation.

As to whether this argument succeeds, readers will judge for themselves. But in making this judgement readers must guard against being seduced into thinking that things have to be the way they are (for example, that human languages must inevitably distinguish sentences from NPs) just because the way things are is so familiar. Avoiding that seduction is tricky but not impossible, requiring a certain exercise of the imagination in order to visualize alternative directions in which language evolution might plausibly have travelled. This is rather like the imagination that a chief executive needs to exercise when thinking about alternatives to her company's current operating procedures. Of course, what many chief executives would do is seek outside advice (for example, calling in management consultants), for the sensible reason that an outsider can often see possible alternatives more clearly than an insider can. In the case of human language, the operating procedures concerned are grammatical patterns; but there is no outsider to whom we can turn for advice, because there is as yet no linguist (from Mars, for example) who is not a native speaker of a human language. Yet an imaginative chief executive can still rethink company procedures even though for some reason no outside consultant is available. Similarly, we can still think about alternative directions in which language might have evolved even though there are

[2] I will follow the standard practice of syntacticians and will make frequent use of 'NP' as an abbreviation for 'noun phrase' in future. What I call 'NPs' are strictly 'determiner phrases' in the sense of Abney (1987); but, in common with many linguists, I will continue to use 'noun phrase' (abbreviated 'NP') in its traditional sense.

no Martian linguists to advise us. It is just a matter of not mistaking the familiar for the inevitable.

The kind of thinking that I am encouraging readers to do in respect of language evolution has a parallel in a kind of thinking that is now commonplace in respect of syntactic structure but that was radically new when Chomsky began to urge its adoption forty years ago. Many of those features of any language that shed most light on the human language capacity, he claimed, are ignored in pedagogical or descriptive grammar books precisely because they belong to all languages (Chomsky 1965). For example, no English grammar book for schools or for non-English-speakers spends time explaining why the interrogative sentence corresponding to the declarative (1) is not (2) but (3):[3]

(1)   The people who are leaving tomorrow will say goodbye tonight.
(2)   *Are the people who leaving tomorrow will say goodbye tonight?
(3)   Will the people who are leaving tomorrow say goodbye tonight?

In accordance with a standard linguists' convention, the asterisk at the start of (2) indicates that it is not a well-formed sentence. Indeed, (2) is so un-English that it requires practice even to read it with fluent natural-sounding intonation. It does not resemble any sort of mistake typically made either by young children or by adults learning English. Yet it conforms exactly to a generalization about declarative–interrogative pairs that one might formulate as (4), apparently well supported by many sentence-pairs such as (5) and (6):

(4)        In an interrogative sentence, the first auxiliary verbform (i.e. form of *be, have, will, can,* etc.) of the corresponding declarative sentence is moved to the front.
(5)   (*a*)   The people are leaving tomorrow.
       (*b*)   Are the people leaving tomorrow?
(6)   (*a*)   The people will say goodbye tonight.
       (*b*)   Will the people say goodbye tonight?

What is wrong with (4), then, as a description of the English declarative–interrogative pattern? The answer is that it is formulated purely in terms of the linear order of words, not the syntactic grouping of words into phrases. In (5) and (6) the word-string *the people* immediately before the first auxiliary verbform (*are, will*) constitutes a complete NP. In (1), however, the string *the people* is not a complete NP; rather, it is part of the NP *the people who are leaving tomorrow*, which also contains the relative clause *who are leaving tomorrow*. A better formulation of the relevant English syntactic pattern, one that correctly predicts that (3) rather than (2) is the interrogative corresponding to (1), is therefore (7):

---

[3]   By 'interrogatives' here I mean only so-called yes/no interrogatives, answerable by *yes* or *no*, not 'WH-interrogatives' containing words such as *who, which, when.*

(7)   In an interrogative sentence, the first auxiliary verbform in the main verb phrase of the corresponding declarative sentence is moved to precede the subject NP.

This formulation is still not 'correct' from the point of view of current mainstream syntactic theory. But it is adequate for our purposes. Above all, it is an improvement on (4) in that it makes it clear that the placement of the auxiliary is **structure-dependent**—that is, it pays attention to the structure of the sentence in terms of its phrasal and clausal constituents, not just to the linear sequence of words. The reason why sentences like (2) are ignored in grammar books, according to Chomsky, is that grammar books ignore features that all languages have in common; and structure-dependence, which (2) violates, is one of those features.

All this will be very familiar to contemporary linguists. But it is relevant to my perspective on language evolution in that it illustrates just the same kind of exercise of imagination as I am urging. In order to establish a point about how language is, Chomsky invited us to imagine a kind of pseudo-English, illustrated by (2), in which a fundamental feature of human language syntax—namely, structure-dependence—does not obtain. Similarly, I will be inviting readers to imagine kinds of language with characteristics fundamentally different from actual modern human language, in order to raise the question why language has evolved the way it has in certain respects.

When Chomsky originally advanced this kind of argument, it had an air of paradox. How odd, it seemed, that characteristics of English (or of any language) which are especially revealing of what all languages share syntactically should be characteristics which no one had drawn attention to before, much less discussed! But this air of paradox has now dissipated, as linguists generally (even ones who disagree with Chomsky on many aspects of the human language faculty) have come to acknowledge how illuminating this approach can be in constructing a theory of language. Likewise, I suggest, any feeling that it is quixotic or pointless to imagine alternative paths for language evolution—even radically alternative paths, involving the most fundamental differences between language-as-it-is and language-as-it-might-have-been—is out of place. Whether this kind of inquiry is profitable or not must be judged by its results. To rule it out in advance as self-evidently fruitless would be to make the mistake of the chief executive who, lacking outside advice, cannot imagine any alternatives to the way in which her company is actually run.

The main obstacle to imagining alternative paths of language evolution can be summed up as anthropocentrism. Being human ourselves, we are tempted to regard the human species as special, set apart from all other animal species, even if we do not believe this consciously. Connected with this prejudice is a temptation to see modern human language as something waiting to be 'discovered' or 'reached' at a certain stage in human evolution, rather like the source of the Nile or the summit of Mount Everest, with all its fundamental characteristics somehow fixed in advance. So central is language to humanness that to say that language could have evolved differently seems tantamount to saying that we humans need not have evolved; rather, a hominid species in many ways like us yet discernibly different might be here instead. This idea naturally makes us uncomfortable. If pressed, we will surely acknowledge that our discomfort is no evidence that the idea is wrong. Even so, one factor encouraging the blinkered view that the way language is is the only way it could conceivably be may be a reluctance to contemplate the possibility of our own non-existence.

## 1.3. Plan of the Book

I approach the subject from a linguistic background, but I presuppose no knowledge of linguistics beyond elementary grammar. Even someone with no more than a vague recollection of what nouns and verbs are should find it possible to follow my argument, with goodwill and a reasonable amount of effort. I have thus tried to make the book accessible to anybody who wants to think seriously about how language may have evolved. Likewise, when presenting evidence from other disciplines, I have tried to do so in such a way as to be comprehensible to the non-expert. This means that some readers are bound from time to time to find my presentation more elementary than they need. I ask readers to bear with me in this. I also hope that in non-linguistic areas I do not misrepresent or distort the facts too grossly, and that any mistakes I make will provoke experts in the relevant fields to do better.

The core of the argument is presented in Chapters 2 and 5. In Chapter 2 I describe those aspects of language whose origin I hope to shed light on, and in Chapter 5 I offer an evolutionary scenario to account for their development. It is in these chapters that most of the specifically linguistic discussion is concentrated. Readers from non-linguistic backgrounds, such as anthropology, primatology, or neurobiology, may find it helpful to look quickly through Chapter 6 before tackling Chapter 2, in order to get some idea of how my approach is situated with respect to recent contributions from those disciplines.

Chapter 3, on philosophical implications, is not essential to the main argument. Nevertheless I urge all readers, not just philosophically inclined ones, to read it. If I am right, it provides a remarkable illustration of how an apparently fundamental aspect of the relationship between language and the world, an aspect that is generally assumed to have a solid basis independent of grammar, may turn out on close examination to lack any such basis. This renders answers to the questions raised in Chapter 2 all the more pressing. In effect, I suggest in Chapter 3 that philosophers as well as language-origin researchers would benefit from adopting the perspective of the linguistic outsider and taking seriously the implications of the possibility that grammar might have been fundamentally different from how it is.

Throughout the book, most of the notes fulfil one of two opposed functions. Some are for the benefit of readers already well versed in the immediate topic, and comment on how my argument relates to other work that they may be familiar with. Others are for the benefit of newcomers to the topic, and provide extra background information that may be helpful. Expert readers may ignore the latter and beginners may ignore the former.

# 2 The Peculiarities of Language

## 2.1. Three Peculiarities of Human Language

In trying to explain aspects of human-language evolution, my focus will be on certain characteristics of human language that are peculiar to it, not shared with other animals' communication systems. That is not to say that shared characteristics are without interest. But, as indicated in Chapter 1, I will be concerned not with all aspects of language evolution but only with some.[1]

It may seem that by formulating the inquiry in terms of communication systems I am already courting controversy. As we will see, some linguists believe that human language has evolved quite independently of animal communication. If they are right, then such resemblances as exist between human language and animal communication systems must be due to convergence rather than to shared origins. But in that case it makes all the more sense to concentrate on those features of human language that do not display this convergence, for those will be features whose presence cannot be explained on the basis that they would have to be present in any communication system. Focusing on these features should, if anything, bias the inquiry towards the conclusion that human language has its origin in something other than communication—the structure of our mental representation of reality, perhaps. Despite this, I will argue in Chapter 5 that these peculiar features of human language can in fact be explained naturally as arising from its communicative function.

I will further narrow the inquiry by focusing on just three peculiarities of human language:

- vocabulary size;
- **duality of patterning**, i.e. the fact that linguistic expressions are analysable on two levels, as composed of meaningless elements (sounds belonging to a finite inventory) and of meaningful ones (words and phrases);

---

[1] The evolution of communication in general has in any case been the subject of a comprehensive recent overview by Hauser (1996).

- the distinction between sentences and NPs.

These certainly do not exhaust the features of human language that are peculiar to it or especially characteristic of it. The linguist Charles F. Hockett published in 1960 a list of thirteen design features of human speech that, though not all unique, are not all found together anywhere else (Hockett 1960*a*, *b*; Hauser 1996: 47–8). Yet, of the three peculiarities that I have mentioned, only one (duality of patterning) appears on Hockett's list. So should we be worried about the discrepancies between Hockett's list and mine?

The answer is no, for two reasons. First, Hockett's list has been in the public arena for over thirty years, so any substantial progress that was to be made by tackling his design features head-on, whether individually or in groups, would almost certainly have been made by now. His list has been widely acknowledged as a stimulus to thinking, but it has not proved so useful as a detailed agenda of subsidiary goals in language-origin research, to be picked off one by one (so to speak). The very paucity of the overlap between Hockett's list and mine may constitute some reassurance that the perspective offered here is new.

The second reason is more subtle but more important. In one sense the Linguistic Society of Paris was right. No matter how much progress may be made in linguistics, anthropology, or any other relevant field, we will never know in detail and for certain how language evolved. But that drawback is just the local manifestation of a drawback that afflicts any science dealing with the past, such as palaeontology or cosmology. In most sciences, the choice between rival hypotheses depends on their relative success in predicting the outcomes of controlled experiments; but in sciences relating to the past the test of a hypothesis is how much of what is currently observed can be deduced from it as a logical consequence. A good hypothesis is one that is both simple and economical in the sense that a relatively large proportion of what is currently observed can be deduced from it, with relatively little reliance on chance or supplementary assumptions. A good hypothesis is also surprising, in the sense that its consequences include facts that do not seem obviously related to one another (Medawar 1967: 125). The more disparate the facts are that a simple and economical hypothesis accurately predicts, the more unlikely it is that these facts are as they are by accident, or for reasons unconnected with the hypothesis. The three peculiarities addressed here are disparate in the relevant sense, yet the scenario put forward in Chapter 5 relates them to one another in a satisfying way, I suggest, and no rival scenario accounts for them so economically.

These three peculiarities are internal to language rather than external. That is, they have to do with linguistic structure (the lexicon, phonology, and syntax) rather than with the cognitive and social functions served by language in human communities. For that reason, they may not seem especially exciting to anthropologists and others who are primarily interested in external factors in language evolution, or in its relationship to human evolution generally. Such readers may be tempted to think that there is nothing in this book for them. But they would be wrong. The question of how language has evolved cannot be divorced from the question of how language has come to acquire the particular structural characteristics that it has. Conceivably, its structural characteristics may all be attributable to external (social and cognitive) factors. The general lack of interest in language evolution on the part of linguists has done nothing to discourage that view. But, if that view is incorrect (as I hope to show), then all approaches to language evolution that ignore details of language structure, including details of grammar, will at best be incomplete and will at worst lead to seriously distorted conclusions. I do not deny the importance of external factors such as brain size, diet, foraging strategies, technology, and social organization; I merely suggest that such factors do not explain everything about how language got to be the way it is. An inquiry such as mine does not compete with inquiries that focus on those external factors. Rather, it complements them by helping to narrow down the range of linguistic phenomena for which an external explanation needs to be sought, and thus should help ultimately to make it clearer precisely what characteristics of humanity (linguistic and non-linguistic) those factors are indeed responsible for.

If external and internal factors complement each other in language evolution, then the second part of the following statement by the primatologist and psychologist Robin Dunbar (1998: 107) must be wrong: 'No doubt non-linguists ought to hesitate before commenting on matters relating to the grammatical structures of languages, but these structures of language are not, in themselves, relevant to questions about the functions of language or its evolution.' Dunbar here prejudges a central question of fact. Whether grammatical structure sheds light on language evolution is a matter to be determined by investigation, not to be settled by fiat before investigation begins. Behind the idea that grammatical structure is irrelevant there lurks perhaps the idea that a kind of language with grammatical characteristics fundamentally different from contemporary human languages is inconceivable. But that is precisely the preconception that I warned against in Chapter 1.

Before offering explanations of my own, however, I need to establish that kinds of language without the three peculiarities on which I am focusing, in particular the sentence/NP distinction, are indeed conceivable. That is the task of the rest of this chapter.

## 2.2. Vocabulary Size

What is known about animal communication systems suggests that distinct calls, to the extent that they can be correlated with specific meanings or contexts of use, are limited to a maximum of about twenty or thirty. The proviso about correlation with specific meanings is meant to exclude vocalization for display, which can indeed be very elaborate. Most Europeans who have lived in suburbs will be familiar with the highly varied song of the male blackbird, delivered while perched on a tree or rooftop, and country dwellers will also have heard the sky-lark, which sings while hovering so high as to be almost invisible. These illustrate vocalization to advertise territorial claims or availability for mating. Readers on other continents will be able to supply alternative examples. But this kind of variety is not a matter of vocabulary size in the relevant sense. In varying its territorial song, the blackbird is not varying the content. At the risk of anthro-pomorphizing in a fashion that may offend animal ethologists, we may say that the blackbird's message is always the same: 'This is my patch; other males keep away!' Human language operates differently. Where the same spoken message has to be conveyed repeatedly (for example, the warning not to leave one's baggage unattended, which is broadcast every ten minutes or so at some airports), we do not expect elegant variation in the style of the blackbird. On the other hand, the number of distinct words with identifiable meanings at our disposal, once we get beyond the first three years of life, is enormously greater than any animal call inventory. How has this difference come about?

Theoretical linguists have not generally taken much interest in vocabulary size. The grammar and phonology that a speaker uses will be much the same whether her vocabulary is 5,000 words or 50,000, and it is grammar and phonology that the theoretical linguist is mainly concerned with. Vocabulary size may be of in-terest to educationists and to applied linguists working in areas such as lexi-cography, second-language teaching, and speech and language therapy; but the question of how and why humans in general have acquired the ability to learn vocabularies as large as they do in normal circumstances is remote from their more practical concerns.

Common-sense answers may seem to be provided by intelligence and brain size. Surely it is natural (one may think) that, as hominids' brains became larger and they became progressively more intelligent, their ability to remember and use a larger vocabulary grew in parallel—an ability that could, of course, manifest itself only when the apparatus for speech had evolved sufficiently, but whose driv-ing force lay in the evolution of the mind and brain, not in the peripheral mecha-nisms for vocalization. The main problem with this kind of answer is that, to the extent that it cannot be disproved straightaway, it merely postpones the major questions. Absolute brain volume does not correlate directly with vocabulary size, for, if it did, people with bigger brains would have larger vocabularies, and there is no evidence of that. Besides, among hominids it is Neanderthals rather than anatomically modern humans who win the prize for the largest average skull capacity, yet it is widely suggested that one reason why Neanderthals lost in the competition with our anatomically modern ancestors may have been some lin-guistic deficiency (Trinkaus and Shipman 1993). And, even if we concede that the relationship between brain size and vocabulary size may not be so direct as common sense suggests, the question still arises: does a large vocabulary really confer such advantages on the individual and the species as to compensate, even in part, for the physical and physiological encumbrance of a large brain?

Before deciding that the answer must surely be yes, it is worth looking at vocabulary size from the viewpoint of adaptive specialization. The forelimbs of both seals and squirrels are ultimately descended from the forelimbs of the first mammal, but they have evolved to cope with completely different tasks. The seal's flippers are good for swimming but useless for picking up nuts. We would be amazed to discover a mammal with the aquatic habits of a seal but whose forelimbs were equipped not only for swimming but also for terrestrial food-gathering. We would be even more amazed if this mammal also had an elongated digit subtending a web of membrane attached to its flank, like a bat, equipping it for a mode of locomotion that it had never used. But the large vocabularies of modern human languages are rather like the forelimbs of this hypothetical mammal. Only in the last 10,000 years have any humans adopted a mode of life other than scavenging, hunting, and gathering, and most human groups have done so, if at all, much more recently than that. Yet every human being is biologically equipped to learn languages with vocabularies appropriate for talking about quantum physics, literary theory, and chemical engineering as well as hunting and gathering. In saying this I am not implying that modern hunter-gatherer communities use smaller vocabularies than other modern communities. In fact, hunter-gatherers have vocabularies that are richly elaborated not only in technical domains of direct economic significance to them, such as botany and the behaviour and anatomy of animals, but also in cultural domains such as kinship systems, clan organization, and mythology. Of course, these technical terminologies themselves are cultural, not biological developments; but the ability to acquire and retain them rests on a biological foundation shared by all humans of whatever cultural and technological milieu.

This ought to surprise us, surely, just as much as we would be surprised to discover a kind of seal that was physically equipped to gather nuts and to fly. If the specialization of the seal's forelimb makes it a more efficient swimmer and so has been encouraged by natural selection, why has not natural selection also encouraged a form of language in humans that is specialized in the same way—that is, in which the capacity to learn and remember words is just sufficient to accommodate the social and economic needs of small bands of individuals living by hunting and gathering, without scope for technical and cultural elaboration or versatility? A biological requirement that our vocabulary should be small in size and limited in content would have the double advantage, seemingly, of freeing up brain capacity for other purposes than remembering words and speeding up the acquisition of vocabulary in infancy. So the large size of human vocabularies is a genuine problem for language-evolution research.

## 2.3. Duality of Patterning

In Section 2.1 I defined duality of patterning as the characteristic of spoken language whereby linguistic expressions are analysable on two levels, as composed of meaningless elements (sounds and syllables belonging to a finite inventory) and of meaningful ones (words and phrases).[2] The level of sounds and syllables is the province of phonology, while that of meaningful elements is the province of grammar and semantics. Has this kind of duality any analogue in animal communication systems? If not, why did it arise in human language? And, since speech is only one of the biologically and culturally available media for linguistic expression, alongside deaf signing and writing, has it any analogue in deaf sign languages and in writing systems?

The short answer to the first question seems to be no. Some animal call systems can plausibly be analysed as involving recombinable elements (Hauser 1996: 278–83; Hauser and Wolfe 1995), but in no system is recombinability clearly evident at two levels, one meaningful and one meaningless. Why then is human spoken language like that?

Certainly, duality of patterning provides one mechanism whereby a language's vocabulary can be extended. Every language can be analysed as having at its disposal a set of contrasting speech sound-types (**phonemes**), ranging in number from about a dozen, as in Hawaiian, to over eighty, as in Ubykh, formerly spoken in the Caucasus (Comrie 1981). But in most languages these phonological resources are underused; phonemes can be combined so as to produce new sound strings that are well formed in terms of the language's phonological structure but which have no conventionally assigned meaning. The assignment of meanings to unused strings of this kind is one way in which new minimal meaningful units or **morphemes** can come into existence. There is thus a sense in which phonemes are building bricks for new vocabulary. On the other hand, if each morpheme were a stretch of sound with no clearly recombinable parts, these building bricks would not be available. New vocabulary items could still be formed, but only by combining existing morphemes so as to produce compounds, or else by modifying them phonetically in ways not describable in clearcut phonological terms as involving the substitution of one phoneme for another.

At first sight, then, we may feel entitled to say that duality of patterning is a direct consequence of vocabulary expansion: once human language had (for whatever reason) set itself on course for a much larger vocabulary than primate vocal call systems, duality was bound to follow. But this inevitability is not so

---

[2] This characteristic is also sometimes called **double articulation** (Martinet 1960). In grammatical terminology many linguists would recognize at least one other kind of meaningful element, the **morpheme**, defined as an element not divisible into smaller meaningful elements; but this does not matter for present purposes.

obvious on closer inspection. In the first place, contemporary languages do not lend much support to the view that duality is essential for vocabulary expansion. Some new words are indeed coined raw from purely phonological resources (for example, *nerd, gizmo, quark*), but these are unusual; the great bulk of new vocabulary is derived from existing vocabulary items. This can be illustrated from the terminology of computing and information technology, where new terms have arisen through extending the meaning of existing words (*mouse, monitor, port*), through compounding (*download, laptop*), through a combination of meaning change and affixation (*computer, browser, internet*), and through blending (*modem* from *modulator demodulator*). All these mechanisms could operate in a language without duality of patterning—even blending, which is proposed as a crucial precursor of duality in a classic article by Hockett and Ascher (1964). Secondly and more importantly, the sign languages of the deaf and some writing systems show in different ways that a linguistic medium can work without any exact analogue of the tightly integrated phoneme inventories of spoken languages. The individual signs of deaf sign languages are certainly analysable into components most of which recur in other signs (Klima and Bellugi 1979), but for some of these components it is hard to establish that they are crucially distinctive in the way that the phonemes are in speech; moreover, it been argued that sign languages can accommodate new gestural elements 'from outside' more freely than spoken languages can accommodate new phonemes (Pulleyblank 1989). And in the non-alphabetic writing system of Chinese, although its characters are analysable in terms of 'signific' and 'phonetic' elements and the number and type of strokes that they contain, it is hard to arrive at a clear-cut 'spelling' for each character in terms of a limited inventory of stroke types and positions (Pulleyblank 1989).

The Chinese state of affairs points up usefully the contrast, in respect of duality of patterning, between how language is and how it might have been. Spoken Chinese, like all spoken languages, is segmentable into phonemes as well as morphemes. But, because written Chinese does not represent the phoneme segmentation, it would in principle be possible for people reading Chinese to relate characters to their meanings directly, bypassing the subconscious phonetic interpretation that seems to be imposed, or at least encouraged, by alphabetic writing systems. However, experiments on Chinese character recognition suggests that this does not happen (Tan and Perfetti 1997). Even skilled readers of Chinese do not pass directly from a character to its meaning, but instead access meaning via phonology, just as readers of alphabetic texts do. So, even when offered an opportunity (so to speak) to process linguistic material in a fashion that bypasses duality, humans do not avail themselves of this opportunity. Why not?

Of the three questions that opened this section, the crucial second question ('Why did duality of patterning arise in human language?') therefore remains unanswered. Since some actual media for linguistic expression lack duality of the kind that spoken language displays, we do not even need to exercise our imaginations to envisage how human language might have evolved without it.

## 2.4. The Distinction between Sentences and Noun Phrases

### 2.4.1. Alternative Syntax 1: No Syntax

It is logically possible for a communication system to exhibit duality of patterning and have a large vocabulary, as human languages do, and yet exhibit no syntactic organization. Meaningful combinations of sounds (words) would be strung together in a rough-and-ready fashion, subject to no grammatical constraints or ordering preferences. To interpret the whole string one would rely solely on common sense or pragmatic clues. In such a communication system (let's call it **'Asyntactic'**) there might be words such as *man, bite,* and *dog,* with just the same meaning and pronunciation as the corresponding English words. Let us suppose also that there is a word *past,* corresponding functionally to the past tense expressed in English in the verbform *bit,* contrasting with *bite.* Asyntactic renderings of the English sentence *The dog bit the man* will include any string consisting of the words *man, bite, dog,* and *past* in any order. Interpreting these strings will be a matter of sorting out what event is most likely to have occurred in a past scenario involving a man, a dog, and an act of biting. In this instance, the most likely event is indeed one corresponding to the English sentence we are trying to gloss. But, if the English sentence had been *The man bit the dog,* translation of it into Asyntactic would seem more difficult. *Ex hypothesi,* no order of words in Asyntactic will encode reliably the fact that the man is the attacker and the dog the victim on this occasion. But a communication system on Asyntactic lines might still have devices to resolve such ambiguities; for example, there might be a word *surprising* whose function is to require an unexpected or less natural interpretation, so that *The man bit the dog* would be rendered by *past surprising dog man bite,* or by any permutation of those five words.

Why has human language not evolved on Asyntactic lines? Asyntactic is, after all, somewhat similar to the 'protolanguage' envisaged as a precursor to modern human language by Derek Bickerton (1990, 1995). Protolanguage will be discussed more fully in Chapter 4. For present purposes it is sufficient to note that, as Bickerton points out, there are contexts where even modern adults use a kind of syntaxless language (for example, when trying to make oneself understood to foreigners or when very drunk), and he argues also that, at the earliest stage in normal language development in infants, syntax should be regarded as not merely rudimentary but non-existent.

An apparently straightforward answer to the question why human languages are not like Asyntactic might be: 'Because Asyntactic cannot distinguish conveniently the roles of participants in an event, as illustrated by the *dog man bite* example.' But ways of mitigating this inconvenience without compromising the language's basic syntaxless character can be imagined, as illustrated by my suggested use of *surprising*. More importantly, this answer makes the fundamental mistake of presupposing that, just because some kind of language is deficient in some respect by comparison with actual human language, the evolution of vocal communication in humans could not have taken that course. This is as if one were to argue that, just because chimpanzee vocal communication is deficient by comparison with human language, it cannot have evolved in chimpanzees. The fallacy is evident. We are tempted to it only because of the kind of prejudice that I warned against in Chapter 1: the assumption that fundamental aspects of language as we observe it must be the way they are by necessity rather than as contingent outcomes of one among many conceivable evolutionary paths.

It is, therefore, not self-evident that human language should have evolved so as to have any syntax at all—at least, any syntax independent of pragmatic interpretation strategies. *A fortiori*, it is not self-evident that human language should have precisely the sort of syntax that it has. In Sections 2.4.2 and 2.4.3 I will discuss two out of the innumerable alternative syntaxes that are imaginable. The reason for choosing these two is to show that the kind of grammar that human languages have could well seem as deficient to an outside investigator (a native speaker of Martian, perhaps) as Asyntactic does to us, and to illustrate a direction in which language evolution might be expected to have gone if it is indeed descended from a vocal communication system something like those of modern primates. The second illustration also lays the groundwork for the account in Section 2.4.4 of what is unexpected about the sentence/NP distinction.

### 2.4.2. *Alternative Syntax 2: Spatiotemporal Coordinates and the Type/Token Distinction*

Most of the things we talk about are locatable more or less precisely in space and time. I say 'most' rather than 'all', because this does not apply to the statement that two and three make five or the statement that, in Lewis Carroll's *Through the Looking Glass*, the Red Queen and Alice have to run as fast as they can in order to stay in the same place. But, outside logical and mathematical truths and explicit fictions, this spatiotemporal locatability generally holds. The sentence *The man bit the dog* cannot be accurately used to describe some state of affairs —more briefly, it cannot be true—unless such an attack indeed took place somewhere at some time. And one can imagine a kind of language (let's call it Spatiotemporal) whose syntax acknowledges this generalization by enforcing mention of a time and a place in every well-formed utterance. In Spatiotemporal a minimal declarative utterance (for convenience let's call it a **complete expression**) would have three constituents, as shown in (1):

(1)   Location in space + Location in time + Object or Event

Possible glosses for *The man bit the dog*, in appropriate circumstances, might be:

(2)   In Christchurch + Yesterday + Man bite dog.
(3)   Somewhere + Past + Man bite dog.

(The internal structure of the third constituent is not important, but I will assume that Spatiotemporal resembles English in that the word order makes it clear who is doing the biting.) The elements *Somewhere* and *Past* illustrate the fact that a specification of place and time must be overtly expressed, no matter how vague. The Space and Time constituents in this respect resemble the subject constituent in an English sentence. If I know that my bicycle has been stolen but do not know the culprit, I can report that fact by saying *Someone has stolen my bicycle*, with the vague *someone* as subject, but I cannot simply leave the subject out, so as to yield *\*Has stolen my bicycle*. (I can, of course, also say *My bicycle has been stolen*, where the use of the passive provides another way of reconciling my ignorance of the thief with the requirement of an overt subject.)

The third constituent in complete Spatiotemporal expressions is given in (1) as 'Object or Event'. This implies that not only (2) but also (4) and (5) are unequivocally well formed:

(4)   In Christchurch + Yesterday + Earthquake
(5)   In Christchurch + Yesterday + Dalai Lama

It is natural to envisage Spatiotemporal operating this way, since both objects and events can be located in space and time. But this characteristic highlights another respect in which Spatiotemporal differs from English. Consider English equivalents of (2), (4), and (5) respectively:

(6)   A man bit a dog in Christchurch yesterday.
(7)   There was an earthquake in Christchurch yesterday.
(8)   The Dalai Lama was in Christchurch yesterday.

These contain a verb (*bit*) or a verblike element, the auxiliary or copula *was*, which expresses tense (the past tense in both instances); *was* also expresses agreement with the subject (a plural subject such as *earthquakes* or *several lamas* would require *were*). On the other hand, of the complete Spatiotemporal expressions (2), (4), and (5), although (2) does contain something verblike—namely, *bite* in its Object-or-Event constituent—(4) and (5) contain nothing corresponding to the English *was*. This is significant because in English, if an expression lacks a verb or copula, it is typically not a sentence; rather it is either ill-formed (e.g. *\*a man a dog in Christchurch yesterday*) or else some other kind of syntactic unit, such as an NP; for example, *an earthquake in Christchurch yesterday* is a well-formed noun phrase in the sentence at (9):

(9)    An earthquake in Christchurch yesterday will probably cause insurance premiums to rise there.

Should complete expressions in Spatiotemporal then be equated perhaps with English NPs rather than English sentences? Because Spatiotemporal is an invented language, that question may seem pointless, inasmuch as we can rig it how we like. But it is not pointless, because limits on how freely we can rig things are imposed by the basic syntactic pattern at (1). An answer emerges when we consider how complete expressions might be combined with one another. Should a complete expression be allowed to appear inside the Object-or-Event constituent of another complete expression? Complex complete expressions of that kind would seem necessary if Spatiotemporal is to be capable of rendering complex sentences of English such as (9). Let us consider what a Spatiotemporal rendering of (9) might look like:

(10)    There$_i$ + Future + [In Christchurch$_i$ + Yesterday + Earthquake] probably cause [There$_i$ + Future + Insurance premiums rise]

The bracketed expressions are well-formed complete expressions that appear here as parts of the Object-or-Event constituent of a larger complete expression consisting of the whole of (10). The subscript *i* shared by *in Christchurch* and the two occurrences of *there* is meant to make it clear that they share the same reference, just as the corresponding English expressions do in (9). In a similar fashion, one might replace one of the instances of *future* in (10) with *future$_j$* and the other with a proform *then$_j$*, signalling temporal coreference.

What is most important about (10), however, are the following two points. First, the kind of embedding illustrated in (10) does not violate the spirit of Spatiotemporal as we have envisaged it, since the third constituent in (10) still reports an Object or Event, albeit a more complex one than in the earlier examples. Secondly, there is no clear answer to the question whether these embedded complete expressions correspond to sentences or NPs in English. In the English sentence (9), which (10) was designed to translate, what corresponds to the first complete expression in (10) is an NP, while what corresponds to the second is a sentence (more precisely, a nonfinite clause[3]), as shown in (11):

(11)    [An earthquake in Christchurch yesterday]$_{NP}$ will probably cause [insurance premiums to rise there]$_{Sentence}$

---

[3] A nonfinite clause is a sentence containing no expression of tense (the grammatical category that is mainly connected with the time at which the action of the verb takes place), such as the suffix *-ed*, which expresses 'past' with most English verbs. Some syntacticians would regard *insurance premiums* as being outside the embedded clause in (11), which would thus consist of just *to rise there*. But that does not matter for our purposes. What is not in doubt is that the embedded element is sentential (or clausal) rather than nominal.

But that is not the only English possibility. In fact, both sentential and nominal renderings for both these embedded expressions can be found, yielding four possible counterparts of (10). The other three alongside (11) are:

(12)   [An earthquake in Christchurch yesterday]$_{NP}$ will probably cause [a rise in insurance premiums there]$_{NP}$

(13)   [There having been an earthquake in Christchurch yesterday]$_{Sentence}$ will probably cause [insurance premiums to rise there]$_{Sentence}$

(14)   [There having been an earthquake in Christchurch yesterday]$_{Sentence}$ will probably cause [a rise in insurance premiums there]$_{NP}$

The last two examples, with the subject position occupied by the nonfinite clause *there having been an earthquake in Christchurch yesterday*, sound somewhat bookish and unnatural; nevertheless they are grammatically well formed. This suggests that the best way of answering the question posed above is to say that, at least on the basis of the examples we have been considering, complete Spatiotemporal expressions display no clear-cut preference for a sentential or a nominal rendering in English, and neither do sentences and NPs in English correspond exactly to any syntactic unit in Spatiotemporal. The tripartite structure posited in (1) seems to lead naturally to a kind of syntax that differs from that of English in a fundamental way.

There is another respect in which Spatiotemporal contrasts interestingly with English. A kind of vagueness that English syntax does nothing to clarify but which will sometimes be hard to express in Spatiotemporal is illustrated in (15)–(17):

(15)   John's lecture on global warming was popular.

(16)   John's lecture on global warming was popular last night; it got a full house even though the weather was bad.

(17)   John's lecture on global warming was always popular, so he was asked to give it year after year.

The vagueness involves the philosophical distinction between types and tokens. A token, whether of an object or an event, has spatiotemporal coordinates; a type does not. In (16) *John's lecture on global warming* denotes a lecture-token, because it refers to a particular occasion; in (17) it denotes a lecture-type, because it refers to no particular occasion or set of occasions. No doubt (17) could not be true unless there is a finite number of occasions on which John delivered his lecture; but knowing that (17) is true does not depend on knowing when those occasions were or even how many there were. This difference between types and tokens entails that the Space and Time constituents in a Spatiotemporal rendering of (16) will be fundamentally different from those in a rendering of (17). In formulating a Spatiotemporal translation of (16), even if one does not know the identity of the hall where John delivered his lecture, one cannot avoid including a component relating to place, no matter how unspecifically, analogous to the indefinite subject that English syntax requires us to include in the sentence *Someone has stolen my bicycle*:

(18)   In some unspecified place + Last night + John's lecture . . . popular . . .

On the other hand, in translating (17), one must characterize both Locations in such a way as to make it clear that they are not merely unspecified but unspecifiable, for example:

(19)   Everywhere, yet nowhere specifically + Always in the past, yet at no time specifically + John's lecture . . . popular . . .

Consider now the English sentence (15). This is vague in that both lecture-token and lecture-type interpretations are possible, depending on whether the context of use resembles that of (16) or (17), but this vagueness presents no syntactic difficulty. English even allows the same expression to have both type and token interpretations in the same context of use:[4]

(20)   John's lecture is always well received, even though it lasted over an hour when I heard it.

On the other hand, a Spatiotemporal rendering of (15) would have to come off the fence on one side or the other because of the requirement that the two Location constituents be overt. It would be impossible (at least without ingenious circumlocution) to carry over into Spatiotemporal the type/token vagueness of (15). That is not to say that type/token vagueness is never possible in Spatiotemporal; but the fact that Location constituents may have the effect of sometimes imposing precision raises the question of whether one could envisage a language whose syntax invariably imposes it.

What is the moral to be drawn from considering Spatiotemporal? We need to ask first whether there is anything about its syntax that would render it ill-suited to the needs of human communication. The answer is surely no. Since most of what we talk about is locatable in space and time, there seems nothing unnatural about a syntactic requirement that complete expressions should contain Space and Time constituents. It may appear inconvenient to have to fill these constituent positions even when we do not know where or when the thing we are talking about is located, or when (as in statements of mathematical facts) spatiotemporal location is inapplicable. But any such inconvenience is no greater than that which

---

[4] This is the reason why I have talked of vagueness rather than ambiguity in connection with types and tokens. In semantic discussions it is conventional to reserve the term 'ambiguous' for words that cannot have more than one sense in any one context (Kempson 1977). Thus *bank*, meaning 'financial institution' or 'edge of river', is ambiguous rather than vague, because sentences like the following are ill-formed: *While Mary was opening an account at a bank this morning, John was sitting on one and fishing.*

English syntax imposes by requiring a filler for the grammatical subject position in a sentence even when we do not know who or what belongs there, as in *Someone has stolen my bicycle*, or when nothing seems to belong there at all, as in *It's raining*. To make the same point another way: if in English and all other languages we found complete expressions with the tripartite structure of Spatiotemporal, it is hard to see any obvious reason why this pattern of syntax should puzzle us. Indeed, it is easy to see how we might be tempted to take it for granted that human language should inevitably have evolved to conform to that pattern.[5] Yet Spatiotemporal differs from English and indeed all languages in such a way that sentences and NPs have no direct syntactic counterparts in it, and also that its obligatory Location components have effects on the expressibility of type/token vagueness. So the moral is: it is far from obvious why human-language syntax is as it is, and not like Spatiotemporal syntax, even though the ramifications of this syntactic choice are considerable.

### 2.4.3. *Alternative Syntax 3: Categorial Uniformity*

In Spatiotemporal, as just discussed, there are no direct counterparts to NPs and sentences in actual human languages, because complete expressions have some characteristics of both. This kind of categorial ambivalence is interesting because it illustrates another direction in which syntax might have evolved. But it is particularly interesting because this evolutionary direction is in some respects a more plausible one than the direction actually taken, so the fact that we did not take it is all the more puzzling—provided we assume that primate vocalizations are relevant to human-language evolution. Again, I acknowledge that that assumption is controversial; but I will argue in later chapters that objections to it are weaker than has sometimes been claimed.

The study of primate communication systems has been revolutionized by the discovery that monkey calls may have objective or referential as well as purely affective or expressive meanings. For example, the calls used by vervet monkeys in the Amboseli National Park in Kenya distinguish between different kinds of predator (snakes, eagles, and leopards) so as to elicit different kinds of evasive action (Cheney and Seyfarth 1990). But no matter how ready we may be to acknowledge the referential character of these calls, there is one respect in which they differ fundamentally from utterances in any human language. Consider a set of possible English translations for the vervets' eagle call:

(21)   An eagle!                     (NP)
(22)   There's an eagle overhead!    (Declarative sentence)

---

[5] Pinker (1994: 117) argues that, in order to express propositions that can be true or false, sentences must indeed contain a syntactic slot for an element referring to time. I will discuss this idea further in Chapter 4.

(23)  Run from the eagle!          (Imperative sentence)
(24)  Take cover in the bushes!    (Imperative sentence)
(25)  To the bushes!               (Prepositional phrase)

Which of these is best? That may seem a silly question, and in one sense it is. It invites us to choose between renderings that differ not only in their lexical content (some mentioning the predator, some the evasive action) but also in their syntactic status: declarative sentence, imperative sentence, noun phrase, or prepositional phrase. The trouble is that there is no obvious ground for choosing between them, because the vervet call system (let us call it Vervetese) has no syntactic categories and no distinctions of sentence type such as between imperative and indicative.[6] Yet the question is useful too, because it provokes another: is it conceivable that a vocal communication system could have evolved which is as elaborate and sophisticated as human language but which is like Vervetese in lacking syntactic category distinctions such as that between sentences and NPs? The characteristics of the Spatiotemporal language in Section 2.4.2 suggest that the answer may be yes, and this is confirmed by the argument to be presented here.

Imagine a vocal communication system, or language, with the following characteristics:

(*a*)  There are simple expressions and complex ones.
(*b*)  A complex expression is formed by combining an appropriate number of expressions (simple or complex) with a following operator. Operators differ according to the number of expressions with which they may be combined; some require one, some two, some three, and so on. We can, therefore, classify operators as one-place, two-place, etc.
(*c*)  All expressions have the same syntactic status. That is, all expressions may appear in the same syntactic contexts, subject only to semantic appropriateness. This language thus differs from English, where the sentence *John arrived yesterday* and the NP *John's arrival yesterday* cannot both occur in the contexts *I think that . . .* and *. . . surprised me.*

Let us call this language Monocategoric, emphasizing the lack of syntactic category distinctions between expressions.[7] A fragment of a vocabulary for a hypothetical Monocategoric with these three characteristics might be as in (26):

---

[6] Jerison (1982: 765, 779) interprets the vervet's predator warning cries as commands. He even goes so far as to say that animal communications are typically commands, and sees this as a central difference between animal communication and human language. But this is wrong. Quite apart from the absence of any objective criteria that might favour (23) or (24) over (21), (22), or (25) as renderings of the eagle call, Cheney and Seyfarth make it clear that vervets have a quite extensive repertoire of other calls that do not resemble commands even superficially: for example, grunts made when approaching dominant or subordinate vervets, or accompanying movement into open country away from the group.

[7] Monocategoric is the same as what in Carstairs-McCarthy (1998b) I called 'Uniformitarian'. The change of name is to avoid any possible confusion with other senses of 'uniformitarian'.

(26)    Simple expressions: snake, you, John, Mary, story
        Operators:
            One-place:      YESTERDAY, DISAPPEAR, SEEM
            Two-place:      SEE (as in *John Mary* SEE 'John saw Mary')[8]
            Three-place:    TELL (as in *John Mary story* TELL 'John told Mary
                            a story')

For clarity, small capitals are used to distinguish operators from simple expressions, just as nouns in written German are distinguished from words of other classes by having a capital initial; but there need be no analogous distinction in spoken Monocategoric any more than there is in spoken German. Examples of complex expressions formed with this vocabulary are in (27):

(27)    (*a*)   [you snake SEE] YESTERDAY
                (i)     'You saw a snake yesterday.'
                (ii)    'your seeing a snake yesterday'
                (iii)   'the snake you saw yesterday'
                (iv)    'you who saw a snake yesterday'
        (*b*)   [[[you snake SEE] YESTERDAY] DISAPPEAR] SEEM
                (i)     'The snake you saw yesterday seems to have disappeared.'
                (ii)    'the apparent disappearance of the snake you saw yesterday'
        (*c*)   John Mary [[you snake SEE] YESTERDAY] TELL
                'John told Mary that you saw a snake yesterday.'

The brackets draw attention to the internal syntax of complex expressions, but they are strictly superfluous because the rules of Monocategoric as set out at (*a*)–(*c*) above determine a unique internal structure for any well-formed expression.[9]

The multiple glosses indicated by the small Roman numerals in (27) may at first seem strange. They are intended to indicate a kind of ambivalence that would naturally accompany consistent grammatical Monocategoricism. As native speakers of human languages, we experience an urge to pigeonhole complex expressions as either nominal (like *the snake you saw yesterday*) or sentential (whether an independent sentence, like *You saw a snake yesterday*, or a nonfinite clause, like *your seeing a snake yesterday*). (See note 3, if necessary, for a reminder of what a nonfinite clause is.) But, taking my cue from the ambivalence of Spatiotemporal expressions like *In Christchurch + Yesterday + Earthquake* (as in (4) and (10) above), I would like to pursue the implications of assuming that Monocategoric is not like an actual human language in this respect. Rather, let us assume that the categorially uniform status of all Monocategoric expressions has a semantic counterpart—namely, the absence of any systematic coding of any

---

[8]  In the English glosses for Monocategoric expressions with no indication of time, the past tense is used. But nothing hinges on this choice of tense.

[9]  Readers who are familiar with the Polish notation for propositional calculus, as presented by e.g. Prior (1962), will detect a resemblance. In that notation, too, brackets are superfluous.

distinction between nominal and sentential readings, or (one may prefer to say) between object and event readings.

At first sight, Monocategoric as so constructed is strangely deficient. After all, talking about a snake is not the same as talking about someone seeing a snake. How could we get by in Monocategoric—to be more precise, how could we do with Monocategoric all the things we do with human languages—if that sort of distinction is not expressible in it? My reply starts with two counter-questions. In practice, will distinctions that are important for efficient communication really be inexpressible in Monocategoric? And does this kind of alleged deficiency really not occur in English and other actual languages too?

In (27) we see the expression *you snake* SEE YESTERDAY in three contexts: as a complex expression on its own in (27*a*) and as part of a larger complex expression in (27*b*) and (27*c*). But in all three contexts the most natural English gloss is unproblematic. In the first context, given that *you snake* SEE YESTERDAY constitutes a well-formed expression, it seems natural to render it by what is unequivocally a well-formed expression in English—namely, an independent sentence. There are certainly discourse contexts in English where an utterance can appropriately consist of something other than an independent sentence, such as an NP or a nonfinite clause. For example, in reply to the questions at (28*a*) and (29*a*), appropriate responses may be the NP at (28*b*) and the nonfinite clause at (29*b*) respectively:

(28)  (*a*)  What's that thing you've got there?
       (*b*)  The snake you say yesterday.
(29)  (*a*)  What are you looking so surprised about?
       (*b*)  Your seeing a snake yesterday.[10]

But grammarians typically distinguish these as incomplete or elliptical sentences (Lyons 1968), by comparison with complete sentences such as *You saw a snake yesterday*. So, in the absence of any information on the discourse content, *You saw a snake yesterday* is the most natural gloss at (27*a*). On the other hand, in (27*b*) the context supplied by the operators . . . DISAPPEAR SEEM forces *you snake* SEE YESTERDAY to be understood as referring to an object rather than an event. Snakes are the kind of thing that can disappear, but snake-seeing occurrences are not. The most natural English gloss is, therefore, one that would be used to refer not to a snake-seeing occurrence but to a snake itself, such as the NP *the snake you saw yesterday*. Finally, in (27*c*) the context provided by the operator . . . TELL and the simple expressions *John* and *Mary* forces *you snake* SEE YESTERDAY to be understood as referring to an event rather than an object. Stories and events are the kind of thing that can be told or narrated, but snakes are not. The most natural English gloss is, therefore, one that would be used to refer to a snake-seeing

[10] Many linguists would label (29*b*) a gerundive nominal rather than (or as well as) a nonfinite clause. The terminology does not matter for present purposes, however.

occurrence, such as the sentence *(that) you saw a snake yesterday*. So, at least in relation to (27), the lack of a sentence/NP distinction in Monocategoric does not put it at a communicative disadvantage to English in practice.

To linguists, factors of the kind that force the choice of reading for *you snake* SEE YESTERDAY in (27) will be familiar as subcategorization requirements and selection restrictions. Subcategorization relates to the syntactic context, selection to the semantic. An example of subcategorization is the distinction between transitive and intransitive verbs within the verb category. Transitive verbs such as *introduce* and *locate* must be accompanied by an NP functioning as direct object while intransitive verbs such as *perish* must not; this is why sentences such as *The hostess spent the whole party introducing* and *Our navigator used to locate very reliably* are ill-formed in English even though it is easy to think of plausible interpretations for them. Selection restrictions involve semantic or pragmatic appropriateness rather than syntax; famous examples of breaches of selection restrictions that were introduced into linguistic discussion by Chomsky (1957, 1965) are *Sincerity admires John* and *Colourless green ideas sleep furiously*. Exactly where the line should be drawn between syntactic restrictions and semantic or pragmatic ones, and indeed whether there is a firm line to be drawn at all, are matters of debate that need not concern us here. The important point is that a word may have two or more possible interpretations, but in a given linguistic context it will usually though not always be the case that selection restrictions will exclude all but one as inappropriate. So, for example, the noun *building* may designate either an activity or a physical object (what the activity of building achieves), as may many other verb-related nouns in English (for example, *construction, painting, improvement, display*); but in (30*a*) and (30*b*) the context forces an activity and an achievement reading respectively:[11]

(30)  (*a*)  The building took longer than we had expected.
      (*b*)  The building collapsed in a heap of rubble.

However, (31) shows a sentence in which *building* occurs that may be compatible with either reading:

(31)   The building on the hillside was a disaster.

Is it the activity that was disastrous, or the physical object that resulted from the activity? A wider discourse context is needed in order to decide, as in (32):

(32)  (*a*)  The building on the hillside was a disaster. Even while it was going on, the increased rainwater run-off began to cause slips lower down.
      (*b*)  The building on the hillside was a disaster. The builder couldn't find a buyer for it and eventually had to demolish it.

---

[11] The distinction that I characterize as one between physical objects and activities is discussed further by Bennett (1988) and Grimshaw (1990), with different terminologies.

These two readings of *the building on the hillside* are in fact parallel to the two readings (ii) and (iii) for *you snake SEE YESTERDAY* at (27a).

A further parallel can be found in actual languages for the multiple readings of *you snake SEE YESTERDAY*. Consider the following French expression:

(33)  le   chat  qui    est tombé par    la   fenêtre
      the  cat   which is fallen  out-of the  window

Which is the more appropriate English rendering: the NP *the cat which has fallen out of the window* or the sentence *The cat has fallen out of the window*? To most readers who know French, the answer will probably seem obvious: *qui* is a relative pronoun introducing the relative clause *qui est tombé par la fenêtre* that modifies *chat*, the head noun of an NP, so (33) must clearly be rendered by an NP in English. But Sasse (1987), citing Wehr (1984), points out that there are contexts in which (33) corresponds rather to an English sentence. He cites the following example from Wehr:

(34)  Que se passe-t-il?—   Le chat qui est tombé par la fenêtre.
      'What's happening?'—The cat has fallen out of the window.'

The question 'What's happening?' is not a question about the cat, such as 'What's the cat done now?' In fact, 'What's happening?' sets up no expectations about what should be mentioned in reply, whether a cat, a window, or anything else. It is therefore the kind of question that is appropriately answered by what Sasse (drawing on the work of the philosophers Brentano and Marty) calls a **thetic statement**. A thetic statement provides information about a whole situation, by contrast with a **categorical statement**, which provides information about a particular aspect of a situation on which attention is already focused. Thetic statements, grammatically differentiated as such, do not always appear where we might expect them to, and, even when they are differentiated from categorical statements, this may be achieved by any one of a range of syntactic and intonational devices, varying from one language to another. What matters here, however, is that an apparently nominal expression like (33) can be used to express a thetic statement in French. Such expressions, when taken out of context, therefore have a kind of ambiguity quite parallel to that of *you snake SEE YESTERDAY* in Monocategoric.

These English and French examples suggest an answer to the second of the two questions that I just posed. Any supposed deficiency in Monocategoric due to the lack of a sentence/NP distinction has parallels in actual languages, of which (30)–(34) illustrate two kinds. So, if one is inclined to dismiss Monocategoric as inadequate for the tasks that human languages perform, one must explain why English and French count as adequate. Expressions that in English and French appear ambiguous in isolation will in practice be clarified by their context, both linguistic and pragmatic, so we can communicate pretty well in English and

French despite these deficiencies; and just the same seems true of Monocategoric, as we have envisaged it. One can envisage Monocategoric expressions containing *you snake* SEE YESTERDAY that are compatible with both an object and an event reading, such as (35), containing the new one-place operator UNUSUAL:

(35)    *[[you snake* SEE*]* YESTERDAY*]* UNUSUAL
       (i) 'The snake you saw yesterday was unusual.'
       (ii) 'Your seeing a snake yesterday was unusual.'

But, just as with (31), the ambiguity will disappear when a wider context is taken into account—for example, when (35) is followed by a Monocategoric expression that could be glossed as 'That species is rare around here' (implying the object reading) or 'One doesn't often see snakes around here' (implying the event reading).

### 2.4.4. Actual Syntax: An Outsider's View

We have looked at two hypothetical language-like systems that differ from human language in having a syntax without an analogue of the sentence/NP distinction. I have argued that such systems 'work' at least well enough, so that one cannot simply allege unworkability as a reason why human language has not evolved in one of those directions. Many readers may feel, however, that, even if those systems do work, a kind of language with a sentence/NP distinction must still work better. The purpose of this section is to argue that that is a human-language speaker's prejudice. To a linguistic outsider such as a Martian, the sentence/NP distinction, far from fostering communicative efficiency, could well seem a pointless encumbrance and its universality among humans quite mystifying.

Imagine that you are listening to someone (call her the Earthling) explaining how human language works to a Martian—an intelligent extraterrestrial creature who communicates by some means quite unlike human language. The Earthling (who knows the basic terminology of syntax) might start by explaining that syntactic units called noun phrases are typically used to refer to objects or events in the world, and are typically combined with other units called verb phrases to form sentences, one of whose functions is to make statements about the objects or events referred to. She might add that statements can be true or false, according to whether they fit the world or not, and that reference too can be either successful or unsuccessful, according to whether the would-be referent exists or not. (An example of a noun phrase with no referent in the twentieth century is *the present King of France.* Logical characteristics of sentences containing such noun phrases have been discussed by Russell (1905) and Strawson (1950).)

The Martian might now reply: 'OK, I get the idea. A noun phrase has one kind of relationship to the world: successful or unsuccessful reference. A noun phrase is combined with a second kind of syntactic unit called a verb phrase to form a third kind of unit called a sentence. A sentence has a second kind of relationship to the world: truth or falsity. Presumably, then, a sentence is combined with some fourth kind of syntactic unit to form a fifth kind of unit, which in turn will have a third kind of relationship to the world, and so on up. In fact, each odd-numbered syntactic unit will have its own kind of relationship to the world, and these relationships can be seen as forming an ordered set such that any odd-numbered syntactic unit $n$ will have relationship $(n+1)/2$ to the real world.'

At this point the Earthling interjects: 'No! Nothing so elaborate! We stop at sentences. We can indeed combine sentences in various ways, but combinations of sentences still just make more elaborate statements, which are still either true or false.'

The Martian now replies: 'I'm confused! Why does your language allow precisely two syntactic units to have their own special kind of relationship to the world? If you don't like overelaboration, why don't you make do with just one? What's so special about the number two?'

This is a good question. In effect, the Martian is asking: 'Why do you need the distinction between sentences and NPs?' At first sight, taking one's cue from the Earthling's mention of truth and reference, one may be tempted to look to them for an answer of a kind not so far discussed. We may be tempted to see it as self-evident that a communication system that does what human language does must inevitably distinguish between mentioning things (or referring) and making assertions about them (or making true and false statements). But, even if we grant for argument's sake that this distinction is important, it does not follow that it must be reflected in syntax. To our hypothetical Martian it might seem just as natural that there should be a distinction in syntactic category between plain assertions and assertions about assertions. The Martian might even argue that this syntactic distinction would serve the useful purpose of signalling the potential presence of opaque contexts (Quine 1960)—that is, contexts where the substitution of one expression for another with the same reference (for example, *Venus* for *the Morning Star*) can change the truth-value of what is said; for example, *Alex believes that Venus is inhabited* may be true even while *Alex believes that the Morning Star is inhabited* is false, if Alex is ignorant of astronomy. Yet the syntax of actual languages, while permitting sentences to be embedded within larger units, does not assign these larger units to a new syntactic category. Why not?

A short answer to this question is that there are many distinctions that grammar might conceivably express but that it generally or consistently neglects. One such distinction is that between tokens and types, already discussed in section 2.4.2.[12] Another is the distinction between activities and achievements,

---

[12] Jackendoff (1983) and Broschart (1997) both make linguistic use of the terms 'type' and 'token', but not so as to draw a distinction like that between the two senses of *John's lecture on global warning* in (16) and (17). They are concerned rather with categorization and with aspects of the distinction between referential and predicative expressions. For them, *John's lecture on global warning* would belong on the token side in (17) as well as (16).

discussed in Section 2.4.3. It is easy to imagine an extraterrestrial community in which all languages encode these distinctions consistently. To language users in such a world it would probably appear scarcely conceivable, at first, that languages could function without reflecting them in their grammar. Yet our own world shows that they can. Conversely, languages in that same world might fail to encode the distinction between referring and asserting. The fact that languages in our own world do have a grammatical mechanism for encoding this does not entail that any communication system that does roughly what human languages do would have to encode it. I will show this by comparing two dialogues, one in ordinary English and the other in a pseudo-English that, like the Monocategoric of Section 2.4.3, lacks the syntactic distinction between sentences and noun phrases. In this pseudo-English, which I will call 'Nominalized English', all English sentences appear as NPs, with their verbs converted into nouns. This has the effect of abolishing any syntactic coding of the distinction between reference and assertion as ways in which linguistic expressions fit the world.

Here is the first dialogue, in ordinary English:

(36)   BILL. Hello. I was sorry to hear you had been ill. You're certainly looking a lot better now!

   ALICE. Yes, I had a nasty bout of bronchitis for three weeks, but I've got over it, fortunately. Just as well, because we've got to get ready for Bridget's wedding next month.

   BILL. Oh, I didn't even know she was engaged!

   ALICE. Yes, he's someone she met in Spain last year. It's going to be a very quiet ceremony, because they're desperately saving money to buy a house. If they can't afford one in Fendalton, they're thinking of moving to a cheaper suburb.

Now here is a Nominalized English counterpart:

(37)   BILL. Greetings. My regret about news of your earlier illness. A definite improvement in your present appearance.

   ALICE. Yes, my three weeks' endurance of a nasty bout of bronchitis, but my fortunate recovery. Timeliness due to the urgency of preparation for Bridget's wedding next month.

   BILL. Oh, my surprising ignorance of her engagement!

   ALICE. Yes, her encounter with him in Spain last year. A very quiet projected ceremony due to their desperate money-saving for house purchase. An entailment by eventual non-affordability in Fendalton of thoughts about relocation to a cheaper suburb.

This dialogue sounds quaint and stilted. But once one has got over its strangeness, it is hard to find any reason why we could not communicate through Nominalized English just as effectively as through actual English. The objection that one is at first inclined to make—that it does not distinguish between mentioning and asserting—cannot be regarded as fatal.

It is important to remember that even in actual English a noun phrase on its own may be interpreted as an assertion. Suppose in the middle of a conversation about something else you see me look out of the window and hear me exclaim 'Gosh! A helicopter!', but on rushing to the window you find no helicopter in sight. You are entitled to be indignant if I insist that I was merely mentioning a helicopter, with no intention of asserting the presence of one. If you are educated in the literature of pragmatics and the philosophy of language, you may well accuse me of violating the Cooperative Principle or the Principle of Relevance, which, according to Grice (1989) and Sperber and Wilson (1995), underlies all conversation; for the only way in which my suddenly mentioning a helicopter can be construed as relevant to our conversation will be if I intend thereby to indicate that a helicopter is suddenly present.

If one is determined to insist that sentences are essential for asserting in English, one might try appealing here to ellipsis of the kind illustrated at (28) and (29). One might argue that, in the imagined context, *A helicopter!* is not just an NP but a sentence, albeit an elliptical one, just as *The snake you saw yesterday* and *Your seeing a snake yesterday* at (28*b*) and (29*b*) would be classified by many grammarians as elliptical sentences. But that appeal will fail because it begs the question. An independent reason for calling (28*b*) and (29*b*) elliptical sentences is that the context provided by the questions at (28*a*) and (29*a*) allows us to identify precisely what sentences they are elliptical versions of—namely, *This thing I've got here is the snake you saw yesterday* and *What I'm looking so surprised about is your seeing a snake yesterday* respectively.[13] But for *A helicopter!* no such unique expansion is available. There are numerous ways in which one might expand *A helicopter!* into a sentence appropriate to the context, such as *There's a helicopter outside!* or *I've just seen a helicopter!* or *Look at the helicopter out there!*; but there is no non-arbitrary way of choosing between them, and so no non-arbitrary way of deciding what sentence *A helicopter!* might be an elliptical version of. In the face of this, the only basis for continuing to insist that *A helicopter!* must count as a sentence would have to be that sentencehood is a necessary condition for asserting. If so, then the claim that a nonsentential expression on its own cannot count as an assertion is guaranteed true by definition, and is therefore vacuous.[14] Of course, it is still empirically true that assertions in English, as in all languages, are usually made by means of sentences. The important question is why—a question that Chapter 5 will address.

---

[13] The differences between these sentences and the corresponding interrogatives include certain demonstrative elements (*I* for *you*, *here* for *there*), but these substitutions are automatic.

[14] In the terminology of Geach (1980: 52), *A helicopter!* counts as the 'independent' use of a 'name'—a kind of use in which the 'name' occurs outside the context of a proposition. Geach agrees with me in distinguishing between 'independent' and elliptical uses.

An odd reflection of the view that assertion presupposes sentencehood (the view that I am rejecting) appears in the editorial conventions of some newspapers. In most newspapers in the English-speaking world one regularly encounters headlines such as *Election victory for Opposition* or *Cancer research breakthrough*. These are syntactically unlike NPs that occur in ordinary speech in that they are telegraphic in style, lacking determiners such as *a*, *an*, and *the*; however, they are unequivocally NPs rather than sentences, because they lack verbs. But some newspapers have an editorial convention insisting that headlines should be sentences. In these newspapers the content of the headlines just quoted would have to be expressed in a form such as *Opposition is victorious in election* or *Cancer researchers achieve breakthrough*. Underlying this convention seems to be a feeling that in order to assert that something has happened a sentence must be used. If that were correct, then readers of newspapers with the more liberal convention, when encountering an NP such as *Cancer research breakthrough*, would be in doubt whether they were being informed of an achievement that had taken place or merely being invited to contemplate an achievement that might take place. But clearly such doubts would be ludicrous. A newspaper that trumpeted *Cancer research breakthrough* over a report of a much more modest achievement would be treated with derision if it tried to excuse itself on the grounds that the headline, being nonsentential, did not constitute an assertion.

My claim that assertion by means of NPs is possible will be reinforced if contexts can be found where it is absolutely general in English usage and where the use of a sentence would be regarded as not merely unnecessary but inappropriate. Such contexts indeed exist. Captions under photographs in newspapers typically take the form of NPs, such as *Senator Edward Kennedy* or *King Hussein of Jordan*; no newspaper insists on *This is (a picture of) Senator Edward Kennedy* or *This is (a picture of) King Hussein of Jordan*. Likewise, at the kind of formal ball at which arriving guests are (or used to be) announced loudly by a footman, the announcement would take the form of an NP: *The Duke and Duchess of Omnium*, not *These people are the Duke and Duchess of Omnium*.

It is characteristic of assertions that they can be mistaken. This characteristic applies just as well to captions and announcements as to sentences. If the footman makes a mistake and roars 'The Duke and Duchess of Omnium!' when it is actually Sir George and Lady Blenkinsop who are arriving, we do not describe him as saying something untrue, but he has certainly said something inaccurate. Our reluctance to use the epithet 'untrue' here merely reflects the fact that we tend to reserve that for sentences (or what sentences express). The close relationship between untruth and this kind of inaccuracy is demonstrated by the practice of the surrealist painter René Magritte, who in several of his paintings exploits the disconcerting effect of deliberately miscaptioning objects that they depict. Sometimes the miscaption take the form of an NP, such as *la lune* ('the moon') under a picture of a shoe, or *la neige* ('the snow') under one of a bowler hat, but in one painting he uses a sentence: *Ceci n'est pas une pipe* ('This is not a pipe') under a picture of a tobacco pipe.[15] The effect achieved by the inaccurate NP labels and by the untrue sentence is exactly the same.

Nominalized English is, of course, a mock-up, and differs from Monocategoric in that, although it lacks the distinction between noun phrases and sentences, it still distinguishes prepositional, adjectival, and adverbial phrases. But it serves to illustrate the point that syntactic coding of the distinction between reference and truth is not vital for successful communication. This conclusion is reinforced if one imagines what questions would arise in the course of the debate on language origins if all humans spoke some version of Monocategoric. Many of the questions that currently puzzle us would puzzle Monocategoric speakers too: how to interpret human fossil evidence and evidence from tools and other artefacts, how human language relates to primate vocalizations, and so on. But it is hard to see why speakers of Monocategoric would ever be inclined to puzzle over their languages' lack of syntactic structures that contrast in the way that sentences and NPs do. Their reaction to the idea that that distinction somehow 'ought' to exist would be like our immediate reaction to the Martian's suggestion that our languages 'ought' to distinguish syntactically between sentences in which a verb phrase is combined with a noun phrase and sentences in which a verb phrase is combined with a sentence. 'We get along perfectly well without such syntactic complexity,' we would tell the Martian—and that is also what the Monocategoric speakers would tell us.

I hope to have persuaded readers that the fact that the syntax of all human languages incorporates a sentence/NP distinction, so far from being self-evident or inevitable, demands explanation. The scene is now set for me to offer an explanation in Chapter 5. But it is appropriate first to address in Chapter 3 a fundamental issue concerning the truth/reference distinction. So far, I have said about this distinction the same as what I have said about the object/event, type/token, and activity/achievement distinctions: the fact that they exist does not entail that syntax must encode them. But in respect of the truth/reference distinction, a more radical possibility presents itself. If a language such as Monocategoric can work quite well without encoding it, does it have a basis outside language at all, or could it rather be a mere by-product of one aspect of how syntax happens to have evolved? Could it be that we do not need the truth/reference distinction; we only think we need it because we are native speakers of human languages, which distinguish sentences (as candidates for truth) from NPs (as candidates for successful reference)? I will argue in Chapter 3 that the answer is yes. That is an adventurous conclusion in that it casts doubt on the handling in Western philosophy of the nature of truth and the relationship of minds, particularly human

---

[15] The paintings referred to are *La Clef des songes* (*The Dream Interpreter*) and *La Trahison des images* (*The Treachery of Pictures*).

minds, to it. To some readers this may already seem too adventurous a conclusion even to contemplate. I would, therefore, like to emphasize immediately that the argument of Chapter 3 is independent of what precedes and follows. There is no inconsistency in rejecting it while agreeing with the rest. One may be persuaded that the evolutionary scenario presented here is plausible while still believing that the truth/reference distinction is valid for reasons unconnected with grammar. On the other hand, if the argument in Chapter 3 is valid, it suggests that one of the reasons why we humans are inclined to regard ourselves as a unique species— namely, that only we have the capacity to apprehend 'truth'—may be bogus. That is because, according to the scenario proposed in Chapter 5, this capacity turns out to have less to do with intellectual superiority than with linguistic by-products of mundane physiological changes in the vocal tract.

# 3 Truth and Reference

## 3.1. Are Truth and Reference Distinguishable Nongrammatically?

In Chapter 5 I will offer an evolutionary explanation for what in Chapter 2 I argued to be a central puzzle about human language: the fact that all languages distinguish grammatically between sentences and NPs. But in Chapter 2 I mentioned what might seem to be a reason why this distinction is not really puzzling at all, so that no explanation of that kind is necessary. We need NPs in order to refer to things or people or events, it might be said, and we need sentences in order to make statements (whether true or false) about the people, things, and events that we refer to. I countered this by arguing that, even if the distinction between truth and reference has a basis that is independent of grammar, that does not explain why it should be reflected so pervasively in grammar, given that we could get along quite well with a language such as Monocategoric or Nominalized English in which the sentence/NP distinction is absent, and given that other philosophically important distinctions lack grammatical counterparts. But I did not challenge the assumption that truth and reference are genuinely distinct as ways in which linguistic expressions may fit the world, irrespective of these expressions' grammatical status.

I will now examine that assumption more closely. Quite a lot hangs on the outcome. If we conclude that truth and reference must indeed be distinguished for nongrammatical reasons, the argument of the following chapters will not be affected. On the other hand, if we conclude that there is no nongrammatical basis for the distinction (that it is a by-product of the sentence/NP distinction, in fact), not only is the central argument of this book reinforced, but one of the main preoccupations of philosophy in the Western world is arguably shown to be distorted. The argument of following chapters will be reinforced because an apparent alternative explanation for the universality of the sentence/NP distinction disappears. And the philosophical preoccupation with establishing the relationship of language to the world (and hence the nature of knowledge in so far as it involves language) has been distorted because of the widespread (though not universal) assumption that the kind of relationship that declarative sentences have with the world (called 'being true' or 'being false') is fundamentally different from the kind of relationship that NPs have with it.

It may seem presumptuous to aspire to say something worthwhile in one chapter about so huge a philosophical topic. Centuries of philosophical writing on the nature of truth cannot be summarized and criticized in so small a space, even supposing I were competent to try. I will in fact concentrate on just three philosophers active between the late nineteenth and late twentieth centuries: Gottlob Frege, Ludwig Wittgenstein, and Peter Strawson. I will also discuss some views of Plato from the fourth century BC, partly because of his enormous influence and partly because of an intriguing parallel that he draws between sentences and syllables (foreshadowing my argument in Chapter 5), which is made much of by the twentieth-century philosopher Gilbert Ryle.

Admittedly, demonstrating that none of these philosophers provides the kind of nongrammatical criteria we are looking for would not demonstrate that such criteria do not exist. On the other hand, it would establish a substantial prima-facie case. The recent three have exerted massive influence on philosophical discussion of language and truth in the English-speaking world during the twentieth century, while Plato is in the special position of being the only Western philosopher of first rank whose work antedates Aristotle's codification of the logic of propositions. So, if a secure nongrammatical motivation for the truth/reference distinction is something that Western philosophy can provide, one or more of these philosophers should surely lead us to it. Yet I will argue that none of them does so.

In my discussion I will not be overly scrupulous about philosophical distinctions between sentences, statements, and propositions. A summary of these distinctions and a justification for ignoring them here can be found in the Appendix.

## 3.2. Frege

Gottlob Frege, who lived from 1848 to 1925, is regarded by some as the most important logician since Aristotle. This is paradoxical, because he was primarily a mathematician. His interest in logic arose from a concern to ensure the validity of mathematical reasoning, and one might therefore expect that he would have no interest in the application of logic to ordinary language. He did indeed criticize ordinary language harshly for its lack of rigour.[1] But he used ordinary language (German) to illustrate his technical use of terms such as *Sinn* ('sense'), *Bedeutung* ('reference'),[2] *Gegenstand* ('object'), *Satz* ('proposition' or 'sentence'), *Gedanke*

---

[1] For relevant quotations and discussion, see Baker and Hacker (1984: 67–76).

[2] In Frege (1980), unlike the two earlier editions of this compilation, the term *Bedeutung* is glossed as 'meaning'. This is unfortunate, because *Bedeutung* has traditionally been rendered 'reference' in translations and discussions of Frege's technical usage. I will stick with the traditional rendering.

('thought'), and *Urtheil* ('judgement'), and it is these illustrations that so profoundly influenced subsequent philosophers of language.

Frege was concerned with relationships between asserted propositions or **judgements**. Examples of judgements (Frege 1980: 2, 3) are:

(1)    Unlike magnetic poles attract one another.
(2)    The Greeks defeated the Persians at Plataea.
(3)    Archimedes perished at the capture of Syracuse.

But it is possible to entertain the idea that unlike poles attract one another without asserting that they do. Frege therefore distinguished between the **content** of a judgement (the idea entertained) and the **assertion** of that content. Only when some content is asserted does a judgement arise. But what sort of content is a content of possible judgement or, more succinctly, **judgeable**? This is an important question for us. The association of judgeability with assertion means that only what is judgeable can be true, so criteria for distinguishing judgeable from non-judgeable content may lead to what we are seeking—namely, criteria for distinguishing truth from other kinds of relationship with the world. And non-judgeable content certainly exists, according to Frege; as an example he cites the 'idea' *house.*

On the basis of these few examples, it may look as if judgeable content is the content of sentences whereas non-judgeable content includes the content of other grammatical units such as nouns. But to derive judgeability from grammar would hardly be appropriate for someone with Frege's views on the imperfections of ordinary language. Moreover, he makes it explicitly clear that in order to be judgeable a content does not have to be expressed by means of a sentence. The judgement at (3) can also be expressed as (4):

(4)    The violent death of Archimedes at the capture of Syracuse is a fact.

Here the content of the judgement is expressed by the NP *the violent death of Archimedes at the capture of Syracuse* and the assertion of this content is indicated by *is a fact.* Indeed, Frege envisages the possibility of a language that would operate entirely in this fashion (1980: 3). Such a language would look rather like Monocategoric or Nominalized English as described in Chapter 2 were it not that (for example) *House is a fact* would be ill-formed in it, since *house* is not deemed judgeable.

But, if grammar is not a secure criterion of judgeability, what is? It has to be acknowledged that Frege is entirely vague: 'the concept indicated by "judgeable-content" is close to the concept or range of concepts expressed by the traditional terms "proposition", "judgement", "assertion", "statement" and "thought"' (Baker and Hacker 1984: 125). This is disappointing. But, even if Frege offers no clear explicit criterion, can we perhaps discover a criterion implicit in his practice? The answer, unfortunately, is no. Rather, we find an array of analyses that are hard to reconcile with one another.

Considering (1)–(4) by contrast with *house*, it looks as if Frege may be relying implicitly on a distinction between physical objects, on the one hand, and states of affairs, on the other. The mutual attraction of magnetic poles, the Greek victory at Plataea, and the death of Archimedes are states of affairs, one might say, while a house is a physical object. An examination of Frege's doctrine of **reference** shows that this is not what he has in mind, however. Frege distinguishes between reference and **sense** in a fashion that can be illustrated by means of his famous examples *the Morning Star* and *the Evening Star* (1980: 29). These expressions differ in sense in just the way that the contrast between *morning* and *evening* suggests: we see the Morning Star at sunrise and the Evening Star at sunset. On the other hand, they have identical reference—namely, the planet Venus. This distinction expresses conveniently two respects in which expressions may differ semantically. The expression *the President of the United States* has the same sense whether it is uttered in 1950 or 1970, but, if used in those years to identify a particular individual, the individual identified (the reference of the expression) differs, namely Dwight D. Eisenhower in 1950 and Richard Nixon in 1970. On the other hand, two expressions that clearly differ in sense, namely *the President of the United States* and *the Allied Commander-in-Chief*, may on appropriate occasions have the same reference—namely, Eisenhower. But the distinction between sense and reference intersects with that between judgeable and non-judgeable content in an at first sight startling fashion. Expressions that can have a reference are not restricted to NPs with a content (or sense) that we might reasonably regard as non-judgeable, such as *the President of the United States*, referring to Eisenhower, or *the Morning Star*, referring to Venus. A sentence too has a reference, according to Frege. Normally this is its truth-value (truth or falsity); but in contexts where the content of a sentence is not asserted (for example, often when it is a subordinate element in another sentence), its reference is identified with its sense. Just as *the Morning Star* and *the Evening Star* refer to the same object—namely, Venus—so sentences (1)–(4) above all refer to one and the same object—namely, truth—which Frege classifies as an abstract object. On the other hand, if (2), for example, is embedded in the larger sentence (5), it refers to its own sense, whereas (5) as a whole refers to truth:

(5)    Herodotus reports that the Greeks defeated the Persians at Plataea.

Notice that the sense of the sentence *the Greeks defeated the Persians at Plataea*, to which that expression here refers, is not the defeat itself, any more than the sense of *the Morning Star* is the planet itself; rather, the sense of any sentence is an abstract object (a **thought**) derived from the words that the sentence contains and in virtue of which the sentence can in appropriate circumstances be true (Frege 1980: 121–2).

This may seem rather convoluted, and the reasoning that led Frege to his view of truth and falsity as objects to which sentences refer need not concern us here.[3] What matters is whether it leads us any closer to a nongrammatical criterion for the truth/reference distinction, in some guise. One way in which it might do so would be if expressions whose content belongs on the state-of-affairs side of the dichotomy between objects and states of affairs are always analysed as referring to either truth, falsity, or their own sense. But that is not the case, as is shown by Frege's analysis of expressions such as the NP *the separation of Schleswig-Holstein from Denmark*. The content of this expression is a state of affairs, surely; but it does not on that account necessarily refer to truth. Objects to which expressions can refer include 'instants and stretches of time' (1980: 71) and indeed anything denoted by an NP with a singular definite article (in English, *the*) (1980: 45). Frege cites the separation of Schleswig-Holstein from Denmark (which took place in 1866) as an example of an instant of time; and it is to that object, not to truth, that *the separation of Schleswig-Holstein from Denmark* refers in the context *After the separation of Schleswig-Holstein from Denmark, Prussia and Austria quarrelled.* Frege freely acknowledges that the same judgement can be expressed with a subordinate clause replacing the prepositional phrase: *After Schleswig-Holstein was separated from Denmark, Prussia . . .* But that simply reinforces his point that grammar is an unreliable guide to logical structure: clauses as well as NPs can refer to objects other than truth or falsity or their own sense— namely, to objects such as instants of time.

That is all very well for Frege, who does not see a need for an explicit criterion for judgeable content and thus for what kind of thing can be true or false. But for us, seeking just such a criterion, the outcome is confusing. To have judgeable content, is it necessary that an expression should be a sentence? Evidently not, since the content of the NP *the violent death of Archimedes at the capture of Syracuse* is deemed judgeable. Is it then sufficient that an expression should be a sentence? No, because the sentence *Schleswig-Holstein was separated from Denmark* can in some contexts refer to an instant in time and thus lack judgeable content. Is it sufficient that an expression should designate a state of affairs, in some sense? No, for the same reason: Schleswig-Holstein's separation from Denmark is a state of affairs, but Frege allows that in talking about it we are sometimes not referring to any of the three things that expressions with judgeable content can refer to— namely, truth, falsity, or their own sense. In fact, the only NPs or sentences whose content belongs consistently on one side of the fence in Frege's discussions (namely the non-judgeable side) seem to be NPs denoting physical objects, people, or places, such as *the house*, *Julius Caesar*, or *the capital of the German Empire*. But remember that physical objects, people, and places have no special shared status in Frege's classification of entities; they are merely a subset of the much larger

---

[3] The reason in fact has to do with Frege's treatment of equality and inequality as functions, in the mathematical sense (1980: 28). Just as $x^2$ is a function mapping each of its possible numerical arguments to a value that is the square of the argument, so $x^2 = 1$ is a function (he says) with a range of just two values: truth when the argument is 1 or $-1$, and falsity when the argument is any other number.

set of 'objects' (in his technical sense), which includes also truth, falsity, and indeed anything, whether concrete or abstract, that an NP can be used to identify. So what after all is the basis for the judgeability distinction? Despite Frege's avowed determination not to let grammar sway him, the only criterion that can be distilled from his practice is in the end a grammatical one. Expressions that are deemed in some contexts to have judgeable content are precisely those that, in German or English, are either sentences or paraphrasable by means of sentences. Expressions that are never deemed to have judgeable content are ones that are not paraphrasable by means of sentences in German (or English: *It houses, *He's Julius-Caesaring*). So truth and falsity as relationships with the world distinct from reference and failure of reference turn out to lack precisely the kind of language-independent foundation that one might reasonably expect of a philosopher who, like Frege, wishes to purge mathematical reasoning of defects imported from ordinary language.[4]

The sceptic may still feel that, if Frege's account of truth and reference is really so unsatisfactory, this ought to have been noticed, if not by Frege himself then at least by commentators. This objection can be answered, however. Commentators have been predisposed to think that the distinction between truth and reference is necessary, whatever shortcomings there may be in Frege's account of it, simply because they are native speakers of some human language and are therefore naturally inclined towards thinking that the sentence/NP distinction, despite the logical imperfections of ordinary grammar, must reflect something fundamental outside language. Indeed, the centrality of sentences as the subject matter of logic is assumed explicitly by Michael Dummett on the very first page of his massive commentary on Frege's philosophy of language: 'the understanding of the fundamental structure of language and therefore of thought . . . depend[s] upon possessing, in a correct form, that explanation of the construction of and interrelationship between sentences which it is the business of logic to give' (Dummett 1981: p. xxxi). This does not mean that commentators have overlooked Frege's vaguenesses. I have already cited Baker and Hacker's remarks about the lack of a clear criterion for judgeable content. And Frege's technical use of the term 'object', exemplified in our discussion of *the separation of Schleswig-Holsten from Denmark*, is also criticized as too all-embracing. From our point of view, though, it is paradoxical that what commentators object to is a trend in Frege's thought that weakens the special status of sentences. Because Frege freely accords object status to anything that a definite NP can identify, he would presumably be willing to recognize an object corresponding to each of the

---

[4] In Straits Salish and other languages of the American and Canadian north-west there is complete or near-complete overlap between the lexical items that can head a sentence ('verbs') and those that can head an NP or determiner phrase ('nouns') (Jelinek and Demers 1994). In such a language the way to say 'That's a house' and 'the house' respectively is something like *That houses* and *that which houses*. It is not clear how Frege would have accommodated such languages if he had known of them; but my argument here does not hinge on them.

nominalized sentences in the Nominalized English dialogue at (37) in Chapter 2.[5] But that is tantamount to recognizing a distinct object corresponding to every judgement (or at least every true one); and it would be a short step from there to questioning whether those other kinds of object that judgement are held to refer to—namely, truth and falsity—are independently needed—which in turn would be a step towards admitting that the truth/reference distinction might be a by-product of grammar. Among the commentators, however, Dummett agrees with Baker and Hacker that Frege's proliferation of objects is dangerous and should be curbed, even if he disagrees with them about how this should be done (Dummett 1981: 70–80; Baker and Hacker 1984: 251–2). Dummett (1981: 7) criticizes as 'a retrograde step' certain developments in Frege's later thought that diminish 'the uniqueness of sentences', and Baker and Hacker (1984: 250) worry about how such developments can be reconciled with 'the sharp differentiation commonly *and rightly* recognized to hold between sentences and names' (emphasis added). So it is not that commentators have missed the weaknesses in Frege's account; rather, it is that their weddedness to sentences and to the truth/reference distinction has been an obstacle to an accurate diagnosis.

I have suggested that Frege's readiness to recognize an object corresponding to every definite NP brings him close to a position where it would be natural to see the truth/reference distinction as superfluous. Why then did he not take that step? In so far as this is a question about Frege's intellectual life history, it is unanswerable. But Frege's terminology provides a clue. Truth and falsity, as we have seen, are objects to which sentences refer. Even a false sentence has a reference—namely, falsity. In this respect, a false sentence is unlike an NP such as *the present King of France*, for that expression has (at least at the end of the twentieth century) no reference at all. So, although the sentence *Ice sinks in water* and the NP *the present King of France* are alike in that they fail to fit the world, that is where their resemblance ends, in Frege's terms. It is not just that the ways in which they fail to fit have different names; rather, their modes of failure differ. In Frege's analysis, an NP such as *the present King of France* fails in a more comprehensive fashion than a false sentence does; for whereas the latter has both a sense and a reference, the former has only a sense. Given Frege's generosity in recognizing objects (an excessive generosity, in the commentators' view), one might have expected him to recognize an object for *the present King of France* to refer to, such as non-existence, perhaps. This object could be the shared reference of all NPs that fail to identify anything, such as *the highest prime number* or *the only skyscraper in New York*. Arguably, an adjustment on those lines would not conflict fundamentally with the rest of Frege's analysis, and could be seen as scarcely more than terminological. Be that as it may, it is not an adjustment that Frege made or even contemplated, so

[5] I consciously ignore the fact that the Nominalized English dialogue is fictitious, so a strict Fregean reaction to it would run up against his unwillingness to recognize fictitious objects. That does not affect the point being made here.

far as we can tell. Possibly this is because the non-identifying NPs that he actually discussed included none denoting objects whose non-existence is a confirmable today by straightforward empirical observation, like our example *the present King of France*. Rather, he limited himself to names of fictitious characters (for example, *Odysseus*) and terms denoting objects whose non-existence is a matter of mathematical proof (*the least rapidly converging series*) or of conjecture (*the celestial body most distant from the Earth*) (1980: 58–62). It was thus easy for him to think of failure of reference as in some way a more marginal phenomenon than falsity, and this may have been part of the reason why he did not devote more attention to the parallels between them.

## 3.3. Wittgenstein

All scholars change their opinions during their lifetime, but Ludwig Wittgenstein (1889–1951) changed his opinions more radically than most, to the extent that some commentators have treated him almost as if he were two people: 'the early Wittgenstein' and 'the later Wittgenstein'. The early Wittgenstein is also sometimes called 'the Wittgenstein of the *Tractatus*', after his *Tractatus Logico-Philosophicus*, mostly put on paper while he was on active service during the First World War and originally published in 1921.[6] Nearly all the published work of the later Wittgenstein appeared posthumously. This reflects the hesitation and diffidence with which Wittgenstein regarded his later work. In 1945 he wrote in the preface to his *Philosophical Investigations*, which was the closest of his later works to completion: 'I should have liked to produce a good book. This has not come about, but the time is past in which I could improve it' (1958: p. viii). Some of this self-deprecation can be put down to fanatical perfectionism, but it also reflects the distrust he had acquired of any systematic presentation of philosophical doctrine such as the *Tractatus* and indeed of the traditional aims of philosophy in general. He now saw philosophy as a kind of piecemeal applied common sense, 'a battle against the bewitchment of our intelligence by means of language', his aim now being, as he picturesquely put it, 'to shew the fly the way out of the fly-bottle' (remarks 109, 309).[7] The results of an activity of this kind were naturally hard to present systematically; but, quite apart from that, certain aspects of Wittgenstein's later views made it almost self-contradictory to try to present them at all, as we shall see.

---

[6] All references here will be not to the original German version, *Logisch-philosophische Abhandlung*, published in *Annalen der Philosophie* (1921) but rather to the English translation by Pears and McGuinness in their bilingual edition (Wittgenstein 1961).

[7] All the main body of Wittgenstein's *Tractatus* and most of his *Philosophical Investigations* are divided into numbered sections or 'remarks'. Citations are located by remarks where feasible, otherwise (if no remark is mentioned) by page.

This change of mind is especially relevant to us, because it can be seen as a loss of confidence in language-as-it-is as a reliable device for representing the world. In principle, that loss of confidence might have led Wittgenstein to think in detail about how language might have been, on the lines that I recommended in Chapters 1 and 2. But both the early and the late Wittgenstein shared a view of language as imposing limits on thought that are not merely difficult but even impossible to transcend. In the *Tractatus* this view is encapsulated in the famous closing remark: 'What we cannot speak about we must pass over in silence' (remark 7). In the *Philosophical Investigations* it is expressed more indirectly, in response to remarks that seem at first to contradict it:

500. When a sentence is called senseless, it is not as it were its sense that is senseless. But a combination of words is being excluded from the language, withdrawn from circulation.

496. Grammar does not tell us how language must be constructed to fulfil its purpose, in order to have such-and-such an effect on human beings. It only describes and in no way explains the use of signs.

Does Wittgenstein then envisage that the withdrawn combinations of words might be restored to circulation, or that language might be constructed according to a different grammar? It seems not. To know what the sense is that the allegedly senseless sentence expresses would require us somehow to 'get behind the words', 'as if there were something coupled to these words, which otherwise would run idle' (remarks 503, 507); but there is no such thing, because when we use a sentence 'nothing is concealed' (remark 435). And as for grammar, to say that it describes the use of signs is not to imply that the use of signs could be any different. Philosophy does not enable us to go beyond the limits set by language-as-it-is, merely to understand better where these limits lie:

119. The results of philosophy are the uncovering of one or another piece of plain nonsense and of bumps that the understanding has got by running its head up against the limits of language. These bumps make us see the value of the discovery.

Here is where Wittgenstein comes close to self-contradiction: philosophy is supposed to be able to show how language misleads us without providing any view of an alternative kind of language that would not mislead us.

The contrast between the early and the late Wittgenstein is directly relevant to our search for a language-independent motivation for the truth/reference dichotomy. This is because the early Wittgenstein propounded a view of the world that seems to provide such a motivation, through his distinction between, on the one hand, **facts** (closely tied to **states of affairs**) and, on the other hand, **objects** or **things**. We are told in the *Tractatus* that 'the world is all that is the case' (remark 1) and 'the sum-totality of reality is the world' (remark 2.063), but this is qualified by remarks that the world is 'the totality of facts, not things' (1.1) and 'the totality of existing states of affairs' (2.04), where by 'state of affairs' is meant not an object but 'a combination of objects (things)' (remark 2.01) or something produced by 'the configuration of objects' (remark 2.0272). States of affairs are thus in a fundamental sense more complex than objects (as remark 2.02 puts it, 'objects are simple'), and constitute an essential intermediate level between objects and the world.

If that is correct, then we can reasonably look to the contrast between objects and states of affairs for a non-linguistic basis for the distinction between reference and truth; and this is indeed what Wittgenstein seems to offer. Truth is introduced into his account as a characteristic of both propositions and pictures (remarks 2.0211, 2.0212, 2.21), but the two are connected by way of **thoughts**, which are 'logical pictures of facts' (remark 3) that find expression in propositions (remark 3.1), so that 'a proposition is a picture of reality' (remark 4.01). The mention of facts and reality in these remarks is crucial. Facts and reality are related to objects not directly but indirectly, through states of affairs. It follows that any linguistic entity that can be described as true must be related to objects in the same indirect fashion; conversely, that any linguistic entity that corresponds directly to an object cannot be described as true. And indeed this is what Wittgenstein says. Propositions never correspond to objects directly; rather objects are 'represented' in propositions by **names** (remark 3.22), so that 'I can only speak *about* them [i.e. objects]: I cannot *put them into words*' (remark 3.221; emphasis in original). The relationship between a name and a corresponding object is one not of truth but of meaning or reference (remark 3.203) (the German verb *bedeuten* used here is the one traditionally glossed 'refer' in discussions of Frege). The distinction between truth and reference therefore seems to have a solid philosophical basis in a distinction that resides in 'the world', quite independently of the language we use to talk about it.

But how solid is this basis really? Wittgenstein seems so confident of the distinction between objects and states of affairs that, although he explores some of its implications in detail, he introduces it by way of bald announcements, without justification. But this very confidence should make us wary: it could be just another example of 'the bewitchment of our intelligence by means of language'. And the details of the distinction, when examined closely, are not reassuring. To say (as Wittgenstein does) that a state of affairs is 'a combination of objects' seems close to saying that it is a set of objects, in the mathematical sense of 'set'. But sets in that sense are not required to have more than one member. Hence Wittgenstein seems to allow for the possibility of states of affairs consisting of only one object. But why then cannot objects be seen as just states of affairs of a particularly simple kind? Certainly, a set containing just one object is not the same as the object it contains. Nevertheless, the possibility of single-object states of affairs raises a question about whether the distinction is really needed. In failing to address this question in the *Tractatus*, Wittgenstein is guilty of a major omission from the point of view of what we are currently seeking—namely, an answer to the question of whether truth and reference are distinguishable nongrammatically.

What Wittgenstein says about propositions and names as linguistic entities is unsatisfactory in a parallel fashion. If states of affairs are combinations of objects, one might expect propositions to be construed as combinations of names. Wittgenstein does indeed say: 'An elementary proposition consists of names. It is a nexus, a concatenation, of names' (remark 4.22). But if 'concatenation' here means something like 'ordered set' in the mathematical sense, then, given that an ordered set, just like an unordered one, can have just one member, Wittgenstein seems to open the door to propositions consisting of just one name. But in that case why cannot we construe a name as just a maximally simple proposition? After all, despite Wittgenstein's denial at remark 3.221 (cited earlier), an object can be 'put into words' inasmuch as we can name it! Here too one might object on Wittgenstein's behalf that a set containing just one name is not the same as the name it contains. But here too we encounter a corollary of Wittgenstein's doctrine (namely, the possibility of single-name propositions) whose implications he fails to explore.[8]

So, reading the *Tractatus* with the question of Section 3.1 in mind, one is left dissatisfied. If Wittgenstein regarded the distinction between objects and states of affairs as too self-evident to require justification, this may mean no more than that he is seduced by grammar. Does Wittgenstein's own later dissatisfaction with the *Tractatus* amount to an acknowledgement of this? And, if so, does it enable the later Wittgenstein to offer a more satisfactory non-linguistic motivation for the truth/reference distinction? Answering the first question properly would require a deeper excursion into Wittgensteinian exegesis than our present priorities warrant; but the answer to the second question is no, as we shall see.

The early Wittgenstein offered a remarkably homogeneous view of propositions: they are all pictures of reality in the sense that a fairly direct mapping should be possible between the parts of a proposition and the parts of the piece of reality to which it corresponds. A famous anecdote illustrates the kind of evidence that weakened Wittgenstein's confidence in this view:

Wittgenstein and P. Sraffa, a lecturer in economics at Cambridge, argued together a great deal over the ideas of the *Tractatus*. One day (they were riding, I think, on a train), when Wittgenstein was insisting that a proposition and what it describes must have the same 'logical form', the same 'logical multiplicity', Sraffa made a gesture, familiar to Neapolitans as meaning something like disgust or contempt, of brushing the underneath of his chin with an outward sweep of the fingertips of one hand. And he asked: 'What is the logical form of

---

[8] Wittgenstein offers a second and seemingly incompatible characterization of elementary propositions in remark 4.24, as 'functions of names'. He probably has in mind here Frege's treatment of the non-name portions of sentences (that is, those portions that are not expressions with identifying reference such as *the Morning Star*) as functions that map their argument (a name) to a truth-value. Be that as it may, this second characterization does nothing to strengthen the case for a non-linguistic basis for the truth/reference distinction.

that?' Sraffa's example produced in Wittgenstein the feeling that there was an absurdity in the insistence that a proposition and what it describes must have the same 'form'. This broke the hold on him of the conception that a proposition must literally be a 'picture' of the reality it describes. (Malcolm 1958: 69)

We need not suppose that the incident on the train amounted to an instantaneous conversion. Nevertheless, Wittgenstein later gave Sraffa's stimulus the credit for 'the most consequential ideas' in the *Philosophical Investigations* (1958: p. viii). For our purposes what is interesting is the direction in which Wittgenstein chose to go once his confidence in his *Tractatus* views had been broken. At least three possible directions can be envisaged. One might have been to seek an alternative view of the world (an alternative metaphysics, one might say) that would avoid the short-comings of the *Tractatus* model but would still provide a language-independent basis for notions such as truth and reference (or meaning). A second might have been to acknowledge that his earlier view of the world had been over-influenced by language-as-it-is but proceed from there to seek reasons why language-as-it-is has acquired the characteristics that make it such an unreliable guide in philosophy. (Relevant reasons might be evolutionary ones, such as this book is concerned with.) A third possibility was to abandon entirely the kind of inquiry that the *Tractatus* represents and to avoid those uses of language that make this kind of inquiry appear worthwhile. The direction in which Wittgenstein actually chose to go was the third.

For our present purposes, that choice is unfortunate. Avoiding uses of language that purportedly lead philosophers astray means forgoing any possibility of arriving at a language-independent basis for the truth/reference distinction. Reference is a kind of meaning, and meaning is part of the dangerous territory that should be entered only for the purpose of erecting defences against 'the bewitchment of our intelligence'. In the very first remark in the *Philosophical Investigations*, Wittgenstein introduces the doctrine that in many if not all contexts the right question to ask about a word is not what it means but how it is used. As for truth and falsity, they are no longer seen as independent of the propositions to which they apply (according to whether these are accurate or inaccurate pictures of reality) but are definitionally linked to the notion 'proposition' itself, inasmuch as 'a proposition is whatever can be true or false' (remark 136), and we have

'p' is true = p
'p' is false = not-p.

To ask for an explanation of truth and falsity that goes beyond this (according to Wittgenstein) would be like asking for an explanation for why in chess it is the king that can be put in check while pawns cannot. No explanation can be forthcoming within the framework of the game of chess, because 'check *belongs* to our concept of the king in chess (as so to speak a constituent part of it)'.

Accepting all this, one could still without any inconsistency look for an explanation for why languages facilitate the expression of propositions, as so defined, and hence look for the genesis of the notions 'true' and 'false' that are linked to them. After all, Wittgenstein is willing to consider explanations of that sort in the context of his chess analogy: the reason why we do not play a game in which pawn capture means victory may be that such a game 'would be uninteresting or stupid or too complicated or something of the kind' (remark 136). And in his extensive discussion of 'language games' Wittgenstein does indeed deal with alternative ways in which language might operate. One of these even has a certain resemblance to the vervet monkey call system discussed in Chapter 2. There the point was made that, even if we accept that the vervets' eagle, snake, and leopard alarm calls have referential content, we cannot sensibly discuss whether they are sentential (either imperative or declarative) or nominal. Similarly, Wittgenstein contemplates a language game with a vocabulary of just the four items *block*, *pillar*, *slab*, and *beam*, used by a builder to give orders to his assistant (remarks 2–20). As Wittgenstein says, it makes no sense to ask whether these items are words or sentences. He explicitly rejects the idea that (for example) *slab!* would have to be analysed as an elliptical or degenerate sentence, short for *Bring me a slab!*, for the good reason that in this language game there exists no sentence *Bring me a slab!* that *slab!* could be regarded as a shortened version of.

A language game can exist, therefore, that lacks the distinction between words and sentences. It might seem a simple step from there to envisaging one that lacks the distinction between names and propositions. If Wittgenstein had taken that step, he might have been led to a radically different view of the nature of truth. But it is a step that he never took. The distinction between names and propositions not only gets carried forward from the *Tractatus* into Wittgenstein's later work but continues to be treated as crucial, even though its linguistic nature might plausibly make it vulnerable to his exhortations against linguistic bewitchment. Wittgenstein argues in the *Philosophical Investigations* that naming by itself is 'not a move in the language-game—any more than putting a piece in its place on the board is a move in chess' (remark 49); in order actually to say something (for example, to describe the colour of a square) one has to use a proposition, even if this proposition consists of just one word (say, *Red*). But that argument is invalid because it rests on an equivocation. There are two senses in which one can name something: one can use its name (so as to refer to it) or one can assign a name to it (so as to label it). In the labelling sense it is certainly true that to name an object is not to say something about the object named; rather, one is setting up the conditions for saying something about it. In the referring sense, however, to name an object may indeed be to say something about it. (Recall our helicopter example from Chapter 2: if I go to the window and utter the NP *A helicopter!*, any hearer will be justifiably annoyed if I then deny any intention of saying anything about a helicopter, or more specifically of saying that one is visible.) Wittgenstein's mistake is to suppose that the distinction between defining (or learning) a term and using it once it has been defined (or learned) motivates a distinction between how names, once defined or learned, relate to the world and how propositions relate to it. But these are quite different distinctions. The fact that the first is well motivated does not show that the second is, any more than it shows that a language game such as the *slab* game must distinguish between words and sentences.

It is pointless to speculate at length about why Wittgenstein considered such a bad argument to be valid. But three clues present themselves. Part of the reason may be that Wittgenstein thinks he has the formidable support of Frege; he equates his own view of names and propositions with Frege's view that a word has meaning only as part of a sentence. But, whatever exactly Frege meant by that, clearly he did not mean that every time a word appears outside the context of a sentence (say, in a shopping list) it is being redefined or relearned.[9]

A second clue is Wittgenstein's near-self-contradictory view of the role of philosophy in relation to language, which I drew attention to earlier. To him it seemed not merely difficult but intrinsically impossible to look at human language from the outside, so to speak, as we have tried to do in this book. The best we can do, he thought, is become more aware of the limits within which language requires us to operate; to attempt more than that is to seek in vain for some hidden essence beneath the surface (remark 92). And one of these limits is the propositional character of language:

93. . . . Why do we say a proposition is something remarkable? On the one hand, because of the enormous importance attaching to it. (And that is correct.) On the other hand this, together with a misunderstanding of the logic of language, seduces us into thinking that something extraordinary, something unique, must be achieved by propositions.—A *misunderstanding* makes it look to us as if a proposition *did* something queer.

One reason why one may think, despite Wittgenstein, that propositions achieve something extraordinary is that they are a feature of a communication system—namely, human language—that is so much more elaborate than any other that has yet evolved.

This brings us to the third clue. Wittgenstein seems to have had little interest in the communication systems of non-human animals and to have been pessimistic about them as topics of research. Animals 'do not use language—if we except the most primitive forms of language' (remark 25); besides, 'if a lion could talk, we could not understand him' (1958: 223). In one late passage in the *Philosophical Investigations* (1958: 184) he does allude to 'the evolution of the higher animals and of man, and the awakening of consciousness at a particular level', but the allusion is so isolated and fragmentary that one cannot make much of it. Sraffa (the economist whose Neapolitan gesture so influenced Wittgenstein) has been

---

[9] I sympathize with Geach's (1980: 52) criticism of both Wittgenstein and Frege on this point.

credited with influencing him towards a more 'anthropological' approach to philosophical problems, so that (for example) his language games are presented not abstractly but in the context of an imaginary social setting where they are played (Monk 1990: 261). But he never supplemented this social perspective with a biological perspective, so as to reflect seriously on why language evolved so as to acquire the characteristics it has.

Despite Wittgenstein's warning against allowing our intelligence to be bewitched by language, it seems fair to conclude that the central place that he gives to the proposition/name distinction, both early and late, reflects just such a bewitchment. Certainly he does not establish the distinction, and hence the distinction between truth and reference, on a non-linguistic foundation of the kind we are seeking.

### 3.4. Strawson

P. F. Strawson is one of the most eminent representatives of the Oxford tradition of analytical philosophy in the second half of the twentieth century. But a particular reason for discussing him in this chapter is that he has devoted much attention, as outlined in Strawson (1994), to the relationship between subjects and predicates, and in particular to the degree of correspondence (or lack of it) between grammatical and nongrammatical criteria for identifying them. This bears on our current concern, in that subjects are typically referring expressions while subjects and predicates combine to form propositions, which can be true or false; therefore, if Strawson can show that the distinction between subjects and predicates has a solid nongrammatical foundation, he has shown that the truth/reference distinction is needed independently of grammar.

Before considering Strawson's views in detail, it is necessary to mention an aspect of them that might seem to render them irrelevant to our present enterprise. His book *Individuals* (1959) is subtitled 'an essay in descriptive metaphysics', which he explains as follows: 'Descriptive metaphysics is content to describe the actual structure of our thought about the world, revisionary metaphysics is concerned to produce a better structure' (1959: 9). If 'the actual structure of our thought about the world' is conditioned in some degree by language-as-it-is, this may seem to imply that Strawson is not concerned with the possibility that language might have been different in any fundamental way and is therefore not interested in any contribution that philosophy might make to explaining its actual characteristics. However, Strawson is concerned to show that the grammatical subject/predicate distinction is sustained by a fundamental ontological distinction—a distinction between kinds of things that exist. At the same time, his announced self-limitation to 'the actual structure of our thought' may help to explain why (as I shall argue) he too fails to supply unequivocally non-linguistic evidence of the kind we are seeking. This failure arises from flaws in his treatment of three issues:

- the relationship between subjects and particulars (a term to be explained directly);
- negation; and
- the relationship between propositions and a certain class of particulars corresponding to the nominalized sentences of Nominalized English in Chapter 2.

### 3.4.1. Subjects and Particulars

A possible view that a philosopher might take of the subject/predicate distinction is that it is purely a matter of grammar and therefore of no interest in philosophy. That is what Wittgenstein's younger Cambridge contemporary, the mathematician and philosopher Frank Ramsey, thought (1925).[10] Strawson puts this radical view on one side, however, on the ground that he wants 'to discover the rationale of the traditional view, *if it has one*' (1959:138; emphasis added).

The rationale that Strawson thinks he can discover involves the distinction between **particulars** and **universals** and the special status that he ascribes to **basic particulars**. The universal/particular distinction, which has a long philosophical pedigree, is drawn by Strawson in *Individuals* (1959) as follows. Particulars include identifiable physical objects, people, and historical occurrences; universals include qualities, properties, numbers, and species. Basic particulars are 'three-dimensional objects with some endurance through time' (1959: 39), or material bodies. These are basic in the sense that the ability to identify particulars of other kinds (events, processes, states, and so on) relies on the ability to identify material bodies. Admittedly, the borderline between material bodies, on the one hand, and events, processes, and states, on the other, is not clear-cut (on which side of the line do rivers and fields fall, for example?), but what matters is that clear-cut examples of basic particulars exist. Particulars are the 'categorial' or non-grammatical underpinning for subjects (as opposed to predicates), and the existence of basic particulars, defined as they are in an entirely non-linguistic fashion, seems to remove any suspicion that this underpinning may be covertly grammatical. As Strawson (1959: 161) puts it: 'There undoubtedly are propositions of a simple kind in which a particular term and a universal term are each introduced and assertively linked; [and] the foundation of the subject–predicate distinction lies in the difference of type or category [i.e. particular versus universal] of the terms introduced into this kind of proposition . . .'.

---

[10] Wittgenstein credits Ramsey alongside Sraffa with having influenced the thinking that led to the *Philosophical Investigations.* Ramsey would certainly have had greater positive influence, not only on Wittgenstein but on philosophers in general, if he had not died in 1930 at the age of 26.

Strawson applies his notion of basic particulars to a question far removed from grammar. It enters into his view of how material bodies relate to personhood. The identification of individual persons depends on their having material bodies, Strawson argues, and the possibility of consciousness thus depends on material bodies too. A disembodied consciousness could not exist, he says, unless it is the consciousness of a person formerly embodied who has memories of that embodied state and who might also 'achieve some kind of attenuated vicarious personal existence by taking a certain kind of interest in the human affairs of which he [*sic*] is a mute and invisible witness' (1959: 116). It is not our business here to decide whether this intriguing claim is correct or not. What the claim shows, however, is that particulars play a role in Strawson's thinking in an area quite independent of language, so that, if he can use them to illuminate the subject/predicate distinction, he will have supplied a motivation for it, and hence also for the reference/truth distinction, which is independent of language too.

How successful, then, is Strawson's use of particulars and universals to illuminate subjects and predicates respectively? Certainly he does not claim that terms designating particulars (typically proper names and NPs with a definite determiner) are always grammatical subjects, or that grammatical subjects are always particular terms. He allows that subjects may be universals, as in:

(6)   Generosity is a more amiable virtue than prudence.

But one association, at least, between universals and predicates is satisfyingly tight, Strawson says: a predicate may never consist entirely of a particular.[11] Besides, even instances such as (6) are to be regarded as untypical; they involve 'analogies' with the more usual pattern in which the subject is a particular (1959: 161, 189).

Strawson takes a serious risk here, however. An appeal to analogy to accommodate more marginal instances of some phenomenon can be successful only if there are independent reasons for thinking that these instances really are more marginal, in some sense. Otherwise, the appeal to analogy will be question-begging and an account based on it will collapse. And I will argue that Strawson's account of the subject/predicate distinction collapses in just this way.

An account of the subject/predicate distinction must accommodate not only universal terms (such as *generosity*) as grammatical subjects but also particular terms (such as proper names and definite NPs) contained within predicates. Strawson recognizes this. Although an expression for a particular such as *John* cannot *be* a predicate, he says, it can be *contained in* a predicate expression such

---

[11] Kinds of proposition in which predicates might be thought to be particulars include statements of identity such as *The Morning Star is the Evening Star*. These are a traditional crux for philosophers. Strawson discusses them too (1959: 242–3). But it is not necessary for me to take a position on his treatment of identity statements, because I will argue that his rationale for the subject/predicate distinction is unsatisfactory for other reasons.

as *is married to John* (1959: 189). This predicate expression is a 'universal-cum-particular' of a kind that involves a 'slight extension' of the 'more fundamental' case where what is predicated of a particular is an ordinary universal containing no particulars (1959: 171–2). Strawson gives few examples to illustrate the distinction between fundamental and extended or analogical instances, but it seems clear that the examples in (7) will count as fundamental while those in (8) will count as involving analogical extension:

(7)  (*a*)  Jean hates tall buildings.
    (*b*)  Jean can't ride a bicycle.
    (*c*)  Jean prefers asparagus.
    (*d*)  Jean admires sincerity.
(8)  (*a*)  Jean hates the Empire State Building.
    (*b*)  Jean can't ride Bill's bicycle.
    (*c*)  Asparagus is Jean's favourite.
    (*d*)  Jean admires her mother.

The propositions in (7) are all of the fundamental kind because their predicates (the parts following the subject *Jean*) contain no expressions that identify particulars, whether basic (material bodies) or non-basic (events, states, etc.). According to (7*a*) it is tall buildings in general that Jean hates, not any specific ones; and what (7*b*) says is that Jean cannot ride any bicycle, not that there are particular bicycles that defeat her. On the other hand, the propositions in (8) all involve analogical extension, according to Strawson. This is because in each of them the predicate contains an expression that designates a particular (*the Empire State Building, Bill, Jean, her mother*), and (8*c*) depends on a further analogy in that its subject (*asparagus*) designates not a particular but a universal.

At this point we are justified in becoming uneasy. Is there any independent reason for counting the examples in (8) as 'analogical extensions' of a 'fundamental' type illustrated in (7)—independent, that is, of the very point that Strawson is seeking to prove—namely, that particulars and universals provide a nongrammatical basis for the subject/predicate distinction? What Strawson needs to supply is evidence that predicates are somehow an unwelcoming environment for particulars, making room for them only with a certain amount of strain or awkwardness. But there does not seem to be anything awkward about (8) by comparison with (7). Is it relevant, perhaps, that in (8) the number of particulars mentioned in each predicate is only one? Conceivably we might feel increasingly uncomfortable about predicates with particulars as the number of particulars increases. A way to test this would be to examine a series of propositions whose predicates contain progressively more particulars, as in (9):

(9)  (*a*)  Jean has put something away.
    (*b*)  Jean has put her bicycle away.

(c)   Jean has put your bicycle away.
(d)   Jean has put your bicycle in the garage.
(e)   Jean has put your bicycle in Uncle George's garage.

Here the number of particulars referred to only in the predicate rises from zero in (9a) to four in (9e), where each of the expressions *Uncle George's garage* and *your bicycle* identifies one particular (the garage and the bicycle) by reference to another (Uncle George and the addressee, identified by *your*). But these examples do not offer the kind of support for Strawson that we are looking for. Certainly the predicates are increasingly complex lexically, but there is no separate increase in strain or awkwardness. For all five examples it is not hard to envisage conversational contexts in which they might be used—although, oddly enough, the example for which it is hardest to imagine a plausible context and which is in that sense most awkward is precisely (9a), whose predicate conforms exactly to Strawson's 'fundamental' type!

These examples highlight an insuperable obstacle to the correspondence that Strawson tries to establish between grammatical and 'categorial' criteria for the subject/predicate distinction. This is the fact that, whatever our criteria for grammatical subjecthood, a simple sentence (one with no sentences or clauses embedded in it) contains only one grammatical subject, but it may contain any number of expressions that identify particulars. Even if one shares Strawson's belief in the 'fundamental' character of sentences in which the subject designates a particular, one is still left with the problem of explaining why just one particular among the many that may figure in a sentence (or, in more strictly linguistic terms, just one particular-identifying expression) should be singled out for a special status. Why one, rather than two or three? Or none at all?

The reason why Strawson never tackles this problem seriously seems to be that he thinks its solution will be trivial. He discusses at length how linguistic expression might be given to a judgement relating to a single particular, but judgements relating to more than one particular are relegated to a footnote: 'the description *could readily be adapted* to cases of judgment relating to pairs, trios, etc., of particulars' (1974: 21; emphasis added). This confident attitude is repeated elsewhere. At one point Strawson discusses the properties of three 'language-types' that are artificially restricted in relation to actual human languages but that illustrate progressively more elaborate kinds of particular-specification and predication (1974: ch. 3). For our purposes, the language-type that is of special interest is one in which sentences can consist of a two-place predicate linking two particular-specifying expressions (Strawson's Language-Type 3 or LT3), as in English *John admires Mary* or *Mary is to the right of John*. In LT3, is either of the two particular-specifying expressions assigned the status of subject, and, if so, on what basis? A convincing answer to that question might yield the kind of motivation for the subject/predicate distinction that we are looking for—one independent of the grammar of language-as-it-is. But Strawson again announces that he will 'pass over' this question, on the ground that a way of revising the definitions of subject and predicate so as to render them applicable to LT3 is clearly possible, and a systematic presentation is unnecessary (1974: 93–4). What these dismissals leave unanswered, however, is the prior question of why LT3, or any language, should need the grammatical subject/predicate distinction at all, as it exists in actual languages.

The inadequacy of Strawson's treatment of such a fundamental issue suggests that his thinking, like that of Frege and Wittgenstein before him, may be influenced more than he realizes by grammar-as-it-is. But there is one aspect of his presentation that may especially have helped to mislead him. This is the rarity, among the English examples that he discusses, of sentences containing more than one expression identifying a particular, and the near-complete absence of sentences containing more than two such expressions, on the lines of our examples (9c–e). If he had considered such examples at more length, he might have been less confident about classifying them as mere analogical extensions of a type illustrated in (9a). One may agree with Strawson that material bodies, as basic particulars, motivate the existence of linguistic expressions that one may call broadly nounlike. (Such motivation may, however, be indirect, via the linguistic expression of predicate-argument structure, as I will argue in Chapters 4 and 5.) But it is a big step from there to concluding, on purely ontological or logical grounds, that just one noun-like expression in each sentence deserves to be singled out for a special 'subject' role; and this is a step that Strawson nowhere adequately justifies.

The task of explaining why there should be just one subject in each sentence will not arise if the focus is not on subjects but on 'subject-terms', understood as terms that identify particulars. A sentence can readily contain reference to more than one particular, so a sentence can readily contain more than one subject-term; and subject-terms may indeed be underpinned ontologically by particulars. Subject-terms, in this sense, are to the fore in much of Strawson's work after *Individuals*, such as *Subject and Predicate in Logic and Grammar* (1974). But for the shift of attention from subjects to subject-terms there is a price to be paid: it diverts Strawson from the goal of providing ontological motivation for subjects in the usual grammatical sense, according to which a simple sentence contains only one subject. Indeed, Strawson himself admits that 'further development' of his theory will be needed to achieve that goal (1974: 138).

The similarity of the labels 'subject' and 'subject-term' in Strawson's usage thus obscures a crucial divergence in meaning. This divergence is further obscured by Strawson's tendency to concentrate on sentences containing no more than one particular-identifying expression. Unfortunately, because this undermines his project of uncovering a non-linguistic basis for the subject/predicate distinction, it also undermines any hope that his analysis of universals and particulars will supply a non-linguistic motivation for the sentence as a grammatical unit, and hence a non-linguistic motivation for truth and reference as distinct relationships to the world.

### 3.4.2. Subjects, Predicates, and Negation

Strawson points out a fundamental asymmetry between individual particulars and 'general characters' (or universals) with respect to incompatibility (1971*a*, 1994: 35–6). Consider one particular (the Eiffel Tower) and one general character (being made entirely of steel). If we assign this character to this particular, we exclude the possibility of assigning to the same particular a multitude of other characters, such as being made entirely of concrete or of papier mâché. On the other hand, we do not exclude the possibility of assigning to the same character any number of other particulars, such as the Forth Bridge or the author's dining-room cutlery set. From the fact that a particular has a certain character, it follows that there are other characters that it cannot have; but nothing follows about other particulars that may or may not have that character.[12]

That is a valid point, but what new light does it shed on the subject/predicate distinction? None, I suggest. According to the argument of the previous section, one may agree with Strawson that there is a distinction between particulars and universals but deny that that explains why syntax should foster a kind of expression in which just one of several particulars is singled out for 'subject' status, the rest being relegated to the 'predicate'. Asymmetry in respect of incompatibility would be relevant, then, if it discriminated somehow between subject particulars and particulars within predicates. But whether in any given sentence the NP *the Eiffel Tower* is a grammatical subject or part of a predicate, the fact that the Eiffel Tower cannot be simultaneously all steel and all concrete is unaffected. So the asymmetry between particulars and universals with regard to incompatibility does nothing to reinforce the alleged ontological basis for the subject/predicate distinction. But it is instructive to consider why Strawson thinks otherwise. This makes it easier to understand (I think) why he overlooks the implications of examples such as (9*b*–*e*) above. Let us begin by considering two facts, A and B.

Fact A is that incompatibility has links with negation, in that (10) entails (11), for example:

(10)   The Eiffel Tower is made entirely of steel.
(11)   The Eiffel Tower is not made entirely of concrete.

The asymmetry in incompatibility means that (10) has no logical connection with (12), however:

---

[12] That statement is a little too sweeping. Among what Strawson (1959) calls 'universals-cum-particulars' there are some general characters that by their nature can be assigned to only one particular, such as being the mother of President Clinton. But for the purpose of the present argument this detail can be ignored.

(12)    The Forth Bridge is not made entirely of steel.

The Forth Bridge and the Eiffel Tower, being particulars, are not mutually incompatible with respect to any universal, as Strawson makes clear.

Fact B is that (13) is syntactically ill-formed in English:

(13)    *Not the Forth Bridge is made entirely of steel.

This is because, in general, NPs cannot be negated in English by the simple device of placing *not* in front of them. But such a construction is allowable when there is an explicit contrast between two NPs, expressed *not . . . but . . .*, for example:

(14)    Not the Forth Bridge but the Tay Bridge is made entirely of steel.

Example (14) demonstrates (if a demonstration is needed) that there is nothing wrong with (13) semantically. Its natural interpretation is 'It is not the Forth Bridge that is made entirely of steel'. What's more, some languages show more latitude than English in permitting this kind of simple negation of NPs, even without an explicit contrast. For example, in Russian, both (16) and (17) are possible as negative variants of (15):

(15)        Ivan prišël.
            'John arrived.'
(16)        Ivan ne prišël.
            'John didn't arrive.'
(17)        Ne Ivan prišël.
            'It wasn't John who arrived.'
     or:    'The person who arrived wasn't John.'
     or:    '*John* didn't arrive [but somebody else did].'

Not surprisingly, this Russian construction is also possible when an explicit contrast is expressed, as in English:

(18)    Ne Ivan prišël, a Pëtr.
        'Not John but Peter arrived.'

Now, what connection is there between Fact A and Fact B? There is a superficial parallel. In virtue of Fact A, universals that may potentially be assigned to the Forth Bridge, as a particular, include incompatible positive and negative pairs, such as 'being made of steel' and 'not being made of steel'; but particulars that may be assigned to the universal 'being made of steel' do not include positive and negative pairs that are incompatible in any comparable fashion, such as the Forth Bridge and some non-Forth-Bridge counterpart. In virtue of Fact B, on the other hand, predicates that can be combined with the NP *the Forth Bridge*, as a grammatical subject, include positive and negative pairs, such as *is made of steel* and *is not made of steel*; but subject NPs that may be combined with the predicate *is made of steel* do not include incompatible positive and negative pairs such as *the Forth Bridge* and *not the Forth Bridge*. It should be clear, however, that the parallel is only superficial. Fact A applies to all particulars and universals, irrespective of what language is used to talk about them. On the other hand, Fact B, as stated, relates only to NPs in English; and, while some languages resemble English in restricting the syntactic negation of NPs, not all languages do so, as Russian shows. Moreover, the reluctance of English NPs to tolerate straightforward negation with *not* has nothing specifically to do with the grammatical subject function, as in shown in (19) and (20), where it is the grammatical object that is negated:

(19)   *We could see not the Forth Bridge.
(20)   *The boat was passing under not the Forth Bridge.

As we would expect in the light of (14), however, both these become acceptable when an explicit contrast is included:

(21)   We could see not the Forth Bridge but the Tay Bridge.
(22)   The boat was passing under not the Forth Bridge but the Tay Bridge.

The fact that Strawson sets so much store by the alleged correspondence between particularhood and syntactic non-negatability may be related to his attitude towards non-subject expressions for particulars, as in (9*b*–*e*). Since these expressions are all in the predicate, and since the predicate is negatable, it is only the non-negatable subject NP that seems clearly to reflect the allegedly corresponding characteristic of particulars. But, as I have shown, the two kinds of non-negatability behave differently (in particular, one is language-independent whereas the other is confined to certain languages), so the apparent parallel is misleading.

A question still remains: even if some languages (like Russian) allow negated subject NPs, why does negation seem so generally to gravitate towards the predicate, and more especially the verb? After all, Strawson is not the only philosopher to whom negating a proposition and negating its predicate seem equivalent (cf. Geach 1980: 58). I will return to this issue when discussing auxiliary verbs in Chapters 4 and 5.

### 3.4.3. Particulars, Propositions, and Nominalizations

In Chapter 2 we considered the relationship between sentences such as (23) and corresponding nominalizations such as (24):

(23)   John arrived yesterday.
(24)   John's arrival yesterday

The central thrust of the argument in Chapter 2 was that the existence of these two kinds of expression in English and in languages generally is a puzzle that needs explaining. It is therefore of interest to see what Strawson has to say about nominalizations such as (24). Does he supply a satisfying non-linguistic motivation for the contrast between (23) and (24)? The answer, I think, is no. Strawson's own account of the parallels between nominalized sentences and other particular-identifying expressions (ordinary NPs, so to speak) tends to weaken, not strengthen, the case for a fundamental difference in role between NPs and sentences (whether nominalized or not), and hence to support the case made in Chapter 2.

Non-basic particulars, as we have seen, include events and processes such as those that are (or could be) designated by the following phrases (Strawson 1959: 200):

(25)   the death of Socrates
(26)   the blow which Peter gave John
(27)   the catch which got Compton out[13]

Using any of these phrases to refer successfully to some event presupposes the truth of a corresponding proposition, Strawson says. These propositions are respectively:

(28)   Socrates died.
(29)   Peter struck John.
(30)   Compton was caught out.

This seems quite plausible. It is hardly surprising that Strawson should see a close relationship between non-basic particulars such as (25)–(27) and certain true propositions. What is more interesting is that he sees the same kind of relationship as subsisting in respect of all particulars, including basic ones. As he puts it: 'in order for an identifying reference to a particular to be made, there must be some true empirical proposition known ... to the speaker, to the effect that there is just one particular which answers to a certain description' (1959: 183). To use an illustration of mine, not Strawson's: I cannot identify a particular by means of the expression *the US president who wore spectacles* unless it is true that only one US president so far has worn spectacles. Even a proper name like *John* 'carries, in use, its own presupposition of fact' (1959: 189); that is, a speaker cannot use it to identify someone unless the speaker knows some fact about him that is sufficient to single him out. Strawson sums up the relationship between particulars and facts metaphorically: 'the particular rest[s] on, or unfold[s] into, a fact.' He adds: 'It is in this sense that the thought of a definite particular is a *complete* thought' (1959: 211; emphasis added). I will return to this notion of completeness shortly.

---

[13] In example (27) the implied reference is to Denis Compton, a prominent English cricketer of the 1950s.

Let us consider from the opposite side the relationship between non-basic particulars and propositions. Just as non-basic particulars such as (25)–(27) 'rest on' facts expressible by propositions such as (28)–(30), so any proposition can provide a resting place for, or be folded up into, a non-basic particular (to use Strawson's metaphors). The Nominalized English version of the conversation between Bill and Alice in Chapter 2 could be viewed as a list of non-basic particulars in Strawson's sense. But now the question posed in Chapter 2 surfaces in a new guise. If there is a non-basic particular corresponding to every proposition, why is it necessary to posit the separate existence of propositions at all? It will not do to respond that propositions (for example, *Socrates died*) are needed in order to constitute a resting place for particulars (for example, the death of Socrates), because this leads us immediately to ask whether propositions too need a resting place; and no satisfactory answer to that question emerges. If a proposition needs a resting place, the question then arises what this resting place in turn rests on, and so on; and any stopping point in this regress must be arbitrary. On the other hand, if propositions are deemed not to need any resting place, that decision seems equally arbitrary; for why should we not accord the same privilege to particulars too? It seems that, once non-basic particulars such as the death of Socrates have been admitted to exist, non-linguistic motivation for the existence of propositions becomes even harder to find.

A way out of the difficulty may seem to be offered by the notion of **completeness**, which Strawson borrows from Frege (Strawson 1959: 152–3). Frege thought that a linguistic expression that refers to an object is 'complete' or 'saturated', whereas an expression that stands for anything other than an object (namely a function, according to his view of the universe) is incomplete. Complete expressions by this criterion include *Archimedes, the capital of Germany,* and *Archimedes perished at the capture of Syracuse,* which refer respectively to the objects Archimedes, Berlin, and truth. Incomplete expressions include *the capital of . . .* and *. . . perished at the siege of Syracuse,* which stand for functions whose values are Berlin and truth when *Germany* and *Archimedes* respectively are inserted in the gaps indicated. Strawson agrees with Frege that both propositions and referring expressions are complete, and predicate-expressions such as *. . . perished at the siege of Syracuse* are incomplete. So far, then, the notion of completeness does not discriminate in any helpful way between propositions and referring expressions. But, Strawson says, referring expressions differ from propositions in that they are simultaneously complete and incomplete. As he puts it: 'the thought of a definite particular, while in one sense complete, is also in another sense incomplete. For when we make the transition from the thought of the fact into which the particular unfolds to the thought of the particular itself, then we are thinking of it as the constituent of some further fact' (1959: 211). This account may seem to offer clear nongrammatical criteria for completeness, through which we may hope to reach our long-sought nongrammatical motivation for the sentence/NP distinction; but the offer does not survive close examination. Let us take the particular in question to be Socrates. According to Strawson, when we make the transition from thinking about our background knowledge of Socrates ('the fact[s] into which the particular unfolds') to thinking about Socrates himself ('the particular itself'), we think of him as 'the constituent of some further fact'—as an actor on stage, so to speak, rather than merely waiting in the wings. Let this further fact be Socrates's death. But, as Strawson himself has shown us, this further fact can be expressed both as a sentence (*Socrates died*) and as an NP (*the death of Socrates*) (our examples (28) and (25)). So, even if we grant that a particular such as Socrates (or a particular-expression such as *Socrates*) is incomplete, it does not follow that the only kind of syntactic frame into which *Socrates* can be inserted in order to achieve completeness is a sentence. An NP will do just as well.

It might be argued that the NP *the death of Socrates* is somehow parasitic on the sentence *Socrates died*, so that only the latter really counts as 'completing' the particular expression *Socrates*. But it is difficult to see how one could argue that without either appealing to the grammatical distinction between the two expressions (and so failing to break out of the circle of purely grammatical criteria), or else assuming the truth-reference distinction whose motivation is what is at issue. Besides, difficulties arise not just with NPs inside NPs, such as *Socrates* in *the death of Socrates*, but with sentences inside sentences. Consider the relationship between the following:

(31)  That Zimbabwe defeated England surprised us.
(32)  Zimbabwe's victory over England surprised us.

Both (31) and (32) have a subject and a predicate. In (32) the subject is a particular, introduced by the NP *Zimbabwe's victory over England*, and as such is incomplete, by Strawson's criterion, just like *Socrates* in (28). But in (31), which says the same thing as (32), the subject is a sentence rather than an NP. Yet sentences normally express propositions, which, according to Strawson, are fully complete, with no tinge of incompleteness. So two sentences with the same meaning can seemingly differ in that one has for its subject an incomplete expression while the other has a complete one. But the sole basis for the difference in 'completeness' is grammatical, so this notion still provides no escape from reliance on grammatical criteria.

In the face of these difficulties, one might perhaps try to salvage a completeness-based account of the truth/reference distinction by modifying Strawson's view of what entities can count as incomplete. Perhaps the subject of (31), though a proposition, is a proposition of a special kind that we are entitled to call incomplete because the sentence that expresses it is subordinate, as indicated in English grammar by its introductory conjunction *that*. But it is still the case that the grammatical category to which (31) as a whole belongs—namely, the sentence category—is the same as that to which its subject belongs. This shows that a 'completing' context can perfectly well belong to the same syntactic category as the expression that it completes. But then the case for preferring *Socrates died* over *the death of Socrates* as a completing context for *Socrates* is weakened still further; for the fact that *the death of Socrates* belongs to the same category as *Socrates* (namely, NP) can no longer count against it, if it ever did.

I have done my best to find within Strawson's descriptive metaphysics a solid nongrammatical basis for the truth/reference distinction and hence for the sentence/NP distinction, but failed. This need not be considered too serious an embarrassment for Strawson, perhaps. Quite apart from the fact that our question is not one he addresses directly, it is open to him to emphasize the self-limitation implied by the term 'descriptive'. Ironically, however, he hinted early in his career at the philosophical importance of an inquiry on the lines of the present chapter, before later apparently losing enthusiasm for it. Writing in 1950 about the 'identifying task' and the 'attributive task' of language (what I have called mentioning and asserting respectively), he says:

There is nothing sacrosanct about the employment of separable expressions for these two tasks. Other methods could be, and are, employed. . . . even the overtly functional, linguistic distinction between the identifying and attributive roles that words may play in language is prompted by the fact that ordinary speech offers us separable expressions to which the different functions may be plausibly and approximately assigned. And this functional distinction has cast long philosophical shadows. The distinctions between particular and universal, between substance and quality, are such pseudo-material shadows, cast by the grammar of the conventional sentence in which separable expressions play distinguishable roles. (1950 [1971*b*: 18])

Admittedly, he later added the following footnote to this passage: 'What is said or implied in the last two sentences of this paragraph no longer seems to me true, unless considerably qualified.' Yet even if the distinction between particulars and universals or between substances and qualities has a non-linguistic basis, it does not follow that a subject/predicate distinction provides the only way of expressing it. The thrust of the argument in later chapters will be that the evolution of this kind of syntax has had more to do with physiology than with ontology; and Strawson does not succeed in countering that thrust.

## 3.5. Plato

The huge opus of the Athenian Plato (*c.*429–347 BCE) is the foundation on which all subsequent Western philosophy rests, directly or indirectly. I will not attempt to comment here on everything that Plato says or implies concerning the truth/reference distinction, but will single out two aspects of his doctrine that, in different ways, are especially relevant to our inquiry. First, the solution that Plato offers in his dialogue the *Sophist* for a dilemma concerning falsity and non-existence seems at first sight to presuppose that truth belongs to sentences for reasons that are not purely grammatical; so if we accept Plato's solution we seem to be committed also to accepting a nongrammatical motivation for the truth/reference distinction. Secondly, Plato notices a structural parallel between sentences and syllables of just the kind that we will discuss in Chapter 5, and it is instructive to see what conclusions he and his twentieth-century commentator Gilbert Ryle draw from this parallel.

### 3.5.1. *Falsity and Non-Existence*

Plato did not embark on philosophy in an intellectual void. His predecessors and contemporaries include Socrates, the pre-Socratic philosophers, and the sophists. Socrates wrote nothing, but is presented as a participant in most of Plato's dialogues. The so-called pre-Socratic philosophers wrote much, not just on philosophy but on physics and astronomy, but their works survive only in fragments and quotations. The itinerant teachers known as sophists sold tuition in various techniques of self-improvement, and many of them seem to have used showy but superficial intellectual fireworks (sophistry, in fact) to attract customers. Plato's dialogue the *Sophist* is concerned with refuting those sophists who alleged that there is a contradiction in asserting that anything can be false—namely, the contradiction of saying that something that does not exist exists.

   This paradox has a serious philosophical background in the work of the pre-Socratic Parmenides (born about 510 BCE), who was concerned with what kinds of things can be deemed to exist and with the relationship between existence and knowledge. His view of what is knowable is narrow, extending only to 'what is and cannot not be' (Coxon 1970). In the *Sophist*, Plato attributes to Parmenides an attitude to paradoxes of the sophists' kind that oddly resembles the later Wittgenstein's attitude to philosophy in general. Wittgenstein argued that, since the traditional questions of philosophy arise through the malfunctioning of language, they should not be embarked on at all. Parmenides' attitude is described by Plato as follows (speaking through the mouth of a Stranger from Elea in southern Italy, one of the dialogue participants and a pupil of Parmenides):

This statement [namely, that falsehoods exist] boldly presupposes that the nonexistent exists; for falsehood could not exist otherwise. But, young man, the great Parmenides always used to testify as follows, from the beginning when I was a boy until the end, speaking each time both in prose and verse:

> This problem, the existence of nonexistent things, can never be tamed;
> You should however bar your thought from that road.
>
> (*Sophist* 237a)[14]

---

[14] This translation is my own.

But in the course of the dialogue the Stranger develops an alternative to Parmenides' simple refusal to tackle the issue. He does this by way of one of the earliest surviving discussions of syntactic structure (*Sophist* 262–4). Sentences (Greek *logoi*) are sequences of words that fit together, such as *A person learns*. Examples of sequences of words that do not fit together and so are not sentences are *walks, runs, sleeps* and *lion, stag, horse*. The first of these consists entirely of verbs and the second entirely of nouns. This draws attention to the fact that the simplest form of sentence consists of a noun and a verb fitted together. Now the Stranger invites Theaetetus to consider the sequences of words *Theaetetus sits* and *Theaetetus flies*. Both of these consist of a noun and a verb fitting together correctly, and are therefore sentences, and they are both sentences about Theaetetus; but only one of them states accurately how things are with him (literally, 'states the existent as it exists': *legei ta onta hōs estin*). This sentence, *Theaetetus sits*, is true (*alēthes*) whereas the other is false (*pseudes*). The Stranger then gets Theaetetus to agree in general that the things that can be true and false are sentences and opinions (which are, so to speak, silent internal sentences). So, falsity being located in its proper realm of sentences and opinions, acknowledging falsehoods to exist involves no contradiction but is just a matter of recognizing the existence of imitations of reality and an art of deception.

To modern readers, this passage may seem to labour the obvious. At the same time, recalling Plato's historical and intellectual context, we are inclined to applaud him for diagnosing the sophists' troublesome paradox (which Parmenides was so reluctant to confront) as arising from confusion between falsity and non-existence. Plato's identification of sentences as the entities to which truth and falsity can be ascribed seems to represent philosophical progress, an escape from sophistic enchantment. But, if that is correct, then the falsity of the sentence *France has a king* (for example) must be quite a different kind of thing from the non-existence of a king of France. So here at last, it may seem, is a philosophical motivation for the truth/reference distinction that is genuinely independent of grammatical contingencies. The motivation is that if we deny the distinction we are back to square one in respect of the sophists' paradox about falsity and non-existence. Are we really willing to reopen an issue that (it may seem) was resolved by Plato more than 2,000 years ago?

This argument fails, however. One may agree that the falsity of *France has a king* (say) is different from the non-existence of a king of France, but at the same time deny that the falsity of *France has a king* is fundamentally different in any other than a linguistic sense from the failure of the NP *the king of France* to refer to anyone. Plato's argument works equally well in relation not just to falsity but to any sort of failure on the part of a linguistic expression to fit the world (any sort of inapplicability, let us say). Suppose the syntax of actual languages were Monocategoric in style, or that the sophists, Parmenides, and Plato all spoke not Greek but a Nominalized Greek analogous to Nominalized English. In such a world the paradox about non-existence and falsity would simply resurface as a paradox about non-existence and inapplicability. A Plato in that world could not refute the sophists by arguing that the only entities which can properly be called false are sentences (and those unspoken sentences that constitute opinions). But he could mount a precisely analogous refutation by arguing that the only entities that can properly be called inapplicable are complete well-formed expressions (the Nominalized analogues of both sentences and NPs) and their unspoken counterparts. It is not necessary here to take a position on whether Plato's way of dealing with the sophists' paradox is successful or not; what matters is that, even if it is successful, his argument provides no underpinning for the truth/reference distinction.

### 3.5.2. Syllables and Sentences

In Chapter 5 I will argue that the sentence/NP distinction arose from a carry-over into syntax of a pattern of organization that evolved in the first instance for the neural control of phonetic articulation, following the restructuring of the hominid vocal tract. Other twentieth-century scholars have noticed the resemblance between sentence structure and syllable structure, though without interpreting it as I have. But Plato noticed the resemblance too, and his exploitation of it has been discussed in some detail by Ryle (1960). Ryle argues that the way in which Plato emphasizes the differences between syllables and individual speech sounds (particularly certain consonants) shows that he had an accurate understanding of the difference between asserting and mentioning (or saying and naming). This is relevant to us because, if Ryle and (on his interpretation) Plato are right, their argument provides another possible extralinguistic basis for the truth/reference distinction. The use that Plato makes of the resemblance between sentences and syllables therefore becomes more than just a curiosity, of only historical interest. I will, however, argue that Ryle's use of of the term 'mention' masks an equivocation similar though not identical to the one underlying the later Wittgenstein's use of the term 'name'. Ryle's mentioning/saying dichotomy, whether or not it can fairly be attributed to Plato, is therefore just as useless for present purposes as Wittgenstein's name/proposition dichotomy.

In the *Theaetetus* (202e–203a) Plato has Socrates conduct a discussion of complex entities and the ways in which they are composed of basic elements. As an illustration, Socrates invites his interlocutor Theaetetus to think about the first syllable of his name, *So-*. Theaetetus agrees that this can be divided into two elements, *s* and *o*, but these elements are not further divisible. A vowel sound such as *o* is relatively 'distinct', but a consonant such as *s* is a mere 'noise' and there are other consonants such as *b* which are not even noises.[15] What Plato seems to mean

---

[15] Although Plato is talking about speech sounds, he uses names of letters of the Greek alphabet to refer to them, and I therefore use letters rather than phonetic symbols here. It would be anachronistic to imply that Plato distinguished clearly between sounds and letters.

here is that [b], like other plosives, cannot be pronounced without some accompanying vowel. This raises the issue of how sounds are combined to form syllables, an issue that is discussed in the *Sophist* (I quote Ryle's translation): 'Some of these [sounds] cannot be conjoined, others will fit together. . . . And the vowels are especially good at combination, a sort of bond pervading them all, so that without a vowel the others cannot be fitted together' (253a). This passage is explicitly recalled at 261d, when the Stranger begins the account of sentence structure discussed above. The explicitness of Plato's connection persuades Ryle that Plato saw the role of the verb in a sentence as exactly analogous to that of the vowel in a syllable. Just as vowels are what combine speech sounds into pronounceable units (syllables), so verbs are what combine words into units that actually say something (sentences). Moreover, the verbforms that Plato uses as illustrations are all, as Ryle puts it, 'live verbs'—that is, finite forms like *flies* rather than participles like *flying* or verbal nouns like *flight*. Ryle therefore attributes to Plato the view that live verbs are essential for saying anything: 'In stating something we combine, at the least, a verb with a noun. By the noun we mention some subject by name; by the verb we assert something about that subject' (Ryle 1960 [1971: 65]). Ryle adds that there is a vital difference between the statement *Brutus assassinated Caesar* and the 'list' *Brutus, assassination, Caesar.* 'The first tells a truth or a falsehood; the second tells nothing at all, though it mentions three things' (1971: 68).

Ryle's view of the distinction between mentioning and asserting seems clearly to entail that being true, a characteristic of what is asserted, is fundamentally distinct from having reference, a characteristic of expressions that merely mention. His argument that Plato noticed the parallel in language-as-it-is between sentences and syllables is, I think, convincing; but Ryle seems to go further, claiming that sentences with 'live verbs', the syntactic analogues of vowels, are essential in order for anything to be said in any sort of language. So is this claim justified?

One way of responding to Ryle is simply to point to the fragments of Monocategoric and Nominalized English presented in Chapter 2. Monocategoric at (27) has no live verbs because it has no verbs at all, only expressions and operators; while the Nominalized English sample at (37) has no live verbs but only verbal nouns (*improvement, endurance, recovery, preparation*, etc.). Would Ryle really insist that in these languages nothing could be said? Conceivably he might argue that in the grammars of these languages certain operators and certain verbal nouns should count as live for his purposes; but that it tantamount to making it true by definition that whenever something is said a live verb is present, which reduces Ryle's claim to vacuity.

There is a more serious flaw in Ryle's position, however. Consider the following remark: 'Live verbs are snatches from speech, that is from the *using* of words. Live verbs could not feature in lists' (1971: 68; emphasis in original). On the face of it, this means that one can produce lists of nouns such as *Brutus, assassination, Caesar* and *lion, stag, horse* but not lists of finite verbforms such as *walks, runs, sleeps*. Yet *walks, runs, sleeps* is just such a list—in fact, precisely the list that Plato uses in an account of sentence structure that Ryle applauds. What's more, Ryle himself gives a list of three live verbs in the very passage where he introduces the term: 'I mean by "live verbs" expressions like "assassinated", "believes" and "will wake up" . . .' (1971: 63). Ryle's self-contradiction arises from confusing two sorts of mentioning. One sort appears in the contrast, long recognized in philosophy and linguistics, between mention and use. Compare (33) and (34):

(33)   (*a*)    *Assassinated* is the past tense form of a verb.
       (*b*)    *Assassination* is a noun derived from a verb.
(34)   (*a*)    Brutus assassinated Caesar.
       (*b*)    Brutus's assassination of Caesar led to civil war.

In this sense, the words *assassinated* and *assassination* are mentioned in (33) but used in (34). In this sense also it is true to say that *Brutus, assassination, Caesar* constitutes a mere list of three nouns that are mentioned, not used. But this is not the sort of mentioning that is meant in the following passage: 'the live verb "flies" in the two-word sentence "Theaetetus flies" does not do the sort of thing that the name "Theaetetus" does (for example, mention someone); it does the asserting of something *about* Theaetetus without which we should not have a truth or falsehood about Theaetetus' (1971: 64; emphasis in original). Similarly, Ryle contrasts 'the *saying-about* that the verb in a sentence does' with 'the *mentioning-of-the-subject* that the nominative of the sentence does' (1971: 66). This second sort of mentioning has nothing to do with lists and is inapplicable to verbs; rather, it is tied to what nouns do when they are not being mentioned in the first sense but rather being used in a sentence.

Because the two sorts of mentioning are so different, it would be fallacious to argue from the need for a mention/use distinction (involving the first sense of mentioning) to a need for a mention/assertion distinction (involving the second sort). Thus it would be fallacious to argue from the mention/use distinction to a need for a distinction between how assertions relate to the world (namely, by being true or false) and how mentioning-expressions of the second sort relate to the world (namely, by referring or failing to refer). In a world where everyone spoke languages like Monocategoric there would still be a place for the distinction between mention and use but none for that between mention and assertion. Ryle's mistake is to think that the second distinction is more solidly based than it is (to think that it is indispensable for saying anything, in fact) because he confuses it with the first. So once again what may have seemed at first like promising non-linguistic evidence for the truth/reference distinction does not survive close inspection.

# 4   Attempts to Solve the Problems

## 4.1. The Search for Explanations

In this chapter we will look at explanations that have been proposed for the three aspects of human language that this book is concerned with—namely, vocabulary size, duality of patterning, and the sentence/NP distinction. I will argue that no previous explanation accounts satisfactorily for any of these aspects of language individually. *A fortiori*, no previous explanation accounts satisfactorily for them all in a unified fashion. Some of the proposals discussed here shed light on the relationship between the syntactic sentence/NP distinction and the lexical-cum-semantic noun/verb distinction, but none of them explains why the sentence/NP distinction arose in the first place, and certainly no other proposal relates it to vocabulary size and duality of patterning in the way that the scenario to be presented in Chapter 5 does.

Several of the alternative explanations discussed here bear on more aspects of language than just its evolution. This raises the issue of whether my own proposal has non-evolutionary implications too. I will argue in Chapters 5 and 6 that it has, and that these implications are broadly confirmed.

## 4.2. Vocabulary Size

This section will be short, simply because vocabulary size has not puzzled researchers on language evolution as much as I believe it should have. Recall a point that was made in Section 2.2: a baby all of whose ancestors have been hunter-gatherers can acquire natively as large a vocabulary as a baby whose ancestors have been city-dwellers for millennia. To express surprise at this is not to belittle the cultural achievements of hunter-gatherer communities; rather, it is to point out how far the biological endowment for vocabulary acquisition in humans everywhere outstrips what one might regard as the minimum for survival. As Premack puts it (1986: 133): 'Human language is an embarrassment for evolutionary theory because it is vastly more powerful than one can account for in terms of selective fitness.'

It may be thought that a reason for the large size of human vocabularies can be found in the organizing principles that link words and classes of words together into a system, whether these principles relate to vocabulary only or to human cognition in general. As Aitchison (1987: 5) says, 'words are not just stacked higgledy-piggledy in our minds, like leaves on an autumn bonfire'. If the link between words A and B is such as to guarantee the existence of words C and D also, and if this kind of guarantee recurs over and over again with different sets of words, then the large size of vocabularies might perhaps be attributed entirely to the way in which they are structured. Links of that kind are certainly influential (Talmy 1985; Cruse 1986). But it is not necessary to explore them in detail here, because there is a certain characteristic of vocabulary that has a more straightforward effect on vocabulary size (as I will show in Chapter 5) but which such links cannot explain. This characteristic is synonymy avoidance.

Words which are **synonymous** are words that mean the same thing. Are synonyms common? One's first reaction may well be to say yes. It is easy enough to think of pairs of words in every open wordclass[1] that seem nearly or completely synonymous, for example:

| (1) | Nouns: | liberty | freedom |
|-----|--------|---------|---------|
|     |        | foe | enemy |
|     |        | bucket | pail |
|     |        | courgettes | zucchini |
| (2) | Verbs: | buy | purchase |
|     |        | seem | appear |
| (3) | Adjectives: | bright | intelligent |
|     |        | gloomy | sad |
| (4) | Adverbs: | nearly | almost |

On closer inspection, however, very few of these words turn out to be completely interchangeable with their alleged synonyms in all contexts. With some the difference is one of style or what some linguists call **register** (Leech *et al.* 1982: 9–10); for example, *purchase* is the sort of word that occurs in legal documents and *foe* is an archaic term now restricted to poetic contexts, so that in everyday colloquial usage only their respective counterparts *buy* and *enemy* occur. With others the difference is one of dialect or regional variation; for example, small vegetable marrows are generally called *courgettes* in Britain and New Zealand but *zucchini* in the United States and Australia. With others there are differences in metaphorical or idiomatic usage; for example, a cake that is soggy in the middle

---

[1] 'Wordclass' means the same as 'part of speech' or, in more recent linguistic usage, 'lexical category'. Open wordclasses are those whose membership can readily be extended by lexical innovation—namely (in English), nouns, verbs, adjectives, and adverbs.

can be called *sad* but not *gloomy*, and one cannot substitute *freedom* for *liberty* in a sentence such as *I am not at liberty to reveal that.* With others still, despite their shared wordclass membership, there are grammatical differences; for example, *appear* can be used without any complement whereas *seem* must have one, so that *She suddenly appeared* is a good English sentence but *\*She suddenly seemed* is not.

What these examples illustrate is that it is difficult to find pairs of synonyms that are perfect in the sense that they are mutually interchangeable in all contexts. This observation is not new. It goes back at least to Michel Bréal's classic *Essai de sémantique* (1897), and a corollary of it has more recently been exploited in an ingenious fashion by Aronoff (1976) in an attempt to explain certain restrictions on the operation of word-formation processes in English. Corresponding to the adjective *curious* there is an abstract noun *curiosity* formed by the addition of *-ity*, a suffix that is quite common (compare *electricity, sensitivity, purity, profundity*, etc.). Why then can this suffix not be used to form a noun *\*gloriosity* corresponding to the adjective *glorious*? Aronoff argues that this is not merely an accidental gap but is due to a general principle whereby lexically stored words block potential interlopers that would have the same meaning. *Gloriosity*, if it existed, would presumably mean much the same as *glory*, and so is blocked by it; on the other hand, there is nothing to block the formation of *curiosity* because there is no pre-existing synonym *\*cury*. The fact that *gloriousness* exists alongside *glory* may seem to pose a problem for Aronoff, but he deals with such examples by restricting blocking so as not to apply to word-formation processes that are completely productive, like *-ness* suffixation, and whose output therefore does not need to be stored in the memory (he argues). But the details of how he copes with apparent counter-examples do not matter. What matters is that the avoidance of synonymy is sufficiently general to provide at least a prima-facie explanation for why certain potential new words strike native speakers as somehow better or more plausible than others.

Does synonymy avoidance really need explaining, whether in terms of childhood vocabulary acquisition or in any other way? One might argue that a language with a proliferation of synonyms would be just too cumbersome for everyday use, and nothing further need be said. But comparing synonymy with homonymy shows that one cannot dismiss the problem so tersely. Synonymy is a kind of many–one relationship between meaning and linguistic expression, involving one meaning with more than one expression. Its converse, involving one expression with more than one meaning, is called **homonymy**.[2] There is no immediately obvious reason why either of these two kinds of many–one relationship should be more undesirable than the other. Yet there is a clear difference in how generally they occur. In English, perfect synonymy is rare, but perfect

---

[2] Some would distinguish homography (identity in spelling irrespective of pronunciation) and homophony (identity in pronunciation irrespective of spelling) as subtypes of homonymy. The only kind of homonymy that I am concerned with here is homophony, reflecting the priority of speech over writing in most areas of linguistic research.

homonymy (as in the pair *bank* 'financial institution' and *bank* 'side of river') is common. Admittedly, in some languages homonymy seems to occur more frequently than in others; for example, the French words *fin* 'end', *fin* 'fine', *feint* 'feigns', and *faim* 'hunger', all pronounced alike, have cognates in Italian (*fine, fino, finge,* and *fame*) which are distinct, reflecting differences in the historical development of the two languages' sound systems. Nevertheless, a general avoidance of homonymy does not seem to be characteristic of any language.

This difference between synonymy and homonymy seems particularly surprising if one views language as a medium for communicating information, in the technical sense of 'information' introduced by Shannon and Weaver (1949). Synonymy, because it allows one meaning to be expressed in more than one way, provides scope for redundancy and hence should help to guard against the loss of information over a noisy channel, one would think. On the other hand, homonymy serves no such useful function, merely increasing the risk of misunderstanding. So, if one were to guess on *a priori* grounds which of the two was the commoner phenomenon, one would probably choose synonymy; yet one would be wrong.

The basis for synonymy avoidance, its relevance to vocabulary size, and its likely role in language evolution are discussed in Chapter 5. For present purposes, what is important is whether it is rendered superfluous as a factor in explaining vocabulary size by any superior rival explanation. The answer is no, simply because no serious rival candidate is on offer. Even supposing that such a rival could be constructed (perhaps out of the semantic organizing principles mentioned earlier), it is hard to see how it could count as superior. Synonymy avoidance needs to be accounted for anyway; so, if (as I will argue) an account of it can also explain vocabulary size, this account will kill two birds with one stone, and will be at least as attractive as any independent explanation.

## 4.3. Duality of Patterning

In Chapter 5, I will argue that duality of patterning is one by-product of the pressure to find contrasting meanings for an increasing diversity of distinct calls. According to that view, hominid calls originally had no individually meaningful parts, so *a fortiori* any consonant-like and vowel-like sounds that they contained were individually meaningless too. These sounds constituted merely an inventory of elements in terms of which calls could be analysed phonetically. In this respect hominid calls originally resembled the songs of certain contemporary North American sparrows and chick-a-dees, analysable as sequences of notes that recur in different combinations but for which no meaning or function has been identified below the level of the song as a whole (Hauser 1996: 47, 97, 278–83). A meaningful level of patterning within the call, intermediate between the whole call and its smallest recombinable components, arose only when some potential calls acquired meaning through analysis as combinations of shorter calls or 'words'.

In this section, I will describe three other factors that have been claimed to underlie duality of patterning, and argue that none of them is fully convincing. This is not to say that they are irrelevant. Any or all of them may have some role in the development of sound–meaning relationships in modern human language. However, none of them is derivable from so economical a set of independently motivated assumptions as the account that I will offer in Chapter 5.

### 4.3.1. Call Blending

Hockett and Ascher, in their pioneering article (1964), attribute duality of patterning to a process of call blending. They invite us to imagine a hominid ancestor in whose repertoire there is a danger call and a food call. Suppose she is confronted with food and danger simultaneously. Rather than produce the food call alone (which Hockett and Ascher represent schematically as ABCD) or the danger call alone (which they represent as EFGH), the hominid produces a blended call ABGH, meaning 'Food but danger!' The partial similarities between this and the older calls allow them to be interpreted in new ways: ABCD can now be interpreted as 'Food and no danger' while EFGH means 'No food and danger'. A different blend of the two old calls, CDEF, will thus mean 'Neither food nor danger'. The call system has now been opened up, in that where there were previously two calls there are now four (AB 'food', CD 'no danger', EF 'no food', and GH 'danger'), and these four are combinable into complex calls. But this kind of increase in vocabulary creates problems through the need to keep each call acoustically distinct. It is in the face of this problem (Hockett and Ascher suggest) that our ancestors made the imaginative leap to phonological segmentation: if a call is a sequence of individually meaningless but interchangeable segments, it no longer has to be distinguished from every other call holistically but can rely on being distinct in as little as one segment, which may be meaningless on its own. Duality thus came about as a response to pressures caused by the opening-up of the call system.

Human language is indeed unique, and 'openness' (in the sense just illustrated) and duality are indeed fundamental characteristics of it. It is not unreasonable, therefore, that Hockett and Ascher should posit unique or at any rate unusual events in the course of its evolution. But their scenario relies on not one but three unusual events. First, they rely on a kind of call blending that would spontaneously occur only seldom and for which there are few if any parallels in contemporary animal communication systems. Secondly, rather than remaining at the level of a slip of the tongue with no subsequent effects, this blending and the consequent semantic reanalysis would have had to be institutionalized and generalized. Thirdly, phonological analysis would have had to be 'invented' later to facilitate call differentiation, thereby creating duality of patterning. No one can say definitely that this sequence of events did not occur. But a scenario in which openness and duality are simply by-products of a constellation of circumstances for which there is independent evidence is bound to be more attractive than one, like Hockett and Ascher's, in which they arise from events that have to be posited specially to account for them.

### 4.3.2. Sound Symbolism, Phonetic Assimilation, and Semantic Drift

The scenario to be presented in Chapter 5 imposes no intrinsic requirement that, at an early stage of language evolution, the smallest individually meaningful elements (proto-words, one may call them) should be short or articulatorily simple. But it may seem natural to suppose that the earliest meaningful elements were indeed short: individual consonant-like and vowel-like sounds, or perhaps consonant–vowel combinations constituting the earliest syllables. The meanings of longer calls would then be derivable from those of the syllables or sounds of which they were composed. In due course, however, a variety of factors would help to obscure the meanings of individual sounds: a sound combination might drift semantically from what its components would imply (just as the English *cupboard* no longer denotes a board for cups), and processes of sound change such as those seen in historical times (particularly the assimilatory effect of neighbouring sounds on one another) would render opaque certain combinations that were formerly transparent. So, as the original meanings of individual sounds or syllables became obscured, these small units would cede to larger units (words or morphemes) their role as the units of semantic patterning, retaining only a phonological role in differentiating these larger units (as /b/ in English is now meaningless, but differentiates *bat* and *bin* from *pat* and *pin*). Thus a dual patterning arose through a gradual loss of meaningfulness at the level of the individual consonant, vowel, or syllable. Versions of such a scenario have been proposed by Stopa (1972), Foster (1978, 1983, 1990), and Pulleyblank (1983).

Sound symbolism is a factor that may seem to count in favour of this scenario.[3] It has often been noticed, for example, that in many languages vowels with a high second formant such as [i] have some association with small size, sharpness, and rapid movement, whereas vowels with a low second formant such as [u] are associated with large size, softness, and heavy, slow movements (Hinton *et al.* 1994: 10). At the same time, the vast majority of words containing [i] and [u] in English, and probably in all languages, lack these clear associations, and there are even some languages where the associations seem to be systematically inverted (Diffloth 1994). But this picture of residual sound symbolism alongside general arbitrariness in sound–meaning relationships is broadly consistent with the

---

[3] 'Sound symbolism' is a potentially confusing term, because the kinds of sound–meaning relationship that it stands for are precisely ones that are not symbolic in Peircean terms (that is, arbitrary or unmotivated) but rather indexical or iconic. However, the term is canonized by usage.

Stopa–Foster–Pulleyblank scenario. The question therefore is whether the scenario is equally plausible when we look at its implications in detail.

What would count strongly in its favour would be the discovery that, across a wide range of protolanguages that cannot be shown to be genetically related by the criteria of conventional historical linguistics, morphemes or roots containing any given sound or class of sounds (say, laterals such as [l] or bilabial plosives such as [p] or [b]) also share some element of meaning to a statistically significant extent. Let us suppose, for example, that in a variety of protolanguages the proportion of roots containing [p] whose meaning involves fatness, roundness, or protrusion is greater than can be attributed to chance, and the same is true of the proportion of roots containing [l] whose meaning involves limpness or weakness, the proportion containing [k] whose meaning involves downward movement, and so on. It would be reasonable then to attribute to the sounds [p], [l], and [k] original meanings something like 'protruding', 'weak', or 'downward'. But statistical significance would be crucial. It would not be enough, for example, just to produce one or two roots from each protolanguage that contained [k] and whose meaning contained a 'downward' element, while ignoring all those roots containing [k] but with quite other meanings. Such minimal exemplification would allow us to associate any sound with virtually any semantic element at random. Determining the threshold for significance would be tricky, but one can imagine circumstances in which it would clearly be exceeded: for example, if the 'downward' meaning appeared in more than half the [k] words in every protolanguage

'Protruding', 'weak', and 'downward' are in fact the original meanings that Foster posits for [p], [l], and [k] respectively, citing roots from Proto-Indo-European and Egyptian. Pulleyblank (1983) agrees with her about [l], while ascribing to [k], at least in a hypothetical precursor of Proto-Indo-European, the meaning not 'downward' but rather 'sharp, point'. Foster (1983) bravely suggests a basic meaning for eighteen consonants (a plosive, a fricative, and a liquid, glide, or nasal at each of six places of articulation) in an Upper Palae-olithic 'Sapiens Language'—meanings supposedly iconically related to articulatory gestures. Pulleyblank more cautiously limits himself to six. Unfortunately, however, although Foster claims support from 'many languages' (1983: 473), neither she, Stopa, nor Pulleyblank presents the vital statistical evidence. Either Foster's or Pulleyblank's proposed sound–meaning associations may be correct—but so may countless other associations, as well as none at all.[4]

It is easy to dismiss such adventures in ultra-long-range linguistic reconstruc-

---

[4] Stopa (1972) claims that the earliest consonants with iconic meanings must have been clicks, and that the Khoisan languages of south-west Africa, in which clicks are common, represent a primitive stage of language evolution. His argument presupposes that phonological and grammatical character-istics can be correlated with levels of cultural sophistication, with Semitic and Indo-European lan-guages at the top and Bushman at the bottom. This view, which Stopa bases on only a tiny sample of languages, is rejected by all serious linguists today, the classic counter-arguments being presented by Sapir (1921).

tion as hopelessly speculative. But, for both Pulleyblank and Foster, a central attraction of their account is that it enables us to trace language back to an earlier human stage when it was fundamentally more iconic than modern language is. Both assume that the meaningful elements at that stage, whether purely vocal or at least partly gestural, must all have been motivated by resemblance to what they designated. As Pulleyblank (1983: 387–8) puts it:

There would have been many . . . kinds of associative symbolism, related either to the sound produced or to the visual appearance of the mouth in producing it. Thus a labial-velar approximant *w* involves rounding of the protruding lips and in this way could symbolize roundness and the associated idea of turning, probably originally combined with a manual turning gesture. Hence, presumably, the use of this consonant in words for 'turn' in both Indo-European and Sino-Tibetan.

But their assumption is a mistake. The transition from a purely iconic to a substantially non-iconic communication system, even if we grant that a purely iconic system ever existed, almost certainly took place long before our australopithecine ancestors, let alone *Homo sapiens*. This is because humans are not unique in using non-iconic, arbitrary signs. Vervet monkeys' alarm calls for leopards, snakes, and eagles do not resemble leopards, snakes, and eagles respectively (Cheney and Seyfarth 1990). The same is true of many calls of other species, both mammals and birds, whose use depends at least partly on identifiable referents in the external world. That fact, together with chimpanzees' signing capabilities, makes it overwhelmingly likely that there was a substantial non-iconic element in whatever call system was used by the common ancestor of humans and chimpanzees, millions of years before Foster's putative Sapiens Language. Even if in fact the vervet call system and human language evolved their arbitrary aspects independently, it would be strange if humans still needed iconic props for communicating at a time when both their brain capacity and their cultural achievements vastly outstripped those of a small monkey. It is easy to be seduced by the idea that using vocal signals whose relationship with their referents is arbitrary must have involved an intellectual and cultural leap that only humans were capable of. However, evidence from animal communication shows that idea to be mistaken.

The sound-symbolic route to duality of patterning has a second apparent attraction, emphasized especially by Pulleyblank; but again the attraction diminishes when examined closely. In attributing meanings to individual sounds, both he and Foster concentrate on consonants and exclude vowels. This is a deliberate omission. Both sympathize with the gesture theory of language origins (which I will discuss later in this chapter), and see the articulatory movements of the tongue and lips in producing consonants as originating from mouth gestures. At that mouth-gestural stage, vowel sounds would have been merely automatic accompaniments of consonantal gestures, enhancing audibility but not independently contrastive. Can we then find in the history or reliably reconstructable prehistory of language any trace of a stage when vowels were non-contrastive? At first sight, we can. Pulleyblank points out that for both the Sino-Tibetan and Indo-European families it is possible to reconstruct a protolanguage with only one vowel—that is, a linguistic stage at which the only vocalic contrast was between the presence of a vowel and its absence. In their paucity of vowels these protolanguages resemble certain contemporary Caucasian languages. For example, Abkhaz has at the phonological level only two vowels (Hewitt and Khiba 1989), while Kabardian has been analysed as having none at all (Kuipers 1960), inasmuch as both the quality and the position of phonetic vowel sounds are claimed to be predictable from the surrounding consonants. So, like Krantz (1988), one may be tempted to regard Kabardian as preserving a feature of an earlier stage of phonetic evolution that we find more widely reflected, naturally enough, in reconstructable protolanguages—a stage when consonants were individually meaningful gestures.

It is only at the phonological level, however, not the phonetic, that the vowel inventories of Abkhaz and Kabardian are so small. As Pulleyblank acknowledges, Kuipers makes it clear that at the phonetic level Kabardian has at least twelve short vowels and five long vowels. In Kabardian, vowels are indeed contrastive in the sense that they provide crucial phonetic cues for identifying neighbouring consonants. And there is no reason to think that vowels were not similarly contrastive in Proto-Indo-European and Proto-Sino-Tibetan, which are located in time no more than 6,000 years ago at the most—long after the larynx had reached its modern low position and much closer in time to ourselves than to the earliest emergence of modern human language, even if we assume for that a date as recent as some anthropologists do (e.g. Noble and Davidson 1996). The phonological peculiarities of these protolanguages, even if the analysis proposed for them is correct, therefore provide no evidence for a putative stage in the evolution of *Homo sapiens* when vowel quality was totally determined by adjacent consonantal articulations. Such a stage may perhaps have existed; but it must have preceded even *Homo erectus*, over 1.5 million years ago, whose vocal apparatus seems to have developed sufficiently to permit some independent control of vowel quality, albeit within a narrower range than today (as will be explained in Chapter 6). And to place the emergence of duality of patterning as early as that involves ascribing to earlier hominids, *Homo habilis* or even australopithecines, the kind of lexical expansion that duality of patterning would accompany—a lexical expansion that would have to have taken place without any of the motivation supplied by the scenario of Chapter 5.

It seems fair to conclude that the sound-symbolic route to duality of patterning favoured by Foster and Pulleyblank is unconvincing on close examination, and is based partly on a mistaken assumption about iconicity. To say this is not to deny that sound symbolism exists (Jakobson and Waugh 1979; Hinton *et al.* 1994), and it may well have existed long before language reached its modern state.

But the evidence does not support the crucial evolutionary role that Foster and Pulleyblank propose for it.

### 4.3.3. Phonological Self-Organization

Why are the cells in a honeycomb hexagonal? At first sight, it seems remarkable that bees, acting purely on biological urges, create such mathematically regular structures. One may be tempted to think that the drive to build cells that are hexagonal rather than (say) circular or square must be genetically imprinted, even though it is hard to see how that shape in particular could have emerged by natural selection. But in fact the choice of shape has nothing to do with biology. When a large number of creatures are building cells side by side, each one pressing outward with virtually equal force against the neighbouring cells, physics and geometry suffice to ensure that the pattern that emerges is hexagonal. Honeycombs organize themselves, so to speak, in a hexagonal fashion without any specific bias towards hexagons in the genes or behaviour of bees.

An important strand in contemporary research on language evolution is the search for similar self-organizing principles to explain aspects of language. Much of this work has centred on how a shared vocabulary and grammar might emerge, given an austere, Spartan set of initial conditions that mimic, more or less, the situation of a pre-linguistic hominid (Batali 1998; Steels 1998). But Studdert-Kennedy (1998) has applied this approach to phonology too, in a way that bears on duality of patterning. He draws attention to the 'particulate principle of self-diversifying systems' propounded by Abler (1989), according to which complex systems (in chemistry and genetics as well as language) typically involve hierarchies of units at various levels, such that the units at a higher level are composed of discrete elements ('particles') at a lower level, but the behaviour and characteristics of the higher-level units are not predictable from that of their components. Thus, in language, the meaning of words or morphemes is not predictable from the lower-level units (the sounds or phonemes) that compose them. Moreover, Studdert-Kennedy cites computer simulations that may seem to show that this characteristic is inevitable. Given a wide choice of consonants and a wide choice of vowels out of which to form meaningful syllables of consonant–vowel shape, there is a tendency for a system to 'economize' by allowing any one consonant to co-occur with a wide range of vowels, and vice versa (Lindblom *et al.* 1983). The initial conditions built into the simulations turn out to favour the 'particulation' of the phonetic material out of which syllables are formed, so as to yield a set of consonants and a set of vowels, each of which is relatively small but with members that are relatively freely combinable with members of the other set. The simulations therefore arrive at broadly the duality that we observe in actual language: meaningful elements ('words') that in turn are composed of recombinable meaningless elements ('sounds' or 'phonemes'). Do these simulations demonstrate, then, that duality of patterning is an aspect of language that can be attributed to self-organization, like the hexagonal cells in a honeycomb? If so, it would be pointless to seek an evolutionary explanation for it.

The answer, I think, is no. Studdert-Kennedy does not claim that a level of individually meaningless recombinable elements must inevitably emerge in any system of communication whatever. Such a claim would clearly be wrong. Many animals have communication systems, but none of these displays duality of patterning of the linguistic kind. It is only when a communication system possesses 'the unbounded scope of reference' of human language (that is, the unbounded range of content for complex messages) that a level of individually meaningless units becomes inevitable, he claims (1998: 206). So, at best, self-organization does not abolish the relevant evolutionary question, it merely rephrases it: not 'How did duality of patterning evolve?' but 'How did a communication system with an unbounded scope of reference evolve?'

That qualification 'at best' needs explaining, and the explanation weakens further the likelihood that an evolutionary explanation for duality can be dispensed with. If one studies the initial conditions of the simulations reported by Lindblom, MacNeilage, and Studdert-Kennedy, one finds that they are not what one might call 'species-neutral'. Rather, they incorporate much that is known about specifically human speech. For example, some consonant–vowel combinations are easier for humans to produce than others, while some are easier to discriminate auditorily than others; and information of this kind was built into the way in which the simulations were run. If the simulations had reflected characteristics of some other species, lacking those human articulatory and auditory biases, one cannot be sure that the same kind of segmental 'particulation' would have emerged. So, in Studdert-Kennedy's scenario, the emergence of the kind of duality that human language exhibits seems to presuppose not just unbounded reference but something like the human vocal tract and the human ear, with their particular aptitudes and weaknesses. This takes us quite far from the kind of pure self-organization exhibited by bees' honeycombs, and much closer to the account that I will offer in Chapter 5, appealing to certain contingencies of human physiology. To seek evidence in language of self-organizing principles that are independent of both biology and culture is certainly worthwhile; but, on present showing, such principles do not render biology superfluous in accounting for duality of patterning.

## 4.4. The Sentence/NP Distinction

Far more explanatory effort has been devoted to syntactic structure than to either vocabulary size or duality of patterning. Many scholars have sought to account for it in terms of factors outside grammar, such as the mental representation of reality or information packaging for efficient communication; and many of these accounts have implications for language evolution. Despite Chomsky's lack of interest, there have also been at least two recent attempts to account for aspects of syntactic structure in more narrowly linguistic terms—that is, to explain why a Universal Grammar that is relatively independent of other mental capacities should have developed certain characteristics rather than others.

To discuss the evolutionary implications of all these proposals with the thoroughness that they deserve would require several books rather than just part of one chapter. What I hope to show here, however, is that all these proposals fall short in one of two ways. Some of them are relevant to aspects of syntactic structure but not precisely to the sentence/NP distinction, while some are relevant to why a kind of syntax incorporating a sentence/NP distinction should be exploited in certain ways rather than others once it had arisen, but do not explain why it arose in the first place.

A recurring theme will be the lack of a consistent relationship between certain aspects of syntax-as-it-is and any representational or communicative function. For example, there is no one thing that all and only grammatical subjects do, or that all and only verbs do. If syntax evolved purely in response to pressures for more sophisticated knowledge representation or more efficient packaging of information, that is at least somewhat surprising. On the other hand, if syntax appropriated neural mechanisms that originally evolved for a quite unrelated purpose, as will be argued in Chapter 5, then what we observe—a rather confusing pattern of many-to-many relationships between syntactic structures and functions—is just what we would expect.

Among the range of uses to which any given syntactic entity gets put, there may be some that predominate. For example, subjects often denote agents, and verbs often denote actions. But that may show only that subjects and verbs, whatever their origin, lend themselves better to some semantic functions than to others. Similarly, if one were given a heap of banisters and treads from a dismantled staircase and told simply to make them into furniture useful in a dining room, one would probably turn the treads into table tops or bench seats and the banisters into table legs, not vice versa. Explaining why particular uses predominate for particular elements of sentence structure—why a banister is more suitable as a table leg than as part of a table top, so to speak—is what functionalist approaches (in the broadest sense) are good at. What they are not so good at is explaining where the raw material comes from; that is, why we should have subjects and verbs in the first place, rather than (say) expressions and operators, as in Monocategoric, or location constituents and object-or-event constituents, as in Spatiotemporal.

### 4.4.1. *Universal Grammar, Propositions, and Predicate–Argument Structure*

Noam Chomsky has famously postulated an innate **Universal Grammar** (UG) to explain why all human languages have characteristics in common, or obey shared principles, that are not plausibly learnable on the basis of the linguistic input to which babies are exposed. But Chomskyan linguists mostly eschew discussion of the evolutionary origins of UG. Exceptions are Frederick Newmeyer (1991, 1998), and Steven Pinker (1994, 1995) with his colleague Paul Bloom (Pinker and Bloom 1990). For this, they have incurred criticism from some Chomskyans (Lightfoot 1991; cf. Dennett 1995). I side with Newmeyer, Pinker, and Bloom, against their critics, on the general issue of whether the evolution of syntax is worth thinking about. But that still leaves scope for disagreement about how and why it happened.

Newmeyer focuses on two contrasts fundamental to spoken language: between sound and meaning, and between the speaker and the hearer. What concerns us is whether his discussion of either of these yields an explanation for the sentence/NP distinction. The speaker/hearer contrast can be disposed of quickly in this context, because the principles of UG that it helps to explain, in Newmeyer's view, are principles concerning not the internal structure of simple sentences but the relationships of sentences (or clauses) to one another. For example, there is a principle of UG that affects the interpretation of sentences (5) and (6), each of which is complex in that it contains an embedded clause (*that/whether we had to get off the bus*). This principle predicts correctly that, although in (5) the scope of *where* is ambiguous, in (6) it is not:

(5)   Where did John say that we had to get off the bus?
(6)   Where did John ask whether we had to get off the bus?

(Sentences (5) and (6) may both be understood as asking about the location of John, but only (5) may be understood as asking about the location of a bus stop.) According to Newmeyer, such principles have evolved to serve the interests of the hearer by excluding certain otherwise conceivable readings of multi-clausal structures and so reducing their ambiguity. But the details of how these principles work are not important here precisely because their sphere of action is multi-clausal. What Newmeyer says about the speaker/hearer contrast cannot explain why simple (uniclausal) sentences exist, distinct from NPs.

What Newmeyer says about the sound/meaning contrast is more relevant. He attributes to it the selective advantage of **autonomous syntax**—that is, a kind of syntax that structures utterances in ways that are independent of and simpler than the ways in which they are structured semantically and phonetically. He makes the point that phonetic structure (involving articulatory gestures, formant frequencies, tone patterns, and suchlike) has no direct relationship with conceptual structure (involving relations of inclusion, such as that between *animal* and *horse*; cross-classification, as in the relationship between *stallion, horse,* and *male*; and predicate–argument structure, as in the relationship between the predicate *kick* and arguments *John* and *ball* in *John kicked the ball*). Phonetic representations are linear and temporally ordered, while semantic representations are hierarchically organized with relationships of dependency (as *John* and *ball* are dependent on *kick*) but with no intrinsic temporal order. To put it crudely, autonomous syntax splits the difference between these two kinds of structure, having some characteristics of each, combined in such a way as to facilitate a mapping between them.

Newmeyer's point about the need for syntax to provide a structural compromise between phonetics and semantics is persuasive. But syntax-as-it-is is not the only compromise that is conceivable. In Chapter 2 we considered two others: Spatiotemporal and Monocategoric, which both lack the sentence/NP distinction. Unfortunately, Newmeyer's account of the necessary tasks of syntax stops short of accounting for that distinction. For example, he says: 'it is a necessary function that arguments need to be kept distinct for each predicate. Putting the matter in fairly crude terms, hearers need to be able to tell what is a subject, what is an object, and what is an indirect object' (1991: 22). But for this comment to serve as an adequate justification for the existence of sentences such as *John gave the encyclopaedia to Mary*, a crucial gap would have to be filled. It would have to be explained why the syntactic entity created by combining *gave* with *John*, *Mary*, and *the encyclopaedia* belongs to a category (namely 'sentence') that is different from that of any of these four components. For a Monocategoric expression such as *John encyclopaedia Mary* GIVE it is strictly speaking inappropriate to use the labels 'subject', 'object', and 'indirect object' because these notions belong to syntax-as-it-is; still, the three arguments of the three-place operator GIVE (namely, agent, theme, and goal) could well be distinguishable by their order. The argument-distinguishing task that Newmeyer imposes could therefore be fulfilled satisfactorily in Monocategoric even though the whole expression would have the same syntactic status as the expressions *John*, *Mary*, and *encyclopaedia* that it contains. The same is true even of the English expression *John's gift to Mary of the encyclopaedia*, within which some syntacticians would be willing to recognize a subject, an object, and an indirect object even though the whole expression is an NP, not a sentence. So the evolutionary scenario offered by Newmeyer is not an adequate alternative to what will be offered in Chapter 5 because, at least in relation to basic sentence structure, it accounts for less.

NPs such as *John's refusing the offer* (as in *John's refusing the offer stunned us*) are called 'propositional NPs' by Newmeyer (1991: 20–1). Presumably he would classify *John's gift to Mary of the encyclopaedia* similarly, because, while clearly related to the sentence *John gave the encyclopaedia to Mary*, it too can appear in larger sentences such as *John's gift to Mary of the encyclopaedia stunned us*. But what precisely is meant by **proposition**? This term recurs constantly in psychological and philosophical discussions of language and of the representation of knowledge, and it is not always clearly distinguished from the terms 'sentence' and 'statement'. Its uses by some philosophers is discussed briefly in the Appendix. Meanwhile, it figures prominently in Pinker and Bloom's (1990) account of the adaptive advantages of grammar.

Before we look in detail at Pinker and Bloom's discussion, it is important to sound a warning. If 'proposition' turns out to mean merely 'semantic content of the kind usually expressed by a sentence', then any appeal to 'propositional representation' or 'propositional structure' to explain the existence of sentences alongside NPs will be circular. Pinker and Bloom teeter on the brink of this circularity when applying to language the doctrine that the complexity of a function counts in favour of regarding any device that fulfils it as adaptive rather than just accidentally useful:

Human language is a device capable of communicating exquisitely complex and subtle messages, from convoluted soap opera plots to theories of the origin of the universe. Even if all we knew was that humans possessed such a device, we would expect that it would have to have rather special and unusual properties suited to the task of mapping complex propositional structures onto a serial channel, and an examination of grammar confirms this expectation. (1990: 714)

Here 'mapping propositional structures onto a serial channel' is presented as a task that language is adapted to fulfil, not as a property of the language mechanism itself. But why should it be precisely in our species, rather than in dolphins or gorillas or cockroaches, that a need to fulfil this task has arisen? After all, if language benefits our own species, it would probably benefit others too! Pinker and Bloom make the mistake here of equating an explanation for how language works with an explanation for why it is humans who have it. One suspects that a reason for this mistake is that 'propositional structures' are so closely associated with sentences that it seems self-evident that the need to express propositional structures could never arise in species that do not use sentences—that is, in any species except humans. But then the fact that language has evolved in humans becomes virtually a tautology, rather than an empirical fact worth trying to explain.

Pinker and Bloom get back on the rails, however, by emphasizing a characteristic of propositions that is logically independent of syntax-as-it-is and that may therefore be a candidate for explaining the sentence/NP distinction: **predicate–argument structure**. This may be defined as the kind of structure that characterizes any expression denoting an action or state (the **predicate**) along with the participants in this action or state (the **arguments**). Thus the sentence *Wellington defeated Napoleon at Waterloo* is an expression with predicate–argument structure, in that it contains a predicate (*defeated*) and three arguments, an agent (*Wellington*), a theme or patient (*Napoleon*), and a location (*at Waterloo*). (Notice that, in this usage, 'predicate' means something different from its meaning in the usage where it is contrasted with 'subject', in terms of which the predicate of the sentence just cited would be *defeated Napoleon at Waterloo*.)

The Monocategoric expression *John encyclopaedia Mary* GIVE has predicate–argument structure too. On the other hand, the English NPs *Mary's encyclopaedia* and *the house at Pooh Corner* lack predicate–argument structure because they denote not actions or states plus their participants but rather objects. The possessor indicated by *Mary's* and the location indicated by *at Pooh Corner* help to identify the encyclopaedia and house in question, but they are not arguments of *encyclopaedia* and *house*, nor conversely are *encyclopaedia* and *house* arguments of *Mary's* and *at Pooh Corner*.

Hurford (1990) asks whether predicate–argument structures (and, by implication, propositions that possess them) exist somehow independently of and prior to language, so that expressing them is an inescapable task of anything that does roughly what human language does, or whether these structures belong merely to language as it happens to have evolved, so that a kind of language without predicate–argument structures is conceivable. Pinker and Bloom in their reply argue that predicate–argument structure derives from the distinction between physical objects and the states or actions that they participate in. This distinction, in turn, is a useful one to express because of certain empirical facts about the world. Cheetahs and gazelles, for example, are relatively stable entities, and they show general consistencies in behaviour that are unaffected by whether a given cheetah or gazelle, on the occasion when one encounters it, is sleeping. Conversely, sleep is a relatively transient state, and animals that are sleeping show general consistencies in behaviour, such as a tendency to stay still if approached quietly, that are independent of the animals' species. It is therefore useful to have separate terms for cheetahs and gazelles and for sleeping, so as to facilitate expressions with predicate–argument structure such as *the cheetah is sleeping*, rather than to have expressions without predicate–argument structure, such as *cheeping* 'cheetah sleeping' and *gazeeping* 'gazelle sleeping', that would obscure those behavioural consistencies.[5]

We need not debate here how satisfactory this is as a response to Hurford. The immediate issue is whether, granting that predicate–argument structure must inevitably be expressed, it must inevitably give rise to the sentence/NP distinction. If predicate–argument structures could be expressed only by sentences, the answer would certainly be yes. But we have already seen that some NPs have predicate–argument structure too. This applies to Newmeyer's 'propositional NP' *John's refusing the offer*, to our example *John's gift to Mary of the encyclopaedia*, and to the Monocategoric expression (another non-sentence) *John encyclopaedia Mary* GIVE. In fact, corresponding to any English sentence whatever with predicate–argument structure we can construct one or more NPs that preserve this structure. For example, corresponding to *Wellington defeated Napoleon*

---

[5] Bickerton (1990: 39) argues on similar grounds for a fundamental distinction between 'entities' and 'behaviours' in our ancestors' mental representation of reality.

*at Waterloo* we have both *Wellington's defeat of Napoleon at Waterloo* and *Napoleon's defeat by Wellington at Waterloo* (since *defeat* as a noun has both active and passive readings), as well as the so-called gerundive nominal with *-ing*, as in *Wellington's defeating Napoleon at Waterloo stunned everybody.* In all of these, the argument status of *Wellington* as agent, *Napoleon* as patient, and *at Waterloo* as location is unchanged. It follows that, in order for predicate–argument structure to be expressed, it is not necessary that a distinction between sentences and NPs should exist. So, whatever else may be said about Pinker and Bloom's treatment of predicate–argument structure, it does not suffice to motivate the sentence/NP distinction.

### 4.4.2. Propositions and Auxiliaries

Pinker and Bloom mention another characteristic that sentences are said to need in order to express propositions: the presence of **auxiliaries**, which 'convey relations that have logical scope over the entire proposition . . . such as truth value, modality and illocutionary force' (1990: 713). Modality encompasses such 'relations' as possibility and necessity, while illocutionary force refers in this context to the distinction between declarative, interrogative, and imperative sentences (or statements, questions, and commands). More recently Pinker has added **tense** to this list—that is, the grammatical expression of the time at which an event takes place (1994: 117). The inclusion of tense is important, because in Chomskyan syntax of the 1980s it is seen as the central or head element in the **inflection phrase** or IP (Radford 1988). It is the presence of the inflection phrase that differentiates sentences from other syntactic units, including NPs, so that in this syntactic framework 'sentence' is really just a less technical term for 'IP'. Consequently, if it can be shown that indicating tense is essential in order to do the sort of thing that language does, the sentence/NP distinction will be motivated on a basis quite distinct from that which I will propose in Chapter 5.

   Pinker argues for the importance of auxiliaries, including in English the modal *will*, in the following terms:

A sentence . . . must express some kind of meaning that does not clearly reside in its nouns and verbs but that embraces the entire combination and turns it into a proposition that can be true or false. Take, for example, the optimistic sentence *The Red Sox will win the World Series.* The word *will* . . . applies to an entire concept, the-Red-Sox-winning-the-World-Series. That concept is timeless and therefore truthless. . . . But the word *will* pins the concept down to temporal coordinates . . . If I declare 'The Red Sox will win the World Series,' I can be right or wrong (probably wrong, alas). (1994: 117)

Pinker is right in thinking that, in order for language to do what it does, some linguistic expressions must be 'pinned down' so as to apply to particular situations or events in the world. (Even vervet alarm calls are pinned down in this way: a vervet uttering the snake call is reacting to a particular snake, not to snakehood in general.) Pinker's emphasis on this function of auxiliaries recalls the function of syntactic tense marking as seen by Steele *et al.* (1981): declarative sentences are generally used to make assertions, and the propositional basis of an assertion, which is 'satisfied' if it 'corresponds to the way the world is', is derived by means of tense from an 'incomplete' propositional basis that, in Pinker's terms, is a timeless concept, not pinned down to temporal coordinates (Steele *et al.* 1981: 170).[6] For both Pinker and Steele, then, being 'pinned down' crucially depends on having tense.

Pinker and Steele make a crucial mistake, however, by failing to notice that sentences (or, in Steele's elaborate formula, the propositional bases of the assertions that declarative sentences are used to make) are not the only linguistic entities that can correspond to the way the world is. NPs can do so too. Examples of NPs that do so are *the present President of the USA, the sum of 9 and 5, the three oldest residents of Buffalo,* and *Wellington's victory at Waterloo.* Examples of NPs that fail to do so are *the present King of France, the largest prime number, the only female resident of Buffalo,* and *Napoleon's victory at Waterloo.* So the discussion by Steele and her colleagues excludes a huge range of expressions that correspond to the way the world is (or purport to do so but fail)— namely, among NPs. And, crucially, these NPs do not generally rely on tense to 'pin them down'. Because they generally lack predicate–argument structure, they have no 'propositional basis' of the sort that, according to Steele's analysis, might depend on tense for derivation from another (incomplete) propositional basis. So, to have syntactic units that correspond to the way the world is, it is not after all necessary to have a distinction between ones that express tense (i.e. sentences) and ones that do not.

It may be thought that a covert reliance on tense is involved in interpreting at least some of the NPs just cited. For example, to interpret correctly *Napoleon's victory at Waterloo,* one must know that the event in question was in the past; to interpret correctly *the three oldest residents of Buffalo,* one must know that it is the city's current population that is presupposed, unless the context indicates otherwise; and so on. But time is not the only thing we have to know about in order to interpret these NPs correctly. We have to know that *Napoleon* refers to the French Emperor, not to a pig in George Orwell's novel *Animal Farm;* we have to know whether *Buffalo* refers to the city in New York State or to one of the several smaller communities of that name in other US states; and so on. Interpreting correctly any sentence or NP on any occasion of use involves conventions of discourse, general knowledge, and a variety of interpersonal and pragmatic factors. But linguists do not insist that each of these factors must have a grammatical counterpart, even a covert one; so to make an exception in favour of tense,

---

[6] Compare, again, the discussion of propositions in the Appendix.

insisting on its presence in any expression whatever that is 'pinned down' sufficiently for us to tell whether it corresponds to the way the world is, would be arbitrary, begging the question in favour of the Steele–Pinker view.

There is yet a further difficulty for the Steele–Pinker view. In our discussion so
far we have charitably assumed that in syntax-as-it-is there is a neat correlation
between tense and sentencehood: all declarative sentences are tensed and no NPs
are. The first leg of this correlation must indeed be correct if sentences are
analysed as inflectional phrases. Whether that is appropriate depends on syntactic evidence, including evidence from languages such as the many varieties of
Chinese in which overt grammatical expression of tense is often or always lacking.
We need not take a position on the matter here. But the second leg of the correlation is certainly wrong. In many languages, some or all of the tenses available for
expression in sentences can also be expressed in NPs that correspond to them.
Although nouns formed from verbs often lack tense, they do not always do so. In
English a present/past contrast is available with gerundive nominals (those
formed with the suffix *-ing*); thus, Newmeyer's example of a propositional NP,
*John's refusing the offer*, has a past-tense version *John's having refused the offer*.[7] In
Finnish this sort of construction is available for the complements of verbs such as
*uskoa* 'believe' and *sanoa* 'say', as an alternative to a subordinate clause with the
conjunction *että* 'that' (Karlsson 1983: 171–2):

(7)   (*a*)   Uskotko,                        että nukut?
                  do you believe   that you sleep
     (*b*)   Uskotko                       nukkuvasi?
                  do you believe   your sleeping (non-past)
                  'Do you believe that you will sleep?'
(8)   (*a*)   Uskotko,                        että nukuit?
                  do you believe   that you slept
     (*b*)   Uskotko                       nukkuneesi?
                  do you believe   your sleeping (past)
                  'Do you believe that you slept?'

The tense contrast between the forms *nukkuvasi* and *nukkuneesi* is indicated by
the suffixes *-va-* 'non-past' and *-nee-* 'past', while their nominal character is indicated by the fact that they carry the nominal second person possessive suffix *-si*
'your' rather than the verbal second person agreement marker *-t* 'you', which
appears in *nukut* and *nukuit*. Such facts suffice to show that, even if Steele and
Pinker were right in thinking that grammatical tense is essential in order to
anchor linguistic expressions to real-world situations, that would not guarantee

---

[7] The auxiliary *have* is generally regarded as a marker of perfective aspect rather than past tense.
However, it expresses past tense in those sequence-of-tense contexts that superimpose past on past: e.g.
*John came* becomes *John had come* in reported speech, in a context such as *Mary said that . . .* It is rea-
sonable to treat *having* in *John's having refused the offer* in the same way.

the evolution of a distinction between sentences and NPs, and so would not render the scenario of Chapter 5 superfluous.

Has our argument against Steele and Pinker been in some respects too successful, however? If tense is really so dispensable, why is it expressed grammatically in so many languages—including allegedly all creoles (the languages that develop when pidgin contact languages are acquired natively) (Bickerton 1981, 1995)? Why, too, is tense expressed in the limited number of ways that Steele and her colleagues describe: as an inflectional modification of the verb, or as an independent element in final, initial, or second position in the sentence? The answers are not obvious. Bickerton, commenting on the prevalence of tense and the absence of relative-clause markers (such as *who* and *which*) in some languages, says:

Why language should need tense markers but not relative-clause markers is something that it is quite impossible to explain in terms of social, cultural, or communicative benefits. Anyone purpose-building a language could make a much better case for a converse state of affairs: relative-clause markers would be obligatory but tense markers could be freely omitted unless time was not obvious from the context or needed to be specified for discourse reasons.... But for some mysterious reason that doubtless lies hidden in the history of brain evolution, language simply reverses the communicative priorities. (1995: 37–38)

The model to be proposed in Chapter 5 has nothing to say about relative-clause markers. If correct, however, it dispels much of the mystery surrounding the evolution of tense markers—which may count as evidence in its favour.

### 4.4.3. *The Thing–Event Space and Cognitive Grammar*

In the world as it is, as Pinker and Bloom (1990) and Bickerton (1990) point out, it is useful for primates such as our scavenging or hunting-gathering ancestors to distinguish between actions-or-states and participants in them, or, in Bickerton's terminology, between behaviours and entities. Pinker and Bloom conclude from that (as summarized in Section 4.4.1) that any kind of open-ended language that our ancestors might develop would naturally be so structured semantically and syntactically as to encode a distinction between predicates and arguments. I pointed out that, even if that is so, it does not inevitably lead to a syntax with a sentence/NP distinction, since predicate–argument structure can just as well be encoded in the complex expressions of Monocategoric and in NPs in English. I want now to deal with a possible rationale for the sentence/NP distinction based not on predicate–argument structure pure and simple but on how predicate–argument structure is prototypically expressed, and I will touch on a possible contribution from the family of linguistic viewpoints known as 'cognitive grammar'.

In Chapter 2 I postulated an imaginary Martian who is surprised that human language provides two different ways in which a linguistic expression can fit the world: by referring (in the case of an NP) and by being true (in the case of a sentence). Could it be that the Martian's surprise will disappear once it appreciates the importance (in the Earth environment, at least) of predicate–argument structure? Perhaps the sentence/NP distinction is motivated by the distinction, among expressions that fit the world, between those with predicate–argument structure and those without. It is not that the correlation is exact. We have already noted that NPs may have an internal predicate–argument structure. Furthermore, there are sentences without predicate–argument structure, such as *Two and two make four* and *Tomorrow is Wednesday*, which do not describe an action or state and so *a fortiori* fail to express any relationship between an action or state and its participants. Nevertheless, it may be felt that, at least prototypically, a sentence is a predicate–argument expression and an NP is not. If this intuition is sound, it may suggest that the sentence/NP distinction can be derived from predicate– argument structure after all, but by a less direct route. In contemporary language, predicate–argument relationships get expressed in sentential form much more often than not. Perhaps that is sufficient to establish predicate–argument structure as the main factor in the origin of the sentence as a distinct syntactic entity, even if the association is not (or is no longer) watertight.

This approach is flawed, however, because it resolves the sentence/NP problem only at the cost of creating two graver problems. The first has to do with those complex expressions, whether sentences or NPs, that do not encode predicate–argument structures. Examples already cited are *Mary's encyclopaedia* and *the house at Pooh Corner*, as well as *Two and two make four* and *Tomorrow is Wednesday*. These illustrate semantic structures of a kind that we may, for the sake of argument, call possessor/possessed, equational, and locational (whether the location is spatial, like *at Pooh Corner*, or temporal, as in *[on] Wednesday*). The problem with this approach is to explain why these other kinds of semantic structure are not endowed with prototypical syntactic encodings of their own. Even if we agree with Pinker, Bloom and Bickerton that the action/participant distinction was important to our ancestors, surely the object/location distinction was important too (it would have been helpful to have a way of representing and communicating where good food sources were), and also the possessor/possessed distinction, given the importance of social relationships in primate groups (to be discussed further in Chapter 6). So why should predicate–argument structure be singled out for privileged syntactic treatment? This approach to the sentence/NP problem suffers from the drawback that it would be equally compatible with a kind of language in which there is a special syntactic structure not just for predicates-plus-arguments but also for two or three other kinds of semantically complex expression—a drawback avoided by the proposal in Chapter 5.

The second problem with this approach has to do with deciding whether a phenomenon is to be counted as involving an action-or-state with participants (hence, semantically, a predicate plus arguments) or not. I use 'phenomenon' here as an umbrella term to embrace both **events**, by which I mean phenomena that would most naturally be designated by an expression with predicate–argument structure, and **things,** by which I mean empirically observable phenomena that would not most naturally be so designated. If predicate–argument structure is to constitute a secure foundation for the sentence/NP distinction, even by an indirect route, then the distinction between events and things must be at least sufficiently clear-cut for us to be confident that it is binary. That is, we must be confident that phenomena cluster around just two prototypes, not one, three, or any other number. If they cluster in some other way, or if the number of prototypes turns out to be indeterminate, then this approach is undermined in that the semantic characterization of phenomena does not after all reveal a binary contrast that the sentence/NP distinction might be taken as reflecting. How, then, is the set of phenomena actually partitioned—in binary fashion or not?

Before offering an answer, I will clarify three aspects of my terminology. First, if the definition of 'thing' did not contain the qualification 'empirically observable', then whatever is designated by certain sentences without predicate–argument structure, such as *Two plus two make four* and *Tomorrow is Wednesday,* would be classed as things. That decision would weaken the case for saying that things (in the technical sense) cluster round a prototype; but it would do so in a fashion that is not vital to my argument, so it seems fairer to exclude such sentences and their content from the present discussion. Secondly, 'event' is deliberately defined so as to include phenomena such as a sleeping cheetah, which is not an event in ordinary parlance but which would naturally be designated by the sentence *The cheetah is sleeping* with the predicate–argument structure *sleep*Predicate *cheetah*Theme. (A more appropriate term would be 'event-or-situation', but 'event' is shorter.) Thirdly, the term that more usually contrasts with 'event' in discussions of this kind is 'object'. I use 'thing' in preference to it only because I have already used 'object' as the partner of 'action(-or-state)' to form a pair of terms for the real-world counterparts of semantic arguments and predicates respectively. There is certainly a considerable overlap between things and objects, as I define them, but it would be question-begging to assume that they are identical, so it is wise to keep the terms distinct.

Clear-cut instances of things, one may think, include physical objects such as the Koh-i-Noor Diamond that have lasted and will last a long time and whose identification does not depend crucially on where they are located. Clear-cut instances of events, by contrast, are phenomena that:

(*a*) involve actions
(*b*) occurring in a specified place
(*c*) at a specified time, and
(*d*) with participants who are identifiable outside that place and time.

An example is the shooting of Archduke Franz Ferdinand by Gavrilo Princip in Sarajevo on 28 June 1914. But how do we classify a phenomenon that has some but not all of characteristics (*a*)–(*d*)?

Consider first the phenomenon designated by the NP *the Niagara Falls*. It certainly has characteristic (*b*), being located on the US–Canadian border between Lake Erie and Lake Ontario. It also has characteristic (*a*), inasmuch as it involves an action (falling) on the part of a participant (water). On the other hand, the participating water lacks characteristic (*d*), in that it is not identifiable outside the context of Niagara in the way that Princip and the Archduke are identifiable outside the context of the assassination—that is, not unless one envisages some procedure for tagging all the water molecules that flow over it. Finally, the Niagara phenomenon lacks characteristic (*c*), inasmuch as the dates of its geological origin and eventual disappearance are not important to its identity.

Consider now a phenomenon that might be designated by the sentence *Sarah poured some water into a bowl.* This differs from the Niagara Falls because it lacks not only characteristic (*c*) but also characteristic (*b*): to accept that the phenomenon exists (or, more conventionally, to believe that the sentence is true) one does not need to know exactly where or when it happened. It also differs in respect of (*d*), becaue one of the participants (Sarah), if she is identifiable at all, will certainly be identifiable in other contexts. On the other hand, this phenomenon shares with the Niagara Falls the action of falling, with water as a participant.

In order to test fairly this approach to the sentence/NP distinction, our classification of the four phenomena so far mentioned (the diamond, the assassination, the waterfall, and Sarah's pouring) must not be prejudiced by linguistic habit, nor by any prior determination to fit them into just two pigeonholes labelled 'thing' and 'event'. But, if we view these phenomena in this linguistically unprejudiced fashion, it is not at all obvious that we will be inclined to fit them into two pigeonholes rather than three or four. And a further example will help to confirm that this uncertainty is not isolated.

Niagara Falls is a phenomenon that is spatially circumscribed, like the assassination of the Archduke, but of unspecified duration. Can one envisage a phenomenon that is temporally circumscribed, again like the assassination, but of unspecified extent in space? An example might be the Second World War, a phenomenon whose impact was worldwide but that differed enormously in intensity from place to place, and that lasted from 1939 until 1945. And while Niagara Falls involves an action (falling) with a rather vague participant (water), the Second World War involves an action-or-state (conflict) with quite precise participants (the belligerent nations) that, like Princip and the Archduke, are readily identifiable outside the context of the phenomenon under consideration. One might expect that the linguistic expressions for both these phenomena would render their action–participant structure overt in predicate–argument structure, and that both would go into the 'event' pigeonhole. In fact, their linguistic renderings in English are both NPs (hence prototypically implying a lack of predicate–argument structure, according to the approach we are examining), and only one of them, namely the Second World War, would in normal usage be classified as an event.

Inspecting the range of what I have called 'phenomena' purely on the basis of their semantic characteristics, it is hard to discern any clustering around just two prototypes based on predicate–argument structure or the lack of it. In fact, phenomena do not look as if they constitute a single continuum or cline at all. Rather, we seem to be dealing with a multidimensional **thing–event space** within which items are situated on the basis of at least four parameters, corresponding to characteristics (*a*)–(*d*). So the binary distinction between sentences and NPs cannot plausibly be explained by appeal to an extragrammatical thing/event distinction. Indeed, the notion of a space whose occupants may have some characteristics of things and some of events, depending on their position within it, suggests that 'thing' and 'event' are decidedly fuzzy notions. Perhaps a thing is simply a monotonous serious of events, as was suggested once by the philosopher Bertrand Russell (1927), or a single slow event, as suggested by the linguist Jim Hurford.[8]

For comment on this issue, it is natural to investigate the considerable philosophical literature on events. But there is apparently little discussion in this literature of phenomena such as the Niagara Falls and the Second World War; and from Bennett's summary (1988) it emerges that most philosophers believe both that there is a bipolar thing/event opposition rather than a multidimensional thing–event space, and that events are conceptually secondary to things and their activities. Does this mean, then, that philosophers provide weighty support for the approach to the sentence/NP distinction that I am here criticizing—the approach that derives it from predicate–argument structure by an indirect route?

The answer is no, I think, because the philosophers do not so much resolve these issues as neglect to discuss them. On the supposed priority of things over events, Bennett himself makes a frank admission:

Someone could have a linguistic/conceptual upbringing that made him competent in talking about how things behave and where they are when, but stopped short of equipping him to use the event concept; nobody could have an upbringing that started at the other end and stopped at the same place. *Or so I confidently believe, though I don't know how to defend my opinion.* (1988: 13; emphasis added)

And on the possible fuzziness of the thing/event distinction, the philosopher Philip Peterson adopts a similar position of firm denial on the basis of unanalysable intuitions, in a tone of truculent discomfort:

I myself think that 'preanalytic intuitions' . . . make it *very* clear that physical objects aren't events and events aren't physical objects, **even if** they both have spatio-temporal characteristics essentially (even exactly the same ones). Any theory which tends to make events and physical objects *appear* to be the same . . . **can't** be true. For it violates a too central preanalytic intuition that we can give up only at the cost of admitting that we don't know what we are talking about, i.e. what our theory is a theory about. (1997: 202; emphasis in original)

---

[8] In discussion at the International Conference on the Evolution of Language, Edinburgh, April 1996.

These philosophers' inability or refusal to analyse or defend their views makes perfect sense, however, if it springs from two facts: (*a*) the fact that, being human beings, they are equipped biologically for just one sort of language—namely, one that insists on distinguishing sentences from NPs, irrespective of whether a clear-cut counterpart of that distinction exists in the outside world; and (*b*) the fact that they are unaware of fact (*a*). Their discomfort arises from a vague but well-founded doubt whether such an outside-world counterpart really exists. In short, these attitudes make sense if the sentence/NP distinction evolved historically for reasons fundamentally independent of the thing/event distinction or of predicate–argument structure, as will be suggested in Chapter 5. 'Admitting that we don't know what we are talking about', as Peterson puts it, may be no more terrible than admitting that we don't know much yet about language evolution.

These philosophical attitudes to things and events are quite similar to those of some contemporary linguists. The terms **cognitive grammar** and **functional grammar** have come to denote a family of approaches that deny that syntax is autonomous in relation to conceptual or semantic structure and that seek to ground grammatical phenomena in cognitive processes with application outside language too (e.g. Langacker 1987, 1990, 1991; Bates and MacWhinney 1989; Lakoff 1991; Deane 1992). For Langacker, the distinction between nouns and verbs reflects a way of thinking about the world (he nicknames it 'the billiard-ball model') that 'no doubt reflects fundamental aspects of cognitive organization' and in which there is a polar opposition between physical objects (of which billiard balls are prototypical examples) and 'energetic interactions' (1991: 13–14). The noun/verb opposition in turn underlies the distinction between NPs and sentences, he says. Yet the noun/verb opposition also gives rise to what Langacker describes as 'two daunting problems' (1991: 15): the extreme semantic hetero-geneity of both nouns and verbs, and the fact that the same piece of content can often be expressed either as a verb or as a noun. Examples of this sort of verb–noun vacillation are easy to find, both within a language (English *It flashed* versus *It emitted a flash*) and between languages (English *It's raining* versus Russian *Idët dozhd'*, literally 'goes rain').

A proposal that makes sense of this vacillation will be offered in Chapter 5. For now, the important issue is what would be necessary in order for the noun/verb opposition, even with the status ascribed to it in the billiard-ball model, to motivate adequately the sentence/NP distinction. The answer is that it would be necessary to show that the noun/verb opposition reflects a fundamentally binary aspect of cognitive organization that (*a*) existed before language did and (*b*) would inevitably lead to sentence–NP syntax rather than to, say, Monocategoric.

There is evidence for an aspect of cognitive organization that arguably fulfils condition (*a*), and that is cited as such by Givón (1995: 408–10)—namely, in the neurophysiology of vision. The nerve fibres from the eyes to the brain split into two streams, known as the P-stream (with two substreams, both terminating in the temporal lobe) and the M-stream (terminating in the parietal lobe) (DeYoe and Van Essen 1988; cf. Hubel 1988).[9] In the P-stream are many neurons that respond to colour whereas in the M-stream there are none; on the other hand, in the M-stream relatively many neurons respond to motion, orientation, and changes in binocular disparity, which is a cue to distance from the observer. One may be tempted to say that the P-stream is specialized for picking out objects while the M-stream is specialized for picking out energetic interactions (to use Langacker's phrase). But, even if that is correct, it is not enough to fulfil condition (*b*). We saw in Section 4.4.1 that predicate–argument structure can be encoded in Monocategoric just as well as in syntax-as-it-is; and an object/action distinction rooted in vision could just as well have Monocategoric as its syntactic outcome, with Monocategoric expressions (whether simple or complex) being prototypical representatives of objects, and operators (whether one-place, two-place, or higher) representing actions. So the neurophysiology of vision may perhaps reinforce the reasons that Pinker, Bloom, and Bickerton offer for our ancestors' discrimination between objects and actions-or-states, but it does not suffice to explain why the sentence/NP distinction evolved.

### 4.4.4. *Topics, Themes, Thetic versus Categorical Judgements, and Processing*

In order to describe adequately how language is used as well as how it is structured, three levels of description must be distinguished: syntactic, semantic, and pragmatic. So far in this book we have been concerned overwhelmingly with syntax and semantics rather than **pragmatics**, which deals with the role played in comprehension by an utterance's context and by the background knowledge and assumptions of speaker and hearers. Yet pragmatic factors have been claimed to underlie some aspects of how grammar works, including basic characteristics of sentence structure. We therefore need to consider to what extent pragmatic factors may motivate the sentence/NP contrast.

Before we embark on this discussion, it may be helpful if I illustrate why the threefold distinction is needed. The vocabulary of syntactic description contains a set of terms for kinds of constituent (phrase or word) such as 'sentence', 'NP', and 'verb', as well as a set of terms for syntactic functions that constituents can perform, such as 'subject', 'object', and 'predicate'. The two sets of terms are necessary because the same function can be performed by more than one kind of constituent (both sentences and NPs can function as objects, for example, as in (9)) and the same constituent can fulfil more than one function (an NP may be an object in one sentence and a subject in another, for example, as in (10)):

(9)  (*a*)  John forgot [the key]$_{\text{NP}}$.
     (*b*)  John forgot [that the key was in his other trousers]$_{\text{Sentence}}$.

---

[9] I am grateful to Daniel Nettle for pointing out the potential relevance of these facts.

(10)   (*a*)   John turned the key.
      (*b*)   The key opened the door.

The vocabulary of semantic description, at the interface between semantics and syntax, contains a set of terms for semantic or thematic roles such as 'agent', 'patient', 'theme', and 'instrument'. These must be distinguished from syntactic functions because constituents with the same syntactic function can have different thematic roles, as in (11), and the same thematic role may be fulfilled by constituents with different syntactic functions, as in (12):

(11)   (*a*)   The door$_{\text{Theme}}$ opened.
      (*b*)   John$_{\text{Agent}}$ opened the door.
      (*c*)   The key$_{\text{Instrument}}$ opened the door.
(12)   (*a*)   The key$_{\text{Instrument}}$ opened the door.
      (*b*)   John$_{\text{Agent}}$ opened the door with the key$_{\text{Instrument}}$.
      (*c*)   The door was opened by John$_{\text{Agent}}$.

In terms of predicate–argument structure, thematic roles distinguish the ways in which the various arguments of a predicate are related to it.[10] Throughout (11) and (12), *John* and *the key* play the agent and instrument roles respectively in relation to the the predicate *open*. But for speakers to use sentences appropriately, it is not enough that they should understand syntax, word meanings, and thematic roles.

Consider the following question–answer pairs, each with two alternative answers given as (*b*) and (*c*):

(13)   (*a*)   So you were all standing on the doorstep. What happened next?
      (*b*)   John opened the door.
      (*c*)   The door was opened by John.
(14)   (*a*)   So what did John do next?
      (*b*)   He opened the door.
      (*c*)   The door was opened by him.

If *he* and *him* in (14) are understood as referring to John, then the predicate–argument structure of all four sentences labelled (*b*) and (*c*) is the same, and exactly the same circumstances could render them true. Why then does (14*b*) sound more appropriate than (14*c*) in reply to (14*a*)—an asymmetry not parallelled in (13*b*) and (13*c*)? Our differing reactions to (13) and (14) reflect neither syntax nor semantics but rather our pragmatic competence, in terms of which an explanation will run roughly as follows. In (14*a*) but not (13*a*) the question directs attention to John and sets up an expectation that the reply should tell us something about him; that is, in the terminology of Li (1976), John is established

---

[10] Notice again that 'predicate' appears both as a syntactic term (where it is usually opposed to 'subject') and as a semantic term (where it is opposed to 'argument'). This usage is confusing but entrenched.

as **topic**, or what Tomlin (1986) calls **theme**. But there is also an expectation in English, as in many languages, that topics or themes should precede what is said about them (the **Theme First Principle**, as Tomlin calls it). Therefore (14*c*) is awkward because, instead of the topic coming first, the new information comes first. On the other hand, (13*b*) is not awkward because (13*a*) does not establish John as the topic. If anything, the mention of the doorstep in (13*a*) makes the door more topic-like than John, so that (13*c*) should be slightly preferable to (13*b*)—which seems to me correct.

Tomlin (1986: 133) suggests that the Theme First Principle has a cognitive basis, which he links with eye movements in visual information processing. Could this cognitive basis suggest an evolutionary origin for the binary structure widely if not universally ascribed to sentences, with terminology such as 'subject–predicate', 'topic–comment' and 'theme–rheme'?

Before we assess this suggestion, it is worth noting that, even if it were true, it would not account fully for the sentence/NP distinction. A requirement that syntax should reflect the topic/comment distinction would not explain why syntax has evolved so as to distinguish the sentence at (15) from the NP at (16):

(15)  The Romans defeated the Gauls.
(16)  the Romans' defeat of the Gauls

One might argue, perhaps, that (15) is most naturally used in a context where the Romans are established as the topic, and the passive counterpart (17) is motivated by the need for a way of saying the same thing but with the Gauls as topic:

(17)  The Gauls were defeated by the Romans.

But nothing in this argument explains why we speak actual English rather than a version of Nominalized English, where the contrast between (15) and (17) is paralleled by a contrast between (16) and (18)—a contrast that exists in actual English too:

(18)  the Gauls' defeat by the Romans

The topic/comment distinction might account for the contexts where (18) is used in preference to (16), but it does not account for why language has evolved in such a way that in actual English (17) exists alongside (18). So, as a would-be explanation for syntax-as-it-is, the topic/comment distinction leaves much territory uncovered.

Even within its limited territory, however, the topic/comment contrast does not provide the evolutionary motivation for sentence structure that we are looking for. If we are to take focus-of-attention seriously as an explanatory basis for syntax, we must derive from it expectations about how syntax should be, without reference to syntax-as-it-is, and then see how many of these expectations match reality. When we do this, we find that the match is poor, as I will show.

When discussing how attention may underlie the pragmatic topic/comment contrast, Tomlin implies that we can pay attention to more than one thing at once—namely, 'certain aspects of the events or subject matter under scrutiny' which 'become either more salient or more important' (1986: 133). This seems intuitively correct. It follows that any syntactic structure motivated by the topic/comment contrast should permit more than one topic per sentence. Examples (19)–(30) illustrate some of the ways in which different elements within the same semantic content can be made the focus of attention, as indicated by the *as-for* phrase:

(19)   John hid the French books under the right-hand table.
(20)   As for John, he hid the French books under the right-hand table.
(21)   As for the French books, John hid them under the right-hand table.
(22)   As for the right-hand table, John hid the French books under it.
(23)   As for the books, John hid the French ones under the right-hand table [but he left the Spanish ones in the cupboard].
(24)   As for the tables, John hid the French books under the right-hand one [but he ignored the ones to the left].
(25)   As for the French material, John hid the books under the right-hand table [but he threw the magazines away].
(26)   As for what John did with the French books, he hid them under the right-hand table.
(27)   As for how the French books got under the right-hand table, John hid them there.
(28)   As for somebody hiding something under the right-hand table, John hid the French books there.
(29)   As for somebody hiding the French books under a table, John hid them under the right-hand one.
(30)   As for John hiding something somewhere, he hid the French books under the right-hand table.

Evidently, our attention need not be limited to just one element in the situation described in (19). Almost any combination of elements (John, the French books, the right-hand table), their properties (being French or on the right) or the activity (hiding) can be the salient aspects about which further information is provided. In respect of the three participants, this is illustrated by the *as-for* phrases in (20)–(22); and, sure enough, in languages where topic status can be encoded syntactically (not merely by a counterpart of the *as-for* method), it will generally be possible to form sentences in which NPs are topicalized that express the content of those phrases. But that is as far as the correspondence between expectations and reality extends. Syntactic topicalization of material such as the counterparts of the *as-for* phrases in (23)–(30) seems to occur seldom, if ever. What distinguishes these from (20)–(22) is that the focus of attention is either less or more than the referent of a single NP. Examples (23)–(25) pick out less, focusing on just some attributes of a participant (such as being books or being French) while leaving out the rest. Examples (26)–(30) pick out more, focusing on some combination of the participants and the activity (hiding).

For the hypothesis that attention-focusing is the cognitive basis for the evolution of a fundamental binary division in sentence structure, this is bad news. If the hypothesis were correct, why should syntactic topicalization always or nearly always be limited to whole single NPs? Examples (26)–(30) showed that the focus of attention may be wider than what can be topicalized grammatically. But we also encounter the opposite kind of mismatch: sentences with the usual sort of binary division but which may be used in contexts where none of their content has already been established as a focus of attention—sentences whose entire content comes out of the blue, so to speak. Examples for which such contexts are easy to imagine are:

(31)   The king's been assassinated!
(32)   It's snowing.

A pragmatically appropriate context for the utterance of (31) is unlikely to be one in which either the king or assassination in general is already the focus of attention. As for (32), one might argue that its use presupposes prior attention to the weather, and indeed there are speech communities in which attention to the weather is nearly always present, at least in the background (Britain is a notorious example); nevertheless, the weather in general is not mentioned in (32), only its current manifestation. In terms of Sasse's (1987) distinction between thetic and categorical statements (mentioned in Chapter 2), both (31) and (32) are pragmatically plausible in contexts where a thetic rather than a categorical statement is appropriate. Indeed, (31) could be a response to the question 'What's happened?'—the same as the question to which the French response reported at (34) in Chapter 2 was the nominal expression *le chat qui est tombé par la fenêtre*.

For focus-of-attention as the evolutionary basis for sentence structure, the difficulty posed by (31) and (32) is that their structure is identical to that of the replies to the questions in (33) and (34)—questions that direct attention to the king and the snow respectively, and for which therefore the appropriate response is a categorical statement, not a thetic one:

(33)   What's happened to the king?—He's been assassinated!
(34)   Is there still snow outside?—It's melting.

If the binary subject–predicate or topic–comment structure of many sentences has really evolved from a cognitive distinction between what we direct our attention to and what we observe about it (in both senses of 'observe'), then this identity of structure is mysterious. Why should the binary pattern have encroached so extensively into the syntax of what we say about situations where our attention is directed nowhere in particular? Languages do indeed exploit various strategies to indicate that a statement is thetic rather than categorical; but there is no single dominant strategy such as we might expect to find if the original prime task of syntax was to distinguish the focus of attention from the rest of what is said. On the other hand, the encroachment of the binary pattern into pragmatically inappropriate territory is quite natural in terms of the scenario which I will propose in Chapter 5.

Finally, let us consider the possible relevance of a principle of syntactic processing, called **Early Immediate Constituents** (EIC) by John Hawkins (1992, 1994). According to this principle, syntax is organized so that the identity of constituents (as NPs, prepositional phrases, relative clauses, and so on) can be recognized by the hearer earlier rather than later as she processes the incoming linguistic string. Hawkins claims that EIC renders redundant pragmatic or cognitively grounded principles such as Tomlin's Theme First Principle. So could EIC be a plausible candidate to explain the evolution of the sentence/NP contrast?

Hawkins's (1994) discussion of EIC is long and complex, and I will not attempt a full evaluation of it here. However, it seems likely for two reasons that the answer to our immediate question will be no. First, Hawkins does not consider the origin of the sentence/NP distinction, so provides no explicit reason for it. It seems likely that his EIC could be complied with in a language lacking the distinction, such as Nominalized English or Monocategoric, just as readily as the Theme First Principle could, as we saw when discussing (15)–(18). Secondly, in order to test the extent to which a given word-order pattern (such as Subject–Verb–Object or Verb–Subject–Object) favours early identification of constituents, Hawkins finds it necessary to appeal to assumptions about the length of syntactic constituents, and to data on the relative length of various constituents in texts in ten languages. But, even if these assumptions are correct and the data are representative, a question arises about what causes what. If EIC is to suffice to account for word-order generalizations by itself, it must be that (to put it schematically) language A is of word-order type M because, in language A, constituent X is generally longer than constituent Y—not that constituent X is longer than constituent Y in language A because language A is of word-order type M. Certainly, whichever is the direction in which causation operates, Hawkins's evidence provides solid support for the relevance of processing factors in syntax. But unless he can show that causation works in the first direction rather than the second, he has not established even that pragmatic factors (such as those which interest Tomlin) are redundant in explaining syntax-as-it-is, let alone that EIC has a significant role in explaining the evolution of the sentence/NP contrast.

### 4.4.5. Protolanguage

Derek Bickerton has in recent years been the most vigorous advocate among linguists of the importance of research on language origins. His books *Language and*

*Species* (1990) and *Language and Human Behavior* (1995) have done much to reawaken interest in the topic. So it is clearly important to assess what he says or implies about the origins of grammar, so far as this bears on the sentence/NP distinction. Because of the wide sweep of Bickerton's proposals, explicitly relating stages of language evolution to stages of hominid evolution generally, this assessment involves two inquiries. We must, of course, consider what Bickerton says explicitly about basic sentence structure; but we must also investigate what he says about the relationship between linguistic and physical evolution, since this may constitute a rival to the scenario that will be presented in Chapter 5.

In Chapter 2, when discussing possible alternatives to syntax-as-it-is, I described a kind of language that I labelled 'Asyntactic', in which combinations of meaningful items were made sense of purely pragmatically, with no syntactic assistance. Bickerton has suggested that a syntaxless kind of language, which he calls **protolanguage**, did indeed arise and is still in use. He sees the following as manifestations of it:

- contact languages or jargons developed in communication between speakers with no shared language, such as Russonorsk (formerly used by Norwegian and Russian sailors in the Arctic), and the early stages of pidgins, before they begin to incorporate identifiable features of the grammar of any of the native languages of their speakers;
- as a special case of this, the *ad hoc* simplified 'touristese' used in attempts to make oneself understood to foreigners (e.g. 'Where bathroom? Water cold! Me want speak manager! Me no pay!');
- the 'two-word' or 'telegraphic' stage of young children's linguistic development, before the rapid acquisition of adult syntax from about the age of $2\frac{1}{2}$;
- the kind of language acquired in later life by people deprived of normal exposure to language before puberty (so-called wild children);
- sign combinations produced by sign-language-trained apes (as described in Chapter 6), and even perhaps by some non-primate species such as parrots under laboratory conditions (Pepperberg 1990).

The shared characteristics of protolanguage in all these manifestations are

a total absence of complex sentences, a lack of correlation between function and word order, frequent omission of subcategorized constituents [i.e. the arguments of predicates], absence of any mechanism for automatically recovering the reference of phonetically null arguments [e.g. the subject of the verb *work* in *John wants someone to work for*], and a complete or all-but-complete absence of grammatical items. (Bickerton 1995: 51)

The stage of human evolution during which protolanguage was the only sort of language in use, Bickerton suggests, was that of *Homo erectus.* Pre-*erectus* hominids were australopithecines and *Homo habilis*, whose tools (or those that survive) were limited to crude choppers. The transition from these early hominids to *erectus* took place between about 2 and 1.5 million years ago. *Erectus* in turn faded away during a second transition that took place within the last 300,000 years. First early *Homo sapiens* and *Homo neandertalensis* appeared, then during the last 100,000 years modern *Homo sapiens* came to replace Neanderthals at the same time as the archaeological record shows a big increase in tool variety and artistic creativity. Bickerton stresses the relative suddenness of these two transitions and the long period of apparent stagnation (more than a million years) between them. The period of stagnation coincides with the dominance of *Homo erectus*—an extremely long period by comparison with that during which *Homo sapiens* has been dominant, yet a period during which cultural change was glacial (Bickerton claims).[11] *Erectus*'s technical achievements were not negligible: in some but not all the areas that they inhabited, they were experts at manufacturing the elegant but enigmatic teardrop-shaped tools known as 'hand-axes', and in some places too they made use of fire. Why then were they so conservative? Because of the cognitive and communicative limitations imposed by proto-language, Bickerton suggests.

Bickerton thus associates two linguistic transitions (from no language to protolanguage, and from protolanguage to full language) with two archaeological transitions (from pre-*erectus* to *erectus*, and from *erectus* to modern humans). From our point of view, it is the second transition that is more obviously important. Because protolanguage had no systematic grammar at all, it cannot have had a distinction between sentences and NPs. The distinction must therefore have arisen in the course of the transition to full language. What then does Bickerton say about the origin of this aspect of modern grammar?

As we have already seen in Section 4.4.2, Bickerton admits frankly that there are some aspects of modern syntax that he cannot explain, such as the universality (or alleged universality) of tense marking versus the optionality of relative-clause marking. But basic clause structure is not so puzzling, he thinks. Like Pinker and Bloom, and like other researchers to be discussed in Chapter 6, he ascribes a crucial role to predicate–argument structure. Mental representation of situations in terms of predicate–argument structure is a prerequisite for knowing who does what to whom. It is therefore a vital component of the kind of social intelligence that, we may assume, was at least as well developed in our immediately pre-linguistic ancestors as it is in modern apes. One thing necessary for the

---

[11] Under the *erectus* label I intend here to include the early species or subspecies *Homo ergaster*. Anthropological discussions about the relationship between *habilis*, *ergaster*, and *erectus* do not seem relevant to Bickerton's claims. The view that little cultural change occurred during the period of *erectus* dominance is based solely on negative evidence: the paucity of relevant archaeological finds so far. But new discoveries of skilfully made wooden hunting spears, about 400,000 years old, in Germany (Thieme 1997) and of possible human settlement (whether *erectus* or archaic *sapiens*) in cold Siberian conditions about 300,000 year ago (Waters *et al.* 1997) suggest that Bickerton may overestimate *erectus*'s conservatism. Evidence that *erectus* survivors may have lingered in Java, alongside *sapiens*, until as recently as 27,000 years ago (Swisher *et al.* 1996) confirms their resilience.

transition from protolanguage to full language was a mechanism for supplying predicate–argument structure with linguistic expression. That mechanism, according to Bickerton (1998: 348), was the syntax of the simple sentence, or clause:

The most basic unit of syntax is the clause. The scope of a clause is determined by what is known as the thematic grid of the single verb that each clause obligatorily contains. Every verb subcategorizes for (obligatorily selects) one, two or three *arguments*, that is to say, nouns or noun phrases referring to some necessary participant in the state or action expressed by the verb, and each of these arguments will have a *thematic role*, that is, will stand in a particular semantic relationship to that state or action.

The sentence/NP distinction is thus a direct consequence of the grafting of predicate–argument structure onto the raw material supplied by protolanguage.

A reader who recalls the discussion of predicate–argument structure in Section 4.4.1 will be able to anticipate my objection to Bickerton here. Sentences are not the only syntactic vehicles through which predicate–argument structure can be expressed. In particular, it may be expressed in forms of language in which nothing corresponding to the syntactic distinctions between 'noun', 'verb', and 'sentence' exists, such as Nominalized English and Monocategoric. Therefore, however much one may be attracted to Bickerton's vision of protolanguage and full language as crucial characteristics of *erectus* and *sapiens* respectively, this vision does not explain why the sentence/NP distinction should exist. Bickerton makes the common mistake, I think, of supposing that certain basic characteristics of syntax-as-it-is, just because they are so basic, could not have evolved in any other way.

That disposes of what Bickerton says about basic sentence structure. But there is another pertinent question provoked by his view of the relationship between language and archaeology. Why should the stage at which protolanguage arose have been the *erectus* stage of human evolution, rather than earlier or later? This question is pertinent, because a rival answer will be proposed in Chapter 5. A proper comparison of the merits of the two answers will clearly have to wait until then. For the time being, I will summarize what Bickerton says.

The capacity for protolanguage must have been latent in our ancestors since at least the human/chimpanzee split, as is shown by the fact that (as Bickerton agrees) chimpanzees can develop it under laboratory conditions. (Chimpanzees' use of sign language and other symbolic communication systems will be discussed further in Chapter 6.) Yet in human evolution, according to Bickerton, protolanguage did not emerge until *Homo erectus* (or shortly before), because it is protolanguage that made possible *erectus*'s cultural advances in toolmaking and in the use of fire (based on evidence from the site at Zhoukoudian, outside Beijing). So why did protolanguage not emerge naturally among australopithecines, for example?

Bickerton distinguishes between 'latent' and 'usable' forms of protolanguage, the latter requiring words (or manual signs) 'to replace the complexities of a concept . . . with a smooth, bland counter that can be manipulated . . . either in thought or in speech' (1990: 145). In order to explain why protolanguage had to wait until *erectus* to become usable, Bickerton appeals to a notion of 'readiness', a stage reached 'most likely at the beginning or the end of the *habilis* period', involving stereoscopic vision, highly developed hands, and some use of stones as tools, along with relative vulnerability to predators and 'a constant need for better information' (1990: 147–53). We cannot be sure that Bickerton's appeal to 'readiness' is mistaken; but one may question both whether this constellation of factors really came into existence just when Bickerton says it did, and whether it was really adequate to trigger an early form of language. The scenario to be presented in Chapter 5, whether right or wrong, is more parsimonious in its assumptions.

### 4.4.6. The Hierarchical Architecture of Complexity

Originators of proposals about how syntax may have evolved disagree on much, but nearly all would agree in placing their work on the scientific side of the science/humanities divide. I do not wish to get embroiled here in discussion of criteria for distinguishing humanities from sciences, or of whether the distinction is really justified at all. I mention it because one scholar, Geoffrey Sampson (1980, 1997), is unusual in combining an interest in language evolution with the view that central aspects of language (particularly semantics, but also syntax) are 'creative' in a way that precludes worthwhile scientific treatment of them. An activity that is creative in Sampson's sense (which is quite different from Chomsky's) cannot be brought within the scope of a hypothetico-deductive system of the kind that contemporary 'Theoretical Linguistics' (as Sampson calls it) aspires to be. Syntax does indeed have a hierarchical structure, but this is only because systems with that structure are more successful in perpetuating themselves than systems without. In support of this view, Sampson adduces Herbert Simon's (1962) argument that complex systems that are adapted for survival share a fundamentally similar architecture, whether the system is a diamond with its constituent molecules or a historical entity like the empire of Alexander of Macedon, with its constituent provinces and satrapies.

Sampson's concern is not to identify a single right answer for how syntax evolved, but to show that answers are available that do not presuppose an innate mental organ such as Chomskyan Universal Grammar. One possible answer, he suggests, posits the building-up of sentences out of holophrastic utterances or 'word-sentences' such as *Up*, *Mountain*, or *John*. These would be syntactically unclassifiable and semantically vague: '"Up" might mean that someone had gone up something, that the honey was high up on the ledge, that the rock needed lifting up, etc. etc.' (Sampson 1980: 148). But word-sentences could be strung to-gether, just as contemporary sentences can, and in due course 'discourses such as "John . . . Up-mountain", "Mary . . . In-cave" would be recognized as com-monly useful, and one kind of subject–predicate structure would become a learned feature of the language'. These strings of word-sentences could them-selves be strung together, and so on. However, Simon's thesis on the architecture of complexity imposes an important testable constraint on how this combination will operate: 'The thesis will predict that complex sentences should be hierarchi-cally structured, with sub-sentential units of the hierarchy being elements that have independent uses as utterances—or which, at least, derive historically from units which once were independently useful' (Sampson 1980:158). The empirical force of that claim is illustrated by a prima-facie counter-example: the verb phrase. Sampson concedes that verb phrases (like *loves the countryside* in *John loves the countryside*) are unusual as independent utterances. In response, how-ever, he questions the validity of the verb phrase as a syntactic unit and hence of the predicate as a syntactic function. All in all, Sampson claims, a Simonian approach to language predicts well the kinds of syntactic features that are common to all natural languages. An innate language acquisition device is super-fluous, because these common syntactic features are precisely those that are favoured by 'the mathematics of evolution' and its preference for decomposable hierarchies (Sampson 1980:163).

If this is true, what Sampson offers is a serious alternative to Chomskyan Universal Grammar. This is not the place to assess empirically whether Sampson's Simonian theory of language can account for everything that any particular version of UG is claimed to account for. However, it can be shown that a Simonian theory is compatible with kinds of syntax other than syntax-as-it-is, and in particular with a syntax that lacks the sentence/NP distinction. Syntax-as-it-is is, therefore, not an inevitable product of 'the mathematics of evolution'.

An alert reader may have wondered what exactly Sampson means when he characterizes *John . . . Up-mountain* in his hypothetical primitive language as 'one kind of subject–predicate structure'. In view of Sampson's scepticism about predicates in the purely syntactic sense, where predicates contrast with subjects, is it predicates in the semantic sense that he really has in mind here—the sense in which they contrast with arguments? If so, then *John . . . Up-mountain* is presum-ably to be analysed as a predicate (*Up*) with two arguments whose semantic roles are location (*mountain*) and theme (*John*). But, if so, the scenario that he describes will by no means inevitably lead to syntax-as-it-is. This is because, as we have already noted, predicate–argument structure can just as well be expressed in Monocategoric. What is more, Monocategoric syntax arguably complies more directly than actual syntax does with the requirement that Sampson derives from Simon, to the effect that every component of an expression should be usable independently.

In actual English syntax, quite apart from the verb-phrase difficulty already mentioned, there is a prima-facie difficulty over relative clauses like *that my brother lent to Mary* in *This is the book that my brother lent to Mary*: the relative clause, though syntactically a sentence, is not usable as an independent sentence. To reconcile this with the decomposability requirement, Sampson posits a process of syntactic change that is 'quite analogous to the situation in biology whereby an organism changes its nature after it has been absorbed into symbiosis with another organism' (1980: 162). But, however convincing this analogy may be, the need to appeal to it would not arise if language had evolved in the direction of Monocategoric, as described in Chapter 2. This is because a Monocategoric expression such as *you snake* SEE YESTERDAY undergoes no change when it is incorporated in larger expressions such as *[you snake* SEE YESTERDAY*]* DISAPPEAR SEEM or *John Mary [you snake* SEE YESTERDAY*]* TELL.

As a rejoinder, Sampson might point out that every complex Monocategoric expression contains an operator as one of its immediate constituents—an element that cannot appear independently, without its due complement of arguments. For example, *you snake* SEE YESTERDAY consists of one expression, *you snake* SEE, plus the one-place operator YESTERDAY; *John Mary [you snake* SEE YESTERDAY*]* TELL consists of three expressions, *John*, *Mary*, and *you snake* SEE YESTERDAY, plus the three-place operator TELL; and so on. Monocategoric therefore fails the decomposability requirement, so would not be a plausible outcome of Simonian linguistic evolution.

This rejoinder is weak, however, because it is not clear that an actual language such as English complies with Sampson's version of Simon's hierarchic architecture any better than Monocategoric does. Consider a sentence such as *You saw a snake yesterday*. Sampson has already cast doubt on the suggestion that this is decomposable into two structures, an NP *you* and a verb phrase *saw a snake yesterday*. In that case, however, the verb *saw* must be an immediate constituent of the whole sentence. But it is no easier to visualize a context for the independent use of *saw* than to do so for *saw a snake yesterday*. *Saw* by itself might be an answer to the question *Did you say that you **saw** a snake, or that you **heard** one?* Equally, however, *Saw a snake yesterday* might be an answer to the question *Did you say that they saw a snake yesterday, or that they expect to see one tomorrow?* So both the verb and the verb phrase can plausibly be used on their own only in response to requests for confirmation, where they are quoted rather than used in the normal manner. In other words, *Saw* here is really '*Saw*', elliptical for '*Saw*' *is what I said*. But, precisely in metalinguistic or quotational contexts of this kind, we would expect Monocategoric too to allow operators to be used on their own, as names for themselves; and as such they would be well-formed expressions. SEE (or rather 'SEE') by itself would thus be a well-formed answer to a question that might be formulated *[you [[[you snake* SEE*] [you snake* HEAR*]]* WHICH*]* SAY*]* QUERY. So, in respect of decomposability, English and Monocategoric emerge on a par.

Admittedly, there may be other actual languages that are more straight-forwardly 'Simonian' in some respects than English is: for example, Chinese, where the literal counterpart of English *Saw* is usable in a wider range of contexts than just requests for confirmation. But this is irrelevant for present purposes. To show that syntax-as-it-is is significantly superior to Monocategoric in terms of decomposability, one would need to show that this superiority is consistent and general, not just sporadic and language-particular.

If we take Sampson's 'subject-predicate structure' to mean 'predicate–argument structure', then, his Simonian model fails to discriminate between syntax-as-it-is and Monocategoric as outcomes of linguistic evolution. But what if we interpret 'subject–predicate structure' to refer to the traditional bipartite structure of the sentence? Sampson's use of the term 'word-sentence' for imaginary primitive holophrastic utterances such as *Up* and *Mountain* points in this direction. But on this interpretation, too, his account of linguistic evolution fails—this time because it begs precisely the question at issue. If one takes it for granted that the prototype of an independently usable composite expression is the sentence, with all that that implies in terms of contrast with other syntactic units such as the NP, then one is bound to neglect the possibility that the sort of complex structure that might result from the combination of holophrastic utterances need not be sentential at all.

This neglect is paradoxical, in view of one of the great merits of Sampson's dis-cussion: his insistence that there is no logical necessity for syntax to be the way it is. He rightly argues that it is illegitimate to interpret a holophrastic utterance, such as one of our ancestors might have produced, as necessarily a kind of ellip-tical version of a complex modern-style sentence (1980: 150). However, apart from asserting that there is no logical necessity for syntax to be hierarchical (a point on which he agrees with Chomsky), he does not contemplate other direc-tions that syntactic development might conceivably have taken.

### 4.4.7. Gesture and Sign Language

Sign languages of the deaf, such as American Sign Language (ASL) and British Sign Language (BSL), are genuine languages in their own right, not mere vague pantomime or derivatives of spoken languages. This has come to be generally rec-ognized by linguists in the last few decades (Klima and Bellugi 1979; Deuchar 1984). But even before this recognition was established there was a current within language-evolution research that favoured gesture over primate call systems as a source for human language (e.g. Hewes 1973, 1976), and the fully linguistic status now accorded to sign languages may be thought to reinforce their evolutionary relevance.

Any proponent of this hypothesis is faced with the task of explaining how and why the switch was made from a primarily gestural to a primarily vocal communication system. It seems fair to say that the explanations offered have been vague. The vocal channel has certain obvious advantages: it can be used when the interlocutors cannot see each other (for example, in darkness), or when the speakers' hands are occupied. But if these are reasons why the vocal channel should have replaced the gestural, they are also reasons against supposing that the gestural channel was ever dominant in the first place. So the main attractions of the hypothesis must lie elsewhere. It is on these that I will concentrate here, with a view to determining whether any of them accounts satisfactorily for the sentence/NP distinction.

The gestural hypothesis has two supposed attractions that do not primarily concern the sentence/NP distinction. One of these involves iconicity. If the transition from iconic to mainly symbolic signing was a major hurdle in language evolution, then (it is argued) this hurdle may have been easier to clear if the original linguistic medium was visual rather auditory, because there is more scope for iconic representation in gesture than in sound. It is easier to imagine how a substantial vocabulary of conventional gestural signs might evolve out of pantomime than how an oral vocabulary of similar size might evolve directly out of vocal mimicry. But this argument presupposes that the use of non-iconic signs is wholly or largely restricted to humans; and, as was noted in Section 4.3.2, evidence from the behaviour of vervets as well as many other animal species shows that that is not so. Besides, if conventionalized gestural signing, as a precursor to spoken language, evolved gradually out of pantomime, we might expect to find reflections of this in the way in which deaf sign languages are used and learned today. We might expect, that is, to find elements of pantomime incorporated seamlessly within sign-language utterances, and to find that infants learning sign languages natively do so via a gradual progression starting from *ad hoc* iconic gesturing. But neither seems to be the case. Infant native learners of ASL do not exploit what Newport and Supalla (1980: 197) call 'the analogue potential of the modality' (i.e. the potential for pantomime), but seem rather to interpret as belonging to a frozen code even those elements of ASL that are partially iconic ('mimetic'). This is consistent with the view that the human capacity to learn language, whether signed or spoken, evolved primarily as a capacity to learn spoken language, in which the scope for iconicity is less.

The second supposed attraction concerns voluntary control. Non-human primates certainly have voluntary control over their hands, even if their vocalizations are automatic; therefore the human ability to speak or keep silent at will may be inherited from a period when speech was subordinate to gesture (it is argued). But again there is a questionable assumption here. The evidence for voluntary control of vocalization among primates is increasing along with the evidence that animals may vocalize in order to deceive (Byrne and Whiten 1988; Byrne 1995); so the apparent need to invoke a gestural stage in order to explain this aspect of human language diminishes.

Armstrong, Stokoe, and Wilcox (1995) address the distinction between words and sentences in a fashion that bears directly on the sentence/NP issue. They do not take the distinction for granted but rather see it as something for which an evolutionary explanation is sorely needed, calling it 'one of the most difficult problems of language evolution' (1995: 156). According to them, 'the seed of language', out of which both words and syntax grow, is the visible gesture (1995: 179). They invite readers to swing the right hand across the body and catch with it the upraised forefinger of the left. This gesture encapsulates a predicate–argument structure, with the swinging grasp as the action, the right hand as the agent, and the stationary finger as the patient. It is from gestures of that kind that the Subject-Verb-Object pattern in syntax evolved (they say), with sentences corresponding to the whole gesture and words corresponding to its parts.

Armstrong and his colleagues (let me call them ASW) are right to see the word/sentence distinction as evolutionarily problematic. Moreover, the fundamental role that ASW attribute to Subject–Verb–Object structure parallels the role that Pinker and Bloom (1990) assign to predicate–argument structure. But this parallel draws attention also to the first of the two important gaps in ASW's account. As we noted in Section 4.4.1, predicate–argument structure can be expressed in an NP as well as in a sentence. Therefore, the fact that a gesture may encapsulate predicate–argument structure does not show conclusively that a form of spoken language evolving out of a sign language composed of such gestures must incorporate a sentence/NP distinction. So ASW's finger-grasping image, just like Pinker and Bloom's image of eating and sleeping cheetahs, is consistent with more evolutionary directions for spoken language than the one actually taken.

The second gap in ASW's account has no Pinker–Bloom parallel. Certainly, the finger-grasping gesture can reasonably be seen as having agent–action–patient structure. But to show that it was from gestures such as that that syntax-as-it-is evolved, it is necessary to show either that the kind of gestural language that was the putative ancestor of spoken language contained no gestures with any structure other than predicate–argument structure, or else that such gestures are irrelevant in evolutionary terms. Otherwise, the question will arise why syntax did not evolve structurally in one of those other directions rather than in the predicate–argument direction.

As a proxy for the putative gestural ancestor we may use a modern sign language (ASW, after all, base much of their discussion on American Sign Language). The question then is: do modern sign languages have signs with an identifiable structure other than predicate-plus-argument? The answer is yes. Several signs in British Sign Language can be regarded as encapsulating a state or activity in a given location. For example, in the BSL counterpart of English *stand* the index and middle finger of one hand are held vertically so as to touch with their tips the flat palm of the other; in the sign for *delicious* the flat hand makes a circular motion over the lower trunk; and in the sign for *imagine* the hand makes a circular motion touching the forehead (Deuchar 1984). So a gestural ancestor could just as plausibly, it seems, have given rise to a Spatiotemporal syntax with location-plus-event structure of the kind described in Chapter 2, rather than to syntax-as-it-is. Why did that not happen? ASW give no answer. Their discussion of the origin of syntax is conducted entirely on the basis of the finger-grasping gesture, neglecting altogether gestures with other structures. It is hard to avoid thinking that a reason for this neglect may be an unconscious bias towards those gestures that seem most closely to resemble syntax-as-it-is. As an explanation of why the sentence/NP distinction evolved, therefore, ASW's theory is at best incomplete and at worst circular.

My discussion here certainly does not exhaust what there is to be said about the evolutionary significance of sign language. There is good evidence that brain lesions of the kind that produce aphasias in spoken language produce parallel disorders in sign language (Poizner *et al.* 1987). This is perfectly compatible with the view of the neural mechanisms for syntax to be put forward in Chapter 5. However, we will also address in Chapter 6 another intriguing possibility about sign language in relation to language evolution—a possibility that cannot be expounded until the scenario of Chapter 5 has been presented.

# 5   A Different Solution

## 5.1. Scope of the Solution

In Chapter 2 I drew attention to three peculiarities of human language that constitute the problem for which I want to offer a solution. These peculiarities are:

- large vocabulary size;
- duality of patterning;
- the distinction between sentences and NPs.

In Chapter 4 I argued that no other proposal about language evolution currently on offer accounts for these peculiarities satisfactorily. The time has now come for me to try to do better.

In Chapter 1, when discussing how my perspective differs from others currently represented in research on language evolution, I said that I would invoke evidence from two apparently unconnected areas: the process of vocabulary acquisition in infancy and the anatomy of the vocal tract. In this chapter I will try to show how this evidence suggests an economical answer to why language possesses those three peculiarities.

An economical answer to this question is not a complete answer to how and why human language evolved. Some issues in language evolution, such as its social role within primate and early hominid groups, are almost entirely independent of the issues that I address here. Others, such as the increase in human brain size, are not independent, so my account is in principle vulnerable to evidence concerning them. But I will argue here and in Chapter 6 that my proposal is consistent with what is known independently about human evolution, and integrates in surprising fashion certain facts about human language that in most other approaches are treated as having nothing to do with each other.

## 5.2. Some Semantic Characteristics of Vocabulary and Grammar

As noted in Chapter 2, all normal human beings have the capacity to acquire by the age of about 6 a very large vocabulary—very large, that is, by the standards of animal communication systems. How do they achieve this? Several decades of research in the study of vocabulary acquisition (a subfield of developmental psycholinguistics with strong links to developmental psychology) allow reasonably confident answers to be given to some aspects of this problem.

In Chapter 2 I mentioned one striking characteristic of adult vocabulary— namely, the rarity of exact synonyms, by contrast with the widespread occurrence of homonyms. In this section I will comment on a second characteristic of adult vocabulary—namely, the rarity of words whose meanings are disjunctive (in a sense to be explained). I will then point to aspects of how vocabulary is acquired in childhood that can be seen as responsible for these two characteristics. But these acquisitional habits turn out to account for some apparently perverse features of grammar too, on the assumption that grammar as well as vocabulary comes within their scope. The very perversity of their grammatical consequences argues that these acquisitional habits are deeply ingrained—perhaps part of our biological endowment. The extensive implications of that possibility are explored in subsequent sections.

### 5.2.1. Disjunctive Categories

In English there are words for different kinds of fruit such as *apple, pear, plum, peach,* and *banana.* In the terminology of lexical semantics (Cruse 1986) these are all hyponyms of the superordinate term *fruit.* But one can visualize an imaginary Disjunctive English that is like English except that its fruit vocabulary is structured differently. Instead of a term for each species there are terms covering two or more species in a disjunctive fashion. Suppose such terms and their English renderings include *pepple* 'apple or pear', *pum* 'pear or plum', *pleana* 'plum or peach or banana'. The English sentence *The bowl contains apples or pears or some of each* can be rendered succinctly as *The bowl contains pepples.* On the other hand, an exact translation of the English sentence *The bowl contains only pears* necessitates recourse in Disjunctive English to a compound noun *pepple-pum* meaning 'fruit that is both an apple-or-pear and a pear-or-plum': *The bowl contains only pepple-pums.*

Few readers will be surprised to hear that no language has been reported (so far as I know) in which any portion of the vocabulary is structured like this. Given that the species of fruit in question are clearly distinct in appearance, it seems intuitively perverse to name them in such a roundabout fashion. But we cannot simply say that what is wrong with *pepple, pum,* and *pleana* is that their meanings are disjunctive.

What Markman (1989) calls the classical model for cognitive categories such as word meanings, analysing them as clear-cut lists of defining criteria, has for some decades faced strong competition from two related rivals: Wittgenstein's family resemblance model (1958) and the prototype model of Eleanor Rosch and her colleagues (e.g. Rosch and Mervis 1975). Wittgenstein (remark 66)[1] pointed out that it is impossible to find any characteristics common to all the proceedings that we call 'games'; rather, these proceedings display a complicated pattern of overlapping resemblances. Rosch likewise argued that within the category 'bird' we regularly distinguish between 'good' or prototypical instances such as robins (which are small feathered flying creatures with the same overall shape as most birds) and more marginal instances such as penguins and ostriches, which lack certain characteristics of the prototype. This shows that the meanings of *game* and *bird* are disjunctive in the sense that alternative ways of qualifying to be a game or a bird exist that cannot be neatly dissected into necessary and sufficient conditions.

Words whose meanings are most commonly discussed from this point of view are nouns, but there is evidence for family-resemblance structure in the meanings of verbs too: Jackendoff (1985) points out that the meaning of *climb* contains the components 'upward' and 'clambering', but that these are disjunct, so as to yield the following pattern of acceptability judgements:

(1)  (*a*)  The boy climbed up the tree.
    (*b*)  The boy climbed down the tree.
    (*c*)  The snake climbed up the tree.
    (*d*)  *The snake climbed down the tree.

Only (1*d*), where both 'upward' and 'clambering' are excluded, is ill-formed.

Disjunctivity is also crucial in metaphor and metonymy. Let us take it that a prototypical crown is an elaborate piece of headgear worn by a monarch as a symbol of sovereignty. We can also use *crown* metaphorically in contexts such as *the crown of the road* or *the crown of his life's achievement*, where the component of sovereignty has disappeared and only the component of topmost position or importance remains; and we can use it metonymically in contexts such as *crown prerogative* or *crown assets*, where all elements of the prototypical crown have disappeared except its association with state authority. Yet if *crown* can mean, roughly speaking, 'headgear *or* topmost part *or* associated with state authority *or* any combination of these', why is 'plum *or* peach *or* banana' (the meaning given for Disjunctive English *pleana*) implausible as a category of fruit?

Markman (1989) reports evidence that suggests that in structuring categories we have recourse sometimes to the classical checklist approach and sometimes to the family-resemblance model. Sorting out the factors that favour one or the other

---

[1]  As explained in Chapter 3, most of Wittgenstein's philosophical writings are divided into numbered 'remarks', and are cited in terms of these rather than page numbers.

is an area of current research in cognitive psychology whose details need not concern us. But there is one important respect in which the disjunctive meanings of *crown* and *pleana* differ. The disjunctive components in the meaning of *crown* are compatible with one another—not surprisingly, since in a prototypical crown they co-occur. This compatibility gives the meaning of *crown* a family-resemblance structure, with a royal crown worn as a symbol of state authority being the prototype. But the disjunctive components in the meaning of *pleana* are not compatible. A fruit cannot be simultaneously a plum and a peach and a banana, or even just a plum and a peach. Consequently it would be impossible to learn the meaning of *pleana* by way of a Roschian prototype, and there are no potentially overlapping components of the kind that yield the family resemblances between games. It seems likely, then, that disjunctive concepts with incompatible components will be especially difficult to learn and especially unlikely to occur as word meanings except artificially—that is, as meanings of explicitly defined technical terms. Bruner *et al.* (1956) report experimental evidence on concept formation that tends to confirm this. This point will be important in Section 5.2.3.

### 5.2.2. Principles Guiding Vocabulary Acquisition

Having noted two general characteristics of word meanings—namely, the avoidance of synonymy and of incompatible disjunctivity—we turn now to possible explanations for them involving how words are learned in early childhood. This will set the scene for describing in Section 5.2.3 how these characteristics manifest themselves, surprisingly enough, in inflectional morphology also. I will then discuss in Sections 5.2.4 and 5.4 their implications for language evolution.

The extent to which children resemble one another in the way in which they acquire their vocabularies is an empirical issue. Conceivably, different children could tackle the task in radically different ways, with few general patterns emerging. However, that is not how things are. Markman (1989) summarizes evidence in favour of a range of more-or-less well supported principles or assumptions by which children are implicitly guided when learning the meanings of new words, including the following:

- **Taxonomic Assumption.** If a word applies to a particular object, it is more likely to apply to other objects of the same type than to objects which typically accompany it (or are thematically related to it). For example, if *dog* applies to a dachshund, it is more likely to apply also to poodles and labradors than to the dachshund's leash, collar and bone.
- **Mutual Exclusivity.** The extensions of word meanings (the classes of things to which they apply) are mutually exclusive (Merriman and Bowman 1989).
- **Principle of Contrast.** Every two words (or, more generally, every two linguistic elements, including minimal meaningful elements or morphemes) contrast in meaning (Clark 1987, 1993).

The Taxonomic Assumption is formulated as a tendency rather than an absolute constraint, implying that it is overridable; but the others are overridable too. Mutual Exclusivity looks like a special case of the Principle of Contrast, and in any case it is overridden when a child learns that, for example, a creature can be simultaneously a poodle, a dog, and an animal. But Mutual Exclusivity is justified as an independent principle by evidence that, when children are presented under certain experimental conditions with the task of guessing what a word means, they will tend to prefer an answer consistent with Mutual Exclusivity rather than the weaker Principle of Contrast. That is why children master the relationship between superordinate terms such as *animal* and hyponyms such as *dog* relatively slowly. This is not the place to review the evidence for these principles in detail, however. I will concentrate rather on how they bear on the issues of synonymy avoidance and disjunctive categories.

Mutual Exclusivity and the Principle of Contrast both provide massive assistance to the learner when confronted with a new word: they allow her to exclude the possibility that this word means the same as any word that she already knows. Consequently, to learn that two words are exact synonyms would involve overriding both principles. The psycholinguistic evidence that supports these principles therefore helps to explain why exact synonyms should be rare. It also leads us to expect that those exact synonyms that do occur should be relatively uncommon words typically learned in adolescence or adulthood, when vocabulary acquisition has slowed and when therefore the assistance of guiding principles to narrow the range of possible meanings is less important. Consistent with this expectation is the fact that, in synonym pairs such as *courgettes* and *zucchini* or *enemy* and *foe*, at least one of the words is relatively unusual and unlikely to be acquired in childhood.

The meanings of *pepple*, *pum*, and *pleana* in our imaginary Disjunctive English, although they comply with the Principle of Contrast, violate Mutual Exclusivity (since, for example, pears belong to the extension of both *pepple* and *pum*) and the Taxonomic Assumption (since none of these terms applies to a single type of fruit). Moreover, the violation of the Taxonomic Assumption is not mitigated by any family resemblance to a central prototype, because the fact that the disjunction is of the incompatible kind means that no central prototype exists. So these two principles lead us to expect that Disjunctive English should be hard to learn. That is not to say that word meanings of the incompatible disjunctive kind are totally non-existent in actual languages. Consider the technical senses of the word *captain*. These include two that can be glossed as 'naval officer of high rank (equivalent to an army colonel)' and 'army officer of relatively low rank'. These senses are incompatible: one cannot be both a naval and an army captain simultaneously. To that extent the meaning of *captain* resembles that of Disjunctive English *pepple*. But these technical senses of *captain* are not the sort of semantic details that are learned in early childhood, and in that respect they resemble the synonymy of *zucchini* and *courgettes*; moreover, the disjunctivity of *captain* is not really a natural semantic development at all, since it arises from the places that the term occupies in an explicitly defined framework of comparative military ranks. So, while *captain* illustrates a kind of word meaning that is hard to reconcile with the Taxonomic Assumption and Mutual Exclusivity, its artificiality means that it is not an embarrassment for them. These two principles jointly lead us to expect that incompatible disjunctive meanings should be rare; and this expectation is correct.

Big questions remain concerning the status of these principles. In particular, are they learned or innate? Whatever their status, they must be entrenched firmly—firmly enough to withstand any pressure to make the linguistic transmission of information (in Shannon and Weaver's sense) more reliable by reducing homonymy and increasing synonymy. This entrenchment is consistent with their being a manifestation of something that we are born with. In the next section I will suggest that evidence from grammar supports this hypothesis.

### 5.2.3. *Vocabulary Acquisition Principles in Inflectional Morphology*

An aspect of many human languages that frustrates learners and puzzles linguists is complexity in **inflectional morphology** (that is, variation in wordshape that expresses grammatical properties, as in the English verbforms *wait, waits, waiting,* and *waited*). For example, anyone who learns German is faced with a range of different plural endings (*-e, -er, -en, -s*) and with the problem of remembering which noun takes which. For example, *Tag* 'day', *Wald* 'forest', *Held* 'hero', and *Park* 'park' form plurals respectively *Tage, Wälder, Helden,* and *Parks*.[2] Because of these differences, these four nouns belong to distinct **inflection classes**. Nouns are assigned to inflection classes on the basis of the affixes they choose to express the eight **cells** in the German nominal **paradigm**—that is, the eight combinations of the two numbers (singular and plural) and four cases (nominative, accusative, genitive, and dative) that are inflectionally relevant for German nouns.

Inflection-class membership is partially predictable on the basis of a noun's gender and the phonological shape of its stem, and strenuous efforts have been made to uncover as much order as possible among the apparent confusion (e.g. Wurzel 1984; Bittner 1988; Köpcke 1988). But a large residue of arbitrariness remains, as in the nouns that I have just listed: they are all masculine, so gender cannot be a factor in determining their choice of plural ending.

Not all languages exhibit precisely this sort of complexity. Nevertheless, it is widespread throughout the world, and can be stable over time. One might expect that linguistic complexity that serves no obvious communicative purpose—that

---

[2] I ignore here the small minority of nouns with foreign plurals, such as *Schemata* and *Celli*. For justification of this, and for a more detailed presentation and discussion of the German facts summarized in this section, see Carstairs-McCarthy (1994).

does not correlate with anything in the extralinguistic world—would be vulnerable to fairly rapid erosion. In some circumstances, this does happen. When a pidgin evolves as a contact language between people from different speech communities, inflection-class differences are among the first grammatical complexities to disappear. But an ordinary (non-pidgin) language may retain arbitrary inflection-class differences for millennia, even while seemingly more useful aspects of grammar, such as the marking of case in nouns or person and number in verbs, disappear.

At first sight, these facts seem to show that, whatever role synonymy-avoidance principles may play in the acquisition of vocabulary, they play no role in the learning of inflectional morphology.[3] That masculine nouns in German choose among four distinct endings that all mean 'plural' seems flatly to contradict Clark's dictum that every two forms contrast in meaning—that is, unless inflectional affixes are outside the scope of her Principle of Contrast. The only way to show that phenomena like German plural inflection comply with synonymy-avoidance principles would be to show that they do contrast after all, in something like Clark's sense. But is there any independent evidence for this?

The answer is yes. Some recent work of my own on inflectional morphology suggests that patterns of inflection-class organization are constrained in such a way as to be neatly describable in terms of an amended version of synonymy avoidance (Carstairs-McCarthy 1994). To show what my claim amounts to, I will show how it bears on two imaginary patterns of inflectional behaviour that are easy to visualize and describe but that are *not* consistent with synonymy avoidance, and also how the actual inflectional behaviour of nouns in German and verbs in the Australian language Warlpiri complies with it.

Imagine a language (call it L1) in which there are six cells in the paradigm for some wordclass. These six cells represent combinations of values for grammatical categories that may be number and case, or person, mood, and tense, or whatever; all that matters for our purposes is that they should be distinct. Imagine also that the fifteen lower-case letters *a* through *o* stand for phonologically distinct affixes. Finally, imagine that these affixes are distributed among words in such a way that there are two inflection classes, Class A and Class B, as illustrated in Table 5.1. According to Table 5.1, any word belonging to Class A has three freely interchangeable variant expressions for cell 1, got by affixing *a* or *b* or *c*, while any word in Class B has two free variants, got by affixing *d* or *e*, and so on. Consider now how a child learning L1 will fare if she is guided by synonymy-avoidance principles. So far we have considered these principles in relation to words without inflectional affixes, but it is a simple matter to extend them to

---

[3] I use 'synonymy-avoidance principles' to mean whatever principles or assumptions governing vocabulary acquisition underlie the rarity of synonymy. Using this term enables me to avoid seeming to prejudge detailed psycholinguistic questions about how Mutual Exclusivity, the Principle of Contrast, and other proposed acquisition principles interact.

TABLE 5.1. *Inflection-class organization in L1*

| Cell | Class A | Class B |
|------|---------|---------|
| 1 | *a* or *b* or *c* | *d* or *e* |
| 2 | *f* or *g* | *g* |
| 3 | *h* | *h* or *i* |
| 4 | *j* | *k* |
| 5 | *l* or *m* | *l* or *m* |
| 6 | *n* or *o* | *o* |

inflected wordforms. The child's expectation will be that the meanings of words consisting of stem-plus-*a*, stem-plus-*b*, and stem-plus-*c* should differ in some respect. If she is guided by Mutual Exclusivity, she will expect further that their denotations should not overlap at all. But even the weaker of these expectations must be overridden if she is to learn L1; what's more, it must be overridden not just occasionally but in respect of every word whose paradigm consists of cells 1–6, and in respect of every cell except cell 4 (where each of Class A and Class B has just one affix). So L1, though easy to visualize, would be a very difficult language to learn. It is, therefore, not surprising to find that languages like L1 do not occur.

The non-existence of inflectional patterns such as in Table 5.1 has been discussed by Pinker (1984). He proposes that they violate a Uniqueness Principle governing the way in which inflectional paradigms are learned: a child will assume that, for every word, there is only one filler (that is, one inflected wordform) for each cell in its paradigm.[4] Once a child has encountered (say) *a* as the cell-1 affix for a particular word, she will be discouraged by the Uniqueness Principle from entertaining the possibility that another affix such as *b* or *c* might also be acceptable for the same word and the same cell. Readers familiar with languages whose inflectional morphology is more elaborate than that of English take the Uniqueness Principle for granted, though probably without realizing it. When writers of pedagogical grammar books say things like '*the* past tense form of verb X is formed with affix Y', their use of 'the' implies that verb X has a unique past tense form; but it is unnecessary to call attention to this uniqueness explicitly because it reflects a characteristic common to all languages. Pinker is concerned with how children learn not vocabulary but grammar, in the light of the fact that they are presented with little if any negative evidence (that is, explicit instruction that such-and-such grammatical formations are wrong). But, as Markman (1989) points out, Pinker's Uniqueness Principle is consistent with Mutual Exclusivity, and can be seen as a grammatical manifestation of synonymy-avoidance principles.

Just as synonymy avoidance in vocabulary is not absolute, violations of the

---

[4] A similar principle, labelled Inflectional Parsimony, is discussed by Carstairs (1987).

Uniqueness Principle occur, but not of a kind that call into question its basic validity. Finnish supplies a fairly extreme example of apparent inflectional profligacy. In standard Finnish, where nouns are inflected for number and case, some nouns have as many as five genitive plural forms: for example, *peruna* 'potato' has genitive plurals (meaning 'of the potatoes') *perunoiden, perunoitten, perunojen, perunien,* or *perunain* (Paul Kiparsky, personal communication). However, it is unlikely that any speaker learns natively in infancy more than one or two of these forms. This is because standard Finnish, like many 'standard' languages, is not learned natively by anyone; it is a kind of artificial compromise between a number of different colloquial varieties and local dialects. For a Finn, mastering standard Finnish is therefore partly a matter of learning which of one's native inflectional forms to suppress and which non-native ones to acquire; but this task is made easier by the standard language's accommodating attitude to 'rival' genitive plural forms. The situation of adult Finns who are comfortable with all five genitive plurals for *peruna* is thus somewhat analogous to the situation of adult speakers of English who are comfortable with both *courgettes* and *zucchini*. Besides, some of the forms are differentiated stylistically, rather like *foe* and *enemy*, or the 'officialese' *purchase* versus the colloquial *buy*. Genitive plurals in *-in* sound more elevated and solemn than forms in *-den*, while forms in *-tten* sound to some speakers more 'natural' than forms in *-den* (Sauvageot 1949; Harms 1957). It is as if, when presented with a profusion of 'synonymous' forms, language learners unconsciously insist on differentiating them somehow or other, and options for this purpose include kinds of stylistic or social nuance that are the raw material of much sociolinguistic research and that often indicate a linguistic change in progress.

Somewhat similar situations can be found in English. Some readers who are native speakers of a variety of English close to the written 'standard' may judge the past tense forms *kneeled* and *knelt* equally acceptable, for example. But this apparent freedom is restricted to only a few verbs (no speaker of such a variety is likely to be comfortable with *feeled* in lieu of *felt* in *He felt ill*, or with *pelt* in lieu of *peeled* in *He peeled the potato*), and even speakers who use both *knelt* and *kneeled* are likely to perceive *knelt* as more 'old-fashioned' or more 'correct', in line with the popular tendency to equate linguistic innovation with decay (Aitchison 1981).

I will turn now to a second imaginary language, L2, which has exactly the same affixal expressions for each cell as L1 has but which distributes them among inflection classes quite differently. This distribution is illustrated in Table 5.2. Whereas in L1 there were just two inflection classes, L2 has five, labelled Alpha through Epsilon. These are distinct in that each differs from all the others in at least one cell; for example, classes Alpha and Beta differ just in cells 1 and 3. More importantly, L2 complies with the Uniqueness Principle in that every word has just one affixed form for each cell. For example, no word in L2 has a choice of *a*

TABLE 5.2. *Inflection-class organization in L2*

| Cell | Alpha | Beta | Gamma | Delta | Epsilon |
|------|-------|------|-------|-------|---------|
| 1 | *a* | *b* | *c* | *d* | *e* |
| 2 | *f* | *f* | *g* | *g* | *g* |
| 3 | *h* | *i* | *i* | *h* | *h* |
| 4 | *j* | *j* | *k* | *k* | *j* |
| 5 | *l* | *l* | *l* | *m* | *m* |
| 6 | *n* | *n* | *n* | *n* | *o* |

or *b* or *c* as its affix for cell 1; rather, a word will take *a* if it belongs to class Alpha, *b* if it belongs to Beta, and so on.

Despite its compliance with the Uniqueness Principle, L2 is still unlike German or any other highly inflected language. Some new teminology will help in showing this. Consider first cell 1. For this cell there are five distinct affixes (*a*, *b*, *c*, *d*, and *e*), so each inflection class has an affix of its own. One can, therefore, think of *a*, *b*, *c*, *d*, and *e* as each expressing not just 'cell 1' but rather 'cell 1, class Alpha', 'cell 1, class Beta' and so on. Let us call affixes of this kind **class-identifiers**. There is one other class-identifier in Table 5.2, namely *o*, which can be thought of as expressing 'cell 6, class Epsilon'. By contrast, all the other nine affixes in Table 5.2 (*f*, *g*, *h*, *i*, *j*, *k*, *l*, *m*, and *n*) are shared by more than one inflection class: *f* by Alpha and Beta, *h* by Alpha, Delta, and Epsilon, and so on. But one of the nine, *n*, differs from the rest in that it is the only affix for its cell apart from the class-identifier *o*. Let's say that an affix whose rivals in the same cell (if any) are all class-identifiers is the **class-default** for that cell. By this criterion *n* is the class-default for cell 6.

In inflectional systems with several inflection classes, is it possible for an affix to be neither a class-identifier nor a class-default? Clearly this is a logical possibility, since it is illustrated by *f*, *g*, *h*, *i*, *j*, *k*, *l*, and *m* in L2. But what do we find in actual languages? It is time to look again at German. As I said earlier, there are eight cells in the paradigm for German nouns (as well as for pronouns, determiners, and adjectives); but of these the only ones that are relevant to the present question are those for which more than one affix is available, namely the genitive singular and the nominative plural.[5] In fact, German masculine nouns are

---

[5] In all nouns, the nominative plural form is the same as the accusative and genitive plural forms; but that does not affect the argument here. In the dative singular the only suffix in general use in modern German is *-en* in Classes D and F in Table 5.3. There is a near-obsolete dative suffix *-e* that may appear on nouns in Classes A, B, C, and E. Arguably Classes D and F are merely subclasses of a single class within which genitive inflection is phonologically conditioned, because all masculine Class F nouns and no masculine Class D nouns end in *-e* in the nominative singular. This fits well with the fact that the only accusative singular suffix for masculines, *-en*, appears precisely in Classes D and F. For an analysis on roughly these lines, see Carstairs (1987). Such an analysis is fully compatible with the claims made here, so it is not necessary to pursue its details.

distributed among six inflection classes, as illustrated in Table 5.3. As Table 5.3 shows, apart from the four nominative plural suffixes there are also three genitive singular ones. Mathematically there are innumerable distinct ways in which one could distribute these seven suffixes among six inflection classes, including many ways in which at least some of the suffixes would be neither class-identifiers nor class-defaults. Let us introduce the term **blurred** for an affix that falls between stools in this way. For example, if *-en* replaced *-es* in the genitive singular of Class A, then both *-en* and *-es* would be blurred. In actual German, however, each of the two cells has a class-default (genitive singular *-es*, nominative plural *-en*), while all the other affixes are class-identifiers. So, if German is typical of actual languages, the answer to the question posed at the beginning of this paragraph seems to be no.

A similar state of affairs prevails in the verbal paradigm in Warlpiri, which has six cells: nonpast, past, imperative, present, infinitive, and irrealis. Verbs are distributed among five inflection classes, as shown in Table 5.4 (Nash 1985; Bavin 1995).[6] Class membership is not predictable on semantic or phonological grounds, so the various suffixes in each cell are prima-facie synonyms, violating

TABLE 5.3. *Inflection classes of German masculine nouns*

| Cell | Class A | Class B | Class C | Class D | Class E | Class F |
|------|---------|---------|---------|---------|---------|---------|
| Gen sing. | *-es* | *-es* | *-es* | *-en* | *-es* | *-ens* |
| Nom pl. | *-e* | *-er* | *-s* | *-en* | *-en* | *-en* |
| e.g. | *Tag* | *Wald* | *Park* | *Held* | *Dorn* | *Name* |
|  | 'day' | 'forest' | 'park' | 'hero' | 'thorn' | 'name' |

TABLE 5.4. *Inflection classes of Warlpiri verbs*

| Cell | Class 1 | Class 2 | Class 3 | Class 4 | Class 5 |
|------|---------|---------|---------|---------|---------|
| Nonpast | *-mi/Ø* | *-rni* | *-nyi* | *-rni* | *-ni* |
| Past | *-ja* | *-rnu* | *-ngu* | *-rnu* | *-nu* |
| Imperative | *-ya* | *-ka* | *-ngka* | *-nja* | *-nta* |
| Present | *-nya* | *-rninya* | *-nganya* | *-rninya* | *-nanya* |
| Infinitive | stem + *-nja* | nonpast + *-nja* | stem + *-nja* | nonpast + *-nja* | nonpast + *-nja* |
| Irrealis | | | Imperative + *-rla* | | |

*Note:* The suffixes are given in Warlpiri orthography; phonetic details do not matter for present purposes. In the nonpast of class 1 verbs, the *-mi* suffix is optional (i.e. a bare stem may occur). In the infinitive, the base to which the suffix *-nja* is attached varies according to the inflection class; but Carstairs-McCarthy (1994) suggests reasons why this kind of stem alternation does not affect the issue of compliance with the Principle of Contrast.

[6] Nash cites unpublished work by Ken Hale.

Clark's Principle. But, just as in German, they are all either class-identifiers or class-defaults. For each of the infinitive and irrealis cells there is a single suffix, which is therefore automatically the class-default, while the nonpast, past, and present cells have class-defaults *-rni*, *-rnu*, and *-rninya* respectively, shared by classes 2 and 4; all the other suffixes are class-identifiers.

Establishing that German and Warlpiri are indeed typical in this respect of course requires the examination of inflectional behaviour in as many languages with inflection classes as possible. Fortunately, an earlier proposal of mine (Carstairs 1983) amounts to a challenge to discover patterns of inflection-class organization of a kind where blurring is most likely to occur; and, inasmuch as no such counter-evidence has been produced,[7] we can be reasonably confident that the absence of blurring in German is more than a coincidence. So let us for the time being take it for granted that blurring does not generally occur—that is, that in all languages with inflection classes each inflectional affix will be expected to be either a class-identifier or the class-default for its cell, and that for this reason L2 is not a possible language. How if at all does this relate to synonymy avoidance?

I said earlier, in connection with Table 5.2, that we could think of the class-identifying affix *a* as expressing not just 'cell 1' but 'cell 1, class Alpha'. Similarly, affix *b* expresses not just 'cell 1' but 'cell 1, class Beta', and so on. It follows that, if class membership counts as part of the "meaning" of the various class-identifying affixes associated with a cell, they are not synonymous. As for class-defaults, they too will differ in "meaning" from their class-identifying rivals: for example, at cell 6 at Table 5.2, *o* will "mean" 'cell 6, class Epsilon' while the class-default *n* "means" simply 'cell 6'. The German genitive singular and nominative plural affixes all avoid synonymy in this way, as shown at (2):

(2)  (*a*)   *-en*     'Genitive singular, Class D'
         *-ens*    'Genitive singular, Class F'
         *-es*     'Genitive singular'
     (*b*)   *-e*      'Nominative plural, Class A'
         *-er*     'Nominative plural, Class B'
         *-s*      'Nominative plural, Class C'
         *-en*     'Nominative plural'

The Warlpiri suffixes can be represented as having similar class "meanings":

(3)  (*a*)   *-mi*     'Nonpast, Class 1'
         *-nyi*    'Nonpast, Class 3'
         *-ni*     'Nonpast, Class 5'
         *-rni*    'Nonpast'

---

[7] The only published challenge to my proposal that I am aware of is that of Nyman (1987). But the challenge can be answered satisfactorily, I think (Carstairs 1988*a*; Carstairs-McCarthy 1991: 234–5).

| | | |
|---|---|---|
| (b) | -ja | 'Past, Class 1' |
| | -ngu | 'Past, Class 3' |
| | -nu | 'Past, Class 5' |
| | -rnu | 'Past' |
| (c) | -ya | 'Imperative, Class 1' |
| | -ka | 'Imperative, Class 2' |
| | -ngka | 'Imperative, Class 3' |
| | -nja | 'Imperative, Class 4' |
| | -nta | 'Imperative, Class 5' |
| (d) | -nya | 'Present, Class 1' |
| | -nganya | 'Present, Class 3' |
| | -nanya | 'Present, Class 5' |
| | -rninya | 'Present' |
| (e) | -nja | 'Infinitive' |
| (f) | -rla | 'Irrealis' |

Given that there are fewer than 150 simple (non-compound) verbs in Warlpiri, this degree of inflectional complexity may seem surprising. Nevertheless, according to Bavin (1995), children learning Warlpiri natively rarely put the wrong suffix on the wrong verb—in fact, they have more trouble learning to indicate case accurately on Warlpiri nouns, even though nouns are not distributed among arbitrary inflection classes. This suggests that inflection class differences really are salient aspects of "meaning" from the children's point of view.

I have put the words "mean" and "meaning" here in scare-quotes deliberately. Some readers may want to object that if we allow a purely intralinguistic notion such as inflection class to constitute part of the "meaning" of an affix for the purpose of testing compliance with synonymy-avoidance principles, then compliance with these principles is rendered all too easy and the principles themselves, at least in relation to inflectional morphology, become vacuous. But that objection, although apparently powerful, fails for two reasons, one more general and one more specific.

The more general reason is that there is independent evidence in favour of intralinguistic "meanings" in morphology. Lass (1990) has pointed out that when two linguistic forms (words or affixes) undergo historical changes that risk rendering them synonymous, one way in which a language may react is not by jettisoning one of them but by creating a new meaning difference to distinguish them, even if this is only an intralinguistic "meaning" difference. Lass invokes here the term 'exaptation' used by Gould and Vrba (1982) to describe what happens when some biological characteristic is put to a use other than that for which it was originally adapted. As Lass puts it, linguistic 'junk' can be 'exapted' to perform new functions, even if these functions are purely intralinguistic, with no communicative or expressive correlate in the world outside language.

A remarkable example of exaptation is what happened to the suffix -*e* on Afrikaans adjectives modifying nouns. In Dutch, the parent of Afrikaans, the presence of this suffix depends on a combination of factors involving the gender, number, and definiteness of the accompanying noun. In Afrikaans, gender has been lost, so one would expect this -*e* to depend just on number and definiteness. Instead, its presence depends now mainly on the structure and phonology of the adjective to which it potentially attaches. Its "meaning", therefore, amounts to redundant signalling of purely grammatical and phonological characteristics of what immediately precedes it. In this respect it resembles a variety of plural endings used in the African language Turkana, which are differentiated in that they redundantly signal information about the shape of the stem of the nouns to which they are attached (Dimmendaal 1987; Carstairs 1988*b*). Maiden (1996) has likewise suggested that patterns of verb-stem distribution in Romance languages that do not correlate neatly with syntactic or semantic features must nevertheless be regarded as "meaningful" intralinguistically because they are both pervasive and productive. So the fact that inflection-class identification constitutes a purely grammatical kind of "meaning" is no ground for excluding it from the functions that an affix can be exapted to perform.

The more specific reason why the charge of vacuity fails is that the intra-linguistic inflection-class "meanings" that I have attributed to class-identifying affixes differ in a crucial respect from the "meanings" that one would need to posit if the blurred pattern of affix distribution illustrated in cells 2–5 in Table 5.2 ever occurred. For those blurred cells, the "meanings" of the affixes would have to include disjunctions, as illustrated at (4):

(4)  (*a*)   *f*    'cell 2, class Alpha or Beta'
          *g*    'cell 2, class Gamma or Delta or Epsilon'
     (*b*)   *h*    'cell 3, class Alpha or Delta or Epsilon'
          *i*    'cell 3, class Beta or Gamma'
     (*c*)   *j*    'cell 4, class Alpha or Beta or Epsilon'
          *k*    'cell 4, class Gamma or Delta'
     (*d*)   *l*    'cell 5, class Alpha or Beta or Gamma'
          *m*    'cell 5, class Delta or Epsilon'

As we have seen, words seldom belong to more than one inflection class, because to do so violates synonymy avoidance in its guise as Pinker's Uniqueness Principle. A disjunction such as 'class Alpha or Beta' is, therefore, of the incompatible kind illustrated for Disjunctive English by *pepple*, *pum*, and *pleana*—the kind of disjunction that is not mitigated by family-resemblance or prototype-based semantics. Even if one were to revise the criterion for class-default status so as to allow one of the two affixes for each cell mentioned in (4) (presumably the most widely occurring affix) to count as a class-default, the other would still be left with an irreducibly disjunctive "meaning". Blurring renders some incompatible disjunctive "meanings" unavoidable. Consequently, if we assume that affixal "meanings" are subject to the same acquisitional constraints as word meanings are, then the absence of blurring in the inflection-class systems of actual languages such as German emerges as neither accidental nor mysterious, but is just what we expect. This outcome supports the view that affixal meanings, including intralinguistic "meanings", are indeed subject to these acquisitional constraints.

It is time to get rid of the scare quotes around "meaning". The difficulty is that simply eliminating them will be unattractive to many semanticists and philosophers, keen to reserve the term 'meaning' for aspects of the relationship between linguistic expressions and the extralinguistic contexts in which they are used. But this difficulty is really only terminological. Let us introduce the new term 'information content' to subsume both extralinguistic meaning and intralinguistic "meaning". Synonymy-avoidance principles can then be reinterpreted on the basis of differences in information content rather than differences in meaning. Given what language is mainly used for, it is not surprising that most differences of information content should be differences of meaning in the traditional, extralinguistic, sense; but the behaviour of inflection classes (along with evidence of the kind cited by Lass) shows that this is not always so.

As I have said, many languages lack inflection-class systems of the German kind. In view of that, the importance that I have attached to the avoidance of synonymy and of incompatible disjunction in inflection would be supported if one could show them to be relevant even where arbitrary inflection-class differences are not an issue. Work on that question is in its infancy, but the signs are promising. Let us suppose that, in some language L3, verbs show no inflection-class differences (equivalently, all verbs belong to one class). Suppose further that L3 verbs have two suffixes for first person singular forms (meaning 'I . . .')—namely, *r* and *s*—and that these are distributed within the verb paradigm on the basis of tense (present, past, and future) and mood (indicative, subjunctive, and conditional). Synonymy-avoidance principles will predict here, as before, that no cell in the paradigm should be filled by two forms, one containing *r* and the other containing *s*; but the affixes *r* and *s* themselves will be guaranteed to differ in information content just by virtue of the fact that they appear in different cells. The question of disjunction avoidance still arises, however. Clearly there is no problem if *r* is restricted to (say) the past forms while *s* appears everywhere else; we can then gloss them respectively as '1st singular, past' and '1st singular', *s* being the default affix that appears only where the more narrowly defined *r* cannot.[8] Now suppose that *r* occurs in the past and the subjunctive; its gloss '1st singular, past or subjunctive' would contain a disjunction, but not an incompatible one, if we assume that in L3 (as in many languages) a verb can be simultaneously past

[8] The kind of priority that *r* has over *s* here is familiar to linguists in the guise of the Panini or Elsewhere Principle (see e.g. Anderson 1992).

and subjunctive. But suppose instead that *r* occurs in the past and the future only. Its gloss must now contain an incompatible disjunction, in that a verbform cannot be simultaneously past and future. If disjunction avoidance is relevant, therefore, we will expect that actual languages resembling the first two versions of L3 may exist, but ones which resemble the third version should not. And evidence from verb morphology in Hungarian, Turkish and Latin tends to confirm this expectation (Carstairs-McCarthy 1998*a*).

In motivating the shift from meaning to information content for synonymy avoidance purposes, I have appealed solely to inflectional morphology. But there are aspects of more conventional synonymy avoidance that point in that direction too. Discussing pairs of apparent synonyms in Section 4.2, I did not in fact argue that they differed in meaning; instead I talked of differences of register (as between *buy* and *purchase*), of metaphorical usage (as between *sad* and *gloomy*), of dialect (as between *zucchini* and *courgettes*), and so on. Clark (1993) lumps these all together as meaning differences, but there are objections to doing so. *Purchase* does not mean 'formal register' in the same way that it means 'acquire in exchange for money', nor does *zucchini* mean 'American or Australian' in the same way that it means 'kind of small marrow'. Both register and dialect, though part of information content for synonymy-avoidance purposes, seem more aptly ascribed to "meaning" in scare quotes than to meaning in the conventional sense.

There is another kind of inflectional "meaning" that is relevant here. I mentioned Lass's (1990) observation that the Afrikaans suffix *-e* has been exapted to supply otiose information about the adjectives to which it is restricted. In the same way, words may avoid synonymy by otiose restriction to particular lexical contexts (by collocational restrictions, in linguistic terminology). The words *addled* and *rancid* are arguably synonymous in the narrow sense, both meaning 'rotten and hence inedible' in relation to food; but they differ in information content inasmuch as *addled* is restricted to eggs and *rancid* to oils and fats. Similarly, *herd*, *flock*, *pod*, *pride*, and *gaggle* all mean 'collection of animals', but they avoid synonymy through their collocations, generally with *cattle*, *sheep*, *whales*, *lions*, and *geese* respectively.

The outcome of this section is both satisfying and paradoxical. It is satisfying in that acquiring word meanings and learning how inflectional affixes are distributed turn out to have much more in common than at first appears. But it is paradoxical in that it shows how a strategy that enormously assists the acquisition of word meanings can perversely facilitate the maintenance of a kind of grammatical complexity that seems entirely pointless. If no languages with arbitrary inflection classes had ever existed, it would never occur to us to wonder why not. Yet inflection-class systems resist erosion with extraordinary steadfastness, and new ones readily come into being when (for example) sound changes render opaque a pattern of affix distribution that had once been clearly describable in phonological terms. The expectation that a difference in shape should indicate a difference in information content is so entrenched in us that, as learners in child-hood, we are ready to count as information for this purpose even something so devoid of extralinguistic relevance as a pattern of affixal choice, or as the internal structure of an adjective (in the Afrikaans instance). It is as if, where no meaning is available to justify a difference in expression, a purely intralinguistic 'meaning' is created. Some implications of this perverse consequence are considered in the next section.

### 5.2.4. *Evolutionary Implications*

If two animal species share a trait that improves their chances of survival in their environment, it is possible that this trait may have been inherited from a common ancestor. On the other hand, the very fact that the trait is adaptive increases the likelihood that it has evolved in the two species separately. For example, the fact that seals and penguins have flippers of similar shape that make them good at swimming under water does not mean that their common ancestor had flippers too; in fact, their most recent shared ancestor must have been some reptile-like creature with forelimbs rather like a modern lizard. In biologists' terminology, the similarity between seals' and penguins' flippers is an instance of analogy or homoplasy (convergent development from different starting points) rather than homology (the sharing of an evolutionary origin). So a biological taxonomist, in classifying species genetically, will not pay attention to superficial similarities of this kind. What will carry more weight is a trait that is not much use to a creature in its present environment. For example, the vestigial wings of an ostrich confirm (if we should be in any doubt) that it is more closely related to eagles and chaffinches than to the earthbound mammals that it now resembles more closely in its manner of living.

Our ability to learn complex patterns of inflection is in some respects like the ostrich's wing. If we lost it, many human languages would be simpler grammatically than they are today; but speakers of them would not be dis-advantaged by that, just as there is no disadvantage in speaking a language that is inflectionally simple now. So, just as the ostrich's wing is best explained as a preservation of something that the ostrich's ancestor had before there were ostriches, it may be that synonymy-avoidance principles can best be explained as the preservation of something that our ancestors had before there were humans (or rather, before there were speakers of human languages of the modern type). If so, it must have been something that was once adaptive, just as the possession of efficient wings is adaptive for most birds. What could that something be?

In trying to answer that question we are in one respect worse off than the palaeontologist interested in ostriches. The palaeontologist has fossils to look at whereas we have not, because language and its ancestors are not body parts with bony substructures. But that is not a serious disadvantage, because synonymy avoidance principles are still adaptive in a clear-cut fashion, unlike ostrich wings: these principles facilitate the learning of extralinguistic meanings, not just intralinguistic "meanings". Is it likely, then, that we have an ancestor for whom it was an advantage to be able to learn extralinguistic meanings quickly, but for whom the mechanism which facilitated this would not also foster the creation of pointless intralinguistic "meanings"? Such an ancestor would be a creature with a vocabulary sufficiently large so that an adaptation which speeded up learning would confer an advantage over competitors lacking the adaptation, but sufficiently restricted so that novel 'words' for which new information content would have to be created would seldom if ever present themselves.

The hypothetical ancestor that I have just described is by no means implausible, because she is not much different from many higher primates today. Vervet monkeys, gibbons, and baboons (for example) all have vocabularies of calls that are restricted in the sense that new calls cannot be freely created, whether by articulatory means (combining 'speech sounds' in new ways) or by syntactic means (combining individual calls in new ways). The main difference, one might argue, is that primate calls do not have to be learned at all, so that an adaptation to facilitate their learning would be superfluous. But this objection is weakened by evidence of the kind that Cheney and Seyfarth (1990) cite, showing that young vervets sometimes utter a predator alarm call in an inappropriate context, and that this mistake is 'corrected' by the failure of adults to echo the call. And it seems likely that this objection will be weakened further as we come to understand more about how primates' use of their call systems changes with age. That a call system is entirely innate rather than learned has tended to be the preferred assumption of zoologists and primatologists when no direct evidence is available; so, as more direct evidence accumulates, the proportion of primate call use in which learning will be recognized as playing a part will tend to increase.

An adaptation for synonymy avoidance in our prelinguistic ancestors seems at least plausible, therefore. Apart from its adaptive role in facilitating vocabulary acquisition, it provides an explanation for the otherwise mysterious propensity of human languages to tolerate certain kinds of inflectional complexity—namely, ones that are consistent with synonymy-avoidance principles. Its plausibility would be increased further if there were evidence that contemporary primates avoid synonymy too, for the closeness of our relationship to them (particularly to chimpanzees) renders it likely that this shared characteristic would be a homology rather than a homoplasy. In Chapter 6 I will discuss in more detail some implications of recent work on the use of sign language and other signalling systems by chimpanzees and gorillas. For the time being it is sufficient to note that the way in which chimpanzees use signs and signalling tokens, though it differs from human language use in the domain of syntax (the domain which has most interested linguists), does not seem to differ markedly as regards sign semantics; that is, no general non-human-like tendency has been reported for chimpanzees to use several different signs to mean the same thing. Moreover, David Premack, a researcher on the cognitive abilities of apes, reports an observation that suggests that chimpanzees are just like human infants in assuming that a new word will mean something different from any familiar word. Premack's experiments involve training chimpanzees to use plastic tokens as 'words', or names for objects. What happens when a chimpanzee is faced with a familiar but so-far unnamed object and, at the same time, an unfamiliar plastic token among an array of tokens? Premack's words, as recorded in an informal discussion, are as follows:

even the stupidest animal rapidly constructs the sentence, 'Give X [the name of the animal] this new piece of plastic.' In other words, the animal requests the unnamed item with the so far unused piece of plastic. Thus the chimpanzees recognize that the potential word, which has not yet been so employed, is the appropriate thing to use in requesting the desired item, which is however not yet named. (Piattelli-Palmarini 1980: 229)[9]

In Sections 5.4 and 5.5 we will be exploring how the hypothesis that our hominid ancestors already observed synonymy-avoidance principles contributes to the larger hypothesis about language evolution that this chapter presents. So it is possible that the plausibility of hominid synonymy avoidance could be enhanced, depending on the attractiveness or otherwise of the larger hypothesis. But the evidence so far presented (and to be amplified in Chapter 6) renders it plausible enough to be worth examining further, irrespective of what the rest of this chapter may reveal.

## 5.3. The Descent of the Larynx

Adult humans are unlike all other mammals in that they cannot breathe while eating or drinking. This is because of the position of the larynx in relation to the throat, nose, and mouth. In adult humans the pharynx (the part of the throat immediately behind the root of the tongue) is a channel shared by food *en route* to the stomach and air *en route* to and from the lungs. Inside the neck, the pharynx divides so that food is shunted into the oesophagus and down to the stomach while air goes through the larynx into the windpipe or trachea, leading to the lungs. When we swallow, the larynx is raised and the epiglottis (a cartilaginous structure above the larynx) helps to prevent food from entering the windpipe. But this is not totally reliable, and the shared stretch of pharynx creates a danger of choking—a danger avoided by other mammals because their passages for ingesting food and for respiration are separate.

The standard mammalian position of the larynx, high up behind the mouth, enables the soft palate (or velum) to mesh with the epiglottis so as to create a

---

[9] I am grateful to Jim Hurford for pointing out this reference to me.

self-contained tube leading from the nose through the nasopharynx (the passage behind the velum) and the larynx to the lungs. This means that liquids and soft foods can pass around the breathing tube at the back of the mouth and reach the oesophagus without any danger of entering the windpipe. Newborn human babies are like all other mammals in this respect, which is why they can breathe while sucking. But at about three months they begin to lose this ability, as the larynx moves towards the lower adult position and the epiglottis and velum move apart.

An obvious question is why, in view of the choking danger, the adult human larynx has evolved away from the standard mammalian plan. I will have more to say about this in Chapter 6. For now, however, I want to concentrate not on the causes but on the consequences of this development, drawing extensively on the work of Lieberman (1984).[10]

Associated with the lowering of the larynx is a change in the configuration of the tongue. In apes and in newborn human babies it is relatively flat, lying entirely within the mouth. In adult humans, however, it is curved so that its back part or root, which is invisible without the help of a dentist's mirror, constitutes the front wall of the pharynx. The result is a radical change in the shape of the passage between the larynx and the lips. In apes and in newborn human babies this passage is relatively straight. In adult humans, however, it is L-shaped, with a right-angle bend sharply demarcating the oral part from the pharyngal part. This change in shape has huge importance for the evolution of speech because it is mainly what makes possible the modern human range of vowel sounds.

In a wind instrument such as a clarinet or saxophone, the reed in the mouthpiece plays a different role from the body of the instrument. When the player blows air past the reed it vibrates, so as to be the source of vibrations transmitted to the surrounding air molecules. These air vibrations are then filtered by the body of the instrument, which amplifies some and damps others, at various frequencies. Some of these frequencies depend on the instrument's shape; it is these that enable us to distinguish whether the instrument being played is a clarinet or a saxophone. One of the frequencies depends on the length of the body of vibrating air that the instrument contains, determined by the number of holes that are stopped by the player's fingers (assisted by various levers and pads on the outside of the instrument); it is this which determines the pitch of the note.

The human vocal tract, including the larynx, can be thought of as another wind instrument, with the vocal folds inside the larynx corresponding to the reed, and the supralaryngal cavities (the pharynx, mouth, and nose) counting as the body

[10] The use that I make of Lieberman's work does not commit me to sharing his controversial view of the vocal tract of Neanderthals and its implications for their speech capacity. In fact, as will appear in Chapter 6, my scenario is compatible with the view that the larynx was already somewhat lowered in *Homo erectus*, hundreds of thousands of years before Neanderthals appeared (Laitman *et al.* 1992). The outline of acoustic phonetics that I present here is restricted to the bare minimum necessary to understand my argument. For more details, see e.g. Ladefoged 1962, Fry 1979, Lieberman and Blumstein 1988, or Clark and Yallop 1995.

of the instrument. But the human apparatus differs from a clarinet in that the pitch of the sound being produced is determined not by the length of the vocal tract but rather by the length and tension of the vocal folds, which vibrate more or less rapidly (producing a sound of higher or lower pitch) according to whether they are tightened or relaxed. However, it resembles a clarinet in that the quality or timbre of the sound produced depends on the shape of the supralaryngal cavities and the body of air that they enclose. In speech sounds, timbre is what distinguishes one vowel from another ([a] from [i], say), even when they are produced at exactly the same pitch and the same volume. It is in terms of vowels that the relationship between timbre and the shape of the supralaryngal cavities is best illustrated.

In acoustic terms, differences in vowel timbre are associated with concentrations of energy at certain frequencies called **formants**. Formants are independent of the fundamental frequency of air-molecule vibration that determines the overall pitch of the vowel; rather, they depend on the filtering characteristics of the supralaryngal body of air. Let us ignore the nasal cavity for the moment and consider only the air in the pharynx and mouth. The right-angle bend at the back of the mouth divides this body of air into two distinct sections, a pharyngal section and an oral section. These sections are what mainly determine the frequency of the so-called **first formant** and **second formant** respectively: the larger the volume of air in the corresponding section of the vocal tract, the lower the formant. (Similarly, the pitch of the note that one can produce by blowing across the top of an empty bottle is lower than the pitch one gets if one reduces the amount of air in the bottle by partly filling it with water.)

Let us see how this works in particular vowels. For the vowel [a] the tongue is low in the mouth, so the oral air volume is large while the pharyngal volume (related to the distance between the larynx and the highest part of the tongue) is small. We will, therefore, expect that the first formant (corresponding to the pharyngal volume) should be high relative to that of other vowels, and the second formant should be low. On the other hand, for [i] the tongue is high in the mouth and its highest part is relatively far forward, so that the oral volume is small while the pharyngal volume is large. The first formant should therefore be relatively low whereas the second formant should be relatively high.

For the first formant, this can be confirmed without any instrumental phonetic equipment by means of a simple experiment recommended by Ladefoged (1993). Tilt your head back so that the skin of the neck is taut, and place your lips and tongue silently in position for each of the vowels [i], [e], [a], [o], and [u] in succession. Meanwhile, use a fingernail or pencil to tap sharply against your taut neck. You should hear a series of tapping sounds that vary discernibly in pitch, being relatively low for [i] and [u] (which both involve a relatively large pharyngal air volume) and relatively high for [a], with [e] and [o] falling between these extremes. To get at the second formant, Ladefoged recommends whispering: the vowel [i], in which the body of air between the highest part of the tongue and the lips is relatively small, has a noticeably higher pitch when whispered than [u], in which the corresponding body of air is enlarged both by pulling the tongue back in the mouth and by protruding the lips.

The picture just presented of the relationship between formants and parts of the vocal tract is admittedly oversimplified. I have said nothing about formants other than the first two, nor about the role of the nasal cavity. But I have said enough to establish the crucial importance of the new L-shaped configuration of the supralaryngal air cavities that arose with the lowering of the larynx. Without the effective division of the oral-pharyngal air into two separate compartments, there would be no clearly defined first and second formants, and without these formants there would be no such clear-cut distinctions in vowel timbre as are found in modern human languages. In other words, until the lowering of the larynx occurred in the course of human evolution, no primate was physically equipped to produce a range of vowel-like sounds encompassing the extremes [i], [u], and [a].[11]

While acknowledging the advantage of being able to produce a bigger variety of sounds, one might argue that a few languages even today make do with only two or three distinct vowels (Lass 1984); so, even if a vocal tract with an undescended larynx is capable of producing only a small range of vowel timbres, that range might still be adequate for a language with a range of phonological contrasts comparable with that of some languages spoken today. To this my reply is threefold.

First, the fact that a modern language may have only a few contrastive vowels need not mean that it does not exploit the full vowel space made available by the lowered larynx; it may mean only that much of the phonetic quality of a given vowel sound is determined by neighbouring consonants, so that vowel sounds play a relatively large role in consonant identification. The Caucasian language Kabardian illustrates this. (The evolutionary implications of such languages, or the lack of such implications, were discussed in Chapter 4.)

Secondly, Lieberman cites evidence from Nearey (1978) that the vowel [i] has special characteristics not shared by other vowels. The precise acoustic characteristics of any vowel naturally varies according to the size of the speaker's vocal tract, so that the formant frequencies of the vowel [ɔ] (as in *horse*) spoken by an American adolescent may be similar to those of the vowel [a] spoken by an adult male. We hear these acoustically similar sounds as different only because their spoken context enables us to calibrate appropriately our auditory interpretation of the acoustic signal. But the formant frequencies of [i], whoever utters it, never

---

[11] It may be objected that certain birds (parrots and mynahs) can mimic human vowels with a vocal apparatus totally unlike that of humans or indeed mammals generally. They do so by producing a kind of sound that is quite different in acoustic terms from human speech, but with certain characteristics that the human ear can interpret as formant frequencies (Lieberman 1984: 156). This does not affect the fact that, among primates, only humans are physically equipped to produce the full human range of vowel sounds.

overlap with those of another vowel spoken by someone with a different-sized vocal tract. Identifying [i] correctly, therefore, does not depend on contextual clues to the speaker's age or sex, and hearing a speaker's [i] is by itself enough to calibrate our interpretation of the other formant combinations that he or she produces. So a form of speech with [i] has an absolute advantage over one without, in that misunderstandings due to misheard vowel sounds are less likely to arise.

Thirdly, the new range of vowel sounds helps to ensure that now, if not before, a kind of vocalization involving regular alternations in sonority is established. The implications of that will be explored in the next section.

## 5.4. Our Ancestors' Dilemma

In Section 5.2 I put forward reasons for thinking it likely that, even before the evolution of modern human language, our hominid ancestors had a vocal call system that obeyed principles of synonymy avoidance—principles that are strong enough in modern languages to encourage the creation of intralinguistic "meanings" such as collocational restrictions and inflection-class distinctions. In Section 5.3 I described the effects of the lowering of the larynx on vocalization potential. I will now describe the dilemma that arises when these two characteristics of a call system are combined—that is, when such an increase in vocalization potential is combined with a strong drive for synonymy avoidance.

Memory capacity is limited, just because brains are finite. This would present no problem for a hominid with a vocabulary of twenty, fifty, or even a hundred calls. But the change in the shape of the respiratory tract, combined with more precise muscular control of the tongue, lips, and velum and of exhalation from the lungs, would mean that the potential call repertoire was vastly increased. Consider the effects of even a modest increase in muscular precision, sufficient to yield potential calls in which a consonant-like onset is combined with any one of three vowel-like sounds close to the extremes of the vowel space: [i], [a], and [u]. Let us assume that control of the tongue is not yet sufficiently precise to allow, for example, contrastive manipulation of the tip and blade of the tongue or contrastive contact at the teeth or the alveolar ridge, but is sufficiently precise to allow a two-way contrast between contact at the front and at the back of the oral cavity—between [t] and [k], roughly speaking. Assume also that muscular control is precise enough for three further articulatory possibilities: lip closure, to yield a [p]-like sound; raising of the soft palate, to yield a distinction between nasal and non-nasal sounds; and finally, with the relatively agile front of the tongue, a distinction between complete and partial obstruction of the airflow, to yield a distinction between a stoplike sound resembling [t] and a fricative-like one resembling [s].

These assumptions are not arbitrary. There is evidence that labial, alveolar, and velar sounds such as [p], [t], and [k] respectively have relatively robust acoustic characteristics—characteristics that do not change much if the place of articulation varies a centimetre or so one way or the other (Stevens 1972, 1989; Carré and Mrayati 1992). And I have already mentioned the evidence cited by Lieberman (1984) that [i] is the vowel most reliably identified when heard, whatever the age or sex of the speaker. In Section 5.6.1 I will discuss evidence from babbling in early infancy, consideration of which has led MacNeilage (1994) to paint a picture very similar to mine of the articulatory repertoire of early humans. But the precise details of the assumptions do not matter. What is important is that they illustrate an articulatory capability intermediate in sophistication between that of a modern ape and a modern human, and therefore not too unlike a stage through which our hominid ancestors must have passed.

Since what we are imagining is an expansion in the vocalization potential of a hominid with a lowered larynx but a still basically apelike call system, it is strictly anachronistic to use here terms such as 'consonant', 'vowel', or 'syllable' that relate to modern human language. With appropriate caution, however, we can describe the potential calls in this hominid's repertoire as including combinations of the eighteen syllables consisting of [p], [t], [k], [m], [n], or [s] followed by [i], [a], or [u].[12] Let us suppose that this hominid's control over exhalation is sufficient to allow vocalizations that are five syllables long—a very modest degree of control by comparison with modern humans, in whose languages far more than five syllables can be uttered in one breath. At first sight the number of potential calls using this articulatory apparatus may not look particularly impressive, especially if possible single syllables are restricted to the eighteen formed by combining one consonant-like and one vowel-like sound. But for longer calls the total increases exponentially, so that five-syllable combinations alone yield 1,889,568 (that is, $18^5$) possibilities. This is the vast increase in the potential call repertoire that the changes in the vocal tract provoke.

It is hardly possible for a call system to operate with a vocabulary of two million calls, each distinct as a whole from the rest in the way that the vervet's eagle call is distinct from its snake call. An educated adult knows somewhere between 50,000 and 250,000 words (Aitchison 1987: 7), so even an exceptionally erudite person is unlikely to have a vocabulary of more than about 300,000 words. Yet the way in which synonymy-avoidance principles affect both the vocabulary and the grammar of contemporary languages shows that, despite the common view that meaning is the senior partner in the sound–meaning relationship, differences in sound between two words or two affixes can instigate the creation of a "meaning" to differentiate them. What's more, as we have seen, the very per-

---

[12] I have assumed that this call system does not use the velar nasal [ŋ], which is less widespread than [m] and [n] in contemporary languages. If we were to include [ŋ], it would increase the repertoire of syllables by three and so strengthen the point that I am about to make.

versity of this effect supports the likelihood that these synonymy-avoidance principles are part of our prehuman inheritance. So the lowering of the larynx presents the hominids who undergo it with a dilemma. On the one hand, synonymy-avoidance principles generate an expectation that the distinct calls now available should contrast in information content; the new repertoire of potential vocalizations should be exploited rather than allowed to go to waste. On the other hand, memory limitations render it impossible for more than a fraction of these distinct calls to be memorized as separate vocabulary items (or, in linguists' terminology, to be lexicalized). How can this dilemma be resolved?

## 5.5.  Resolving the Dilemma: Vocabulary Expansion and Duality of Patterning

For a creature with a built-in expectation that distinct calls should differ in information content, there is one obvious strategy for mitigating, if not resolving entirely, the dilemma posed by an increased articulatory repertoire. That strategy is to create more calls. So, if our ancestors already observed synonymy-avoidance principles, a lower larynx and a more agile tongue would have triggered pressure for the brain to accommodate a larger call vocabulary. What's more, this pressure would have been independent of our ancestors' cognitive abilities or social structures at the time. It could have operated so as to facilitate the learning of more calls than were immediately needed—that is, more calls than necessary to achieve an advantage over competitors in the current physical and social environment.

The idea that an organism might be better at some task than it needs to be, in some sense, sounds paradoxical. But it is not hard to find among animals examples of skills that are apparently overdeveloped in this way. In their natural habitats dolphins have no need to jump through hoops suspended in the air, and sea lions have no need to balance spinning balls on their snouts; yet the ability of both to do so is exploited in aquatic circuses. Natural selection penalizes a creature when its survival skills are worse than its competitors'; it does not penalize a creature when it can do better than it needs to survive, provided that this special aptitude does not come at the price of inferiority in other more crucial skills.

We have here an answer to the problem posed in Chapter 2 concerning vocabulary size. I will restate the problem here. Even if we assume the most recent possible date for human language to have attained all its modern characteristics (that is roughly 50,000 years ago, shortly before the latest possible date for the migration of *Homo sapiens* to Australia), it is still the case that for most of its existence all its users have been hunters and gatherers, and many of its users are hunters and gatherers even today. Why then has it evolved in such a way that there is no difference between a child from a hunter-gatherer community and a child from Silicone Valley in respect of their ability to acquire natively the vocabulary of electronics or literary theory as well as elaborate kinship systems? Cultural and technological changes have created the need for a massive expansion in vocabulary that is relatively recent. Cultural and technological changes are much more rapid than biological ones, however, so the biological framework within which humans learn vocabulary is much older. One might, therefore, have expected this expansion to run up against in-built limits on vocabulary size and perhaps also content. Why has it not done so?

That expectation rests upon an assumption: that the potential size of our hominid ancestors' vocabulary depended solely on their most basic environmental and social needs. But the fact that the expectation is not fulfilled suggests that the assumption is wrong. By contrast, cultural development uninhibited by any vocabulary size limits is just what we will expect if, as I have suggested, potential vocabulary size is driven not by environmental or social factors but rather by inherited synonymy-avoidance principles. If hominid vocalization has always been subject to a requirement that any potential call that sounds different from every other call should be available to mean something different, then the potential for a much larger vocabulary was an immediate consequence of the development of the modern human vocal tract. Well before 50,000 years ago, the linguistic prerequisites for a twentieth-century vocabulary were satisfied. All that had to happen was for culture and technology to expand to fill the available space, so to speak. And the sophistication of Upper Palaeolithic cave painting and tool manufacture suggests that that expansion began early.

What I am suggesting may seem to involve an inversion of the common-sense relationship between linguistic meaning and speech sounds. Meaningful strings of speech sounds (morphemes and words) exist to express a content whose independence of them is shown by the fact that it can also be expressed in writing. What's more, meanings can be expressed by manual signs, as in deaf sign languages. So, in the linguistic partnership between meaning and sound, if either of the two partners has seniority, it must surely be meaning, one may think. But we have already seen reason to doubt whether this is always so, in the shape of the intralinguistic "meanings" created to guarantee synonymy avoidance in inflectional morphology. In the partnership between meaning and sound, sound may sometimes take the lead, so as to stimulate the discovery or invention of new meanings.

I am not suggesting that, as language evolved, extralinguistic meanings were accumulated arbitrarily. We need to distinguish between the pressure for vocabulary expansion to take place and the directions in which this expansion might proceed. There is plenty of scope in this scenario for cognitive, social, cultural, and technological factors to exert an influence—an issue to which I will return in Chapter 6. All I am suggesting is that, thanks to inherited synonymy-avoidance principles, the capacity for a much larger repertoire of distinct vocalizations introduced a new kind of pressure for this expansion to take place.

Pressure arose for a bigger vocabulary, then. But limitations on memory and practicalities of learning meant that vocabulary expansion by itself could not blot up all the new calls that the vocal apparatus could now produce—a total in millions, even assuming the limited articulatory possibilities posited in Section 5.4. Conceivably, therefore, our ancestors might have stopped at a call system in which new potential calls were lexicalized to the extent that memory allowed, but many others were left unused. Our ancestors would then have had a call system much larger than than of any modern non-human primate, but still like that of modern primates in being closed: that is, the number of calls in it would be finite, with no mechanism for creating new ones.

At a stage of hominid evolution like that pictured in Section 5.4, a large but closed call system may appear at first quite a plausible outcome. After all, one may think, closure has its parallel in English, where many conceivable words are not used: for example, we have *bat, tab, but, tub, bet,* and *bit,* but not *teb* or *tib.* But if we visualize such an outcome in terms of concrete examples, it appears less plausible. Let us assume that the calls that have been lexicalized include [tipu] and [naka] but not [tipunaka]. It is immediately evident that there is a way of using [tipunaka] in the call system without it being lexicalized: it can have a meaning derived from or related to those of [tipu] and [naka] separately. Whether such a combinatorial meaning for [tipunaka] in particular would 'make sense' or be pragmatically useful does not matter. What is clear is that there are sure to be some non-lexicalized potential calls that are homonymous with strings of calls whose semantic combination is pragmatically useful. That being so, two reactions are relatively unlikely: either that the users of this call system would austerely refrain from using these useful combinations, or that they would lexicalize them (that is, assign to them meanings not derivable from those of their constituent calls). It is more likely that they would continue using such a call, but treat it as a call of a new kind: a complex call that is made up of two or more shorter calls and that therefore does not need to be remembered as a separate vocabulary item. In this way the dilemma of Section 5.4 is resolved. A way has been found whereby a large proportion of the potential call repertoire can be put to use, in accordance with synonymy-avoidance pressures, without imposing an intolerable burden on the memory or an impracticable task on the learner.

This new call system has now acquired two characteristics that are prominent in Hockett's (1960*b*) list of design features for human language. First, it has transformed itself from a closed system to an open one, because meaningful calls are no longer limited to the finite vocabulary of lexicalized calls. Secondly, calls are now analysable into recurring constituents at two levels. Our hypothetical [tipunaka] is analysable in articulatory and acoustic terms as containing seven sounds from the system's repertoire of six consonant-like and three vowel-like sounds, each of which can occur in other calls but is individually meaningless. It is also analysable as a string of two smaller calls, [tipu] and [naka], each of which is meaningful. In other words, the system has acquired duality of patterning. But to account for the development of openness and duality I have not needed to invoke any special factor or influence. They have emerged as direct consequences of the resolution of the dilemma posed by memory limitations, synonymy-avoidance principles, and the reconfiguration of the vocal apparatus. On grounds of economy, this may reasonably be counted in favour of the scenario presented here.

## 5.6. Resolving the Dilemma: a Phonological Source for Syntax

The picture painted in Section 5.5 is of a stage of language evolution at which some longer potential calls are rendered usable through being analysed as strings of shorter calls. But a huge question still remains. Precisely how will the combined meaning of these strings be determined? This is a question about syntax.

We have already seen in Chapter 2 that there are numerous conceivable syntaxes for a communication system with a vocabulary and a phonology like those of a human language, including some syntaxes that, though coherent and practical, are quite unlike syntax as it is. But the kind of syntax that human languages actually have is not a mere random choice from among the conceivable alternatives. Rather, I shall argue that its main features constitute a natural outcome of articulatory innovations due to vocal-tract changes. This may seem a surprising suggestion. Why should the evolution of articulatory phonetics correlate in any way with that of sentence structure? But the very fact that such a correlation seems improbable means that, if one can be established, it is all the more likely to reflect a genuine causal connection.

### 5.6.1. Syllables: Psychological Reality and Phonetic Motivation

A consistent articulatory characteristic of human speech, distinguishing it from other primate vocalizations, is that it involves rapid alternations in the width of the vocal tract, from wider to narrower and back again. Sounds or sound clusters whose production hinders or blocks the free flow of air from the lungs alternate with sounds in which the air can escape relatively freely. The auditory correlate of this is a pattern of rapid alternation in the **sonority** of the sounds produced, where by sonority is meant 'loudness relative to that of other sounds with the same stress, length and pitch' (Ladefoged 1993: 245). In phonology, a broad consensus has been reached to the effect that speech sounds can be ranked in a sonority hierarchy on the lines of Table 5.5 (see e.g. Kenstowicz 1994: ch. 6, and references there). Language-particular variations in this hierarchy exist, but they are limited to refinements within a given rank; for example, some languages treat

Table 5.5. *The sonority hierarchy*

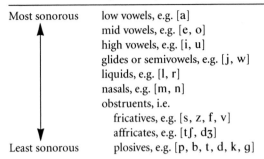

| Most sonorous | low vowels, e.g. [a] |
| | mid vowels, e.g. [e, o] |
| | high vowels, e.g. [i, u] |
| | glides or semivowels, e.g. [j, w] |
| | liquids, e.g. [l, r] |
| | nasals, e.g. [m, n] |
| | obstruents, i.e. |
| |    fricatives, e.g. [s, z, f, v] |
| |    affricates, e.g. [tʃ, dʒ] |
| Least sonorous | plosives, e.g. [p, b, t, d, k, g] |

all obstruents as equally low in sonority while others treat fricatives as more sonorous than plosives. The most sonorous sounds are thus those produced with least obstruction in the vocal tract above the larynx—namely, vowels (especially low vowels); the least sonorous sounds are those in which the egress of air from the lungs is for a time blocked completely by a tight contact made at the lips or between the tongue and some point on the roof of the mouth while the soft palate is raised to seal off the nasal cavity.

Ladefoged's definition of sonority is acoustically imprecise inasmuch as loudness is an auditory notion, not subject to direct instrumental measurement. Even so, the sonority hierarchy is firmly established as a tool of phonological analysis because of its link with the notion **syllable**, which I have already used in discussing the hypothetical ancestral pre-language of Section 5.4. This notion is not purely technical, being part of the ordinary vocabulary of every educated person. That alone is an indication that it deserves to be recognized as a psychologically real unit of phonological structure; and this is confirmed by the fact that people in all communities seem to have no difficulty in counting syllables, which is why syllable-counting is a feature of so many conventions for versifying.

The link between sonority and syllables is as follows. The number of sonority peaks in an utterance (that is, the number of sounds such that the immediately adjacent sounds are lower in the sonority hierarchy) corresponds closely to the native speaker's intuitive judgement of the number of syllables.[13] It follows that, if in any language we examine words that native speakers agree to be monosyllabic, we nearly always find that a graph of the sonority of the sounds that the word contains shows a pattern such that no sound is higher in sonority than any sound intervening between it and the most sonorous sound. For example, the

---

[13] I say 'corresponds closely' rather than 'corresponds exactly' because of examples like English *sprints*, which is monosyllabic but which, if fricatives are deemed more sonorous than plosives, has three sonority peaks (on s, i, and s). Prima-facie mismatches of this kind fall into clearly defined categories, however, so as to encourage confidence that they do not reveal a basic flaw in the syllable–sonority correspondence. For relevant discussion, see e.g. Selkirk (1982), Paradis (1991), and references quoted by Kenstowicz (1994).

English word *plant* begins with a plosive [p] from which the sonority graph rises via the liquid [l] to the vowel [a] before declining again to the nasal [n] and the plosive [t].

Establishing the number of syllables in an utterance does not by itself establish whether any clear-cut boundaries between syllables can be drawn, and if so where. But again, there is remarkable agreement on this question among native speakers, whether or not they know anything about phonological theory. If people speak very slowly in order to try to make themselves understood to a foreigner, they may well insert pauses even inside words; but these pauses will not be random. For example, speakers of English will have no difficulty in agreeing that the word *instruction*, pronounced [ɪnˈstrʌkʃən], contains three syllables corresponding to the sonority peaks [ɪ], [ʌ] and [ə]; but they are also likely to agree that the most natural pausing places, or syllable boundaries, are where the dollar signs are: [ɪn$strʌk$ʃən].

The first of these two boundary decisions is worth looking at closely. This is not the only decison that would yield strings of sounds pronounceable independently as English syllables, for both [ɪns$trʌk] and [ɪnst$rʌk] also meet that criterion. To describe the reason that a phonologist is likely to offer for our preferred decision, I need to introduce some more terminology. Let the most sonorous sound in a syllable (the sonority peak) be its **nucleus**, let any sounds within the syllable that precede the nucleus constitute the **onset**, let any which follow it constitute the **coda**, and let onsets and codas together be called **margins**. The principle on which speakers of not only English but all language operates in determining syllable boundaries can be stated as follows:

(5) **Onset Maximization.** Subject to what the syllable patterns of a language allow, marginal sounds are assigned to onsets rather than to codas.

Let us see how this works in our example *instruction*. This contains the string of four marginal sounds [nstr]. We cannot assign them all to an onset, because [nstrʌk] is not a possible syllable in English—not surprisingly, since it would contain two sonority peaks, on [n] and on [ʌ]. The nasal [n] must therefore belong to a coda. But the remaining string [str] can be assigned in its entirety to an onset, because [strʌk] is a possible English syllable (indeed, it constitutes the actual word *struck*). That being so, we need explore no further, since any alternative demarcation will assign more sounds to a coda than is necessary in order to comply with Onset Maximization.

The fact that Onset Maximization applies not just to English but to all languages suggests that it reflects something in our biological endowment. Three further observations tend to confirm this. First, Onset Maximization implies a priority of onsets over codas such that we may expect to find some languages lacking syllables with codas (if their syllable patterns allow all marginal sounds to be assigned to onsets), but we will never expect to find a language lacking syllables with onsets. And this is correct (Jakobson 1962: 526; Clements and Keyser 1983). Languages such as Maori in New Zealand and Etsako and Urhobo in west Africa allow no codas (Laver 1994: 35), so that all syllables end in a vowel; but no language has been reported which allows no onsets. Secondly, even in languages where codas are permitted, the inventory of sounds that are permitted in codas is often smaller than that of sounds in onsets, and I know of no reports of languages where the coda inventory is larger. For example, in Mandarin Chinese (Putonghua) possible onsets include obstruents, liquids, nasals, and glides, but possible codas include only nasals and one glide. Thirdly, the first approximations to adult words that babies produce during what Locke (1993) calls the 'reduplicated babbling' stage resemble syllables consisting of just a single-consonant onset and a nucleus. As Locke (1993: 176) puts it:

This stage refers to the onset of well-formed syllables.... Babbled syllables typically involve closures that are released into an open vocal tract, giving the impression of a consonant-vowel syllable (such as [da]) that may be produced repetitively ([dadadada]). [At the variegated babbling stage] infants display sounds having several different points of articulatory closure within multisyllabic strings (such as [daba]).

This aspect of babbling underlies the often-repeated suggestion that in many languages a word like [ma] has come to mean 'mother' through adult over-interpretation of a typical babbled syllable.

Showing that the syllable needs to be recognized as a unit in the phonology of modern human languages does not by itself demonstrate any motivation for it at a stage in the evolution of speech before the development of the full modern articulatory repertoire, such as what we may call the [tipunaka] stage pictured in Section 5.5. What we would like to find is an articulatory or acoustic motivation that would be equally applicable to that earlier stage. Phoneticians have been cautious about identifying syllables on purely phonetic as opposed to phonological grounds, pointing out that syllables do not identify themselves clearly in instrumental recordings or in the measurement of air pressure from the lungs during speech (Lieberman and Blumstein 1988; Clark and Yallop 1995). Even so, there are good reasons to think that the subdivision of utterances into syllables would be justified at the [tipunaka] stage too.

One reason is linked to babbling. Why do babies tend to say [da] or [ga] rather than [ad] or [ag]? A possible answer is that releasing a closure by lowering the tongue involves less precise muscular control than forming a closure by raising the tongue to a particular point on the roof of the mouth. This answer seems as plausible in relation to earlier humans exploiting to the full an archaic speech apparatus as to babies learning today to exploit a more modern one. But, whatever the correct answer, it is reasonable to suppose that those articulatory combinations that are easiest for modern babies are among those that appeared early in speech evolution. So Onset Maximization would have applied then too.

But, since onsets are onsets of syllables, it follows that syllables too appeared early.[14]

A second reason has to do with a factor that we have not so far considered—namely, the acoustics of the speech signal. Some of the earliest work on speech synthesis during the 1950s by the Haskins Laboratories in New York had a straightforward practical purpose: to devise a procedure whereby written material could be converted into speechlike sounds for the benefit of blind people (Lieberman 1984). But this project encountered obstacles much more formidable than the vagaries of English spelling. An articulatory phonetician transcribing the English words *Dee* and *do* will have no hesitation in using the same symbol [d] for the consonantal onset in both. But when an acoustic phonetician looks at a spectrographic analysis of these syllables, revealing the amount of acoustic energy at various frequencies, she finds no common element corresponding to [d]. As we have seen, vowels are distinguished acoustically by formants, related to the acoustic filtering properties of the vocal tract above the larynx. Consonants are identified by interpreting transitions (rises or falls in frequency) at the ends of vowel formants. But the transitions involved in [di] and [du] are different. If one removes the transitions from [di] and splices them onto the vowel formants from [du], the result does not sound much like [du], and vice versa. Moreover, there is no way of removing the vocalic element from either syllable so as to leave an element that will sound like [d] by itself, with no accompanying vowel. So long as enough is left to be interpretable as speech at all, it will be interpreted as [di] or [du], as the case may be. Speech perception, therefore, does not involve matching neatly distinguished segments of the acoustic signal with sounds, one by one, as alphabetic writing systems and even phonetic transcriptions may tempt us to think. Rather, our brains perform a complex analysis whereby quite different acoustic stimuli can be interpreted as the same sound, and one acoustic stimulus may signal two sounds (a consonant and a following vowel) inextricably (Liberman *et al.* 1967).[15]

This kind of analysis is not peculiar to humans, in that many animals hear the calls of their conspecifics differently from all other sounds. It is reasonable to suppose that our ancestors at the [tipunaka] stage did so too. The point of mentioning acoustic phonetics, then, is that it supports the relevance of the syllable at that stage in language evolution. The [t] in the call that I transcribed as [tipu] would not be identifiable as such independently of the [i] that immediately follows it. On the other hand, the identification of this [t] would not involve the [u] at the end of the call. That is not to say that it is impossible for a segment to be

---

[14] We will see in Section 5.6.2 that approaches to syllable structure currently exist in which onsets (and rhymes and nuclei) are acknowledged but syllables as such have no theoretical status. But that does not affect the point being made here: the probable early appearance of those phonetic and phonological phenomena that are generally described in terms of syllables.

[15] For a more detailed introductory account of the acoustic fusion of consonant and vowel, see Lieberman and Blumstein 1988: 145–7. This fusion leads us to expect that there should be articulatory overlap too. For discussion of that aspect, see e.g. Kent (1983) and Lindblom (1983).

affected by another that is not immediately adjacent; languages with systems of long-distance assimilation such as vowel harmony and umlaut show that this can indeed happen. The point is rather that the acoustic effect of a vowel on an immediately adjacent onset consonant is inescapable. And this kind of acoustic inseparability correlates with syllable membership, as we have characterized it so far: a marginal sound and a nucleus that are acoustically separable in the sense that the marginal sound is identifiable without giving any hint of the identity of the nucleus (as [t] in my example is identifiable without involving [u]) must belong to separate syllables. So, because acoustic separability and inseparability are features of the [tipunaka] stage, so too is the syllable in so far as it correlates with them.

This section has been devoted to showing that to talk of syllables at the stage in language evolution envisaged in Section 5.5 is legitimate. But I have not said anything about the internal organization of syllables beyond introducing a subdivision in terms of nucleus, onset, and coda. In the next section I will discuss this internal organization. The ground will then have been fully prepared for a comparison between syllables and sentences in Section 5.6.3.

### 5.6.2. Syllables: Internal Organization

As we have seen, a syllable has a nucleus that corresponds to a sonority peak, and it may also have an onset or a coda or both, constituting margins. Furthermore, the syllable's sonority contour normally slopes down from the nucleus towards the margins, and onsets have priority over codas by Onset Maximization, as stated at (5). But there is more to be said. Do syllables have any internal constituents? Three logical possibilities are presented at (6), (7), and (8):

(6)

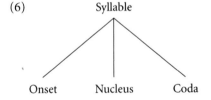

(7)

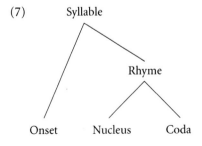

(8)

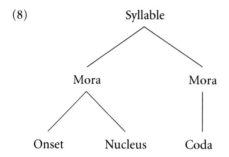

In fact, all three have been advocated in recent phonological discussions. The structures at (6) and (8) represent minority views, advocated by Clements and Keyser (1983) and Hyman (1985) respectively. The structure at (7), by contrast, is more traditional (Fudge 1969) and still represents the mainstream view (Blevins 1995). There is even a fourth view, according to which only onsets, rhymes, nuclei, and perhaps codas have any theoretical status, and 'syllable' is simply an unofficial shorthand for a rhyme together with any adjacent onsets not attached to another rhyme (Kaye *et al.* 1990; Harris 1994). This diversity of opinion may look disappointing. However, everyone agrees on the existence of three asymmetries, which are what matters to us:

- between nuclei and margins;
- between the two kinds of margin; and
- between the syllable itself (whether officially recognized or not) and its constituents.

Disagreements concerning the relative importance of these asymmetries and details of their handling in phonological theory need not concern us.

The asymmetry between nuclei and margins consists in the fact that the nucleus, being a sound of relatively high sonority, is what defines the presence of a distinct syllable, and in most languages a syllable consisting of a nucleus alone is possible. French furnishes several examples of nucleus-only syllables that also constitute complete words belonging to open wordclasses, such as *eau* [o] 'water', *haie* [ɛ] 'hedge', *août* [u] 'August'. Sequences of nucleus-only syllables (forming sonority plateaus rather than peaks) are often disfavoured, but they are not universally outlawed; for example, the Hungarian word *barátjaiéi* [ˈbɒraːcɒieːi] 'ones belonging to his or her friends' contains six syllables of which the last three contain no margins. On the other hand, a syllable with no nucleus is a contradiction in terms. In the Imdlawn Tashlhiyt dialect of Berber a syllable can consist entirely of plosives, at the bottom of the sonority hierarchy; but even there one of the plosives can be identified as the nucleus (Dell and Elmedlaoui 1985, 1988; Prince and Smolensky 1993).

The main asymmetries between onsets and codas have already been mentioned:

onsets are maximized, some languages permit no codas at all, and the inventory of possible codas in a language tends to be smaller than that of possible onsets. Some languages even require that all syllables contain an onset, such as Senufo (Clements and Keyser 1983: 28). Compulsory onsets are probably more widespread than is often realized. A language may require that a nucleus that would otherwise be syllable-initial must be preceded by a default onset whose identity is always predictable, such as in German, where an apparently onsetless syllable such as *Obst* 'fruit' in fact begins with an obligatory glottal stop, or abrupt opening of the vocal folds: [ʔoːpst]. Because such default onsets do not contrast with other sounds and are often omitted in conventional spelling, it is easy to overlook their significance for syllable structure. There are, however, other important onset–coda asymmetries, which are reflected in (7) and (8) respectively.

The structure at (7) implies that the nucleus has a closer relationship with the coda than with the onset, so as to form a constituent called the rhyme. The evidence in support of this analysis comes from phonotactic constraints and from slips of the tongue. Phonotactic constraints are constraints on sound juxtapositions; they can be thought of as phonological analogues of the collocational restrictions mentioned in Section 5.2.3, whereby *a flock of cows and *a herd of sheep sound odd. In many languages constraints on possible nucleus–coda combinations are more stringent than constraints on onset–nucleus combinations. Thus in English every onset–nucleus combination seems possible. Gaps can certainly be found, in the shape of combinations that do not occur among actual English words; for example, no English words (so far as I know) contain the combinations [skrɔi] or [ðu]. But these gaps can reasonably be seen as accidental; [skrɔi] does not sound un-English, and [ðu] perhaps does so only because [ð] as an onset occurs only in syntactically and semantically restricted sets of closed-class words such as *the, that, then, though*. By contrast, there are systematic onset–coda constraints whose breach yields definitely un-English-sounding results. For example, diphthongs and 'long' vowels such as [u] and [i] cannot occur with [ŋ], with the nasal-plosive clusters [mp] and [ŋk], or with most liquid-plosive clusters such as [lt], [lk], [lp], so that combinations like [uŋk], [iːmp], [eilt], [aulp], and [ailk] are impossible.[16] The relative frequency of nucleus–coda constraints is to be expected, however, if the nucleus and coda form a constituent within the syllable (namely the rhyme), with its own well-formedness conditions.

This structure also implies that the onset is an immediate constituent of the syllable whereas the coda is not. That leads us to expect that, in slips of the tongue that involve switching sounds between syllables, onsets should be switched more readily than codas. Removing the onset from a syllable will leave a compete constituent (the rhyme) behind, whereas removing the coda will leave a fragment (the onset and part

---

[16] In ordinary English spelling the first four of these, if they occurred, would probably be represented *oonk, eemp, ailt,* and *owlp*. The fifth is not spellable!

of the rhyme) that does not form a constituent. And this expectation is confirmed by the fact that spoonerisms involving onsets (e.g. *dat and cog* for *cat and dog*) are much more frequent than switches involving codas (e.g. *cag and dot*), an onset–coda pair (*cad and tog* or *gat and doc*), or nuclei (*cot and dag*) (Fromkin 1973).

The structure at (8) is motivated by considerations of syllable weight. In many languages, a distinction between light and heavy syllables plays a part in determining relative prominence or stress. Typically, a light syllable is one with a short nucleus and no coda, while a heavy syllable has a coda, with or without a long nucleus. Even though the location of word-stress in English is notoriously complex, it is not random, and syllable weight plays a part in determining it. This can be illustrated through the stressing in English of certain loanwords from Russian. In Russian, the stress on the surname *Rozhdéstvensky* and the word *bábushka* 'grandmother, old woman' lies on the second and first syllable respectively. Most native speakers of English, however, are inclined to stress the second-to-last syllable (*Rozhdestvénsky, babúshka*), and have to make a conscious effort if they want to stress these words in the Russian way. This is because the penultimate syllables (*-ven-, -bush-*) contain codas and are therefore heavy, so tending to attract stress. The same phenomenon can be seen by comparing the words *sedítion, aquátic,* and *inhíbit,* whose stressed syllables are light, with *refléction, distémper,* and *indúlgent,* whose stressed syllables are heavy. In the first group of words, a native speaker of English can without difficulty shift the stress on to the first syllable if she tries to, and many other words with light penultimate syllables exist in which the first syllable is actually stressed, such as *pólishing, héretic,* and *ácrobat.* But shifting the stress in the second group of words sounds much less natural, and it is hard to find actual words that display that combination of penultimate heaviness with antepenultimate stress.[17]

In (8), the term **mora** is used to denote a unit of weight: a light syllable is monomoraic while a heavy syllable is bimoraic.[18] What is important for present purposes is that the onset is always attached moraically to the nucleus. This reflects the second kind of asymmetry between onsets and codas: onsets have no effect on syllable weight. Never, in English or any other language, is stress attracted to a syllable because that syllable has a particular kind of onset. In terms of the structure at (7), syllable weight depends on the rhyme alone.

There are thus two differences between onsets and codas that have motivated the structural analyses illustrated in (7) and (8) respectively. Although these analyses seem at first contradictory, they agree in assigning a special or privileged place to

---

[17] Some readers may wonder why *pédantry, cálendar, wárranty,* etc. sound quite natural. In these words the coda consonant that renders the penultimate syllable heavy is the coronal (i.e. tongue-blade) nasal [n], and there is evidence that coronal sounds often flout generalizations that apply to other places of articulation (Paradis 1991). Genuine counter-examples to the weight constraint alleged here are (in my pronunciation) *stálactite* and *stálagmite.*

[18] The possibility of superheavy or trimoraic syllables in a few languages does not affect the argument.

onsets. The onset is separated from the rest of the syllable both in that it contributes nothing to syllable weight and in that it is relatively unconstrained phonotactically.

The third and final asymmetry, that between the syllable and its constituents, may seem so obvious as not to be worth mentioning. However, it differentiates the syllable from many other hierarchically organized structures. The arithmetical expression 3 + (8 ÷ 2) can be viewed as having two constituents, 3 and 8 ÷ 2, of which the second also has two constituents. In that respect it resembles the syllable as presented at (7). One can even envisage a diagrammatic representation for it mimicking (7):

(9)

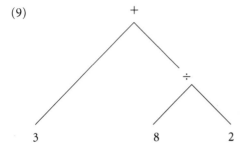

But a crucial difference between (9) and (7) is that in (9) the entities represented at the terminal nodes (3, 8, and 2) and at the two branching nodes are all of the same kind: they are all arithmetical expressions. Consequently they can be interchanged without rendering the expression ill-formed. We can substitute a simple expression (say, 4) for 8 ÷ 2, and we can substitue a complex expression (say, 4 − 1) for 3, and what results is still an arithmetical expression. But nothing comparable can be done with syllable structure. We cannot replace a nucleus with an onset, or a coda with a rhyme, and still have a well-formed syllable. Above all, we cannot nest syllables in syllables, by filling the onset, nucleus, or coda position with a syllable. These asymmetries are not usually pointed out in handbooks of phonological theory, simply because it is unlikely that any student of phonology is ever tempted to wonder whether syllabic constituents are interchangeable and if not, why not. But they will turn out to be important in the next section.[19]

### 5.6.3. The Syllable as a Model for Sentence Structure

Compare the structure at (7) with that at (10), which represents a traditional view of the syntactic structure of a simple English sentence such as *John saw Mary* or (an example much discussed in Edward Sapir's classic book *Language* (1921)) *The farmer killed the duckling*:

---

[19] The view of the phylogeny of syllabically organized speech expounded in Sections 5.6.1 and 5.6.2 seems consistent with that of MacNeilage (1998), who argues that the open–close oscillation characteristic of speech may originate in the oscillation involved in chewing and swallowing.

(10)

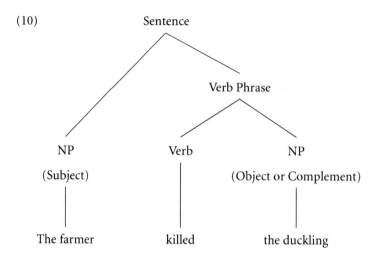

A broad similarity between the two structures has been noticed more than once. Four reactions to this similarity are possible. First, we may regard it as a coincidence, shedding no light on how language really works. Secondly, it may be a manifestation in two distinct domains (syntax and phonology) of a single principle of linguistic organization that is more fundamental than either domain. Thirdly, it may be due to the influence of syntax on phonology. And, fourthly, it may be due to the influence of phonology on syntax. The fourth view probably looks at first sight the least attractive. Nevertheless I will argue that it is correct; but first I will explore apparent attractions of the other three views.

Most contemporary linguistic theorists probably subscribe to the first view. This is partly because few linguists work in both syntax and phonology, so parallels between them are not high on their agendas, but partly also because it is easy to find prima-facie evidence suggesting that any such parallels are accidental. The order of the constituents illustrated in (10) is not universal: Subject–Verb–Object or **SVO** is the normal order in English and many other languages, but **SOV** order is about equally widespread and **VSO** occurs in about 11 per cent of the world's languages, while orders in which the object precedes the subject, though very rare, are attested (Tomlin 1986). On the other hand, the Onset–Nucleus–Coda order of constituents in the syllable is invariable. Moreover, there is no direct association between syllable structure and sentence structure within a language; for example, there is no evident tendency for 'nucleus-final' languages (ones whose syllables contain no codas) also to favour the verb-final (SOV) sentence pattern, or vice versa.[20] But when presenting my

---

[20] New Zealand Maori and several other Polynesian languages seem in fact to illustrate the very opposite situation. Their syllables lack codas and so are nucleus-final, yet their basic constituent order is arguably VSO.

own view later I will argue that these objections are less substantial than they at first seem.

The approach to phonology developed by Jonathan Kaye, Jean Lowenstamm, and Jean-Roger Vergnaud (1990) and the somewhat similar approach of John Harris (1994) take syntax–phonology parallels seriously. In the Principles-and-Parameters version of Chomsky's syntax developed during the 1980s (Chomsky 1986*a*, *b*), two prominent notions are 'licensing' and 'government'. It is not necessary to explain here exactly what these mean in the context of Chomsky's syntax. What is important is that they figure in these approaches to phonology too. Kaye, Lowenstamm, and Vergnaud (who call their approach **Government Phonology**) see this as a deep commonality between syntax and phonology, ascribable to some aspect of the innate language organ that is neutral between the two domains. The evolutionary origins of this commonality are not discussed, however.

The psychological and neurological approach to language developed by Patricia Greenfield (1991) could hardly be more different from that of Kaye and his colleagues, except that she too notices the parallel between what she calls 'sound combination' and 'word combination' (1991: 541), and she too sees it as not primarily tied to either. For her, what underlies both is a neural mechanism for combining objects and using tools, in respect of which humans have diverged from other primates in the course of their evolution. I will, therefore, defer further discussion of Greenfield's views until Chapter 6, where we will consider how this chapter's proposals relate to evidence from biological anthropology.

Levin (1985) explores a different phonology–syntax parallel, involving the relationship between phrases and their heads (between nouns and NPs, for example). Ever since Jackendoff (1977), syntactic phrases have been widely seen as **projections** of head elements belonging to categories such as 'noun' or 'verb', and non-head elements in phrases are subject to restrictions that are held to apply uniformly to phrases of all kinds. In the most influential version of the theory, three levels of projection exist. These can be represented schematically as X, X′ ('X-bar') and X″ ('X-double-bar'), where X stands for any category. Because of this terminology, this model of syntactic constituency is generally known as **X-bar theory**. At (11) and (12) I give simplified X-bar representations of the structure of the sentence *The enemy destroyed the city* and the NP *the enemy's destruction of the city*.[21]

---

[21] Readers familiar with syntactic theory will recognize that I have oversimplified, in that in (11) I have represented the sentence as the maximal projection of the verb, rather than of Infl or Comp. But for present purposes it is sufficiently accurate to regard the verb as the head of the sentence.

(11)

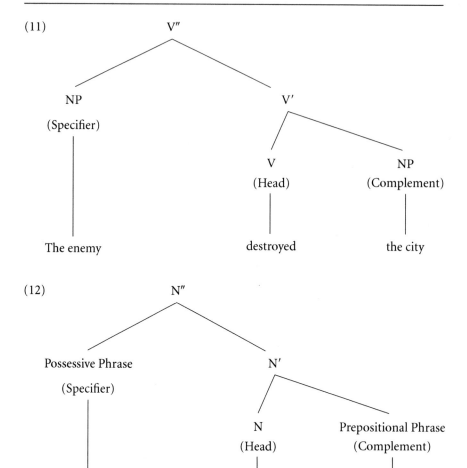

(12)

The terms **specifier** and **complement** are labels for syntactic functions, just like the more familiar 'subject' and 'object', but unlike 'subject' and 'object' they are held to apply to any kind of phrase. Thus the syntactic role played by *the enemy* in (11), which would be termed traditionally 'subject', is held to be the same as the role played by *the enemy's* in (12): they are both specifiers. Likewise, *the city* in (11) and *of the city* in (12) are both complements. More complex sentences and phrases may contain other kinds of nonhead constituent, causing there to be more single-bar and double-bar nodes than in these examples; but specifiers are always daughters of the highest double-bar node (the **maximal projection**) and complements are always daughters of the lowest single-bar node, as here.[22] I need not trouble non-syntactician readers with more details than this. The important point is that, according to Levin, the resemblance between (11) and (12) on the one hand and (7) on the other is not an accident: the nucleus is the head of the syllable (equivalently, the syllable is the maximal projection of the nucleus), the rhyme is the single-bar projection of the nucleus, the coda is the complement of the nucleus, and the onset is the specifier.

It does not matter whether X-bar theory is fundamentally neutral between syntax and phonology, as licensing and government are said to be by Kaye and his colleagues, or is fundamentally syntactic. What matters is that Levin sees sentences and syllables as structurally parallel. Both her approach and that of the Government Phonologists are therefore economical, in the sense discussed at the start of Chapter 2. Because of the overlap beween their mechanisms for describing syntax and phonology, their theories do more with less. This is an attractive feature. But they share a drawback too. Neither theory has anything to say about language evolution. Licensing, government, and X-bar theory are presented as characteristics of the language faculty without any time dimension and without any discussion of where they may have come from. This does not count as a criticism in terms of the authors' aims, which are to describe how language is, not explain how it came to be the way it is. But it means that the parallels between syntax and phonology that they note are not approached in a way that might shed light on why the sentence/NP distinction has evolved.

What about the fourth alternative: that the resemblance between (10) and (7) is due to the influence of phonology on syntax? Something like this has been proposed by MacNeilage *et al.* (1984): they point out that, just as syllables provide frames for the insertion of segmental content (that is, individual speech sounds), so sentences provide frames for the insertion of morphological content (mor-phemes). However, they do not pursue in detail possible structural correspondences between syllables and sentences, as I will in the following sections.[23]

I will argue that the three asymmetries of syllable structure discussed in Section 5.6.2 have quite close parallels in the structure of sentences in language-as-it-is—parallels closer than to anything in the structure of Spatiotemporal and Monocategoric, which I presented in Chapter 2 as alternative conceivable paths for syntactic evolution and, in the case of Monocategoric, a more likely path at first sight than the one actually taken. So, since the syllable appeared as a unit of phonetic and phonological organization as soon as the lowered larynx and other

---

[22] In the 'Minimalist' syntax developed by Chomsky during the 1990s (Chomsky 1995), the terminology is substantially changed, but the basic architecture of phrase structure is retained, along with the notions 'complement' and 'specifier'.

[23] Liberman (1970) similarly points to parallels between syntactic and phonetic coding, but he does not argue that phonetic coding is in any sense more fundamental.

vocal-tract changes made a more modern style of vocalization possible, it is reasonable to conclude that the neural organization underlying syllable structure was co-opted to provide a syntax for strings of 'words' when the need became pressing. It was natural, therefore, that syntactic structure should possess features reminiscent of syllable structure. This resemblance was neither accidental nor analogical but rather homological in the evolutionary sense: that is, it came about because sentence structure had originally the same biological basis in neural organization as syllable structure had.

### 5.6.4. *Compliance with the Syllabic Model: Spatiotemporal and Monocategoric*

The three syllabic asymmetries (labelled for convenient reference) are:

(A)  between nuclei and margins;
(B)  between the two kinds of margin; and
(C)  between the syllable itself (whether officially recognized or not) and its constituents.

Let us now put aside so far as possible what we know of how syntax either operates or might operate, and consider what characteristics we will expect a syntax to display if it is modelled on a syllabic structure with these asymmetries. I will present as A′, B′, and C′ the syntactic counterparts of all three asymmetries in turn, using 'word$^P$' as the syntactic counterpart of '(speech-)sound' and 'sentence$^P$' as the syntactic counterpart of 'syllable'. I will also speak of 'vocabularies$^P$' of words$^P$ so defined. (One can think of the superscript $p$ as meaning 'derived from phonological structure'.) This will help readers to begin thinking immediately about how far these expectations are fulfilled in syntax-as-it-is, since the degree of fulfilment depends on how closely the behaviour of these syllable-derived words$^P$ and sentences$^P$ corresponds to the behaviour of actual words and sentences.

**Syntactic Asymmetry A′.** On the basis of the discussion of syllabic asymmetry A in Section 5.6.2, we will expect to find a syntactic position resembling the nucleus in two respects. First, just as the nucleus is an obligatory constituent of all syllables in all languages, so this nucleus-like position is obligatory in each sentence$^P$. Secondly, just as the sounds that can fill the nucleus position are largely distinct from (because more sonorous than) the sounds that fill the marginal positions, the words$^P$ that can occupy this nucleus-like position are largely distinct from those that can occupy the marginal positions. This distinctness is not absolute, however. Just as a sound relatively low in sonority (a nasal consonant, say) is nuclear if the adjoining sounds are even less sonorous, so a word$^P$ that usually occurs in a marginal position occupies the nucleus-like position if the adjoining words$^P$ differ from it in some respect that can reasonably be regarded as a syntactic or semantic counterpart of sonority.

**Syntactic Asymmetry B′.** Onsets and codas are substantially alike in terms of the sounds that can occur in them but onsets are privileged in relation to codas by Onset Maximization and by the fact that onsets are found in all languages while codas are not. Sentences[^P] thus have marginal positions that are substantially alike in terms of the classes of words[^P] and word[^P]-clusters that can occur in them. The onset-like position is, however, privileged in that, unlike the coda-like position, it occurs in all languages, and most sentences[^P] contain it.

**Syntactic Asymmetry C′.** Just as a syllable cannot contain a syllable in lieu of onset, nucleus, or coda, so a sentence[^P] cannot contain a sentence[^P] in lieu of its nucleus-like position or any margin-like position.

Even partial compliance with these expectations is not easily achieved. To see this, consider first the hypothetical Spatiotemporal syntax that we discussed in Chapter 2. Spatiotemporal does not exhibit Asymmetries A′ or B′ at all. In each of its complete expressions, not one but three constituents (or positions) are obligatory—namely, the two location positions and the object-or-event position. Complete expressions are thus not like sentences[^P]. Moreover, there is no overlap between the sorts of phrases that can appear in any of these positions. There is, therefore, no parallel with the overlap in vocabulary[^P] between onsets and codas predicted by Asymmetry B′, nor with the substantial but not complete distinctness of nuclear and marginal vocabulary[^P] predicted by Asymmetry A′. In terms of Asymmetry C′, although it is impossible for a complete expression of Spatiotemporal to constitute the whole of one of the three constituents of a larger complete expression, one or more complete expressions can indeed appear as subconstituents inside the object-or-event position, as illustrated at (10) in Chapter 2. We might plausibly also allow complete expressions to appear inside one of the locational positions, as in (13):

(13)  In Wellington + During (In Christchurch + Yesterday + Earthquake) + Small tremors.
'During the earthquake in Christchurch yesterday, there were small tremors in Wellington.'

Because of this scope for embedding one complete expression inside another, Spatiotemporal exhibits Asymmetry C′ at best imperfectly. So my scenario for syntactic evolution suggests a reason why no modern language resembles Spatiotemporal. The absence of Asymmetries A′ and B′ and the only partial presence of Asymmetry C′ shows that Spatiotemporal is an improbable outcome if syllabic organization provides the model for syntax.

Consider now how Monocategoric fares. A Monocategoric expression also has no counterpart of the single obligatory nucleus-like position that Asymmetry A′ predicts. In a complex expression such as *you snake* SEE we cannot equate this position with that of the operator SEE, because a well-formed Monocategoric expression can be simple, with no operator at all (e.g. *snake*, which might be uttered in a context where the best English gloss would be something like 'There's a snake'). Nor can we equate the nucleus-like position with either of the operator's arguments, *you* or *snake*, because the choice between them would be arbitrary. There is in any case no expectation that a complex expression should contain just one argument; rather, it will have one, two, three, or more, depending on the valency of its operator. As for vocabulary, Monocategoric at first sight exhibits Asymmetry A' inasmuch as the vocabularies of operators and simple expressions are distinct; but this distinctness is total, with no counterpart of the partial overlap that Asymmetry A' allows for. And a Monocategoric expression does not exhibit Asymmetry B', because, however many arguments accompany its operator, none is privileged except in the trivial sense of coming first. Finally, the possibility of an expression occurring as a constituent in a larger one is built into Monocategoric syntax as one of its fundamental features, so Asymmetry C' is entirely absent.

In Chapter 2 I pointed out that the predator-specific alarm calls used by vervet monkeys could not sensibly be classified as nominal or sentential, because there is nothing in their call system to motivate such a distinction. I also pointed out that everything we can use English for could also be accomplished by means of a language such as Nominalized English or Monocategoric, in which the nominal/sentential distinction is lacking too. It follows that, if human language is descended from something like a primate call system, there is no stage in its evolution at which the sentence/NP distinction would have had to emerge in order for it to express everything that modern human language can. The question therefore arises why human language did not evolve in something like the Monocategoric direction. Why, in other words, did a syntactic distinction evolve which, from a Monocategoric point of view, looks like a needless complication? That is a question to which I can now suggest an answer. Monocategoric, just like Spatiotemporal, is not the sort of language that we would expect to evolve in an environment where syntax was modelled on syllable structure, so as to favour the three asymmetries.

The absence of any germ of the sentence/NP distinction in animal communication systems has been seen by some scholars as favouring a totally different conclusion—namely, that animal communication systems have nothing to do with human language. (This is sometimes called the **discontinuist** view.) But the argument just presented already removes what some have seen as a support for discontinuism. The existence of non-Monocategoric syntax in modern human languages may not after all be an obstacle to regarding them as homologous with primate vocal communication. But can we say more positively that the kind of non-Monocategoric syntax that human languages actually have is what we would expect if Asymmetries A', B', and C' played a role in its origin? That is the question to which we now turn.

### 5.6.5. *Compliance with the Syllabic Model: Syntax-as-it-is*

We certainly do not find a perfect match between characteristics of modern syntax and the expectations which flow from Asymmetries A', B', and C'. But we find a match that is much closer than for Spatiotemporal and Monocategoric—and too close to be regarded plausibly as accidental. The evolutionary scenario being explored here leads us to expect a close match not between syllable structure and *modern* syntax, but rather between syllable structure and the kind of syntax that developed at that stage in language evolution when vocal-tract changes and synonymy-avoidance principles jointly created a need for a syntax of some sort. We cannot test the closeness of that match directly. What we can do, however, is consider whether the kind of syntax that the asymmetries predict is a plausible candidate to be the ancestor of syntax-as-it-is.

One can derive from the three asymmetries a more detailed checklist of characteristics indicating compliance with them:

(i)  Every text is analysable into sentences such that each sentence obligatorily contains a nucleus-like position.

(ii)  This nucleus-like position is filled by a class or classes of words that are substantially but not completely distinct from the classes of words that fill constituents occupying the margin-like positions.

(iii)  Substantially the same classes of words are found in all constituents occupying margin-like positions.

(iv)  Some non-nuclear constituent or constituents are privileged in onset-like fashion.

(v)  A sentence cannot occupy the nucleus-like position in a larger sentence.

(vi)  A sentence cannot occupy a margin-like position in a larger sentence.

It would have been a waste of time to apply this checklist to Spatiotemporal and Monocategoric because of the impossibility of identifying nucleus-like and margin-like positions in those languages. But in the syntax of modern human languages, we find four characteristics on the checklist that are arguably universal (namely, (i), (ii), (iii), and (v)), one (namely, (iv)) that is open to more than one interpretation but that on at least some interpretations is extremely widespread if not universal, and only one (namely, (vi)) that does not fit at all. Let me justify this assessment in more detail.

Characteristic (i) is exhibited in any language where every simple sentence contains a position filled by a verb or verblike element identifiable as such by its syntactic or morphological behaviour. (The significance of the qualification 'or verblike element' will be discussed further in Section 5.6.7. For the time being, the distinction is not important.) It is generally true of English and indeed of every language in which the sentence, defined as a complete syntactic unit headed by a verb or verblike element, is a minimal complete non-elliptical expression. It is logically possible that, in some language, verb-headedness should be a criterion for sentencehood, but many stretches of any text or utterance should not be analysable in sentential terms. An example would be a language whose syntax permits both verb-headed sentences and complex expressions of the Monocategoric kind. The fact that no language has been reported as behaving like this shows that the pervasiveness of characteristic (i), with the nucleus-like position as broadly verbal, is an empirical finding, not a platitude.

There is a superficially powerful objection that needs to be rebutted. Many texts or discourses contain syntactic strings that, whether we call them sentences or not, do not contain anything verblike and are not parts of verb-headed sentences either. Here are some examples, of which (16) and (17) are Russian:

(14)    ALICE. What made that rustling noise?
        BILL. A snake.
(15)    Gosh! A helicopter!
(16)    Moj     brat —     student.
        my      brother    student
        'My brother is a student.'[24]
(17)    Moj     brat       bolen.
        my      brother    ill
        'My brother is ill.'

In the little dialogue at (14), Bill's reply to Alice is an NP and contains no verb. Does it not therefore show that English after all lacks characteristic (i)? But Bill's reply is elliptical, in the sense introduced in Chapter 2. That is, it is a sentence with parts left out, appearing in a context that shows clearly what the missing parts are. We can restore the missing parts from Alice's question, so as to produce *A snake made that rustling noise.* Crucially, this restored sentence does contain a verb—namely, *made.* So apparent exceptions involving ellipsis need not be regarded as genuine exceptions, because from every elliptical sentence one can reconstruct a complete sentence with an identifiable verb. The parasitic status of elliptical sentences is confirmed by the fact that it is easy to envisage an English text or dialogue where no sentence is elliptical (it might sound long-winded but it would still be recognizably English), but one cannot envisage an English text (a text in actual English, that is, not in Nominalized English) where all the sentences are elliptical.

The example at (15) is of a different kind. In Chapter 2 I imagined (15) being uttered in the middle of a conversation in which there had been no mention of helicopters. I suggested that it would be arbitrary to deny that it asserts something (namely, that a helicopter is present), even though it cannot be regarded as an elliptical sentence because there is no way of restoring the complete sentence of

---

[24] The dash in the Russian example is an orthographic convention in sentences without a copula. In speech, a short pause may occur in that position.

which it is an elliptical version. But if it is neither an elliptical nor a complete sentence it is not a sentence, so we seem again to have English evidence that does not fit characteristic (i). Example (15) is unusual in another way, however: it is an exclamation. Those who take a discontinuist view of language evolution are commonly happy to admit that some human utterances, such as involuntary cries of pain, delight, and suchlike, are indeed related to animal vocalizations (Burling 1993). Hybrids between human language and animal calls are cries that are involuntary but lexicalized, such as swear words. Evidence that swear-word use is somehow distinct from ordinary language use is the fact that swear words are spared by some forms of aphasia that affect ordinary vocabulary and that they behave as if they were non-linguistic cries in some language disorders such as Tourette syndrome. So, whether or not the discontinuist view is correct in general, there is evidence that ordinary linguistic units (words or phrases) can sometimes be uttered spontaneously outside the syntactic framework of modern human language, and it seems reasonable to put exclamations in this category. An exclamatory NP may in appropriate circumstances make an assertion, but that is not evidence that ordinary English syntax must allow for non-elliptical elements outside the framework of complete sentences.

Examples (16) and (17) are typical of sentences in many languages that, unlike English, do not insist on a copula (some form of *be* or its equivalent) in the absence of any other verbal element. This is not contrary to characteristic (i), however, because this characteristic refers to the presence not of a wordclass but of a position, and characteristic (ii) leads us to expect that words other than verbs may occupy this position—words that are relatively low in the syntactic or semantic counterpart of sonority mentioned in Asymmetry A' but that may nevertheless be higher in the scale than any neighbouring marginal word. Being low in the syntactic counterpart of sonority may be interpreted as not being a verb. I have not said what the semantic counterpart of sonority might be, and will continue to defer that issue until Section 5.6.7. For the time being, an analysis of (16) and (17) in terms of which *student* 'student' and *bolen* 'ill' occupy a nucleus-like position can be defended on two grounds. First, in tenses other than the present tense an overt copula appears:

(18)  Moj    brat     byl      studentom.[25]
      my     brother  was      student
(19)  Moj    brat     budet    bolen.
      my     brother  will-be  ill

It would be arbitrary to deny the existence of a nucleus-like position in (16) and (17) but admit it (with *byl* and *budet* as occupants) in (18) and (19). Secondly, the

---

[25] When there is an overt copula, as here, it is usual for a predicative noun to appear in the instrumental case (*studentom*) rather than the nominative (*student*) (Borras and Christian 1959: 10–12). That does not affect the point being made.

string *moj brat student* has two possible interpretations in Russian: one as in (16), and one as an appositional construction, corresponding to English *my brother the student*, as in (20):

(20)  Moj      brat       student    čital          knigu.
      my       brother    student    was-reading    book
      'My brother the student was reading a book.'

In this appositional interpretation *moj brat student* can also appear as an exclamation, just like *a helicopter* in (15):

(21)  Moj brat student!
      'My brother the student!'

Example (21) can be interpreted as making an assertion, just as (15) can: it means something like 'My brother the student is here, unexpectedly!' This is clearly a different assertion from what (16) would normally express. But the difference is no surprise if (16) is a sentence containing a nucleus-like position while (21) is not. So the two interpretations constitute evidence for two distinct syntactic analyses, and thus indirectly for an analysis of (16) that is consistent with characteristic (i).[26]

Characteristic (ii) is exhibited in any language where verbs or other occupants of the nucleus-like position are syntactically or morphologically distinct from the class or classes of words that typically occupy marginal positions, yet where nonverbs (or words that are clearly derived from nonverbs) can sometimes occupy this position too. Doing so may or may not involve acquiring morphological marks of verbhood. Instances where a purportedly nuclear nonverb does not acquire verbal morphology include the Russian examples (16) and (17), where *student* 'student' and *bolen* 'ill' remain morphologically a noun and an adjective respectively. Examples of nonverbs acquiring morphological marks of verbhood can be illustrated in English by the verbal counterparts of the nouns *father* and *shelf* and the adjectives *thin* and *fat*—namely, the verbs *father*, *shelve*, *thin*, and *fatten*, as in (22)–(25):

(22)  King George VI fathered two daughters.
(23)  The library staff shelved all the books.
(24)  The chef thinned the soup with stock.
(25)  The farmers fattened the livestock before selling them.

The past tense marker *-ed* shows that these all acquire verbal inflectional morphology. In addition, *shelve* and *fatten* exhibit verb-forming derivational

---

[26] Another syntactic analysis according to which (16) and (17) are consistent with characteristic (i) is an analysis where the nucleus-like position is occupied not by *student* and *bolen* but by a zero alternant of the copula that appears overtly in (18) and (19). I do not reject that analysis; but to resort too readily to zero constituents in the present discussion would risk begging the question. That is why I have suggested arguments for a nucleus-like position in (16) and (17) that do not depend on positing a zero copula.

processes—namely, the voicing of the final fricative (found also, for example, in the verbs *prove, wreathe,* and *house* [hauz]) and the suffixation of *-en* (found also in the verbs *shorten, stiffen,* and *redden*). To the extent that all languages resemble Russian and English in allowing words that are basically nonverbal to occupy the nuclear position, with or without acquiring verbal morphology, they exhibit characteristic (ii).

In syllable structure, just as a sound of relatively low sonority can occupy the nuclear position, so a sound of relatively high sonority can occupy a margin. This situation is illustrated by the glides [j] and [w] (the initial sounds of the English words *yes* and *wet*), which are routinely analysed as differing from the high vowels [i] and [u] only in their position in the syllable. That leads us to expect that, if the syllabic model is correct, words that are basically verbal should sometimes occupy margin-like positions. And that is correct also. Many verbs such as *sing, walk,* and *dance* have counterparts that are both syntactically and morphologically nominal, in the sense of being capable of plural inflection in English (*songs of the Auvergne, our walks in the forest, Saturday-night dances in the village hall*).

All languages also exhibit characteristic (v): no whole sentence can occupy the nucleus-like position in a larger sentence. This does not perhaps appear surprising. However, one can envisage a kind of syntax in which the replacement of a verb by a suitable sentence might add emphasis, for example, so that (26) and (27) would be emphatic alternatives to (22) and (23):

(26)    King George VI [he had two children] two daughters.
(27)    The library staff [everyone tidied the heaps of stuff away] all the books.

The nonexistence of such sentences is correctly predicted by Asymmetry C′.

With regard to characteristic (vi) the picture is different. In all languages sentences are found embedded in margin-like positions, as in (28) and (29):

(28)    [That he had two children] surprised us all.
(29)    I hope [that everyone tidied the heaps of stuff away].

There is thus one major mismatch between modern syntax and what the syllabic model predicts. This may seem a prima-facie embarrassment for the model, albeit mitigated by the fact that Spatiotemporal and Monocategoric comply with it no better in this respect. But I will defer further discussion of this mismatch until Section 5.6.10, after we have explored in detail how to interpret the notions 'margin-like' and 'onset-like' that appear in characteristics (iii) and (iv).

### 5.6.6. *Margin-like Positions in Syntax*

In Section 5.6.3 I mentioned the broad resemblance between the traditional representation of syllable structure in (7) and the syntactic structure of many

English sentences, as illustrated with Sapir's *The farmer killed the duckling* at (10). If we take this resemblance at face value, we will equate the onset-like position with the syntactic subject and the coda-like position with the object. As I noted earlier, however, this equation seems vitiated by the fact that a large proportion of the world's languages are verb-final (SOV) and a smaller though still significant proportion are traditionally analysed as verb-initial (VSO). A second apparent difficulty is that the notion 'subject' is notoriously difficult to define satisfactorily in a cross-linguistic fashion, and some linguists argue that there are languages in which a privileged grammatical status should be assigned not to the subject but to the **topic** (very roughly, an NP designating something or someone whose identity is known to both speaker and hearer) (Li and Thompson 1976; Comrie 1989).[27] A third and very obvious apparent difficulty is that, even in languages where identification of subjects is uncontroversial, there are many sentences which consist of more than just a subject NP, a verb, and an object NP. However, these difficulties diminish when the implications of the syllabic model are examined more closely.

Let us put aside the superficial parallel between the phonological and syntactic structures at (7) and (10) and consider how onset-like privileges, as specified in characteristic (iv), might in principle manifest themselves in syntax. The following options are possible:

(*a*)   All margin-like material (i.e. everything nonverbal) appears before the verb (mimicking onset maximization in syllable structure), so that the verb is final in the sentence.

(*b*)   Only one syntactic constituent appears before the verb, so that the verb is the second constituent of the sentence with everything else following it (mimicking the fact that onset material is 'weightless' for the purpose of distinguishing between heavy and light syllables), but there is no special constraint on what the preverbal constituent should be.

(*c*)   The constituent that appears immediately before the verb belongs obligatorily to a particular syntactic category or has a particular syntactic function.

(*d*)   One particular argument of the verb (one of the NPs designating a participant in the action or state indicated by the verb) has a special syntactic status (such as 'subject') that differentiates it from all the other arguments collectively.

These options differ in how the privilege is accorded, mimicking variously the syllable onset's initial position, its prenuclear position, the contrast between its near-obligatoriness and the coda's optionality, and the contrast between how it and the coda relate to the nucleus. Some of the options are logically compatible;

---

[27]   For further discussion of the topic/comment distinction, see Section 4.4.4.

for example, it is logically possible for a language to have both a 'verb-second' requirement (option (*b*)) and NPs with the special status of subjects (option (*d*)). This compatibility will turn out to be significant for the incidence of various word-order types.

It is worth contrasting what the implications would be if codas rather than onsets were privileged in syllable structure. Options (*a*), (*b*), and (*c*) would be replaced by options (*a'*), (*b'*), and (*c'*):

(*a'*)   All margin-like material (i.e. everything nonverbal) appears after the verb, so that the verb is initial in the sentence.

(*b'*)   Only one syntactic constituent appears after the verb, so that the verb is the second-to-last constituent of the sentence with everything else preceding it, but there is no special constraint on what the postverbal constituent should be.

(*c'*)   The constituent that appears immediately after the verb belongs obligatorily to a particular syntactic category or has a particular syntactic function.

What evidence is there that any of options (*a*)–(*c*) are chosen in actual languages, and that options (*a'*)–(*c'*) are avoided?

Consistent with option (*a*) is the fact that, as already mentioned, a high proportion of the world's languages prefer or require that the verb should be final in the sentence. Examples are Turkish, Japanese, and (in subordinate clauses) German. Notice that option (*a*) imposes no limit on the number of constituents that may precede the verb. This is quite appropriate from the point of view of mimicking the syllable. A nucleus usually contains just one vowel, or two in the case of diphthongs or so-called long vowels; on the other hand, a margin may contain a cluster of more than two consonants, as in English *sprints*, or (admittedly an extreme case) Georgian [prts'kvna] 'to peel', which has an onset cluster of six (Laver 1994: 34).[28] So the syllable model for syntax leads us to expect that margin-like positions should often contain not single words[p] but clusters, and nothing in the model imposes an expectation that such a cluster should constitute a single phrase.

The existence of verb-initial languages (the minority with preferred VSO order) is consistent with option (*a'*), and so is superficially problematic for the syllabic model. But, quite apart from the relative infrequency of these languages, their

---

[28] The fact that the relative sonorous liquid [r] intervenes between the obstruents [p] and [ts'] shows that there are two peaks of sonority in this word, on [r] and [a]. It might therefore be expected to contain two syllables, not one. But the behaviour of Georgian native speakers (for example, when counting syllables for the purpose of versification) shows clearly that it is monosyllabic. It must be acknowledged as another illustration, alongside English *sprints*, that sonority gradients from nuclei to margins are not always smooth. It is probably not an accident that the consonant [r] on which the anomalous sonority peak occurs is coronal, since coronals have a propensity to 'break the rules' (Paradis 1991).

verb-initial character is not a mirror image of the verb-final character of SOV languages. In the languages that are most often used to illustrate the VSO pattern, various factors conspire to dilute their verb-initial character. First, no language (so far as I know) is so consistently verb-initial as some are consistently verb-final; all 'VSO' languages seem to tolerate sentences in which a nonverbal element is fronted, for purposes of emphasis or topicalization. Secondly, many of the sentences that are often cited as verb-initial in fact have an onset-like position occupied by a grammatical function word such as a particle indicating aspect or tense, as in Maori at (30) (Head 1989) and Welsh at (31) (Rhys Jones 1977):

(30)  (*a*)  Kua          kōrero   ngā wāhine.
              perfective   speak    the women
              'The women have spoken.'

      (*b*)  I            kōrero   ngā wāhine.
              past         speak    the women
              'The women spoke.'

      (*c*)  E            kōrero   ana          ngā wāhine.
              progressive  speak                 the women
              'The women are speaking.'

(31)         Fe           fytodd   Tom          frecwast da.
              past         eat      Tom          breakfast good
              'Tom ate a good breakfast.'

One might interpret these as sentences in which onset-like privilege is given to the initial particle, pushing the verb to second position, in accordance with option (*b*), discussed below. Thirdly, the initial 'verbal' element may be an auxiliary, separated from the lexical verb by an NP that functions as subject and that is therefore privileged in relation to the lexical verb in accordance with option (*c*), as in Welsh again (Rhys Jones 1977):

(32)  (*a*)  Mae          Tom  yn darllen  llyfr.
              be-present   Tom  reading     book
              'Tom is reading a book.' or: 'Tom reads a book.'

      (*b*)  Roedd        Tom  yn darllen  llyfr.
              be-past      Tom  reading     book
              'Tom was reading a book.'

But in any case, for a VSO language to manifest characteristic (iv), option (*d*) is always available. The implications of this will be considered in connection with option (*d*) later.

I have not so far mentioned the view that verbs can be in initial position only as a result of a syntactic movement—a raising of the verb into an empty syntactic position (McCloskey 1996 and references there). Such analyses have been proposed for reasons quite independent of the syllabic model for syntactic evolution.

In effect, they treat the initial position of verbs or auxiliaries in declarative sentences in VSO languages as derived, much like the initial position of auxiliaries in 'yes/no' questions in English—a phenomenon that in Section 5.6.10 below I relegate to a later stage of syntactic evolution. For me to set too much store by such an analysis to explain VSO order might seem like a too eager resort to a convenient dodge for explaining away uncomfortable data. Nevertheless, if the analysis can be justified on independent grounds, it has the significant consequence that all modern VSO languages can be regarded as irrelevant for the purpose of testing the predictions of the syllabic model.

Consistent with option (*b*) is the so-called **verb-second** phenomenon observed in several Germanic languages and much discussed by syntactic theorists (Haider and Prinzhorn 1986). This is the requirement in many syntactic contexts that the verb (or a verbal element such as an auxiliary) should be the second constituent of the sentence. The following examples illustrate this phenomenon in German:

33) Wilhelm ist gestern abend mit seiner Mutter zum Bahnhof
     William is yesterday evening with his mother to the railway station
     gegangen.
     gone
     'William went to the railway station with his mother yesterday evening.'

(34) Gestern abend ist Wilhelm mit seiner Mutter zum Bahnhof gegangen.

(35) Mit seiner Mutter ist Wilhelm gestern abend zum Bahnhof gegangen.

(36) Zum Bahnhof ist Wilhelm gestern abend mit seiner Mutter gegangen.

These examples differ in respect of emphasis or focus, but apart from that the gloss provided for (33) applies equally to them all. In all of them, too, the verbal auxiliary *ist* is the second constituent. What precedes *ist* is always a phrase, but the kind of phrase does not matter: it may be nominal (*Wilhelm*), adverbial (*gestern abend*), or prepositional (*mit seiner Mutter, zum Bahnhof*). Apart from *ist*, there is a second verbal element in (33)–(36): the participle *gegangen* 'gone'. A striking fact about this participle in the context of the present discussion is that it is always final. So it is fair to say that, in this kind of sentence, German uses both option (*a*) and option (*b*) simultaneously as ways of privileging an onset-like element. This need not surprise us. What German shows (in terms of the syllabic model) is both that more than one syntactic homologue of onset-privileging became established in the human biological endowment for syntax, and that more than one of these homologues can manifest itself in a single language. (In Section 5.6.7 I will discuss further the significance of the distinction in German and many other languages between two kinds of verbal element—namely, auxiliaries and lexical verbs.)

By contrast with option (*b*), option (*b′*) seems never to be chosen. The asymmetry between second position and second-to-last position that the privileging of onsets leads us to expect seems to be absolutely general. In this respect the syntactic facts reflect syllable-based predictions exactly.

Option (*c*) is manifested by Hungarian. The position immediately before the verb stem is reserved for the **focus**—that is, the central component of the comment that the sentence expresses about its topic. This allows for contrasts like the following (where the verbform *elfutott* 'ran away' contains a prefix *el* 'away' that may be separated from the verb stem, and where focus is indicated by italic type) (Abondolo 1987):

(37)　A pék　　*el*futott.
　　　 the baker　*away*-ran
　　　 'The baker ran away.'
(38)　*A pék*　 futott el.
　　　 *the baker*　ran away
　　　 'It was the baker who ran away'
(39)　El　　 *a pék*　　 futott.
　　　 away　*the baker*　ran
　　　 'As for running away, it was the baker who did it.'

The negative particle *nem* 'not' and constituents containing it, when present, are normally assigned to the focus position:

(40)　A pék *nem* futott el.
　　　 'The baker didn't run away.'
(41)　*Nem a pék* futott el
　　　 'It wasn't the baker who ran away.'
(42)　A pék *nem* el futott, hanem *be*futott.
　　　 'The baker didn't run *away*, he ran *in*.'

By contrast, option (*c'*), which accords a consistent special status to the position immediately following the verb, is not chosen by any language, so far as I know. At first sight it may seem to be exemplified by languages in which a verb must be immediately followed by its direct object (its complement, in the terminology of X-bar theory). This is generally the case in English, so that *\*John crashed yesterday his car* and *\*The Queen welcomed at the airport the President* are not natural alternatives for *John crashed his car yesterday* and *The Queen welcomed the President at the airport*. But the special status of the direct object is not consistent in the relevant sense, because there are verbs without direct objects. I will elaborate on this observation when discussing option (*d*).

Option (*d*) is manifested in any language where a subject or topic NP is distinguished syntactically from the verb's other arguments. This is the option that in a sense deviates furthest from the syllabic model, since the form of privilege that it accords to an onset-like constituent does not require this constituent to precede the verb. By the same token, the deviation is lessened if the subject or topic does precede the verb. It would therefore not be surprising if we found languages in which the order subject-before-verb is chosen, perhaps simultaneously with option (*c*), so as to place the subject not merely before but immediately before the verb. Sentence structure in such languages would conform to more than one interpretation of what it means to 'privilege onsets' in syntax. And indeed languages in which subjects usually precede verbs are the vast majority. The only exceptions are OVS and VOS languages, which are very rare, and VSO languages, which (as we have seen) are relatively uncommon. And the compatibility of option (*d*) with the other options suggests why this should be so: verb-before-subject languages are ones where compliance with characteristic (iv) is less thoroughgoing or less obvious than it might be.

Because the kind of privilege that an NP derives through option (*d*) has its roots in syllable structure, there is no reason to expect it to have any consistent semantic, pragmatic, or cognitive rationale. And indeed we find none. Although in many languages one NP in every sentence seems to stand out from the others in a way that encourages us to label it 'subject', reliable universal criteria for subjecthood are notoriously lacking (Li 1976). If the basis of syntax is cognitive, or even if it springs from an entirely autonomous Chomskyan language organ, this is a paradox. But if, as the syllabic model claims, the basis for the existence of subjects resides ultimately in the physiology of the vocal tract, there is no reason to expect that this privileged element should correlate consistently with anything non-phonological. The second of the apparent difficulties mentioned at the start of this section therefore disappears. Subjects are syntactically and semantically messy because their ultimate motivation does not lie in syntax or semantics at all; rather, they are leftovers from syntax's phonological substrate.

What has option (*d*) got to do with the fact that there are verbs without direct objects? The point is that there is an asymmetry between objects and subjects that can be seen as a further parallel between syntax and syllable structure. I mentioned earlier that in some languages a syllabic onset is obligatory. In German, for example, a glottal stop provides a default filler for any onset position that would otherwise be empty. There are also languages where in most contexts a subject must be provided for every verb, even if it contributes nothing semantically. Contrast the English sentences at (43*a*) and (44*a*) with their Italian counterparts at (43*b*) and (44*b*):

(43)  (*a*)  It was raining.
      (*b*)  Pioveva.
(44)  (*a*)  It's true that they've left.
      (*b*)  È      vero    che     sono    partite.
             is     true    that    have    left

English verbs need an overt subject whereas Italian verbs do not, so where nothing else is available English resorts to a dummy subject *it* (or in some contexts *there*, as in *There seems to be a power cut*). But there are no languages that insist on dummy objects. These would be languages in which, from a purely syntactic point of view, there are no intransitive or objectless verbs. In a version of English with dummy objects rather than dummy subjects we would encounter sentences such as (45) and (46) instead of (43a) and (44a):

(45)   Was raining it.
(46)   Is true that they've left it.

If we reject the syllabic model for syntactic evolution, there is no obvious reason apart from historical accident why this subject–object asymmetry should exist. But dummy subjects are just what we will expect to find in a language where characteristic (iv) manifests itself through simultaneous choice of options (c) and (d), with the 'special syntactic function' for the purpose of option (c) being the subject function. At the same time, the syllabic model suggests no reason to expect dummy objects, so, if the model is correct, their absence is no surprise.

So far we have been considering characteristic (iv), which is concerned with what distinguishes onset-like behaviour in sentence structure. It is time to turn to characteristic (iii), which is concerned with what all non-nuclear material has in common, whether onset-like or not. In syllables, the sounds that can appear in the coda (if any) are of the same broad class as those that can appear in the onset—namely, consonants—and the coda repertoire is nearly always a subset of the onset repertoire. (Instances like the velar nasal or *ng* sound in English, which can appear in codas but not onsets, are rare.) In syntax, similarly, there is no systematic disjunction between material that is privileged in onset-like fashion (whichever option is chosen) and material that is not so privileged. For example, there is no language in which NPs can appear solely in non-subject functions, being replaced in the subject function by phrases of some other kind whose head words are derivationally related to nouns, perhaps, but whose syntactic characteristics and those of the phrases they head are significantly different from those of nouns and NPs respectively—for example, by being head-final while ordinary NPs are head-initial. That is not a particularly far-fetched possibility. One can easily envisage a kind of language in which onset-like privilege is based on option (b) (i.e. verbs are in second position), and the head of any phrase is required to be at whichever end of the phrase is closest to the verb. For the English example at (47), glosses available in such a language might include the three illustrated in (48), where the bracketing draws attention to their constituent structure:

(47)        My brother parked your old bicycle in Bill's garage.
(48)   (a)   [my brother] parked [[bicycle old] your] [in [garage Bill's]]
       (b)   [your [old bicycle]] parked [brother my] [in [garage Bill's]]
       (c)   [[Bill's garage] in] parked [brother my] [[bicycle old] your]

To grammatically aware speakers of such a language it would no doubt seem quite natural that heads of phrases should be situated as close to the verb (the head of the sentence) as phrasal integrity allows. Indeed, if all languages had this kind of mirror-image structure, it would scarcely occur to us that they might be otherwise. So the fact that no language is like this calls for an explanation, if possible. And characteristic (iii) supplies one, inasmuch as this kind of fundamental contrast between preverbal and postverbal syntax would violate it.[29]

### 5.6.7. *Verbs, Auxiliaries, and the Syllabic Model*

In Section 5.6.5 I suggested that the sentential counterparts of syllabic nuclei were verbs or verblike elements. For the purpose of the argument there, which focused on form or structure rather than content, it was necessary to establish only that such counterparts existed. I did not discuss the semantic implications of the fact that it is verbs—words that typically denote predicates rather than arguments—that occupy the nucleus-like position, rather than, say, nouns. But in the light of the discussion in Sections 4.4.1 and 4.4.2, this may seem like a significant omission. Even if predicate–argument structure does not explain the sentence/NP distinction, something needs to be said about the way in which predicates and arguments are mapped onto the sentential positions that the syllabic model provides. This is especially so since the mapping follows a consistent pattern: predicates occupy the nucleus-like or verbal position and arguments appear elsewhere.

Consider a piece of semantic content formed by combining a predicate *kick* with an agent *boy* and a patient *ball*. The distinction between objects and actions or states is not clear-cut (a point that was discussed in Section 4.4.3).[30] Even so, for reasons such as those of Pinker and Bloom cited in Section 4.4.1, some such distinction is cognitively useful, and it is at least sufficiently clear-cut for no one to quibble about classifying boys and balls as objects and kicking as an action. When this semantic content is to be expressed in terms of a kind of syntax with the syllable-derived characteristics described in Chapter 3, is there any reason why *kick* rather than *boy* or *ball* should gravitate towards the nucleus-like position?

The answer is yes. With the action *kick* in nucleus-like position, expressed syntactically by a verb, there is room to accommodate both its arguments *boy* and *ball* in marginal positions in the same clause (with one or both of them receiving onset-like privilege through one of the options described in Section 5.6.6). On the other hand, if one of the arguments (let's say, *boy*) is placed in nuclear position, then fitting *kick* and *ball* around it involves greater deviation from the syllabic model, as I will show.

---

[29] It may seem as if this mirror-image syntax parallels the sequencing of marginal material within the syllable on the basis of sonority. But the parallel is only superficial. In syllables, even in languages that permit codas, an onset cluster may lack a mirror image in the coda (for example, in British English Received Pronunciation there are no coda clusters [rC] corresponding to onset [Cr]) and vice versa (for example, in all varieties of English there is no onset cluster [pm] corresponding to coda [mp]). Moreover, the ordering *bicycle old . . . garage* in (48a), with an adjective sandwiched postverbally between two nouns, shows that there is in this hypothetical language no consistent 'sonority' relationship between wordclasses like that between (say) liquids and stops.

[30] Throughout this section, 'object' means 'physical object' rather than 'grammatical object (direct or indirect)'.

Let us assume first that the semantic content $boy_{Agent}$ $ball_{Patient}$ $kick_{Predicate}$ is still to be expressed in a single sentence. With *boy* as nucleus, the repertoire of elements from which margin-like items can be drawn will have to be varied enough to encompass both *ball* (designating an object) and *kick* (an action)—in effect, a repertoire so varied as to include the whole spectrum of semantic content from the object end to the action-or-state end. But in that case sentence structure fails to reflect a salient characteristic of syllable structure: the distinction between elements that typically occur in nuclei (vowels) and ones that typically occur in margins (consonants). Certainly, as we observed in Section 5.6.2, typically nuclear material, such as the high vowels [i] and [u], can sometimes appear in margins as [j] and [w], and typically marginal material, such as liquids and nasals (e.g. [r, l, n, m]), can sometimes appear in nuclei; but this never compromises the relatively high sonority of nuclei *vis-à-vis* margins. Even in Imdlawn Tashlhiyt Berber, with its generous tolerance for consonantal nuclei, a sequence such as [ir] can be syllabified in only one way, with the more sonorous [i] as nucleus and the less sonorous [r] as margin (Prince and Smolensky 1993). Similarly, in English, typically verbal content can sometimes be expressed in nominal form (e.g. *song*, *dance*, *walk*) and typically nominal or adjectival content can sometimes be expressed verbally (e.g. *father*, *shelve*). Even when this happens, however, something akin to the normal 'sonority gradient' is maintained, so that we do not find an NP expressing an action or state as an argument of a verb designating a physical object. Thus, if in any language sentences such as *The carpenter shelved a building* and *The boy balled the kick* are interpretable at all, it is certainly not as paraphrases of *The carpenter built some shelves* and *The boy kicked the ball.*

From these considerations it emerges that the most plausible semantic equivalent of the sonority hierarchy is an object–action hierarchy, with action lying at the high end. Notice that this conclusion does not depend on any new assumptions. It is an automatic corollary of the syllabic model, when combined with Pinker and Bloom's observations about the origin of predicate–argument structure. If humans represent events mentally in terms of stable objects and transient actions or states, then many events will be represented semantically as involving a single predicate with more than one argument. That being so, all that is required to ensure that the single predicate will gravitate towards the nucleus and its arguments towards the margins is the syllable-derived requirement that the material that occupies margin-like positions should be both relatively homogeneous and relatively distinct from what occupies the nucleus-like position.

The classification of experience in terms of objects and actions (or in terms of a spectrum with these as endpoints) may be largely independent of syntax-as-it-is (though with the proviso that it may be syntax that imposes a one-dimensional spectrum in preference to a multidimensional space, as argued in Section 4.4.3). The noun/verb dichotomy is not independent of syntax, however. Rather, it arises from a filtering of the object–action spectrum (or the thing–event space) through a kind of syntactic structure that emulates the nucleus–margin asymmetry within syllables.

There is a second conceivable way in which the syllabic model might be reconciled with nuclear status for *boy*. This would be to invert the correlation between sonority and the action–object hierarchy so as to put objects, not actions, at the high end. Then not only *boy* but also *ball* would have to occupy a nucleus-like position. A consistent contrast between typical occupants of margin-like and nucleus-like positions would thereby be achieved. But since the syllabic model allows room for only one nucleus-like position per sentence, *boy*$_{\text{Agent}}$ *ball*$_{\text{Patient}}$ *kick*$_{\text{Predicate}}$ could be expressed only by a concatenation of two sentences—something like *boy kick, kick ball*. Working out the details of how such a syntax might work is superfluous, however, because the failure of syntax-as-it-is to develop in that direction is not surprising. Event-representations with multiple arguments being so common, it is natural that a single-clause syntactic representation for them would be preferred over a multiple-clause representation. So, since a single-clause representation is available if one locates predicates rather than arguments at the nucleus-like position (as we do), it is natural that the way of relating predicate–argument structure to syllable-derived sentence structure should be the one actually chosen.

There is, therefore, nothing arbitrary, in terms of the syllabic model, about the fact that it is actions or states that are typically expressed in the nucleus-like position while objects are typically expressed in the margin-like positions. In terms of this model, that is how the syntactically defined wordclasses 'verbs' and 'nouns' evolved semantically as 'doing-words' and 'thing-words' respectively. But in Section 5.6.5 I talked not only of verbs but also of 'verblike elements', and the time has come to explain that qualification. The account offered here associates verbs with auxiliaries in such a way as to make sense of similarities in their syntactic behaviour—similarities that, in Pinker and Bloom's account, appear accidental.

Syllables as such are meaningless, whereas sentences are meaningful. This has somewhat awkward implications for a kind of syntax that requires a nucleus-like position in every sentence to be filled by a word drawn from a special class 'verb', distinct from the classes that typically figure in margin-like positions. If sentences are to be sufficiently versatile to allow us to say whatever we like, the specialness of this class cannot be such as to impose too great semantic constraints on its members. To the extent that verbs answer to the very general characterization of denoting actions or states, semantic specialness is certainly kept to a minimum and versatility promoted. But there are many sentences in whose meaning one is hard pressed to find anything even so vague as an action or a state, such as *Two and two make four* or *Tomorrow is Wednesday*. What a syllable-derived syntax really needs in order to ensure maximum semantic versatility, one may think, is for nucleus-like positions to be filled (or at least fillable) by a class of items that are so bleached of lexical content that, for any predicate–argument structure whatever, at least one of them will be appropriate. These items, if they exist, will be verblike syntactically, in that material with onset-like privileges will be positioned in relation to them in the same way as it is positioned in relation to verbs, as described in Section 5.6.6. Furthermore, just as it is possible for onset-like privileges to be exercised in a sentence in more than one way (as, for example, in a language that has both syntactic subjects and a second-position requirement for verbs), so it should be possible for the syllabic nucleus to be emulated in two different ways in the same sentence, once by a verb with lexical content and once by a member of the lexically empty verblike class. These expectations about suitable occupants for the nuclear position arise naturally from the syllabic model. Are they fulfilled, then? Do languages generally show any evidence of a class of items of this lexically empty verblike kind?

The answer is yes. The characteristics just outlined fit well the class of auxiliaries as described by Steele *et al.* (1981), Pinker and Bloom (1990), and Pinker (1994). The positions that auxiliaries occupy correspond exactly to the positions that verbs are predicted to occupy as a consequence of the onset-privileging options described in Section 5.6.6—with just the same proviso about sentence-initial position, not predicted by the syllabic model but available in some languages to auxiliaries as well as to verbs. (In the four languages Luiseño, Lummi, Japanese, and Egyptian Colloquial Arabic examined by Steele *et al.* (1981), only Egyptian Arabic allows sentence-initial auxiliaries.) Moreover, the expectation that some sentences might have two nucleus-like positions, one occupied by a verb and one by an auxiliary, is instantiated in German (33)–(36) above. Here the lexical verb *gegangen* is at the end, implying option (*a*) for privileging onset-like material, while the auxiliary *ist* is in second position, implying option (*b*).

This account of why languages have auxiliaries with the characteristics noted by Steele *et al.* (1981) seems superior to that of Pinker and Bloom in two respects: it accounts for the parallels between their behaviour and that of lexical verbs, and it avoids assigning to auxiliaries a fundamental role in propositional structure that on close examination turns out to be dubious. It may be that, if Pinker and Bloom were to address the verb-auxiliary parallels explicitly, they could produce convincing reasons for them quite independent of the syllabic model. It is hard to see what those reasons might be, however, because the reason that they suggest for the sentential positions favoured by auxiliaries—namely, that they 'convey relations that have logical scope over the entire proposition' (1990: 713)—is inapplicable to lexical verbs.

Relations with alleged propositional scope include 'truth value, modality and illocutionary force'. Pinker later extends the list to include tense, and indeed, as we have seen, gives pride of place to tense in 'pin[ning] down to temporal co-ordinates' the concept that a tenseless proposition expresses (1994: 117). But we noted in Chapter 4 both that tense fails to discriminate between sentences and NPs and that many more factors than tense (or 'temporal coordinates') are important in pinning down either a sentence or an NP to something in the world that it is meant to correspond to. This shows that the semantic content of the auxiliary constituent is too narrow for the task that Pinker ascribes to it. We are entitled to ask, for example, why auxiliaries never express location as well as time, since pinning a proposition down involves pinning it down in space too. In fact, if the pinning-down task is grammatically as important as Pinker claims, it is surprising that syntax has not evolved in the direction of Spatiotemporal, as described in Chapter 2, rather than in the direction of syntax-as-it-is.

The range of semantic content typically expressed by auxiliaries is also too wide for Pinker's purpose, in that it includes elements that certainly do not 'have scope over the entire proposition'. Consider (49) and (50):

(49)    Eggs seem to disappear from Lucy's fridge quite quickly. She must eat two eggs every day.
(50)    The doctor has put Lucy on a special diet. She must eat two eggs every day.

The word *must* is traditionally classified as a modal auxiliary. In contemporary mainstream syntactic theory it will be analysed as incorporating a tense element (present) with which is combined a modal element MUST. But there is a crucial semantic difference between the tense element and the modal element. The tense element can plausibly be regarded as having scope over the whole second sentence in both (49) and (50). But one cannot say the same of MUST. In (49), where the second sentence can be paraphrased as 'It must be the case that Lucy eats two eggs . . .', it is plausible enough to analyse MUST as having sentential scope: 'MUST [Lucy eat two eggs . . .]'. But in (50), where an appropriate paraphrase is 'Lucy is obliged to eat two eggs . . .', MUST has scope only over the verb phrase *eat two eggs every day*. To analyse (50) as expressing the semantic structure 'MUST [Lucy eat two eggs . . .]' would be as arbitrary and unjustified as to analyse it as expressing the structure 'EGGS [Lucy must eat two every day]'.

The difference between the two instances of *must* has long been familiar to philosophers and linguists, who distinguish between **epistemic** and **deontic** uses of modals: *must* is epistemic in (49) but deontic in (50). A similar distinction applies to uses of *may*, *can*, and other modals, not only in English but in other languages. What matters here is that, despite their differences in scope, they are identical in their syntactic location. Therefore one cannot explain the auxiliary status of the epistemic *must* in terms of its sentential scope unless one has some plausible story about why the deontic *must*, without sentential scope, is an auxiliary too. Conceivably such a story might take the form of reasons why epistemic uses should be regarded as primary. But that would seem hard to square with evidence from language change, to the effect that expressions that were once exclusively deontic in character acquire epistemic uses, but not vice versa (Bybee *et al.* 1994).

Nor are modals the only items typically located among auxiliaries that have less than sentential scope. Negation, which Pinker (1994: 117) cites as typically sentential, in fact has a range of possible scopes, rather as modals have. Even a seemingly straightforward negative sentence such as (51) has a range of readings, of which (52) is just a selection, from among which the appropriate reading is determined by stress, intonation, and context:

(51)    Peter hasn't lost his bicycle.
(52)  (*a*)    NOT [Peter has lost his bicycle] ('. . .; I don't know where you got that idea from!')
  (*b*)    Peter [NOT [has lost his bicycle]] ('. . .; he just decided to walk for a change.')
  (*c*)    Peter has [NOT [lost his bicycle]] ('. . ., but he's certainly forgotten where he put his skateboard.')
  (*d*)    Peter has lost [NOT [his bicycle]] ('. . ., but his skateboard.')
  (*e*)    Peter [NOT [has]] lost his bicycle ('. . ., but he will soon if he isn't careful.')
  (*f*)    [NOT [Peter]] has lost his bicycle ('. . ., Bill has.')
  (*g*)    Peter has lost [NOT [his]] bicycle ('. . ., he's lost Bill's.')

In (52*a*) the scope of -*n't* is indeed the whole sentence, but in (52*b*–*g*) it is not. This illustrates the strong propensity in English for *not* to gravitate to the auxiliary, even when its scope is much less than the whole sentence. (Contrast this with the Hungarian pattern, illustrated at (40)–(42), where *nem* 'not' immediately precedes whatever constituent it negates.) This propensity is another embarrassment for any theory of auxiliaries that sees them as primarily sentential in scope. It also perhaps helps to explain why philosophers such as Strawson are so insistent that, in a fundamental sense, only 'predicate-terms', not 'subject-terms', are negatable (as we noted in Chapter 3).

I do not pretend that a syllable-based account of auxiliaries accounts for every feature of their behaviour. But if one sees them as an answer to the problem of providing nucleus-like material for any sentence, whatever its content, then three of their semantic characteristics fall into place neatly. First, their meanings are extremely general in the sense that they can be readily combined with almost any lexical content. Secondly, they are more like semantically bleached verbs than semantically bleached nouns. For just the same reason that verbal content typically lies far from the object end of the spectrum between objects and actions-or-states, so auxiliaries stand for very general non-objects (including negation) rather than for very general objects (such as 'thing'). Thirdly, because actions and states are more transient than objects, it is natural that pinning action-and-state expressions (verbs) down to particular actions and states in the world should rely relatively heavily on mention of time, while the corresponding task for object expressions (nouns) should rely less on time and more on place. It is, therefore, not surprising that some auxiliaries, being verblike, should relate to time but none should relate to place. The widespread appearance of tense among auxiliaries and among categories expressed inflectionally on verbs is understandable without any need to attribute to it a unique role in 'pinning down propositions'.

It is worth remembering at this point how the syllabic model for sentence structure was originally motivated. It was presented as an expectation about how syntax should evolve, at a stage in language evolution where a need for some kind of syntax became pressing. Evidence considered in previous sections suggests that this expectation is largely fulfilled. But that evidence did not include detailed facts about auxiliaries in contemporary languages. So the fact that the syllabic model succeeds as well as it does in accounting for both the existence and the characteristics of auxiliaries as a category is a welcome bonus, and adds significant weight to its case.

### 5.6.8. *Verbs and Direct Objects*

In Section 5.6.2 I mentioned that, according to the dominant current view, the nucleus and the coda of a syllable form a constituent called the rhyme, as represented in (7). However, I have not so far suggested any sentential counterpart to the rhyme. This is so that my catalogue of syllable-derived expectations shall reflect aspects of syllable structure that are as uncontroversial as possible. I have talked of an asymmetry between the onset and the coda, and of how this asymmetry might manifest itself in syntax, but I have not assumed that the nucleus forms a unit with either the onset or the coda.

That decision has an air of proper caution, but one could argue that it makes the task of testing the syllabic model easier than it should be. Let us assume that the majority opinion is correct, and that the rhyme is a genuine constituent of syllable structure. In that case the model leads us to expect, in most if not all languages, some sentential counterpart not only of the various asymmetries discussed in earlier sections but also of the rhyme as a constituent. What might this constituent look like?

I have suggested that there is more than one way in which the onset-coda asymmetry might be mimicked syntactically. Similarly, there is more than one way in which syntax might be expected to mimic the nucleus–coda bond. One way would be for the nucleus-like element (a verb or auxiliary) to form a constituent with all the marginal material that follows it. Another would be for the nucleus-like element to have a specially close bond with an adjacent constituent, preferably an immediately following one. Are either of these expectations fulfilled?

A verb-initial or auxiliary-initial constituent consisting of everything except the onset-like material is arguably just what we find in many SVO languages, such as English. These are languages in which there is not only SVO order but also evidence for a major syntactic break between an NP functioning as subject (or topic) and a verb phrase (VP) functioning as predicate (or comment). For English, this structure is illustrated at (10), reproduced here for convenience:

(10)

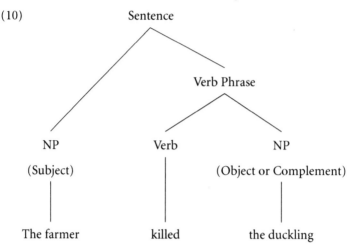

However, it is the second kind of mimicry that is more immediately pertinent, because it is a conceivable evolutionary basis for the tendency for **Verb–Object Bonding**. As evidence for this tendency, Tomlin (1986) adduces a range of phenomena in various languages:

- the incorporation of object nouns into verbs, so that, for example, a verb-form analogous to *fishcatch* will mean 'catch fish';
- the inseparability of verbs from their object NPs;
- the impossibility of moving an object NP away from its verb in question-formation or topicalization, for example;
- the frequency of idiomatic expressions consisting of a verb and an object NP, and the rarity of ones consisting of a verb and a subject NP;
- the widespread occurrence of verbs with **cognate objects**, i.e. objects that essentially repeat the semantic content of the verb (*sing a song, die a (glorious) death, dream a dream*);
- the creation of new verbs by borrowing a word from another language and treating it as the object of an indigenous verb with a very general meaning such as 'do' (e.g. Turkish *telefon etmek* 'to telephone', literally 'telephone do');
- phonological fusion of the object NP with the verb.

What is important to us about Verb–Object Bonding is its cognitive grounding—or rather the lack of it. As we saw in Chapter 4, Tomlin seeks cognitive grounding for word-order principles, and tries to derive his Theme-First Principle from attention-focusing; but for Verb–Object Bonding he frankly admits that he can see no cognitive basis (1986: 74, 134). The lack of any such basis is no surprise in terms of the syllabic model, however. Verb–Object Bonding may be just another example of something that happens in syntax for reasons that have to do fundamentally not with semantics, pragmatics, or independent syntactic factors but with syllable structure.

This is not to say that, in any given language, Verb–Object Bonding must always lack an identifiable function. For example, in languages that allow but do not require the incorporation of objects into verbs, the contrast is often exploited as an indication of definiteness: *fishcatch* 'catch a fish' versus *catch fish* (with unincorporated object) 'catch the (previously mentioned) fish'. But the syllabic model encourages us to expect no general function common to all instances of Verb–Object Bonding, and indeed no general function apears to exist. In this respect, the behaviour and status of 'objects' in syntax resembles that of 'subjects'.

### 5.6.9. Topicalization and Cognitive Grammar: Some Syllable-Derived Implications

In Sections 4.4.3 and 4.4.4, I suggested that neither the topic/comment distinction nor the cognitive partitioning of experience invoked by Langacker and his colleagues contributed much to motivating the sentence/NP distinction. In this section I will briefly suggest how contributions may flow in the other direction: the sentence/NP distinction, viewed as a derivative of syllable structure, may help to explain otherwise puzzling features of both topicalization and the linguistic structuring of experience. What I say here is no more than an outline. It seems worth saying, even so, because it illustrates ways in which our understanding of how syntax relates to semantics and pragmatics may be helped by the hypothesis that, in certain basic respects, syntax is as it is for a semantically and pragmatically quite irrelevant reason—namely, a restructuring of the vocal apparatus.

In Section 4.4.4, we noted that the topic of a sentence in a strictly informational sense (the shared knowledge on which the speaker offers a comment) may occupy both more and less than an NP. Yet, when topicalization is grammaticalized (that is, when the topic of a sentence is systematically identified by syntactic means), this topicalization is always or nearly always limited to whole single NPs. Why should this be so? The syllabic model suggests an answer: syntactic topicalization is one strategy for fulfilling the expectation that some margin-like element should be privileged, in onset-like fashion. The fact that only margin-like elements can be thus privileged explains why verbs cannot be syntactically topicalized in the same way as NPs, even though verbal content may quite well be part of 'shared knowledge', as in Examples (28)–(30) of Chapter 4. And the expectation that the privilege should settle on a clearly identifiable constituent (unless the verb-final strategy for 'maximizing the onset' is chosen) explains why syntactic topicalization should be restricted to single NPs.

We also noted in Section 4.4.4 that, even when the entire content of a sentence constitutes a comment in the informational sense (that is, when the sentence expresses a 'thetic judgement'), it is typically not differentiated in any fundamental syntactic fashion from a sentence expressing a 'categoric judgement'. Thus, in languages where a syntactic distinction between subjects and predicates is justified, thetic judgements typically exhibit just the same binary subject–predicate structure as categorical judgements do. This may seem puzzling. But the encroachment of the binary structure into pragmatically inappropriate territory is just what the syllabic model leads us to expect. Whether a statement is thetic or categorical, the sentence that expresses it must conform to a syntax that mimics syllabic asymmetries. Nicolas Ruwet, in a thorough discussion of the syntax of weather expressions such as *It's snowing*, talks aptly of 'a conflict between our experience and the analytic demands of syntax' (1991: 103). The syllabic model provides what Ruwet does not: a suggestion about the evolutionary origin of this analytic straitjacket.

I mentioned in Section 4.4.3 the 'two daunting problems' for cognitive grammar cited by Langacker (1991: 15): the semantic heterogeneity of both nouns and verbs, and the fact that the same piece of content can often be expressed either as a verb or as a noun. Examples of this sort of verb–noun vacillation are easy to find, both within a language (English *It flashed* versus *It emitted a flash*) and between languages (English *It's raining* versus Russian *Idët dozhd'*, literally 'goes rain'). The discussion in Section 5.6.7 shows how these problems are substantially solved by the syllabic scenario: from the semantic point of view, verbhood and nounhood are two ends of a continuum that is the syntactico-semantic counterpart of sonority within the syllable. To say this is not to reject the cognitive approach to grammar, but rather to assist it by identifying aspects of grammar that the cognitive approach need not attempt to explain, simply because a fundamentally different kind of explanation is available for them.

Many languages possess lexical wordclasses other than nouns and verbs. But the reason why it is just these two classes that are apparently universal (rather than three classes, twelve, or just one) need not be that the world or our perception of it is fundamentally structured that way. It may rather be simply that syntax evolved in its early stages so as to copy the distinction between precisely two classes of sounds: consonants (typically marginal in the syllable) and vowels (typically nuclear). And the reason why the same content can vacillate between nominal and verbal expression is fundamentally the same as the reason why I used the word 'typically', not 'always', in talking about the syllabic roles of consonants and vowels. Just as a sound of middling sonority may be marginal in one syllable and nuclear in another (provided that the margins are occupied by sounds even lower on the sonority hierarchy), so the same piece of content may be sometimes nominal and sometimes verbal (provided that margin-like positions in the sentence are occupied by items even lower on the object–action hierarchy—that is, closer to the object end). The coexistence of *It flashed* and *It emitted a flash* is therefore no longer a problem. What would be a problem, for the syllabic model as much as for cognitive grammar, would be the discovery of some variety of English in which it is natural to express the same content in a form such as *It flashed an emission* or *An emission flashed from it.*[31]

### 5.6.10.   Early versus Modern Syntax

When discussing the semantic heterogeneity of subjects, I described them as leftovers from syntax's phonological substrate. The term 'leftover' needs emphasizing. In checking modern syntax against the expectations of the syllabic model, we are using modern syntax as a proxy for what the syllabic model more directly relates to: the kind of syntax that arose at the stage of language evolution when vocal-tract changes, leading to vocabulary growth and duality of patterning, created a pressing need for it. It is hardly likely that modern-style syntax should emerge suddenly in its full complexity at that point. Therefore it is only to be expected that there should be some discrepancies between what the syllabic model predicts and what we observe today.

A prominent discrepancy concerns characteristic (vi), according to which no embedding of sentences in margin-like positions should occur. Yet all modern languages permit this kind of embedding. The question to ask, then, is whether sentence-embedding is the sort of departure from the original syntactic groundplan that might reasonably be expected to have arisen during the course of syntactic evolution after it had been kick-started by syllable structure. In evolutionary terms, this amounts to asking whether a change in the biological substrate for language that would permit embedding is the sort of change that would confer an advantage on those humans experiencing it, such that the genetic basis for the change would be likely to spread throughout the population. The answer to that question must surely be yes. (More detailed suggestions about why this change happened when it did will be offered in Section 6.2.4, while detailed discussion of how various aspects of complex sentences may have evolved is offered by Kirby (1999).) On the other hand, it is much less clear whether the development of the sentence/NP distinction or the privileging of part of each sentence in one or more of the various ways listed under options (*a*)–(*d*) would confer any comparable advantage. If Monocategoric and Spatiotemporal can work just as well as modern human syntax, the answer must be no. So those are characteristics of language whose source is more plausibly sought in whatever non-syntactic raw material was put to use in evolving syntax originally. And an advantage of the

---

[31] For a different view of the parallels between the verb/noun and vowel/consonant contrasts, see Taylor (1996: 84–5).

syllabic model is that the non-syntactic raw material that it posits does provide sources for these two otherwise puzzling characteristics of modern human syntax.

Another prominent discrepancy between what the syllabic model predicts and what we observe in modern languages concerns the movement of constituents, whether in simple or complex sentences. An example is the fronting of the auxiliary in English to form yes/no interrogatives, e.g. *Did my brother park your old bicycle in Bill's garage?* as the interrogative counterpart to (47). The syllabic model has nothing to say about this phenomenon. Indeed, it may have struck the reader that I have ignored interrogative and imperative sentence-types entirely, concentrating solely on declaratives. If my intention had been to account for every aspect of syntactic evolution, that would be a serious drawback. But the sentence/NP distinction, which is my sole syntactic concern, is neutral between sentence-types. Moreover, there is evidence that declarative sentences are 'privileged', perhaps for reasons to do with conceptual structure rather than communication (Newmeyer 1995). So if any sentence-type has evolutionary priority, it will be the declarative. It is thus the declarative type that the syllabic model must be measured against.

At this point it is worth comparing my approach to the development of fully modern syntax with that of Bickerton. According to the syllabic scenario, there existed a clear-cut stage in syntactic evolution beyond protolanguage but before the fully modern stage. This scenario therefore allows more room for manœuvre in marrying linguistic evolution with palaeoanthropology. We may agree with Bickerton that the transition to *erectus* probably coincided with some linguistic advance. We may also agree that traces of a syntaxless protolanguage survive today. We need not, however, deny protolanguage to the australopithecines or to *Homo habilis*; for, as Bickerton agrees (1990:145), protolanguage need not have awaited duality of patterning and the articulatory benefits of a reconfigured vocal tract. Correspondingly, we need not insist that the evolution of grammar did not begin until the appearance of *Homo sapiens*.

Two elements in Bickerton's account that are fully compatible with mine are his emphasis on language as an 'engine of thought' and his scepticism about any generalized increase in 'intelligence' as a prerequisite for language. Ironically, however, my account carries this emphasis further than Bickerton's. In my framework, there is no need for a 'latent protolanguage' in the mind that must await complex conditions of 'readiness' before it can come into use, and that in turn requires a radical neural restructuring in order to give rise to true language. Rather, central features of true language (an enlarged vocabulary and a syntax incorporating a sentence/NP distinction) were by-products of a development that had nothing directly to do with the brain, the mind, or intelligence—namely, a change in the shape of the vocal tract. The only 'mental' factors invoked in this chapter have been a synonymy-avoidance mechanism and an awareness of predicate–argument structure (as an outgrowth of social intelligence)—both of them factors that humans share with other apes.

What I have not yet offered, however, is any account of why that change in the vocal apparatus should have taken place. When I discussed the descent of the larynx in Section 5.3, I explicitly avoided that question. But it is one of the questions that will be tackled in Chapter 6.

# 6  Apes, Anthropology, and the Brain

## 6.1. Kinds of Complementary Evidence

In Chapter 5 I presented a scenario for language evolution that accounts economically for three characteristics of modern human language:

- large vocabulary size;
- duality of patterning;
- the distinction between sentences and NPs.

As I said there, this scenario does not attempt to cover all aspects of how and why language evolved. What is more, the vocal tract changes to which I attributed such importance were presented without any discussion of archaeological or anatomical evidence for their timing or for their relationship with other potentially relevant factors such as brain size, tool use, or culture. The picture that I presented is, therefore, incomplete.

That is not, of itself, a criticism. Human language is a complex phenomenon and we must expect any complete evolutionary explanation for it to be 'multifactorial', as Bradshaw and Rogers (1992) put it. What I have offered is an account according to which certain seemingly independent aspects of language are joint consequences of the interaction of two factors: vocal-tract changes and synonymy-avoidance principles. But clearly my account cannot be correct unless it is at least consistent with what we know about the factors that I have so far neglected.

In this chapter I will discuss how well my scenario fits the evidence from three areas: biological anthropology, brain neurophysiology, and studies of the linguistic abilities of our closest primate relatives, the great apes. Conceivably, evidence from any of these three areas could seriously weaken the case presented in Chapter 5. For example, it could turn out that there is incontrovertible evidence for modern syntax with a sentence/NP distinction even before the evolution of the modern adult human vocal tract, or that this kind of syntax can be successfully learned by apes, or that the brain mechanisms for controlling phonetic articulation and syntax are so distinct that there is no question of the latter evolving from the former. I will argue, however, that the evidence from all these areas is consistent with my scenario, and that the scenario also suggests intriguing new ways of interpreting certain evidence from research on aphasia and on sign language.

## 6.2. Archaeology and Biological Anthropology

A succession of fossil discoveries and theoretical developments have made the anthropological and archaeological study of human origins an exciting field in recent decades. It is inevitable that some of this excitement should have found expression in proposals about language evolution. Yet, for all this interest, one surveyor of the field (Richards 1987: 205) has commented with disarming frankness that 'the timing of the origin of language is anyone's guess'. In discussing the evidence here I will certainly not try to resolve specifically anthropological uncertainties.[1] Instead, I will restrict myself to evidence that bears on the scenario proposed in Chapter 5. The conclusion that will emerge is that the three aspects of language that this scenario seeks to explain are not accounted for better by any specifically anthropological proposal, and nothing in the anthropological evidence conflicts with the scenario. At the same time, some anthropological evidence may complement the scenario by dealing with aspects of language evolution that it does not cover, such as social motivation for a more elaborate and versatile vocal communication system.[2]

### 6.2.1. The Timing of Archaeological and Linguistic Developments

The importance that I have attributed to vocal-tract changes presupposes that there is no evidence for language with essentially modern syntax, incorporating the sentence/NP distinction, before the larynx was lowered. This presupposition is correct, for a reason that is almost too obvious to need stating. Direct evidence for modern-style syntax does not appear until the first surviving written records, dating from around 7,000 years ago in Egypt and Sumeria (modern Iraq); but the Egyptians and Sumerians were anatomically modern humans with lowered larynxes, and so were their predecessors for many thousands of years, since it is clear that both the people responsible for the artistic explosion of the Upper Palaeolithic around the western Pyrenees in Europe and the people who crossed the sea to Australia about 60,000 years ago were anatomically modern.

---

[1] Henceforward in this section I will use 'anthropological' as short for 'anthropological or archaeological or both'.

[2] For introductory surveys of human evolution, see Foley (1995) or Mithen (1996). For a more popular account, see Stringer and McKie (1996).

That is not the only issue of timing that affects my scenario, however. If the scenario is correct, then vocal-tract changes should have led to vocabulary enlargement and a sentence–NP syntax fairly directly—or, to put it more realistically, there should have been a period of fairly close interplay between anatomical and linguistic changes. So it would be embarrassing for this scenario to find evidence of a long interval (thousands or hundreds of thousands of years) after the lowering of the larynx and before the emergence of modern-style language. Does such evidence exist, then? The answer is no—unless one relies heavily on elaborate fossil artefacts as indicators of the appearance of modern-style language, or uses the term 'language' idiosyncratically, or interprets in a questionable fashion the theory that all modern humans are descended from people who came out of Africa within the last 200,000 years or less. I will look at these possibilities in turn.

There is no such embarrassing interval if Lieberman (1984, 1991; Lieberman and Crelin 1971) is right about the articulatory limitations of *Homo neandertalensis*, and if these limitations were shared by all earlier hominids. Lieberman thinks that Neanderthal vocal tracts were configured in such a way that they could not produce the full modern range of speech sounds, particularly vowels, and suggests that a major reason why Neanderthals lost ground to modern humans, despite having a bigger brain and a more robust physique, was their relative inferiority as speakers. Although Lieberman's interpretation of the Neanderthal evidence is supported by Krantz (1980), it is generally rejected by biological anthropologists and anatomists (Burr 1976; DuBrul 1977; Duchin 1990; Houghton 1993; Schepartz 1993).[3] Furthermore, even if Lieberman is right, that would support the late appearance of fully modern speech capacities in our ancestry only if modern humans are descended (at least in part) from Neanderthals. But that is inconsistent with the increasingly dominant anthropological view, according to which Neanderthals were cousins of modern humans rather than their ancestors. For present purposes, it is sufficient to note that, if Lieberman is right, that poses no problem for my scenario.

Let us then explore the consequences of supposing that Lieberman is wrong, and that among humans much earlier than anatomically modern *Homo sapiens* the reconfiguration of the vocal tract was already sufficiently advanced to permit a modern or nearly modern repertoire of speech sounds. Again there is no problem for our scenario, provided that it is possible for a form of language incorporating syllable-based aspects of syntax to have become established as soon as the larynx embarked on its descent. On this possibility anthropologists' opinions

---

[3] Duchin (1990) argues that Lieberman overestimates the importance of the position of the larynx for modern human speech and underestimates that of the oral cavity. Lieberman, Laitman, Reidenberg, and Gannon (1992) contest this. Nevertheless, Laitman, Reidenberg, and Gannon are willing to accept that the lowering of the larynx began long before the appearance of modern *Homo sapiens* (Laitman *et al.* 1992).

differ. One school of thought points to the abundant evidence of tool manufacture by *Homo erectus* as evidence that they must have had language. Another school of thought, however, argues that the use and manufacture of simple tools does not presuppose human-like language, because chimpanzees that lack language can nevertheless use twigs to probe for ants or termites and hammerstones to crack nuts, and because tool manufacture can be learned by imitation. Furthermore, according to this view, the long period of more than a million years during which one of *erectus*'s preferred tools, the so-called Acheulean hand-axe, underwent almost no change shows that *erectus* did not experience the kind of cultural evolution that language makes possible. There was, therefore, an interval of well over a million years after the vocal tract had begun to move to its modern configuration but before language had evolved into an adequate vehicle for transmitting culture.

This second opinion seems problematic for our scenario. On closer examination, however, it turns out to presuppose an unsustainably close relationship between language and the archaeological record. The experience of the last two and a half centuries shows that enormous changes in material culture and technology can occur without any accompanying change in language except of the most superficial kind—namely, the acquisition of new vocabulary. The grammar of English is essentially the same in 1998 as it was in 1750. So it is arbitrary to assume that in prehistory things were different, and that a period of relatively rapid cultural and technological innovation such as the Upper Palaeolithic in Europe must necessarily have been a time of rapid linguistic evolution. Conversely, it is arbitrary to assume that the development of a syllable-based syntax of the kind described in Chapter 5 must have left in the archaeological record traces that would be both immediate and substantial. Even if one regards hand-axe technology and the use of fire as insufficient evidence for some form of language, one must acknowledge that *erectus* almost certainly used more tractable materials, such as wood and hides, more extensively than they used stone; and there is no telling what degree of sophistication they may have reached with those perishable materials. The very few wooden artefacts that do survive from pre-*sapiens* times, such as the 400,000-year-old hunting spears from Germany (Thieme 1997), are certainly well beyond what any uncontroversially languageless creature is known to be capable of.

In recent years, the scholars who have most consistently and vigorously defended a late date for the origin of language are Iain Davidson and William Noble (see e.g. Davidson and Noble 1993; Noble and Davison 1996). Their principal focus is on the archaeological evidence for when humans first made objects with symbolic significance, where 'a symbol is anything that, by custom or convention, stands for something else' (Noble and Davidson 1996: 5). They argue that it is only when the users of vocal or gestural communication discovered its symbolic significance that language may be said to have come into existence. They thus support the discontinuist side in the debate over whether or not there is evolutionary continuity between animal and human vocal communication, since 'humans are unique, under natural conditions, in being creatures who communicate using symbols' (Noble and Davidson 1996: 8), and 'the focus is on what happened when hominids first expressed themselves in ways of which they were *aware*' (Noble and Davidson 1996: 20, emphasis added). But in tying the term 'language' to awareness of symbolism, Davison and Noble ensure that their discussion is irrelevant to the kind of issue which concerns us here.

Davidson and Noble's interpretation of 'language' has two strange consequences. First, it is not clear whether even today all normal human speakers can be said to use 'language' in their sense. Many children are arguably not aware of the symbolic nature of words because they are not aware of the arbitrariness of the relationship between a word and what it stands for. Among adults, the same applies to Socrates, as presented in Plato's dialogue *Cratylus*, when he argues that there are necessary connections between words and things. And the taboo in some communities against using the name of a recently dead person or words that resemble that name (Dixon 1980) may be an indication of a similar attitude, precluding achievement of what Davidson and Noble call 'language'. Secondly, according to them, language has an 'all-or-none' character, since nothing can be 'half-discovered' (Noble and Davidson 1996: 8). Language therefore cannot have evolved gradually. That does not mean that they think that language sprang into existence suddenly from nowhere, for they distinguish between language and what they call 'critical precursor abilities that allowed linguistic behaviour to emerge' (Noble and Davidson 1996: 141). What it does mean, however, is that language evolution in my sense is in their terms rather the evolution of these 'critical precursor abilities'. But then their claim that language emerged late in human evolution clearly does not impinge at all on the substance of the scenario presented in Chapter 5. It is not that Davidson and Noble have a view of syntax (say) that conflicts with the syllabic model; rather, they operate with a definition of language in which syntax plays no part, so any apparent conflict between their account of symbolism and my account of duality of patterning, vocabulary size, and the sentence/NP distinction turns out to be almost entirely terminological.[4]

The last possible piece of evidence on timing involves the 'out-of-Africa' theory of recent human prehistory. According to this theory, everybody alive today is descended from a small group of people living in Africa somewhere between

---

[4] The differences are perhaps not entirely terminological. Davidson and Noble are less inclined than I am to see anything language-like in vervet alarm calls (Cheney and Seyfarth 1990). But this is not so much because they and I disagree about the substance of what vervets can and cannot do as because, in their terms, the absence of evidence that vervets are consciously aware that their calls mean something shows that vervet calls are non-linguistic by definition.

200,000 and 100,000 years ago, without any genetic admixture from elsewhere. If that is correct, the question arises why these people and their descendants, in the course of their migrations, did not interbreed with the humans they met. These other humans would have included other *Homo sapiens*, so children produced from such unions would almost certainly have been viable and fertile. Could it be that what discouraged interbreeding was that the people from Africa had language, or a more advanced variety of it? This might also account for the Africans' success in supplanting other human populations. But if we posit an early date for the lowering of the larynx, the scenario of Chapter 5 implies an early expansion in vocabulary and development of syllable-based syntax too, which would have affected not only people in Africa but everyone at the level of *sapiens* and even *erectus*. So there seems at first sight to be a timing discrepancy between the 'out-of-Africa' theory and the syllabic model for syntax.

Even if the 'out-of-Africa' theory is correct, however, the demise of the non-African populations need not have had anything to do with syllable-based sentence structure. Rebecca Cann, one of the researchers who first cited evidence from mitochondrial DNA in favour of a relatively recent common ancestor in the maternal line (Cann *et al.* 1987), has more recently suggested that the apparently near-complete disappearance of those populations may have been due to new infectious diseases brought by the migrants (Cann *et al.* 1994). The older humans may thus have suffered the same tragedy as the Hawaiians, whose number fell by a factor of about 100, from around two million to 20,000, in less than two generations after Captain Cook's arrival there in 1778.[5] In any case, even if there was a linguistic factor in the migrants' success, it could well have been not syllable-based sentence structure but rather sentential recursion (the capacity to embed sentences inside sentences), for reasons discussed in Section 6.2.4. The possibility that our recent ancestors from Africa may have been the first users of fully modern language is quite consistent with the possibility that a basic syllable-derived syntax may have evolved hundreds of thousands of years earlier.

Some researchers have argued for a rather different kind of linguistic component in the 'out-of-Africa' scenario. Let us suppose that the methods of historical linguistics enable us to reconstruct some words of 'Proto-World', the most recent common ancestor from which all contemporary languages are descended (Ruhlen 1994). Let us suppose also that the date at which Proto-World was spoken can be established as roughly contemporary with the 'out-of-Africa' migration. Both these suppositions are highly dubious (Carstairs-McCarthy 1997). But, even if they are correct, what might they tell us about how language evolved?

If Ruhlen is right, then Proto-World must have been at least modern enough to

---

[5] More recently, however, Cann (1995) has seemed inclined to re-emphasize language as a likely factor in the success of the migrants from Africa.

contain words entirely made up of recombinable speech sounds, like the words of modern human languages but unlike the call systems of other primates. On the other hand, grammatical structure of the kind that modern languages possess could have developed thousands of years previously, or could be yet to develop thousands of years in the future. The parent language whose vocabulary Ruhlen thinks is fragmentarily reconstructable was indeed original in one sense; but that does not constitute evidence that it was original in any sense pertinent to language evolution. The only hint that this parent language may have been novel in an evolutionary sense comes from palaeoanthropology, not linguistics; so Proto-World speculations add no independent weight to the linguistic implications of the 'out-of-Africa' scenario.

It seems fair to conclude that no evidence from the palaeoanthropological record relating to the timing of vocal-tract changes conflicts with the scenario presented in Chapter 5.

### 6.2.2. The Original Impetus for Vocal-Tract Changes

Even if the timing of vocal-tract changes (so far as it can be determined) is consistent with the syllabic model, it may still be thought that that model is deficient in not supplying a motivation for them. Why should the larynx have begun to lower in the first place, if not in response to selective pressure for better speech?

This question can be answered satisfactorily, however. Evolutionary theory, in most of its modern versions, does not assert that a genetically conditioned anatomical innovation will occur only if it is adaptive; it asserts rather that the genetic basis for that innovation will maintain itself and perhaps spread within the population only if it is not maladaptive. Evolutionary theorists do not deny that creatures may be born with genetically conditioned deformities that diminish their chance of survival; they merely assert that the genetic underpinnings for such deformities will be unlikely to thrive within the gene pool because their unfortunate bearers are likely to be relatively unsuccessful at reproducing. And the first step towards a lower larynx could have been just such an innovation 'out of the blue'—but one that was able to maintain itself because it was not significantly maladaptive (choking is, after all, a relatively rare occurrence), and because it proved also to have novel advantages involving vocalization.

There are besides other factors, quite independent of selection for linguistic ability, that may have encouraged a 'low-position' allele of the gene for larynx position. One such factor is bipedalism. Given that humans and chimpanzees share a common ancestor who lived sometime between 5 and 7 million years ago, what were the earliest differences to emerge subsequently between our ancestors and those of chimpanzees? The answer will certainly include the adoption of an upright stance and bipedal gait, in view of the evidence for this in the Laetoli footprints from 3.7 million years ago and the skeleton of the australopithecine 'Lucy', who died about 3 million years ago (Foley 1995). The likely relevance of bipedalism for the larynx is pointed out by Aiello (1996*b*: 279):

In bipedal hominines[6] the spinal cord enters the brain case from below rather than from behind, constricting the space for the larynx between the spinal cord and the mouth. This together with the reduction of the face in early *Homo erectus* . . . in relation to the australopithecines [owing to the incorporation of meat in the diet, requiring less chewing] would be expected to necessitate a lower larynx particularly in these later terrestrially committed bipedal hominines.

The constricting effect of the position of the spinal cord in bipedal hominines favoured the development of an arched, or flexed, skull base, by comparison with the flatter skull base observed in apes. The relevance of this basicranial flexion to the position of the larynx is confirmed by evidence from contemporary mammalian species: a relatively high degree of flexion generally correlates with a low position of the larynx (Laitman and Reidenberg 1988). So it is reasonable to conclude that human bipedalism (perhaps in conjunction with the 'reduction of the face' mentioned by Aiello) encouraged a lowering of the larynx, independently of any encouragement emanating from the evolution of speech itself (DuBrul 1958, 1976, 1977; Schepartz 1993). Indeed, the larynx-lowering effect of bipedalism has even been confirmed experimentally in research on rats (Riesenfeld 1969). The lowered larynx also facilitated mouth-breathing, and hence more rapid transfer of bigger volumes of air than was possible with the nose alone. This would have been useful in sustained bipedal running—an important new element of the savannah lifestyle that bipedal hominids came to adopt.[7]

A quite different but still language-independent reason for larynx-lowering is suggested by Elaine Morgan (1982, 1989) in the context of her Aquatic Ape Theory. According to this theory, many apparently unrelated characteristics that distinguish humans from other primates, such as hairlessness, subcutaneous fat, bipedalism, and face-to-face copulation, can be parsimoniously accounted for if it is assumed that our ancestors came to be adapted to a semi-aquatic existence during a period when the sea level was high. The lowering of the larynx allows the velum to be raised so as to form a seal with the back wall of the nasopharynx, thus reducing the risk of water entering the lungs through the nose during swimming. However, Morgan's theory is not widely accepted among biological anthropologists, so I emphasize that it is not the only possible source of a language-independent impetus for the lowered larynx.[8]

Lieberman (1991) questions the importance of bipedalism, on the ground

---

[6] 'Hominine' is a term for pre-*sapiens* humans used by those researchers who think that 'hominid' is more properly applied to a wider grouping including at least some apes.
[7] I am grateful to Jeffrey Laitman for pointing this out.
[8] Some non-anthropologists have found it puzzling that most anthropologists reject the Aquatic Ape Theory so firmly (Richards 1987; Dennett 1995).

that people who have an abnormal basicranium with an elongated hard palate (sufferers from Apert's syndrome) can still walk upright. But this is a weak argument. For genetically controlled characteristics to spread within a population (say, a slightly shorter palate or a slightly lower larynx than average), it is not necessary that the advantage enjoyed by the individuals who possess these characteristics (say, slightly less expenditure of effort in maintaining an upright posture) should be massive or immediately obvious. Evolution can work through the accumulation over many generations of the effects of a characteristic whose advantage at the level of the individual, though genuine, is tiny. Conversely, the disadvantage suffered by an individual in whom these accumulated effects are absent, for whatever reason, need not be so devastating that it is impossible to compensate for. A short man can play basketball and may even play it well; but that does not prove that, in respect of adaptedness for basketball-playing, there is no difference between him and a tall man. Similarly, the fact that even a person with a somewhat australopithecus-like basicranium may be able to walk upright does not prove that, in respect of adaptedness for upright posture, there is no difference between her and a person whose basicranium is normal.[9]

### 6.2.3.  Tool Manufacture, Accurate Throwing, and Speech

Syntax involves hierarchical organization: the combination of words into phrases and the combination of these phrases into larger units, according to principles some of which differ from one language to another but some of which seem to be common to all humans. The production of speech (even the most casual speech) therefore involves planning, in some sense; it cannot be simply a matter of stringing together words chosen one at a time. But these characteristics of hierarchical organization and planning are not peculiar to language. Other patterns of behaviour can be analysed in similar terms, and at more than one level: the level of individual actions (picking up a flint, positioning it firmly, hitting it with a hammerstone to chip off a flake, and so on) and the level of the neural impulses that control such actions. Could it be, then, that the syntactic organization of language is a byproduct of the mastery by humans of patterns of non-linguistic behaviour that are relatively complex at one or both of these levels—complex, that is, by comparison with what other primates are capable of? If so, the neural control of syntax could involve the cooption or exaptation of parts of the cortex that originally had another function, just as in the syllable model, but the function in question would be different. It is important, therefore, to explore how attractive such a non-linguistic source for syntax may be as an alternative to the syllabic model.

[9] The weakness of Lieberman's argument here ironically resembles the weakness of Wind's argument, discussed in Section 6.3.2, by which he purports to show that vocal-tract changes contributed nothing significant to language evolution.

An example of the hierarchical organization of actions is at (1), which illustrates the structure of the action sequence of dipping a spoon in some food and carrying the food with the spoon to the mouth. This represents a more advanced stage of spoon use by a child than at (2), where (2*a*) stands for simply the grasping of a spoon (Greenfield 1991: 540).

(1)

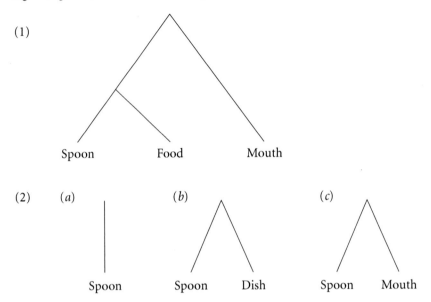

Spoon        Food        Mouth

(2)    (*a*)            (*b*)            (*c*)

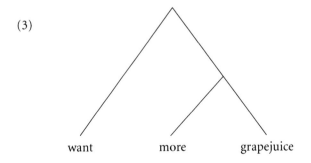

        Spoon        Spoon    Dish        Spoon    Mouth

The kind of branching structure illustrated at (1) is similar, in some sense, to that shown in (3) and (4), also taken from Greenfield (1991), where the items hierarchically linked are syntactic and phonological respectively:[10]

(3)

want            more            grapejuice

---

(4)                                  ball

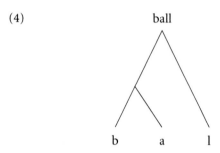

                              b        a        l

Greenfield sees similarities such as this as evidence (though not the only evidence) for two related suggestions: that object manipulation and linguistic structure are controlled by the same neural mechanisms in early childhood before neural specialization takes place, and that in evolutionary terms they are homologous.

One way of looking at Greenfield's proposal is as a weaker version of the syllable model for syntax. To manipulate the articulatory apparatus is to manipulate objects. So is there any evidence that syntax exhibits parallels with the pattern of manipulation of the articulatory apparatus in particular, rather than with the pattern of manipulation of objects in general, such as dishes, spoons, and food? If Greenfield is right, the answer must be no. That means that the distinction between sentences and NPs, which is central to the fact that all human languages are as they are rather than like Monocategoric or Spatiotemporal, must emerge from general hierarchical patterns for object manipulation such as (1).

This is precisely where Greenfield's account fails, however. The simple action which one can represent as [Spoon Food] (the left-hand constituent in the hierarchical structure of (1) ) is different from the more complex action represented by the whole of (1). But it is not a different *kind* of action, in the sense in which a verb phrase is a different kind of syntactic unit from a sentence. Likewise, Greenfield's version of syllable structure at (4) is not labelled in such a way as to bring out the fact that (for example) the onset consonant *b* has a different status in relation to the whole syllable than the nuclear vowel *a* does. And this lack of labelling is not just an oversight on Greenfield's part. In her caption to (3), she says: 'Nodes are not labeled in order to avoid a commitment to a particular theoretical description. The important point about [(3)] (which would not be disputed by any theory) is that *more* plus *grapejuice* forms a single complex unit, which, in turn, relates to *want*' (1991: 533). But this emphasis on hierarchical structure by itself, ignoring the status of the constituents within it, precludes Greenfield from drawing attention to precisely the differences between the syllable and its constituents that, according to the syllabic model, underlie the difference in status in syntax-as-it-is between the sentence and its constituents.

That there should be some similarities of the kind illustrated in (1)–(4) is hardly surprising, given that none of the structures there contains more than three

ultimate constituents and that (1) and (4) exhaust the available ways of organizing three items in a binary-branched hierarchical structure. But Greenfield might
still be able to make a strong case for an object-manipulation source for syntax,
despite the objections so far raised, if there were evidence of parallels between the
two kinds of structure even where the number of ultimate constituents was larger
and where therefore the range of possible branching structures was larger too. Yet
it is just at this degree of complexity that, according to Greenfield, object manipulation and syntax diverge. As she puts it: 'Developmental information about
grammars of action and language suggests that programs for combining objects
become increasingly differentiated from programs for combining words (linguistic grammars) starting around two years of age' (1991: 541). It is hard to avoid the
conclusion that, once one gets beyond parallels that are mathematically inevitable
because of the small number of items involved, evidence for a general-purpose
hierarchical organization of behaviour manifested in both object manipulation
and language vanishes. Greenfield is correct in drawing attention to the fact that
the manual motor area of the cortex is next to the the orofacial area, and the orofacial area in turn is next to Broca's area, which is widely seen as having a special
role in the grammatical organization of speech. But the manual motor area is not
directly next to Broca's area; and this lack of contiguity counts against the suggestion that the manual motor area (as opposed to the orofacial area) has something
directly to do with how language is learned. The evidence seems rather to support
the more sceptical view of the anthropologist Thomas Wynn, who argues that
'there is, in fact, no equivalent to linguistic syntax in tool behavior, thereby
seriously weakening the potential of prehistoric tools to inform us about
language' (1993: 390).[11]

The neurobiologist William Calvin (1989, 1992, 1993) suggests that syntax
evolved not from how slow-speed object manipulations are organized in tool use
but from how high-speed neural impulses are organized for accurate throwing.
He points out that throwing a stone accurately enough to hit a small target (a
rabbit, say) is a purely human accomplishment; chimpanzees may throw stones
and branches when they are angry or excited, but they do not use stone-throwing
to kill or immobilize their prey when hunting. Furthermore, achieving accuracy
cannot be simply a matter of responding to neural feedback during the throw,
because this feedback is too slow. Human brains must, therefore, have evolved so
as to improve accuracy by different methods—by using many neurons in parallel
to reduce the inherent unreliability of individual neural impulses, and by devel-
oping a 'serial buffer' in which a chain of motor commands can be stored ready
for execution, somewhat as a chain of commands is stored in the instruction roll
of a player piano.

The neurological details do not matter to us, however, so much as what Calvin

---

[11] For a more sympathetic assessment of Greenfield (1991), see Maynard Smith and Szathmáry
(1995).

sees as their implications for language evolution. The neural sequencer for throwing and similar high-speed skills was coopted for language, he thinks, in such a way as to provide the germs of syntactic category distinctions: 'One can imagine a manual-brachial sequencer being adapted to simple kinds of language. A verb is usually a stand-in for a movement. And the targets of a ballistic movement are examples of nouns: "Throw at that rabbit!" or "Hit that nut." This seems just like the predicate of a sentence: the verb and its object.'(1993: 238–9). Calvin thus tackles an aspect of syntax that Greenfield neglects. In suggesting an evolutionary reason for why syntax should differentiate nouns from verbs, he in effect supplies labels for some of the nodes in the hierarchical structures that Greenfield leaves unlabelled. Does Calvin's ballistic model for syntax then achieve all that the syllable model does?

The answer is no, for two reasons. First, as Calvin admits, nothing in the planning of ballistic movement supplies any obvious precedent for the role of the subject NP in sentence structure. In the syllable model, by contrast, making one NP the subject is one way of mimicking in sentence structure the kind of privileged status that onsets have in syllable structure (as we saw in Chapter 5). Secondly, the ballistic model, unlike the syllabic model, does not explain why actual syntax is not like Monocategoric. The movement/target distinction in throwing could be regarded as a precedent not merely for the verb/noun distinction but also for the distinction in Monocategoric between operators (such as HIT, THROW) and simple expressions (such as *rabbit, nut*). But recall that in Monocategoric there is no difference in status between a simple expression, such as *snake*, and a complex expression, such as *you snake SEE*; their freedom to appear as arguments of operators within larger expressions is governed purely by semantic and pragmatic considerations, not syntactic ones. It follows that Calvin's ballistic model is compatible with a kind of syntax in which there is no distinction between sentences and NPs. In that crucial reflect it is inferior to the syllabic model, according to which the sentence/NP distinction is the syntactic reflex of the syllable/margin distinction.

Calvin's approach nevertheless complements the syllabic model in a useful way. Although the lowering of the larynx is the most prominent of the physiological changes that triggered syntactic development according to the syllabic model, it is not the only one. It would have had much less effect on the human vocalization repertoire if the tongue, lips, and soft palate had not acquired the agility that they exhibit in speech. And Calvin's ballistic model suggests a source for that agility. Of course the tongue, lips, and soft palate are not used for throwing; but the area of cortex most closely implicated in controlling movement of the tongue and lips is next to that which controls the hand, and the idea that finer neural control of hand movement could have leaked across so as to yield finer control of the tongue and lips too seems compatible with what we know of how the cortex works. So more accurate throwing could indeed have contributed to the development of syntax, but by a more indirect route than Calvin suggests.

The idea that syntax has its origin in the brain mechanisms for speech motor control in particular, rather than (say) manual motor control, is not new, having been outlined by Lenneberg in his pioneering work on the biology of language (1967). Its most vigorous recent exponent is Lieberman (1991). But Lieberman makes a mistake somewhat similar to Calvin's: he too underestimates how much there is to explain. As he puts it: 'Brain mechanisms adapted to handle the complex sequential operations necessary for speech production would have no difficulty in handling the comparatively simple problems of syntax' (Lieberman 1991: 107–8). But, as Chapter 2 showed, the problems of syntax are not simple, inasmuch as many kinds of syntax are conceivable that differ markedly from the kind that actual languages have. The syllabic model proposed in Chapter 5 to explain certain aspects of syntax is entirely consistent with Lieberman's emphasis on motor control for speech, but it goes further than anything proposed by Lieberman towards explaining why syntax is as it is.

### 6.2.4. Brain Size and Encephalization

Harry Jerison, a pioneer of research on brain size in relation to body size, introduced the term **encephalization quotient** to mean the ratio of the brain size of a species to that of other related species with the same body size (Jerison 1973). Before calculating this quotient, one must decide what to use as a measure of body size (for example, weight, volume, or surface area), and what to count as related species (for example, whether to compare humans to apes, to all other primates, or to all mammals). Fortunately we need not be too concerned with these issues, because on every basis of calculation the human encephalization quotient is high. It has been said that our brains are about three times as big as they would be if we were average primates of the same size (Wills 1993: 265). So when did this brain expansion take place, why did it take place, and what does it have to do with language?

To the second and third of these questions nobody has suggested more than tentative answers. It is not surprising, therefore, that nothing known about brain size conflicts with the syllabic model for language evolution. But the issue is still worth some attention, because some answers recently posed for the 'why' question complement the syllabic model nicely.

The 'when' question is the one to which it is easiest to give a relatively clear-cut answer. Brain enlargement over the last three million years has not been a steady process. Rather, there have been two bursts of relatively rapid enlargement, the first of which took place between about 2 million and 1.5 million years ago and the second of which took place within the last 500,000 years (Aiello and Dean 1990; Aiello 1996*a*). These correspond to two important transitions: the replacement of australopithecines by *Homo habilis* and subsequently *Homo erectus* as the dominant human, and the emergence of *Homo sapiens*.[12] In contrast, during the 1.5 million years of dominance by *Homo erectus*, brain size increased only slightly. Why the two bursts, and why the intervening stasis?

Aiello and Wheeler (1995) have suggested an explanation for the first in terms of diet. Brain size comes at a cost, because the brain and the digestive system are both expensive to maintain by comparison with other parts of the body. It follows that, so long as poor diet imposes the necessity of an elaborate and expensive digestive system to extract sufficient nutrients from it, brain enlargement will be hampered. On the other hand, once diet improves so that digestion can be accomplished more cheaply, metabolic energy can be released to service a more expensive brain. It is, therefore, not a coincidence, they suggest, that the earliest hominids for which there is evidence of a significant amount of meat in the diet are *Homo habilis* and *Homo erectus*.

Why then did brain enlargement not continue steadily throughout the *erectus* period? Why instead was there a long period of stasis before the relatively sudden 50 per cent increase in cranial capacity during the last quarter of a million years? Seriously tackling those questions would take us too far from the theme of this book. But there is one possible story which satisfyingly links Aiello's and my perspectives on language evolution, as well as the ideas on brain–language 'coevolution' put forward by Terrence Deacon, which will be discussed further in Section 6.3.2.

Recall that the scenario presented in Chapter 5 did not purport to explain why modern syntax is as it is in all respects, but only why it incorporates the sentence/NP distinction. Recall also that modern humans' aptitude for speech involves not just a low larynx but also fine motor control of the tongue, lips, and velum and precise control of exhalation. Let us suppose that *Homo erectus* had at least a partially lowered larynx, as argued by Laitman and colleagues (1992). Let us assume also that her control of neither articulation nor exhalation was as precise as ours. These assumptions are reasonable if, as Calvin suggests, *Homo erectus* only gradually acquired the kind of 'serial buffer' for accurate control of throwing that could then be coopted for control of the vocal organs, and if, as Aiello suggests (1996a, 1996b, citing MacLarnon 1993), *Homo erectus* was not neurally equipped for fine control of respiration. It follows that *Homo erectus* may have been able to produce utterances whose grammar incorporated a sentence/NP distinction, but her slow articulation and her difficulty in prolonging exhalation would have kept her sentences short. So, just as the cost of maintaining a digestive

---

[12] Many anthropologists now prefer a more fine-grained classification of the varieties of human formerly lumped together as *Homo erectus*. Thus, *erectus* is distinguished from *Homo ergaster* at the earlier end of the period, and from *Homo heidelbergensis* at the later end. But no one has suggested precise linguistic correlates for these distinctions (so far as I know), so they do not matter for our purposes.

system suitable for a poor diet inhibited brain enlargement in australopithecines, limitations on spoken language may have inhibited further language-driven brain enlargement in *Homo erectus*.

Once those limitations had been removed, however, as better breath control facilitated longer utterances and as improved accuracy in throwing yielded more rapid articulation as a by-product, the kind of brain–language coevolution that Deacon envisages could have accelerated again, as part of the transition from *erectus* to *sapiens*. Scope for longer sentences may also have facilitated the appearance of a central feature of modern syntax that the syllabic model does not explain: **recursion**, or the embedding of sentences in sentences. By this time, too, it seems reasonable to suppose that the neural mechanisms for syllable structure and sentence structure, although still closely allied, may have become sufficiently independent so that the lack of any parallel to recursion in syllable structure would not have inhibited this innovation in syntax. The transition from *erectus* to *sapiens* would thus coincide not with the simultaneous appearance of all the characteristics of modern syntax (as some proponents of a late date for language origin seem to think), but rather with the enrichment of the syllable-based syntax already in place by the new characteristic of recursion. The kind of language that *sapiens* had at her disposal would be by no means wholly novel, but its versatility would be enormously enhanced by the removal of any specifically grammatical upper bound on the length of a well-formed expression, and this new scope for linguistic elaboration would provide new ways in which people with bigger brains could enjoy a selective advantage.[13]

The story just presented is admittedly speculative. It is also incomplete, inasmuch as there were certainly other factors involved in the development of the structure and use of language, some of which will be touched on in the next section. But it reinforces the fact that a plausible palaeoanthropological context for a stage of language evolution such as is presented in Chapter 5 can be found. In Section 6.2.2 I argued that language-independent reasons are available for the larynx-lowering that (I suggest) provoked an increase in vocabulary, duality of patterning, and a new kind of syntax. In this section I have looked at what might have happened after that stage, suggesting some language-independent reasons why one further characteristic of modern syntax—namely, recursion—may have had to wait a further million years or so.

### 6.2.5. *Social Functions of Language*

In the study of language-as-it-is, two generally recognized subdisciplines are sociolinguistics, which deals with how languages are used in communities and

---

[13] Reynolds (1983) seeks to relate language evolution to a Rubicon in tool manufacture: the development of composite or hafted tools, allowing what Reynolds calls an 'externalized grip'. It is tempting to see a parallel between hafted tools and recursive syntax.

social groups and with attitudes to linguistic differences, and grammatical theory, which deals with how languages are structured.[14] Most of the issues that are to the fore in sociolinguistics at any one time are independent of those that grammatical theorists are currently debating, and vice versa. One can distinguish likewise between the evolution of the social functions of language and the evolution of its structure. This book is about certain aspects of language structure. Even so, it is relevant to consider whether any social functions of vocalization or vocal communication may have influenced the evolution of language structure, either as to substance or as to timing.

Activities that may be carried out more efficiently with the help of language, and that have, therefore, been proposed as spurs to language evolution, include the following:

- foraging and food-sharing (Parker and Gibson 1979);
- cooperative tool use (Gibson 1993);
- territorial marking (Jerison 1982);
- choice of mate (Miller and Todd 1998);
- social intelligence (Worden 1998);
- vocal 'grooming' for the maintenance of relationships and solidarity within the group (Dunbar 1996).

It seems fair to say that the pendulum of opinion concerning what language would have predominantly been used for among early hominids is swinging away from the information-sharing function emphasized by Gibson towards the social-interaction function emphasized by Worden and Dunbar. Dunbar's approach also links language evolution to encephalization and group size. Population growth and increases in group size would have meant that the mutual physical grooming to which chimpanzees and some monkeys devote considerable time would have become altogether too time-consuming if some method could not be found to groom several individuals at once; and human language evolved as just such a method.

The extent to which these proposals impinge on the subject matter of this book depends on the extent to which the functions and structure of language are interdependent, and in particular the extent to which grammatical structure has evolved in response to social function. Robert Worden (1998) has suggested that syntactic structure is indeed an outcome of social interaction: hierarchically organized 'scripts' for social situations were historically the model for hierarchically organized syntax. That suggestion is not compatible with the scenario proposed in Chapter 5; nevertheless, Worden's approach may complement our scenario rather than conflicting with it, as I shall explain.

In Chapter 4, when discussing Pinker and Bloom's and Bickerton's views

---

[14] Some linguists restrict 'grammatical theory' to syntax and morphology (word structure), but I intend a wider sense here, including also phonology, semantics, and vocabulary.

of grammatical evolution, I agreed that some mental representation of predicate–argument structure was almost certainly present in pre-linguistic hominids. But I argued there that the linguistic expression of predicate–argument structure does not require a distinction between sentences and NPs, and so is by itself not enough to account for the evolution of syntax-as-it-is rather than (say) Monocategoric. Now, Worden's 'scripts' are essentially representations of predicate–argument structure; therefore, as evolutionary precursors of sentence structure, they suffer from precisely the same inadequacies.

That said, Worden's proposal and the other socially based proposals complement the syllabic model by making suggestions in an area where that model is silent—namely, the semantic domains that would tend first to be colonized by new vocabulary. In Chapter 5 I suggested reasons why a lowered larynx would trigger an increase in vocabulary, but I said nothing about what the new 'words' would mean. The average non-anthropologist probably has an image of 'cavemen' as creatures with a small vocabulary focused on the mundane struggle to stay alive; they would have words for 'mammoth' and 'spear' and 'kill' but perhaps not for 'stroke me!' or 'nice!' or 'dominant male'. Dunbar in effect suggests reasons why the average non-anthropologist is wrong. But they are reasons that a researcher whose focus is on linguistic structure can happily accept, because they are independent of his concerns.

Language can be used to convey information and to reinforce group solidarity, but it can also be used to tell lies. This observation underlies a rather different kind of socially based approach to language evolution. Other primates sometimes display 'Machiavellian intelligence', deceiving each other for selfish advantage—or at least they behave in a way that is naturally described in that fashion unless we reject it as too anthropomorphic (Byrne and Whiten 1988). Moreover, human language is a particularly handy tool for deception, since it is under fully voluntary control and its use is almost cost-free in energetic terms. So we face a paradox. Given that it is easy to tell lies, and given the likelihood that selfish individuals will lie so as to prosper at the expense of others, why should I believe anything that anyone says? The most rational assumption on my part is that the other person is trying to trick me. Yet, unless there is a shared assumption that most people tell the truth most of the time, it is hard to see how language could become established as a social institution. Any physiological or psychological explanation for why language structure should have evolved in one way rather than another is pointless (it may seem) unless we can resolve this paradox and explain why language should have evolved at all.

One possible response, from the point of view of the concerns of this book, is a single brisk sentence: the fact that language *has* evolved shows that any barriers imposed by the possibility of deception were not insuperable. But that is perhaps too brisk. There is interest even from our point of view in considering how the paradox may be resolved, because that may be relevant to dating the stages of language evolution. The solutions proposed to this problem involve complex interactions among a range of factors (Knight *et al.* 1995; Power and Aiello 1997; Knight 1998). Common to these solutions is an emphasis on the special burden placed on human females, in comparison with other primate females, by brain expansion combined with bipedalism. Bipedalism promoted a narrowing of the pelvis, so that childbirth would have become more troublesome even without the added complication of brain expansion. As it was, bigger brains and narrower pelvises meant that babies had to be born relatively immature and helpless, needing longer and more intensive parental care than in other primates. This, in turn, meant that females with young babies were more dependent on other group members (particularly males) to provide food and to share responsibility for child-rearing. Language is seen as part of a web of biological and cultural factors, including also concealed ovulation and the invention of myths and rituals surrounding menstruation (with red ochre pigment used to simulate menstrual blood), that had the combined effect of enforcing male contributions to the welfare of their mates and offspring and using the role of language in ritual to counteract its inherent untrustworthiness.

Again, it is not necessary for us here to take a view on every detail of this kind of account. What matters is the date it implies for the emergence of the kind of ritual-oriented language that it posits. Power and Aiello suggest that there is evidence of regular and widespread ochre use among *Homo sapiens* in southern Africa by about 110,000 years ago, and less widespread use dates from much earlier. On the other hand, Neanderthals do not seem to have used red ochre until the period when they were in cultural contact with modern *Homo sapiens*. This suggests a social reason for a second burst of linguistic evolution, complementing the physiological and neurological ones suggested in Section 6.2.4, and compatible with them in date. It also suggests a further reason why Neanderthals were less successful than modern *sapiens*—namely, their probable lack of a sham menstruation ritual.

The upshot is that the social factors underlying language evolution by no means render superfluous the approach pursued in this book. At the same time, my relegation of social factors to one section of one chapter by no means reflects the importance they would assume in a complete account of all aspects of language evolution, beyond the scope of this book. Meanwhile, it is encouraging to find that evidence from archaeological and fossil sources on the likely dating of linguistic developments seems mutually consistent, and also consistent with my scenario.

## 6.3. The Brain

Until recently, our understanding of the brain mechanisms that underlie language derived entirely from observing what goes wrong when various parts of the brain are deformed or damaged. More recently, three other sources of evidence have become available: responses of conscious patients to electrical stimulation of various parts of the brain during surgery; magnetic resonance imaging (MRI), which can provide much more detailed pictures of cross-sections of the brain than are possible with X-rays; and positron emission tomography (PET), which measures minute changes in blood flow so as to show which part of the brain is most active during different linguistic tasks.[15] One kind of evidence is, of course, not available for ethical reasons: we cannot deliberately damage chosen areas of a person's brain solely to observe the effects, any more than we can deliberately rear children in artificial environments where their exposure to language is abnormal. This is one reason, although not the main reason, why clear-cut correlations between particular brain structures and particular aspects of language have proved tantalizingly elusive. Nevertheless, correspondences do exist, as I will show in Section 6.3.1, including some that are promising for the syllabic model.

We know something too about brain evolution. Relating that to language evolution is even more tricky than exploring how language is controlled in the modern human brain, but I will explore in Section 6.3.2 a recent suggestion about how the brain has been reorganized in the course of language evolution. (The issue of brain size has already been discussed in an anthropological context in Section 6.2.)

### 6.3.1. Neurological and Linguistic Correspondences

There are three independent correspondences between the syllabic model for syntactic evolution and the neurological basis of language. These correspondences tend to confirm the syllabic model in the sense that, although the model does not predict them in detail, their absence would have required extraneous explanation of a kind that turns out to be unnecessary.

The first correspondence concerns the broad characteristics of Broca's and Wernicke's aphasia. In 1861 Paul Broca found a lesion in the frontal lobe of the left hemisphere of the brain of a patient who could say nothing except one syllable. Not all people with Broca's aphasia are as silent as Broca's original patient, but they all suffer more or less from **agrammatism** (speech that is syntactically disjointed, with grammatical words such as determiners, conjunctions, and auxiliaries left out), and their speech tends to be slow and effortful. On the other hand, their understanding of what is said to them is good (with important qualifications that we will come to shortly). Carl Wernicke later gave his name to the effects of a lesion further back in the left hemisphere, in the temporal lobe and part of the parietal lobe. Wernicke's aphasics can speak fluently, but what they say is rambling

---

[15] For a layperson's introduction to the brain's role in language, see Pinker (1994). For a wider-ranging but still introductory treatment, see Calvin and Ojemann (1994). Both books also provide more detailed references.

and empty, with many nonsense words. Moreover, by contrast with Broca's aphasics, their understanding is poor.

These two types of aphasia are relevant to the syllabic model in the following general respect. If the evolution of syntax had nothing to do with the evolution of speech, there would be no reason to expect that articulatory disturbances should be associated with disturbances of syntax rather than of vocabulary. In other words, there would be no reason to expect that slow and laboured articulation should generally accompany the agrammatism of Broca's aphasia rather than the lexical confusion of Wernicke's. So the fact that the associations are as they are fits the syllabic model.

The second correspondence concerns the functions of certain adjacent parts of the cortex (or outer layer) of the brain. The syllabic model presupposes a certain versatility or plasticity on the part of different areas of the cortex. It would be futile to suggest that the sentence/NP distinction might be a by-product of the syllable/nucleus distinction if the functions of given areas of cortex were rigid and immutable, for then the neural mechanisms that control articulation in speech could never acquire any role in syntax. But there is considerable evidence for the necessary plasticity, at the level both of the individual and of the species.

At the level of the individual, the most striking evidence comes from the effects of massive brain damage in early infancy. Although in most individuals (including left-handers) the main centres for the control of language are located in the left hemisphere, a child who suffers massive left-hemisphere damage in infancy can nevertheless acquire a considerable command of language (Dennis and Whitaker 1976; Isaacs *et al.* 1996). It is as if some capacity for language development is innately present in parts of the brain remote from the normal language centres, but this back-up capacity withers unless it is called upon as a result of damage to the normal mechanisms early in life. Moreover, there are parts of the cortex whose function may change in one individual over time, owing to changes in the demands placed on them by the body parts with which they are connected. Exercising one finger can increase the area of cortex devoted to controlling it, and in blind people the cortex areas for finger control are larger than average (Calvin and Ojemann 1994: 188 and references cited there).

At the level of the species, the possibility of recruiting for syntactic purposes parts of the brain that originally had other functions is widely agreed (see e.g. Calvin 1989), although opinions differ on what these other functions were. Suggestions include the hierarchical organization of activities such as toolmaking or throwing (see Section 6.2.3) or 'a generalization of neural mechanisms that gradually evolved in the motor cortex to facilitate the automatization of motor activity' (Lieberman 1984: 67). But if the syllabic model for syntax is correct, we will expect to find Broca's area next to an area of cortex associated with a particular domain of motor activity—namely, that of the lips, jaw, and tongue. And this is indeed what we find. Behind Broca's area, the frontal lobe is separated from the parietal lobe by a cortical furrow called the central sulcus (or Rolandic fissure). Just behind Broca's area, between it and the central sulcus, is the motor strip, which controls movement in various parts of the body, while just behind the central sulcus is the sensory strip, which registers tactile sensations from the same areas. The crucial fact for our purposes is that the part of the motor strip closest to Broca's area controls not (for example) the legs or the hands but rather the tongue, jaw, and lips. This is exactly what we expect if the neural mechanisms recruited to control syntax at the stage of language evolution with which Chapter 5 was concerned were mechanisms whose original function was to control articulation and the structure of syllables as phonological units.[16]

The third correspondence is more subtle and will take longer to describe. It concerns aspects of the agrammatism that is associated with Broca's aphasia. The contrasting symptoms associated with damage to Broca's and Wernicke's areas were originally interpreted as meaning that Broca's area was responsible for speech production whereas Wernicke's area was responsible for comprehension. In recent decades, however, this neat dichotomy has come to be rejected. More fine-grained experiments on Broca's aphasics have revealed a tendency to mis-interpret sentences in which the choice of lexical items does not by itself render only one interpretation plausible (Zurif 1995). Consider the following pair of sentences, with *mouse* and *boy* emphasized:

(5)   It was the *mouse* that the cat chased.
(6)   It was the *boy* whom the girl chased.

For a sentence whose open-class vocabulary consists of just the three words *chased*, *mouse*, and *cat*, like (5), there is only one sensible interpretation, irrespec-tive of its grammar, just in virtue of our general knowledge about cats and mice. On the other hand, a sentence containing the three words *chased*, *boy*, and *girl* could mean either of two things, because both girls and boys can chase one another; the correct interpretation of (6) therefore relies crucially on grammar. And it turns out that Broca's aphasics do significantly worse on interpreting sentences like (6), where the range of likely interpretations is not narrowed down by the choice of vocabulary. It therefore seemed for a while reasonable to con-clude that, in Broca's aphasia, syntax was disrupted in comprehension as much as in production (Caramazza and Zurif 1976). The old view of Broca's and Wernicke's aphasia as involving a production/comprehension dichotomy was thus replaced by one involving a new but equally neat dichotomy, between grammar and vocabulary.

This new view has, however, been challenged by evidence that Broca's aphasics whose comprehension is disrupted in the way just described can nevertheless do surprisingly well when asked to judge as 'good' or 'bad' sentences that differ in

---

[16]  The same fact is cited by Jerison (1982: 765) as evidence against the view that spoken language evolved from gesture.

grammaticality—not perfectly well, but much better than would be expected if their aphasia affected their entire command of grammar (Linebarger *et al.* 1983; Bates *et al.* 1991: 134–5). If they simply ignored grammar altogether, one would expect them to accept as 'good' any string whose open-class words can jointly be made sense of in some pragmatically plausible fashion. One would, therefore, expect them to accept all the sentences in (7)–(10), including those starred as ungrammatical:

(7)  (a)  I want you to go to the store now.
    (b)  *I hope you to go to the store now.
(8)  (a)  I hope you will go to the store now.
    (b)  *I want you will go to the store now.
(9)  (a)  Mary ate the bread that I baked.
    (b)  *Mary ate the bread that I baked a cake.
(10) (a)  How many birds did you see in the park?
    (b)  *How many did you see birds in the park?

Examples (7) and (8) illustrate the difference between *want* and *hope* in respect of the kind of clausal complement they permit; (9) illustrates the unacceptability of 'gapless' relative clauses; and (10) illustrates the impossibility of moving a specifier (*how many*) out of its NP (*how many birds*). But, on the basis of their lexical content alone, they can all be made sense of; (9*b*) might mean, for example, the same as *Mary ate the bread and I baked a cake*. Yet these judgement tasks are among those on which Linebarger and her colleagues found that their agrammatic patients did well, with a pattern of acceptability judgements close to that of normal speakers. But three tasks on which the patients did less well as a group involved reflexives and tag questions (*isn't he?*, *doesn't it?*, etc.), as illustrated in the following pairs:[17]

(11) (a)  I helped myself to the birthday cake.
    (b)  *I helped themselves to the birthday cake.
(12) (a)  The famous man himself attended the ceremony.
    (b)  *The famous man itself attended the ceremony.
(13) (a)  The little boy fell down, didn't he?
    (b)  *The little boy fell down, didn't it?
(14) (a)  John is very tall, isn't he?
    (b)  *John is very tall, doesn't he?

A reason for this discrepancy in performance has been suggested by Mauner, Fromkin, and Cornell (1993). Before considering it, however, I will explore

---

[17] The words 'as a group' are important. Among the four patients studied, only one did consistently less well on all these three judgement tasks (involving reflexives, subject tags, and auxiliary tags) than she did on any of the other seven judgement tasks that were posed. This variability in performance within an already small group makes it risky to regard any interpretation as firm.

whether there is any viable suggestion that fits the syllabic model for sy
evolution. Recall that, as emphasized in Chapter 5, this model does not se
explain every aspect of modern syntax but only those aspects that can plausibly ~
ascribed to the carry-over into syntax of structural characteristics of the syllable.
There is far more to modern syntax than this. But if the syllable-derived aspects
of syntax are the oldest, we should not be surprised to find that they are governed
by somewhat different neural mechanisms than the more recent accretions, and
are differently affected in aphasia. For example, we may find that the sort of aphasia that affects phonetic production also disrupts relatively fundamental aspects of
sentence structure, such as identifying which NP is privileged (through being
subject or topic, for example), while sparing finer syntactic niceties whose biological basis is more recent. If so, we may find that someone with this sort of
aphasia can correctly identify ungrammatical sentences as 'bad' because of violations of these finer niceties, even though she fails comprehension tests that
depend on correctly identifying a sentence's verb and its subject. For such a
person, a relatively intact sensitivity to those grammatical details that are not
derived from syllable structure may conceal a void where mastery of basic
sentence structure should be. The question now is whether the pattern of acceptability judgements displayed by Linebarger's agrammatic patients is consistent
with this suggestion.

It seems reasonable to answer yes, at least provisionally. I will illustrate in relation to (7)–(14) the sort of considerations that will be relevant. Examples (7) and
(8) are entirely consistent with my suggestion, because the difference in the sentential complements of *want* and *hope* is a parochial English matter rather than a
fundamental matter of clause structure, so is among the syntactic niceties that I
suggest may remain intact in agrammatic aphasia. Example (9) is likewise
accounted for by a parochial feature of English grammar—namely, the fact that
English uses the gapping strategy rather than the resumptive-pronoun strategy in
relative-clause formation. What this means can be seen by comparing (9*a*) with a
Greek translation:

(15)   I   María   éfage   to   psomí   pu   to   épsisa.
     the   Mary   ate   the   bread   that   it   I-baked

The Greek relative clause *pu to épsisa* contains a pronoun *to* 'it' that refers back to
(or 'resumes') the noun that the relative clause modifies—namely, *psomí* 'bread'.
The English version at (9*a*) contains no such resumptive pronoun, because we
cannot say *Mary ate the bread that I baked it*. But the fact that Greek differs from
English in this respect shows that neither language's behaviour can plausibly be
regarded as part of the syllable-derived syntactic substructure. Therefore the gap
in the relative clause in (9*a*) belongs to a branch of syntax that may plausibly be
spared even while syllable-derived aspects are disrupted, and the absence of the
gap in (9*b*) is something that a Broca's aphasic can be expected to notice as 'bad'

even while she has difficulty in understanding argument structure (who does what to whom) from its encoding in simple sentences.

The aphasic's insensitivity to basic sentence structure may make (10*b*) seem at first sight a strong candidate to be passed as 'good', as being a blend of *How many did you see in the park?* (where *how many* is the patient or 'theme' argument) and *Did you see birds in the park?* (where *birds* is the theme argument). The only thing wrong with (10*b*), we may think, is that it seems to contain one theme argument too many. Why is it, then, that Linebarger's patients tend to identify (10*b*) correctly as 'bad'? My suggested answer involves recalling that, in Broca's aphasia, although some syntactic abilities are disrupted, pragmatic abilities seem to be unaffected. That is why patients cannot consistently pick out the right picture to match (6) but can do so with (5), which is pragmatically unambiguous. Presented with a sentence about seeing something in the park, even though they will be oblivious to syntactic clues identifying particular NPs as agent or theme, they will still expect to find one NP that plausibly designates someone who sees and one that designates something that is seen. The problem with (10*b*) is that it seems to have three NPs jostling for these two jobs—namely, *how many*, *you*, and *birds*, so in correctly classifying it as 'bad' an agrammatic patient may be relying on pragmatic factors rather than on grammar, whether syllable-derived or not.

The poor performance of Linebarger's patients on (11*b*) follows from their inability to identify which NP is syntactically privileged, I suggest. This entails an inability to interpret correctly any grammatical indicator that some other NP has the same reference as the syntactically privileged one. In (11*b*) the reflexive pronoun *themselves* is just such a grammatical indicator. The element *-selves* indicates that the subject NP (syntactically privileged in English) must refer to the same individuals as *themselves* does, and must therefore be plural too. But an aphasic who cannot identify which NP is the subject will inevitably be unable to spot a mismatch in number between a subject NP and a reflexive pronoun, and is therefore likely to overlook the 'badness' of (11*b*). Insensitivity to syntactic privilege is also crucial to (13), involving one kind of tag question. Correctly classifying (13*b*) as 'bad' involves sensitivity to the subject NP in the sentence to which the question is tagged, so that the inappropriate subject pronoun in the question (*it* in (13*b*) ) can be recognized as such. But sensitivity to subjects belongs to the basic syllable-derived core of syntax that is damaged in Broca's aphasics; so it is no wonder that they tend to go wrong on subject pronouns in tags.

Damage to the syllable-derived core of syntax involves also damage to the recognition of the nucleus-like position and hence of the status of its verbal occupants. This leads us to expect that in tag questions Broca's aphasics should be just as bad at spotting inappropriate pro-verbs (forms of *be*, *do*, and *have*) as at spotting inappropriate pronouns. And examples such as (14) show that this expectation is correct.

That leaves (12). In (12*b*), the pronoun *itself* within the NP *the famous man itself* has an emphatic function rather than a reflexive function as an NP on its own, like the pronouns *myself* and *themselves* in (11). Syllable-derived syntax is, therefore, not relevant in (12), and I can suggest no reason why some or all of Linebarger's patients should fail to detect anything wrong with (12*b*). But it appears that Linebarger and her colleagues lumped examples with emphatic pronouns and with true reflexives together for testing purposes, so it may be that a finer-grained test that discriminated them would reveal divergent patterns of judgement.

At the risk of oversimplifying, I will sum up as follows what I suggest is going on with Linebarger's patients. At least the following three factors play a part in the receptive processing of any sentence:

(*a*) pragmatic expectations about what the sentence should mean, based on its lexical content and our general knowledge (such as our knowledge that cats generally chase mice, not vice versa);

(*b*) interpretation of syllable-derived aspects of sentence structure, including recognition of the very fact that it is a sentence (with a verbal or quasi-verbal head) rather than some other kind of unit such as an NP, and identification of any constituents with onset-like privileges such as subjecthood or immediate preverbal position;

(*c*) interpretation of non-syllable-derived aspects of grammar, such as relative-clause-formation strategy or choice among types of clausal complement (e.g. *I hope that you will go* versus *I want you to go*).

In patients with the kind of aphasia where the syllabic organization of speech is damaged, leading to slow and effortful articulation, factor (*b*) is damaged too (I suggest), but factors (*a*) and (*c*) may be spared. This kind of damage may be compared to that suffered by a wooden-framed house in which the structural timbers have been eaten by termites while the roof and weatherboards are intact. The damage to the studs and joists is masked by the soundness of the cladding, just as the comprehension deficits of Broca's patients are generally masked in normal conversation and become evident only under laboratory conditions. Moreover, just as the cladding may compensate more or less well for weakness of the structural timbers, depending on how it is designed and how solidly it is constructed, we should not be surprised to find that non-syllable-derived aspects of grammar may compensate more or less well for deficits in the syllable-derived aspects. This means that we should not be surprised to find that Broca's aphasia manifests itself in rather different ways in languages that differ in their use of inflectional morphology or in the freedom or rigidity of their word order, for example.

Cross-linguistic differences in manifestations of aphasia have indeed been found (Bates *et al.* 1991). However, one symptom of Broca's aphasia seems to be common to speakers of all languages so far investigated—namely, that verbs suffer worse than nouns. This is true both for languages where verbs are elaborately inflected for tense, person, and so on, such as Hungarian, and for languages where verbs are not inflected at all, such as Chinese. Such a finding is just what we will expect, in terms of the syllabic model; for, if Broca's aphasia involves damaged access to both syllable structure and its syntactic homologue, then verbs, whose syntactic status is the counterpart of the status of the nucleus within the syllable, should be particularly vulnerable.

In broad terms, Linebarger's finding of a mismatch between comprehension and grammaticality judgements among English-speaking aphasics is supported in a later study by Beverly Wulfeck (1988). Wulfeck's study differs from Linebarger's in two main respects. First, the subjects' comprehension was tested on the same sentences as were used in the grammaticality-judgement task. This enabled Wulfeck to check how well an individual's performance on the two tasks is correlated, in relation to sentences of any one type. The correlation turns out to vary from one individual to another and from one sentence type to another. It seems clear, however, that semantic and pragmatic factors affect comprehension much more than they affect grammaticality judgements—a finding that seems consistent with the tripartite view of linguistic processing just outlined, in which a pragmatic factor (*a*) is distinguished from grammatical factors (*b*) and (*c*). The second difference is that Wulfeck explored a narrower range of syntactic constructions, consisting of just tag questions, reflexives, simple subject–verb–object sentences, and sentences with centre-embedded relative clauses (as in *The mouse [that the cat chased] died*, where the relative clause is bracketed). This difference is unfortunate for our present purposes, since Wulfeck ignores most of those aspects of grammar which, according to my analysis, are clearly not homologous with syllable structure. Her study is, therefore, not much help in testing the prediction that, in Broca's aphasia, syllable-derived grammar (corresponding to factor (*b*)) should be affected significantly worse than non-syllable-derived grammar (factor (*c*)).

My suggested explanations for Linebarger, Schwartz, and Saffran's findings have advantages, I think, over those proposed by Mauner and her colleagues (1993). The latter attribute the aphasics' performance to an impairment in the syntax of 'referential dependency'—that is, an impairment in the ability to interpret those syntactic elements (anaphoric pronouns and traces left by the syntactic movement of NPs) that are required in normal syntax to have the same reference as certain other NPs. But their account suffers from three drawbacks. First, to account for the agrammatics' blindness to inappropriate auxiliaries in tag questions such as (14*b*), Mauner and her colleagues are forced to extend the notion 'reference' to cover items that are verbal rather than nominal and that are words rather than phrases—an extension that, in terms of their Chomskyan syntactic framework, is *ad hoc*. Secondly, they offer no reason why it should be referential dependency in particular that is impaired, rather than any other aspect of syntax.[18] Thirdly, and perhaps most crucially, they offer no reason why syntactic deficits should tend to co-occur with articulatory impairment. The syllabic model has none of these drawbacks.

This concludes my discussion of the third correspondence between what the syllabic model for syntax predicts and what the neurological underpinnings of language reveal. Considering that the model was not proposed with aphasia in mind, the overall correspondence is gratifyingly close, and suggests an explanation for the Linebarger data that is at least as economical and well-fitting as any other on offer.

### 6.3.2. Brain–Language Coevolution and Vocal-Tract Changes

It has seemed to some researchers that there is an insuperable obstacle to deriving human language from a primate call system. This is the fact that the brain structures that control primate vocalization seem to be different from those that control human speech (Myers 1976; Bradshaw and Rogers 1992: 326–8). Surgically removing the homologue of Broca's area (or what seems to be the homologue of Broca's area) in rhesus monkeys does not affect their ability to vocalize. Facts such as these have been interpreted as showing that voluntary vocalization is controlled by the brain's neocortex and involuntary vocalization is controlled quite separately by the supposedly older limbic system. Yet, unless Broca's area is at least potentially relevant to voluntary vocalization at the stage in language evolution visualized in Chapter 5, the correspondences just described, whatever their modern significance, cannot be regarded as supporting the syllabic model for sentence structure.

I will not attempt a complete survey of current views on the role of Broca's area or its homologues in other primates, much less a balanced evaluation of them. For present purposes it is enough to point out that the doctrine just summarized is under attack (Steklis 1985). The three million years or more during which brains have evolved in human ancestry since the earliest australopithecines provide plenty of time for parts of the cortex to acquire new functions (Deacon 1989, 1992, 1997), and indeed 'for many features of language to have arisen, flourished, and perished without trace' (Deacon 1992: 77). Newman (1992) has drawn attention to similarities between intonation contours in adult speech, in babies' cries, and in the 'isolation call' of many primates (the call made by a young monkey or ape when separated from its mother); he attributes these similarities to the shared involvement of the brain region known as the anterior cingulate gyrus. Likewise,

---

[18] Deane (1992), from a cognitive-grammatical standpoint, tries to explain the Linebarger data in such a way that the role of referential dependency is not accidental but rather a consequence of the central role played in language (he thinks) by the inferior parietal lobe. But the inferior parietal lobe is some distance away from Broca's area; so Deane faces a prima facie difficulty in explaining why this area has not generally been implicated in syntactic deficits.

Deacon argues that the brain areas for controlling vocalization in humans and other primates are linked through neural connections via the prefrontal cortex, which includes the part of the brain associated with certain 'higher' mental functions: maintaining mental images of things in their absence and planning sequences of actions (Calvin and Ojemann 1994: 141–2).

Human brains differ from other primate brains not just in overall size but in the relative size of various internal parts, and one part that is especially large in humans is the prefrontal cortex. Deacon (1992, 1997) suggests that this enlargement is due to the coevolution of brain and language through mutual feedback. Restricting the term 'language evolution' to purely sociocultural processes of language development, independent of brain mechanisms, he sums up this feedback as follows: 'subtle biases in the conditions for language evolution may become amplified through their influence on brain evolution and subtle biases introduced by cognitive limitations or neurological predispositions may become amplified through their influence on patterns of language evolution' (Deacon 1992: 50). The scenario presented in Chapter 5 can be seen as involving mutual amplification of just this kind. It is unrealistic to suppose that the larynx was fully lowered to its modern adult position before it had any effect in terms of an increase in vocabulary size and hence a need for duality of patterning and for syntactic organization. That is why I posited an intermediate stage of articulatory development in which only part of the modern range of articulatory possibilities was available. But even this involves an oversimplifying assumption, useful though it may be for expository purposes. It is not that the larynx was lowered in two stages rather than one. Rather, the gradual expansion in the vocal repertoire (involving improvements in breath control and articulatory precision as well as repositioning of the larynx) acted in concert with neurologically based synonymy-avoidance principles to amplify pressure for vocabulary expansion—so perhaps encouraging expansion of the prefrontal cortex, which today has a role in word association. But limitations on the number of new vocalizations that could be learned, stored, and used as wholes would in turn create conditions that would amplify any predisposition for the neurological mechanism underlying syllable-based phonology to widen its field of responsibility. This mechanism could supply a kind of syntactic organization that, by providing systematic and reliable interpretations for relatively long vocalizations construed as strings of 'words', would help to increase the advantages of the changes in the vocal apparatus that made such longer vocalizations possible. So some of the effects of the vocal-tract changes feed back as encouragement for the changes to be maintained and enhanced.

I have presented the syllabic model for syntactic development as consistent with Deacon's view of the brain. It may seem that, in doing so, I run up against Deacon's own scepticism about vocal-tract evolution as a major factor in brain–language coevolution. Responding to Lieberman, he urges us not to underestimate the articulatory range of an ape-like vocal tract. Even though an undescended larynx precludes the modern range of vowel contrasts, there would still be scope for kinds of vocalization involving contrasts between consonantal and vocalic sounds (he says), with a greater reliance on various kinds of redundancy than in modern languages, compensating for 'relatively more vague' speech-sound distinctions (Deacon 1992: 75; cf. 1997: 358).

This apparent disagreement is mainly a matter of emphasis, however. The syllabic model purports to account for only certain aspects of syntax, and there is plenty of scope to seek explanation for other aspects elsewhere. The scenario presented in Chapter 5 does not posit any crucial evolutionary Rubicon before which 'language' did not exist, for the whole discussion both there and in Chapter 2 presupposes that it is worthwhile to investigate the implications of assuming no radical discontinuity between primate vocalization and human language. Besides, believing in the significance of vocal tract changes for syntactic evolution by no means commits one to believing that the sentence/NP distinction was absent from the forms of language used by all our ancestors until anatomically modern humans (*Homo sapiens sapiens*) appeared on the scene. As Deacon himself points out, there is evidence that the larynx was already lowered to a significant extent before even archaic *Homo sapiens*. Larynxes, being soft tissue, are not preserved in fossils, but Laitman, Reidenberg, and Gannon claim to have established a correlation between the position of the larynx and the shape of the basicranium (the base of the skull) strong enough to allow them to conclude that already in *Homo erectus*, by more than 1.5 million years BP, the larynx was lowered sufficiently to introduce the modern human risk of choking but to provide also the compensatory advantage of 'an expanded supralaryngeal portion of the pharynx available to modify initial layngeal sounds. As a result, the variety of sounds *H. erectus* could have produced was greater than that possible for the earlier australopithecines' (Laitman *et al.* 1992: 393). Deacon (1992) quotes a personal communication in which Laitman suggests more precisely that adult *Homo erectus* would have had a larynx in a position equivalent to that of a modern 5-year-old—not so low as in a modern adult, but low enough to produce a range of vowels including [a], [u], and the crucial [i], whose calibrating function is emphasized by Lieberman.

Laitman's basicranium–larynx correlation has been challenged by other biological anthropologists (Schepartz 1993)—but with the implication that he underestimates, not overestimates, the extent of larynx-lowering in *erectus*. So it seems safe to conclude that at least the beginnings of syllable-derived motivation for a sentence/NP distinction can be dated as far back as the first quarter of the two-million-year period that Deacon posits for brain–language coevolution on the basis of archaeological and neurological evidence. This is sufficient to establish syllable structure as an early competitor among the various neural predispositions, cognitive limitations, and behavioural factors whose interplay Deacon sees as evolutionarily relevant to language. It is, therefore, sufficient to establish its broad consistency with Deacon's approach to brain–language coevolution.

More importantly, my scenario supplies an answer to a question that Deacon has posed more recently (1996, 1997): why is human language unique in the sense that no non-human animal makes even the most rudimentary communicative use of symbols that are combinable in a rule-governed but open-ended fashion? Deacon's answer is: because only humans are capable of 'symbolic reference', which he attributes to the uniquely human expansion of the prefrontal cortex. Deacon argues at length (1997) that 'symbolic reference' involves a range of characteristics certainly not present in call systems such as that of vervet monkeys. For example, he claims that a word cannot have 'symbolic reference' unless it is used in the context of other words in a phrase or sentence, and that symbols derive their meaning from their relationship with other symbols, so that 'symbolic reference' presupposes a relatively complex vocabulary.

Deacon's appeal to 'symbolic reference' does not satisfactorily answer the question that he himself poses, however. If 'symbolic reference' presupposes the combination of words in sentences and phrases, then to claim that syntax has evolved because of 'symbolic reference' clearly risks circularity. To break out of the circle, Deacon needs to suggest an evolutionary rationale for specific syntactic phenomena. The closest that he comes to this is in a discussion of the 'complementary functional roles and phrase components of language'—namely, subject and predicate, topic and comment, agent and action, or 'operator' and 'operand': 'The earliest symbolic systems would necessarily have been combinatorial and would have exhibited something like this operator–operand structure (and probably subject–predicate structure) right from the start. . . . In other words, some form of grammar and syntax has been around since the dawn of symbolic communication' (Deacon 1997: 334). But, as we saw in Chapter 2, 'some form of grammar and syntax' need not be syntax-as-it-is. In particular, one can conceive of a kind of syntax (namely, Monocategoric) that certainly differentiates operators from operands, and would be perfectly adequate for expressing semantic predicate–argument relationships, but which lacks a sentence/NP distinction and therefore has no subject–predicate structure, inasmuch as that presupposes sentences. What we need is an answer not just to the question of why syntax should be 'combinatorial' but to the question of why it has the particular combinatorial structure that it has. Deacon admits that there is much in language that his account ignores: 'Most of the details of modern languages have other later evolutionary causes' (1997: 409). But this amounts to saying that his account, for all its possible value in relating brain structures with cognitive developments, offers no rival answer to the questions that the syllabic scenario addresses.

Some scholars have gone further than Deacon in downplaying the importance of the vocal tract in language evolution. Wind (1976, 1989) goes so far as to assess its importance as virtually zero. As he puts it:

[A]fter removal of the epiglottis, (parts of) the tongue, palate, teeth, or lips, and in many other pathological conditions of the vocal tract, man is usually still able to make himself understood by his vocalizations. . . . Let us . . . assume that a whole chimpanzee vocal tract would be transplanted into a human individual while its nervous system would remain human. . . . only the encoding speed would be slightly lower than in most other humans, but for the rest such speech would hardly differ from the normal. (1976: 626)

Wind's optimistic guess about this chimpanzee–human hybrid contradicts the findings of Duchin (1990) concerning the size, shape, and musculature of the chimpanzee tongue. But in any case it is a mistake to treat our resourcefulness in compensating for pathological defects as evidence that normal conditions are evolutionarily irrelevant. One might as well argue that the ingenuity with which arm and hand defects are overcome by many victims of the thalidomide tragedy shows that there is no advantage for humans in having normal arms and hands.

Even if a kind of vocalization incorporating consonant–vowel alternations developed before the modern or *erectus* range of vowel distinctions was made available by the lowering of the larynx, that does not weaken the claim that the lowering of the larynx was significant for the evolution of syntax. Let us allow, for the sake of argument, that speech went through an evolutionary stage with something like the range of consonants posited in Section 5.4—that is, [p], [t], [k], [m], [n], and [s]—but with no independent control of vowel quality. Recall now one of the factors mentioned in Chapter 5 as underlying the importance of syllables in modern languages—namely, the acoustic inseparability of the onset consonant and the nuclear vowel. This inseparability entails that the execution of a sound sequence such as [pi], [ka], or [tu] must be planned as a unit; it cannot be a matter of instructing the lips or tongue to produce the consonant and separately instructing them to produce the vowel. But in a form of speech where there is only a narrow range of vowel timbres whose distribution is almost entirely if not entirely determined by surrounding consonantal articulations, this combined planning of consonantal and vocalic articulation would not yet be generally necessary. Therefore, that form of speech would lack an important articulatory–acoustic motivation for recognizing the syllable as a unit in terms of which the neurological control of speech must operate. It is only when vowel and consonant articulation have achieved some independence—effectively, when the larynx has begun to be at least partially lowered—that the need arises for a kind of phonological organization that differentiates between the syllable and its constituents. It is conceivable that language may have gone through a stage (presumably before *Homo erectus*, if Laitman and his colleagues are right) when consonantal elaboration was, so to speak, ahead of vocalic.[19] But the syllabic model commits us to saying that at that stage, if it existed, the sentence/NP

---

[19] The existence of languages with only one or two phonemic vowels, or even none at all, has been seen by some scholars, including Deacon (1992), as evidence that there was such a stage. But in Section 4.3 I argued that these languages have no special relevance for evolutionary questions.

distinction in syntax would not yet have arisen. I can see no evidence that Deacon or Wind might adduce to disprove that corollary of the model.

It may still seem that an approach that highlights the importance of vocal-tract changes, such as mine, has a disadvantage in relation to one which downplays their importance, such as Deacon's. Deacon's scenario suggests a clear reason why the larynx should have lowered—namely, to facilitate speech as a mode of expression for the kind of language that was coevolving with the brain. But Deacon's scenario enjoys an advantage only if no alternative motivation can be suggested for the lowering of the larynx. In fact, as we saw in Section 6.2.2, there is ample alternative motivation, involving bipedalism and rapid breathing. It seems fair to conclude that Deacon's suggestions about brain–language coevolution complement the syllabic scenario usefully in areas that that scenario has nothing to say about, such as the role of the prefrontal cortex, but do not provide a viable alternative account of the evolution of those aspects of language that the syllabic scenario is concerned with.

### 6.3.3. Mental Representations, Conceptual Structure, and (Dis)continuism

We have already noted that two of the labels that have come to be used in order to categorize theories of language evolution are 'continuist' and 'discontinuist'. Continuist theories are those that posit an evolutionary continuity between human language and an ancestral vocal call system, so that modern language is a cousin of the contemporary call systems of other primates. Discontinuist theories deny this continuity, so must seek the origin of language somewhere else. The alternative source posited by Bickerton (1990) and Wilkins and Wakefield (1995) is a mental structure for the representation of reality. Bickerton calls this structure the 'secondary representational system' (SRS) to distinguish it from the 'primary representational system' that is directly tied to sensory input. Colour-blind people differ from people with normal vision in respect of the visual component of their primary representational system, but they may all share the same secondary representational system, which in Bickerton's view is closely tied to language; it is in fact the 'latent protolanguage' of Sections 4.4.5 and 5.6.10. The kind of mental representation that Wilkins and Wakefield see as relevant is relatively independent of language, and more akin to the 'conceptual structure' (CS) posited by Jackendoff (1983). What matters to us, however, is whether either of these representational systems successfully accounts for the sentence/NP distinction in syntax.

Central to Wilkins and Wakefield's scenario is the cortical configuration known as the **parieto-occipito-temporal junction** (POT), which is peculiar to humans. On the basis of data from comparative primate neurology and from palaeoneurology (the reconstruction of brain structure from fossil endocasts and from marks on the interior surface of fossil skulls), they conclude that the POT developed at about the stage of *Homo habilis*, owing to cortical refolding due in turn to the expansion of the parietal lobe in the brains of our hominid ancestors. The significance of the POT is its alleged role in the human ability 'to identify distinctive properties of presented data and then to characterize these properties in sufficiently abstract form that they are generalizable across situations' (Wilkins and Wakefield 1995: 169). Other primates can make cross-modal perceptual associations so as to allow them to identify by sight an object that they have previously only encountered by touch, and vice versa; but only humans (it is claimed) can perform the more abstract tasks of identifying the characteristics that disparate objects share and of forming concepts that are not merely cross-modal but amodal, or independent of perceptual modality.[20] Another peculiarly human cortical feature (Wilkins and Wakefield claim) is Broca's area, 'whose inherent specialization is the hierarchical structuring of information' (1995: 170) and which also first appeared in *Homo habilis*. The POT and Broca's area, therefore, made possible jointly for the first time a mental map of the world in which concepts could be both cross-classified through shared properties and hierarchically related (e.g. as superordinate versus hyponym or whole versus part). This mental map (essentially the same as Jackendoff's 'conceptual structure') was a necessary though not a sufficient condition for the development of language (1995: 177).

We have already seen that Bickerton does not address the issue of why language evolved in the direction of syntax-as-it-is rather than alternatives such as Spatiotemporal or Monocategoric. Do Wilkins and Wakefield have more to say? At first sight, the answer is no. Discussing how CS facilitated the construction of a lexicon among 'primitive language-capable learners', they add: 'It falls outside the scope of the lexical learning theory to predict how the learner moves from the acquisition of lexical entries to aspects of the syntactic component. It also falls outside the scope of this target article to speculate on how language evolved once the emergent capacity and CS came into existence' (1995: 179). Nevertheless they regard their view of the role of Broca's area as broadly compatible with that of Greenfield (1991) (discussed in Section 6.2.3), according to which hierarchical structure in both syntax and phonology is directly related to the organization of sequences of actions, such as grasping a spoon, dipping it into a bowl, and lifting it to the mouth. To that extent they support Greenfield's account of the origin of syntax. But I have already criticized that account as too vague in that it neither discriminates among different conceivable patterns of binary branching nor motivates the sentence/NP distinction. So Wilkins and Wakefield have, after all, no more to offer on the question at issue than Bickerton has.

[20] It is not clear to me how this alleged limitation of non-human primates squares with Premack's (1976) success in training chimpanzees to classify objects as the same or different in respect of categories such as colour or shape. For the sake of argument, however, I will assume that Wilkins and Wakefield are correct.

Wilkins and Wakefield's account suffers a particular weakness in respect of Broca's area. For them, Broca's area is above all the brain centre for hierarchical organization. The fact that it also plays a big part in controlling the speech apparatus is from their point of view merely an accident. As they put it, 'nothing [in their account] precludes the evolutionary development of a close association between Broca's area and aspects of vocal tract control' (Wilkins and Wakefield 1995: 177), but nothing in their account requires it either. In the scenario of Chapter 5, by contrast, the fact that Broca's area has a role in vocal-tract control as well as in syntax is far from accidental. In Chapter 5, the original linguistic function of Broca's area is seen as motor control of the articulatory apparatus. Broca's area's role in the hierarchical organization of syntax was a by-product of that, when the kind of structure that came naturally to the syllable was applied also to strings of meaningful items. For Wilkins and Wakefield to show that their account is superior, despite their failure to relate the phonetic and syntactic roles of Broca's area, it would be necessary for them to show that its role in hierarchical organization (as opposed to motor control) was definitely acquired before the larynx was lowered sufficiently to increase the vocalization repertoire in the fashion described in Chapter 5. But they produce no such evidence.

The syllabic model for sentence structure says nothing precise about the content and structure of the vocabulary, as opposed to its size. The model is, therefore, consistent with Wilkins and Wakefield's view of the special role of the POT in allowing amodal concepts to develop and hence of influencing the repertoire of possible meanings for words, once language evolution had reached a point where the term 'word' can appropriately be used. In that sense, the syllabic model and Wilkins and Wakefield's model are complementary rather than conflicting. But underlying Wilkins and Wakefield's account, like Bickerton's, is a rejection of the syllabic model's continuist assumptions. The reconfiguration of the vocal tract at a stage when our ancestors' vocalizations were akin to modern primate calls cannot be relevant to language evolution if, as they and Bickerton insist, primate call systems have nothing to do with human language.[21] If they are right, therefore, the supposed advantages of the syllabic model must be illusory. Any parallels between syllable structure and sentence structure must be coincidental, and if rejecting the syllabic model means that for the time being we have no precise answer to the questions posed in Chapter 2 about duality of patterning and the sentence/NP distinction, at least we will no longer be seduced by false answers. So it is timely to assess how strong the discontinuist argument is.

There are certainly vast differences between animal call systems and human language. The question is whether these differences are such as to render an evolutionary connection either impossible or highly improbable. Five general (or

---

[21] Wilkins and Wakefield allow that *Homo habilis*'s vocal call system may have furnished the phonetic shape of a few of the original lexical items.

supposedly general) characteristics of animal calls once seemed to weigh against them as percursors of language:

(*a*)  they are closed rather than open;
(*b*)  they are affective or emotive rather than referential;
(*c*)  they are innate rather than learned;
(*d*)  they are iconic rather than symbolic;
(*e*)  they are involuntary rather than voluntary.

I said 'once seemed' rather than 'seem' because the trend of discoveries since the late 1970s has weakened the force of all five.

The openness of human language (the fact that an infinite variety of things can be said in it) was not one of the peculiarities posed for discussion in Chapter 2. Nevertheless, the scenario presented in Chapter 5 shows one route whereby a finite repertoire of calls could have opened out into a system in which an un-limited variety of complex expressions could be produced. On the other side of the coin, some animal communication systems have been claimed to possess a kind of 'syntax' in that segments of calls can appear in different orders, and even though these order contrasts have not yet been shown to be meaningful, it would be premature to rule out the possibility (Hauser and Wolfe 1995).[22]

The supposed generality of characteristics (*b*) and (*c*) has been decisively over-turned by evidence that some vervet monkey calls are associated with objective features of the environment and that their correct use depends partly on learning. These facts were established in the early 1980s by Cheney and Seyfarth (1990), building on work by Tom Struhsaker and Peter Marler; but neither of these features is limited to the calls of vervets or even of primates (for example, it has been known for some time that some birdsong is learned rather than innate) (Hauser 1996). Certainly, vervet monkeys' calls are impossible to classify syntactically (are they nouns or verbs, declarative or imperative?); but that reveals no more than that their call system does not have the kind of grammar that human languages have.

So long as it was thought that animal calls never had external referents, the question of whether such calls were iconic (resembling their referents in some way) or purely symbolic (i.e. arbitrary) did not arise. Besides, common sense seemed to suggest that the possibility of a purely arbitrary or conventional link between a vocal signifier and its meaning must have constituted a major intellec-tual Rubicon that only humans have been able to cross. That is perhaps why one still encounters both the notion that animal calls are 'largely iconic', so as to have characteristic (*d*) (Bickerton 1995: 17; cf. Brandon and Hornstein 1986), and the notion that human language must have had largely iconic beginnings (Foster

---

[22]  If the syllabic model for sentence structure is correct, no such animal 'syntax' can be homologous with human. The immediate issue, however, is whether such opening ever occurs, not with the form it takes.

1978, 1983; Armstrong *et al.* 1995; Harnad 1996). But much evidence from animal communication research (not only from vervets) demonstrates that, if non-iconic referential vocal signals constituted an evolutionary Rubicon, it was a Rubicon that was crossed long before hominids evolved.

Characteristic (*e*) is hard to test in conditions of the kind required for statistically solid, replicable experiments. How can we tell when an animal utters a call by choice, so to speak, and when it utters it as an automatic response to a stimulus? For as long as it was generally accepted that the neural underpinnings of human language and of animal calls were evolutionarily unrelated, it seemed natural to assume that voluntary vocalization was peculiar to humans. But in Section 6.3.2 I pointed out that this unrelatedness no longer seems so obvious. Besides, it now seems clear that primates can utter or suppress calls so as to 'mislead' conspecifics and thus gain a private advantage, such as access to food or a mating opportunity (Byrne and Whiten 1988). Whether or not this means that primates have beliefs about each other's beliefs, it certainly suggests that their vocalizations are not always involuntary in the sense of being rigidly tied to narrow stimuli.

If a strong case could be established for the discontinuist thesis, then the continuist status of the syllabic model might weigh against it more heavily than its accounting for the sentence/NP distinction would weigh in its favour. But the case for the discontinuist thesis looks increasingly weak. Consequently, the Bickerton and Wilkins–Wakefield models do not render the syllabic model superfluous. They are almost certainly right in emphasizing the importance of representational systems and conceptual structure for some aspects of language evolution, but not for the aspects with which this book is mainly concerned.

### 6.3.4.  *The Grammatical Structure of Sign Language*

I argued in Section 4.4.7 that the evidence in favour of the gestural theory of language origin was weak. However, I promised to address in Chapter 6 an intriguing possibility concerning sign language in relation to language evolution—a possibility that could not be expounded until the scenario of Chapter 5 had been presented. The time has come to fulfil that promise.

Let us suppose that syllables and sentences are linked in ontogeny as well as phylogeny, so that a child will not acquire a syntactic sentence/NP distinction unless she also acquires a syllable/margin distinction in speech. If that is true, one will predict that in deaf people the maturation of Broca's area (and perhaps other brain areas) will take a slightly different course than in hearing people, and that in sign language as acquired natively by the deaf there will be no sentence/NP distinction. The findings of the last three decades, emphasizing that sign languages are genuine languages, may seem to prove that prediction false. But the alternative syntaxes explored in Chapter 2 show that languages are imaginable in which the sentence/NP distinction is lacking. So the fact that a sign-language expression is well formed and that its content would be rendered by a sentence in a spoken language (e.g. *John's bicycle was stolen*) is not by itself sufficient reason for calling it a sentence, with the implication of contrast with another kind of sign expression called an NP (e.g. an expression that would correspond to *the theft of John's bicycle*). What then would be suitable criteria for distinguishing sentences from NPs in sign language, and are these criteria met?

I do not know of any attempt to address these questions directly. Certainly, in ASL some signs denoting objects, such as CHAIR, are derived morphologically from signs denoting actions, such as SIT. (I use small capitals here to indicate English glosses of ASL signs.) Supalla and Newport (1978) describe this by saying that some ASL nouns are derived from verbs. But these 'nouns' and 'verbs' could equally well figure as expressions and operators in a sign-language version of Monocategoric, so their existence does not of itself establish that ASL has a sentence/NP distinction. If my questions about sign-language sentences and NPs have not been addressed, that may be merely because the pervasiveness of the sentence/NP distinction in spoken languages makes it seem natural to assume that it must figure in sign languages too. Yet there are conceivable answers to these questions that could provide strong confirmation for the syllabic model. If suitable criteria for distinguishing sign-language sentences from NPs can be identified, and if these criteria are met in all sign languages, that will be no great surprise, for it will show merely that the neurological basis for syntax in deaf and hearing people is identical. On the other hand, if no suitable criteria can be identified, or if no such criteria are met, this will be evidence that the ontogeny of the sentence/NP distinction does indeed depend on the acquisition of syllable structure in speech, and hence powerful new evidence that sentences and syllables are indeed homologous.

Some intriguing indirect evidence exists. Recall that in Monocategoric the expression *you snake* SEE YESTERDAY (Example (27a) in chapter 2) could be glossed in English by a sentence ('You saw a snake yesterday'), an NP headed by *snake* ('the snake you saw yesterday'), or an NP headed by a gerundive nominal ('your having seen a snake yesterday'). I pointed out that the apparent inconvenience of such ambiguity had parallels in actual languages, and could usually be resolved by contextual cues. Nevertheless, that kind of 'ambiguity' is not general in spoken languages—after all, if it were, there would be no sentence/NP distinction to explain. But many expressions in ASL seem to be systematically ambiguous in much the same way as the Monocategoric expression. Consider (16):

(16)   RECENTLY DOG CHASE+ CAT

In isolation, this is most naturally glossed in English as a sentence ('Recently the dog chased the cat'), and it would seem natural therefore to classify the ASL expression as a sentence too. Yet in the following context this expression must be glossed as an English NP:

(17)   [RECENTLY DOG CHASE+ CAT] COME HOME
       'The dog that recently chased the cat came home.'
       'The cat that the dog recently chased came home.'

In the context of (17), (16) functions like an NP containing a relative clause, the head of the NP being either of the two nouns in the clause.

One way of describing this situation is to say that in (17) RECENTLY DOG CHASE+ CAT really is a relative clause with an internal head. This is the style of analysis favoured by Liddell (1978, 1980), from whom these ASL data are drawn. He points out that in (17) RECENTLY DOG CHASE+ CAT is marked as subordinate by a characteristic facial expression (head tilted back, eyebrows raised, upper lip tense), and that relative clauses with the same internal-head pattern and the same potential for ambiguity are found also in some spoken languages, such as Diegueño (indigenous to San Diego County in California). But, in the light of our discussion of *you snake* SEE YESTERDAY in Monocategoric, it would be rash to exclude the possibility that RECENTLY DOG CHASE+ CAT, in both (16) and (17), is neither a sentence nor an NP but akin to a Monocategoric expression—a syntactic unit of a kind not found in spoken languages.

If there is indeed no genuinely syntactic distinction between sentences and NPs in ASL, we will expect that any detailed study of 'NPs' in ASL should reveal their structure to be identical with that of ASL 'sentences'. Recent work by Dawn MacLaughlin (1997) suggests that, at the very least, the two structures are closely parallel. In particular, verbal agreement with subjects and objects in ASL 'sentences' mirrors agreement with possessors and possessees respectively in possessive NPs such as the ASL equivalent of *Bob's friend*. Comparing *Bob's friend* with the signed 'sentence' equivalent to *Bob hit Ross*, MacLaughlin points out that, within the 'signing space' in front of the signer's body, the location of subject and possessor alike (*Bob* in both our examples) is indicated by the tilt of the signer's head, whereas the location of object and possessee alike (*Ross* and *friend* in our examples) is indicated by the direction of the signer's eye gaze. The structural resemblance between 'sentences' and 'NPs' is reinforced by further subtle evidence involving the cooperation of manual and non-manual signs (head movements and facial expressions).

Admittedly, MacLaughlin herself does not question the applicability of the sentence/NP distinction to ASL. I must emphasize that, in raising doubts about it, I am by no means advocating a reactionary view of sign languages as not being really languages in their own right, or as being intrinsically narrower in their expressive range than spoken languages. The fact that sign languages are fully-fledged languages does not entail that their grammar must parallel that of spoken languages in all respects, however. Secondly, ASL signers do not need to rely solely on context in order to resolve the ambiguity of sentences such as (17). Liddell describes various mechanisms for doing so, such as a quick nod accompanying the sign for the 'head noun' (DOG or CAT). One can envisage analogous focusing devices in Monocategoric, to distinguish between the readings 'You saw a snake' and 'the snake that you saw' for *you snake* SEE. But such devices need not compromise the basic categorical uniformity of *you snake* SEE, any more than the stress contrast in English between *You saw a* SNAKE and *You* SAW *a snake* affects the fact that they are both sentences. Similarly, the fact that there are devices for distinguishing different interpretations of DOG CHASE+ CAT in ASL does not of itself demonstrate that DOG CHASE+ CAT must in different contexts belong to different syntactic categories.

I do not pretend that this brief discussion of a small range of facts in just one sign language shows that throughout such languages a sentence/NP distinction is lacking. What I hope to have shown, however, is that the question of whether the distinction exists there is by no means nonsensical, and that it deserves serious attention because of its implications for the relationship between syllables and sentences in ontogeny and phylogeny.

## 6.4. Apes and Language

Apes (including chimpanzees, bonobos or pygmy chimpanzees, gorillas, and orangutans) are our closest living animal relatives. If any animals are capable of acquiring and using human language to any extent, apes should surely be among them. On the other hand, they cannot produce the human range of speech sounds, at least partly because their vocal tracts are configured differently from ours. This inhibited attempts to explore their linguistic potential until the 1960s, when Beatrix and Allen Gardner conceived the idea of teaching chimpanzees to use ASL (Gardner *et al.* 1989*b*). At about the same time, David Premack began to train a chimpanzee to communicate by means of plastic tokens (Premack 1976, 1986), and later Duane Rumbaugh initiated a project involving a keyboard of arbitrary symbols or 'lexigrams' that a chimpanzee could press (Rumbaugh 1977). Sign language has also been explored as a means of communication with a gorilla (Patterson 1978) and an orangutan (Miles 1990).[23]

These experiments attracted considerable attention in the ordinary media during the 1970s. They also provoked a sometimes acrimonious debate among linguists, psychologists, and primatologists. Do they demonstrate that what seemed to be the most important cognitive barrier between human beings and other animals is after all an illusion? Or do they merely illustrate a propensity for overenthusiastic misinterpretation on the part of researchers who do not understand

[23] Wallman (1992) provides a convenient catalogue of the various experiments. His highly negative interpretation of them is, of course, controversial.

how human language really works? If one thinks of the possession of language in all-or-nothing terms, it may seem necessary to take sides. On the other hand, if one is exploring (as we are) a scenario according to which the characteristics of modern human language evolved only gradually out of a primate vocalization system, one will not find upsetting the possibility that apes may manifest some of these characteristics and not others. What matters here is whether there is anything in the ape language experiments that bears on the three characteristics of language whose origin we are mainly concerned with (our large vocabulary, duality of patterning, and the sentence/NP distinction), or which either confirms or disconfirms the suggestion that synonymy-avoidance principles are part of our primate inheritance.

It is easy to show that the ape language evidence is compatible with our proposal in respect of vocabulary size and duality of patterning. The vocabularies of signs, tokens, or lexigrams acquired by apes have never been reported as approaching in size the vocabulary of even the average 4-year-old child, let alone that of a human adult. Moreover, since apes do not speak, their use of language can shed no light on duality of patterning. The ape evidence is therefore consistent with the view that these two characteristics of human language are by-products of something that apes lack—namely, a lowered larynx. But on synonymy avoidance and the sentence/NP distinction there is more to be said, and this will occupy the next three sections.

### 6.4.1. Synonymy Avoidance by Chimpanzees

In Chapter 5 I quoted Premack's comment that chimpanzees, when presented with a so-far unused plastic token and a familiar but so-far unnamed object, will consistently associate the new token with the unnamed object. In other words, they rule out straightaway the possibility that the new token may be a new name for an already named object. This is consistent with an observation of Sue Savage-Rumbaugh (1986), reporting on the behaviour of the chimpanzees Sherman and Austin at a stage when they were quite used to associating lexigrams with objects. For one or two weeks before the introduction of a new food item that would eventually have to be named, several new unassigned lexigrams would be placed on the lexigram keyboard; however, the two chimpanzees would ignore these until the new food item appeared, at which point one chimpanzee would spontaneously choose one of the unused lexigrams to designate it, and the other chimpanzee would follow his lead (1986: 174–5). These observations suggest that chimpanzees share synonymy-avoidance principles with humans and that these principles are therefore likely to be part of our biological inheritance dating from before the chimpanzee–human split, five million or more years ago.

It would be nice to be able to report confirmatory findings from systematic studies of apes directed precisely to this question, comparable with the studies by

Marchman, Clark, and others on word learning by human infants. Unfortunately, this is not possible. But the lacuna has more to do with the way in which apes have been taught than with any scepticism about synonymy avoidance on the part of the researchers. Apes' exposure to new vocabulary items, whether ASL signs, plastic tokens, or lexigrams, has been crucially unlike the normal exposure of hearing human infants. In the normal human situation, exposure to new words is not rationed; children hear not only their own caregivers talking to them but also other adults and older children talking to each other. By contrast, those chimpanzees trained on artificial sign systems (as in Premack's, Rumbaugh's, and Savage-Rumbaugh's studies) have been introduced to new signs only gradually, in a carefully controlled and monitored fashion. Even the apes who have learned ASL signs have done so, directly or indirectly, from human teachers who have often not been native speakers of ASL, so the teachers' vocabulary has often been more or less limited, preventing them from engaging in fluent ASL conversations with other humans on a wide variety of topics in the apes' presence. In these circumstances it is natural that the focus should have been on introducing words or signs with clearly distinct referents (whether objects or activities) rather than investigating explicitly whether apes will readily learn more than one word or sign with the same referent. Despite this, some further work of Savage-Rumbaugh (1986) with the chimpanzees Sherman and Austin can be interpreted as confirming that chimpanzees are as reluctant as humans are to conclude that two vocabulary items are perfectly synonymous.

In her fascinating account of several years' interaction with Sherman and Austin, Savage-Rumbaugh reports more than once that a task that had seemed to involve merely a straightforward new application of old lexigram knowledge turned out to be unexpectedly difficult for them. The chimpanzees, despite seeming to know the requisite object–lexigram associations and despite being rewarded for good performance, were sometimes strangely obtuse at grasping what they had to do to get the rewards. In due course, two factors emerged that help to account for this seeming obtuseness. One is that chimpanzees' use of lexigrams is overwhelmingly oriented towards requesting. It is not that they cannot develop an awareness of words as names in non-request contexts, as human infants do, nor that they cannot develop a habit of using lexigrams to announce or comment on their own actions (what Savage-Rumbaugh (1986: 324–8) calls 'indicating') ; it is just that these developments are slower to emerge than in human infants. The second factor is that, in order for a chimpanzee to learn what lexigrams mean, the outcomes of pressing different lexigram keys must be different. As Savage-Rumbaugh (1986: 108) puts it: 'They could not accurately select *different* symbols from trial to trial when shown different foods if the results of selecting these different symbols were always *the same*; that is, if they received social praise and a single food common to all trials' (emphasis added). These two factors combine to yield a neat explanation of the chimpanzees' obtuseness.

Imagine a training routine of the kind just described by Savage-Rumbaugh. To the human experimenter, this routine seems clearly to involve two parts: first, a naming test (choosing a lexigram for a displayed object), and, secondly, the granting or withholding of a reward according to whether the chosen lexigram was right or wrong. For the human experimenter the connection between the lexigram and the reward is indirect, mediated by the requirement that the chosen lexigram be the one that "means" the displayed object. For the chimpanzee, on the other hand, the routine is just another way of requesting rewards; it is the reward, not the displayed object, that is the "meaning" of any lexigram. So, if the same reward is given even when different lexigram keys are pressed (depending on what object is on display), it will seem to the chimpanzee as if different lexigrams have the same "meaning". But that should not happen in a communication system constrained by synonymy-avoidance principles. So, assuming that the chimpanzees are biologically endowed with the expectation that such principles should be observed, their bewilderment is understandable. Attributing synonymy-avoidance principles to chimpanzees leads us to predict that attempts to train them should be successful only when pressing different lexigram keys yields different outcomes, not just from the teachers' naming-oriented point of view but from the chimpanzees' own request-oriented point of view—and this is just what Savage-Rumbaugh and her colleagues discovered.

### 6.4.2. *The Nature of Apes' Sign Combinations*

The Chomskyan approach to language is called 'generative grammar' because of its emphasis on the human ability to generate combinations of words that are wholly novel yet reliably interpretable in virtue of their syntactic structure. Correspondingly, during the early years of the ape language debate, a claim that some chimpanzee had attained a degree of linguistic competence was seen by most theoretical linguists as of interest only if it was interpreted as meaning that the ape had displayed a human-like ability to create new sign combinations with predictable meanings. Yet, since human syntax was held to be constrained by an innate Universal Grammar, the possibility that apes might have some capacity for language seemed to imply that Universal Grammar might be in part shared with apes—a possibility that many linguists found disturbing, in the light of Chomsky's view that human language is fundamentally different in kind from any animal communication system. It is not surprising, therefore, that controversy raged and still rages over the interpretation of chimpanzees' sign combinations such as WATER BIRD or CRY HURT FOOD. Did they show that a chimpanzee can create new compound words, meaning 'swan' and 'radish' respectively (Fouts and Rigby 1977)? Or could they be merely unstructured concatenations of individual signs (Terrace 1979; Wallman 1992)?

As always, our concern here is not to decide who is right but to explore how the facts bear on the language-evolution scenario of Chapter 5. This scenario does not presuppose that chimpanzees should be unable to combine signs in regular ways. Accepting the scenario, therefore, does not commit one to insisting that WATER BIRD is a mere concatenation rather than a linguistic or quasi-linguistic unit. What the scenario does presuppose, however, is that apes' sign combinations should not show evidence of a kind of syntax in which there is a clear-cut difference in structure or function between sentence-like and NP-like units; for, if they did show such evidence, it would be proved that the distinction cannot be a by-product of syllable structure. What kind of structure, then, do apes' sign combinations have?

Two facts about apes' sign combinations make this question seem difficult to answer: they are generally short (strings of more than two signs are unusual and often contain repetitions), and they do not contain morphological markings of the kind that distinguish clearly in English between an NP such as *John's arrival yesterday* and a sentence such as *John arrived yesterday*. The corpus of ape utterances certainly contains some that look sentence-like, such as WASHOE WANT CEREAL (Washoe being the Gardners' first ASL-trained chimpanzee) or BABY DRINK MORE COFFEE, signed by a watching chimpanzee when her trainer was pretending to give coffee to a doll (Gardner *et al.* 1989*a*). It also contains some that look more like an NP or compound noun, such as MORE MILK or the already mentioned WATER BIRD. But others are hard to classify, such as METAL HOT (used of a cigarette lighter) or OUT HOME MILK DAR (Dar being another of the Gardners' trainees). Even in respect of the apparently clear cases, our classification of them has more to do with their English glosses than with internal evidence. Did the chimpanzee who signed BABY DRINK MORE COFFEE really mean it as a sentence ('The baby is drinking more coffee') rather than as an NP ('Wow! A baby drinking more coffee!')? I can see nothing in the reported ape language data that would allow us to answer that question. But its very unanswerability resolves our earlier question about whether apes' sign combinations show a clear-cut sentence/NP distinction. It seems impossible to draw any such distinction in a principled way, without allowing oneself to be influenced by the syntactic status of plausible English glosses.

Ape language experimenters, responding to scepticism about apes' syntax, sometimes invoke the similarity between many ape sign combinations and the telegraphic or 'two-word' speech of very young children (Brown 1973). When a young child says *Give doggie* or *Baby table*, we do not deny that she is using language, albeit in an immature way. What then entitles us to deny that chimpanzee sign combinations such as CHASE DAR or PLEASE BLANKET OUT are examples of language use too? This is a fair objection so long as what is at issue is language in a wide sense rather than, as here, language with a particular kind of syntax. The resemblance between apes' sign combinations and the telegraphic stage of infant speech, even if we grant that it exists, is irrelevant for present purposes because both of them crucially lack the clear-cut sentence/NP distinction of adult spoken language whose evolution we are trying to account for. I emphasize the absence of that distinction in chimpanzees' signing not in order to belittle what chimpanzees are capable of nor to deny them some capacity for language, provided this capacity is freed of any essential tie to humanness. I emphasize it only in order to show that chimpanzees' sign combinations are perfectly compatible with a view of language evolution according to which the sentence/NP distinction did not emerge until several million years after the date of chimpanzees' and humans' most recent common ancestor.

So far we have been considering chimpanzees' success in acquiring the syntax of a *human* language (ASL). But what happens if an ape reared in an environment of language use is left to his own devices, so to speak? One could argue that it is in this situation that any capacity for syntactic organization would most clearly manifest itself. And this is the situation of the bonobo (or pygmy chimpanzee) Kanzi, exposed to language by Savage-Rumbaugh and her colleagues in conditions quite unlike Sherman and Austin (Savage-Rumbaugh and Lewin 1994; Rumbaugh and Savage-Rumbaugh 1996). The baby Kanzi accompanied his mother while Savage-Rumbaugh and her colleagues were trying with little success to train her in lexigram use, but he himself simply watched and listened to what was going on. Later, when separated from his mother for four months, he began spontaneously to use lexigrams for intentional signing. Savage-Rumbaugh decided, therefore, simply to observe how Kanzi's sign use developed, given access to a lexigram keyboard and plenty of interaction with humans but with no explicit training of the kind that Sherman and Austin had received. She recorded and analysed all Kanzi's sign combinations, including combinations of lexigrams and pointing gestures, made during nine hours of daily observation over the five months from April to August 1986 (Greenfield and Savage-Rumbaugh 1990, 1991). This yielded a corpus of 1,422 combinations.

Two important points emerge from the analysis. First, Kanzi developed preferences for combining particular types of sign in particular orders; secondly, some of these order preferences differed from those of his human interlocutors, and so could not have been learned from them. Greenfield and Savage-Rumbaugh conclude that Kanzi took significant steps towards inventing a syntax of his own, and that his achievement may shed light on the process whereby a syntax for human language was first invented by our remote ancestors.

Before looking in more detail at Kanzi's sign combinations and at Greenfield and Savage-Rumbaugh's evaluation of them, let us consider what bearing they may have for our scenario. As we have seen, there is no evidence of a sentence/NP distinction in the ASL combinations of Washoe and her successors. Even if there had been, however, one might argue that that these chimpanzees had merely copied this structural distinction from the human language that they had been exposed to. But, if Kanzi's combinations show evidence of such a distinction, that argument is not available, since some of his combinations of lexigrams or of lexigrams and gestures are not based on any human model. Evidence of a sentence/NP distinction in Kanzi's sign use could, therefore, be a severe blow to our scenario. On the other hand, there is nothing in our scenario that conflicts with the possibility that Kanzi may invent rules of sign order, and we have no reason to object to calling such rules 'syntactic'. Whether a bonobo syntax exists does not matter to us; what matters is the nature of that syntax, if it exists.

The regular patterns that appear in Kanzi's signing are summarized in Table 6.1. There are two invented rules, one requiring lexigrams to precede gestures and the other requiring action signs to be ordered according to the order in which Kanzi wishes the actions to take place. The first rule gives clear priority to the communicative mode (lexigram or manual sign) over any syntactic or semantic factors, and the second sheds no light on how to analyse those sign combinations concerning which the sentence-or-NP question chiefly arises—namely, combinations of two signs one of which is semantically verblike and the other nounlike. So these rules hardly justify attributing to Kanzi a syntax with a sentence/NP distinction. To say this is not to disagree with Greenfield and Savage-Rumbaugh, for they make no such claim for Kanzi's syntax. It establishes, however, that no matter how generously we interpret Kanzi's syntactic inventiveness, his achievement does not conflict with the syllabic model.

TABLE 6.1. *Kanzi's syntactic rules*

| Rule | Example |
| --- | --- |
| *Learned rule* (based on human lexigram users' order) | |
| Action precedes object | BITE TOMATO, SLAP BALL |
| | |
| *Invented rules* (independent of human users' orders) | |
| Lexigram precedes gesture | |
|     action–agent | CHASE person, TICKLE person |
|     entity–demonstrative | BANANA dem., COKE dem. |
|     goal–action | AUSTIN go, TOOLROOM come |
|     object–agent | BALLOON person, PEACH person |
| | |
| Action precedes action, sign order corresponding to order of performance | CHASE HIDE, TICKLE BITE |

*Notes*: Small capitals represent lexigrams. 'Person' represents a gesture pointing to a particular person. 'Dem.' represents a demonstrative gesture.

Greenfield, Rumbaugh, and Savage-Rumbaugh argue that Kanzi's experience sheds light on human-language evolution in two ways: it shows how syntactic rules can be invented, and it shows that syntax need not be 'biologically predetermined'. As Savage-Rumbaugh and Rumbaugh (1993: 106) put it:

any brain capable of understanding the problem of determining which noun is to be linked to which verb in a complex utterance would have to come up with syntax, and that syntax would have to have certain features (for example, verb–noun units . . . ). Moreover . . . it would seem inevitable that completely *independent* non-innate solutions to the problem would necessarily show some overlap.

It is at this point, I think, that they go beyond what can legitimately be concluded from Kanzi's achievement. They make no effort to respond to arguments for innateness resting on aspects of grammar that the learners' linguistic exposure is insufficient to determine—so-called poverty-of-stimulus arguments developed over many years by Chomsky and others, and alluded to in Section 1.2. But more pertinent to our present concern is their assumption that the direction in which syntax has evolved, and which provides the framework for their terms 'noun' and 'verb', is effectively the only direction in which it could have evolved. The arguments presented in Chapter 2 show that that assumption is risky, and one can even construe Kanzi's syntax as reinforcing the risk. If our ancestors had invented syntactic rules like Kanzi's, based on communicative mode and on the temporal order of actions, can we be confident that their descendants would inevitably have developed a syntax incorporating a sentence/NP distinction? The answer must surely be no—unless we presuppose precisely the sort of extrasyntactic impetus that the syllabic model supplies.

### 6.4.3. A Bonobo's Understanding of Spoken English

All the early work on ape language concentrated not on what apes could understand but on what they could say (or sign). This is not surprising. Use of ASL signs and lexigrams can be observed directly, but understanding of them cannot. Even in respect of human infants, studies of speech production heavily outnumber studies of comprehension. But it is *a priori* likely that a child may understand a word or a syntactic construction some time before she first uses it. Savage-Rumbaugh's work with Sherman and Austin was designed partly to rectify this imbalance in respect of chimpanzees, since her training routines enabled her to record not just when a given lexigram was used but whether it was used in an appropriate context.

Interest in comprehension increased markedly when it was discovered that the bonobo Kanzi, unlike chimpanzees or any other animals, could understand spoken English sentences with a high degree of accuracy even in the absence of contextual cues. (The proviso about contextual cues is important; many animals, including domestic pets, sometimes behave as if they understand spoken language, but their understanding turns out on close examination to be restricted to a few expressions used in stereotyped situations.) Because Kanzi showed signs of understanding spoken English unexpectedly well, Savage-Rumbaugh and her colleagues set out to compare systematically his comprehension at age 8 with that of a human child, Alia, aged 2 (Savage-Rumbaugh *et al.* 1993). Most of the test material took the form of spoken English requests in a variety of syntactic formats, such as 'Get the rubber band that's in the bathroom', 'Put the water on the vacuum [cleaner]', and 'Can you put the money in the potty?'. The pragmatic oddness of many of the requests (to put money in a potty, for example) was deliberate, so as to reduce the reliability of guesswork as compensation for defective understanding. The outcome was that 72 per cent of Kanzi's responses were judged correct (as against 66 per cent of Alia's), confirming that his understanding of English extended to recognizing lexical items incorporated in sentences.

For us as for Savage-Rumbaugh, the important issue is whether Kanzi understood not just words but syntax. Arguably, Kanzi's correct response to the request 'Pour the water on the vacuum', for example, might reflect no more than an understanding of the words *pour, water,* and *vacuum* (or even just *water* and *vacuum*) and an understanding that he was supposed to do something involving all (or both) their referents. But the tests included pairs of sentences which differed syntactically rather than lexically, such as 'Make the doggie bite the snake' and 'Make the snake bite the doggie' (the doggie and the snake being soft toys). Kanzi responded correctly to 79 per cent of these paired sentences (33 out of 42); and his sensitivity to word order was even better than this suggests, because his nine incorrect responses included some in which the error was lexical rather than syntactic.

What impressed Savage-Rumbaugh most, however, was the difference in Kanzi's response to requests of the type 'Go to location Y and get object X' (identified as 'type 5B') and to requests of the type 'Go get object X that's in location Y' (identifed as 'type 5C'). Object X was always available near at hand as well as in location Y, so that there was always a choice of places from which to get it and so scope for error in responding to the request. In response to half of the type 5B requests, Kanzi went first to the object X nearby, and needed further prompting in order to go to location Y. In response to the type 5C requests, however, 'Kanzi typically did not even glance at the array [of objects] in front of him. Instead, he headed directly for the specified location [Y], suggesting that he had deduced from the structure of the sentence itself that there was no need to search for the object [X] in the array in front of him' (Savage-Rumbaugh *et al.* 1993: 89–90). Moreover, since *that's in [location Y]* is a relative clause, Savage-Rumbaugh *et al.* (1993: 100) conclude that, at least in type 5C sentences, Kanzi has mastered recursion; he is not only sensitive to syntactic relationships in simple sentences (it seems), but also capable of responding appropriately to at least some complex sentences. Finally Savage-Rumbaugh concludes: 'While we cannot yet explain why Kanzi has so easily acquired skills that were formerly assumed to be the sole province of *Homo sapiens*, the fact that he has done so should cause us to reconsider many of our standard assumptions regarding brain development and function' (Savage-Rumbaugh *et al.* 1993: 251).

If Savage-Rumbaugh's interpretation is correct, the scenario of Chapter 5 is in trouble. The development of modern-style syntax did not need to wait until such anatomical developments as the lowering of the larynx, for even the complexity of recursion is within the competence of a bonobo—within his receptive competence, at least. But, although Kanzi can fairly be said to have some syntactic competence, Savage-Rumbaugh goes too far in assimilating it to syntactic competence of the modern human kind.

Let us consider first Kanzi's success with sentences such as 'Make the doggie bite the snake'. When Kanzi hears one of these, it is reasonable to expect him to decide who should bite whom in a way that is consistent with one of his own syntactic rules, if possible—that is, with one of the rules, summarized in Table 6.1, that Savage-Rumbaugh distils from his productive use of lexigrams and gestures. The 'lexigram-before-gesture' rule is hardly applicable, in any of its versions, and nor is the 'action–action' rule. That leaves the 'action-before-object' rule. Given that *bite* denotes an action and that *the snake* immediately follows it, we will expect Kanzi to interpret the snake as the thing to be bitten and the dog, by default, as the biter. And this yields the correct response. In fact, an interpretive strategy based on assuming that actions immediately precede their objects, although only moderately reliable in English generally, is highly reliable for the sentences that Kanzi heard. So Kanzi's relative success in interpreting them, though striking, does not necessarily imply any syntactic competence beyond that of his lexigram use. Admittedly, the 'action-before-object' rule was probably learned from his human caregivers, as Savage-Rumbaugh and Greenfield say, rather than invented. But one can hardly claim on such a slender basis that he learned the sentence/NP distinction too, especially since (as we saw in the previous section) his invented rules do nothing to support it.

What of Kanzi's purported mastery of recursion, exemplified in type 5C sentences such as 'Go get the apple that's in the microwave'? At first sight, this may seem to nullify the objections that I have just put forward. If Kanzi has learned to put a sentence inside a sentence, *a fortiori* his syntax must be described in terms of sentences! But Savage-Rumbaugh's claim is undermined by the availability of a much more conservative explanation. All the relevant relative clauses are of one form *that's in the [location Y]*. There is, therefore, nothing to prevent Kanzi from interpreting *that's in the* as a preposition, like *from*, or even failing to interpret it at all. The fact that *the apple* immediately follows *get* is enough to show him that it is the apple that he must get, not the microwave. Given that Kanzi can evidently distinguish *get* and *take* as involving movement towards and away from where he now is, that leaves only one plausible role for the microwave—namely, as the current location of the apple. This is not to deny that an explanation is needed for the difference in Kanzi's responses to type 5C sentences and to type 5B ones of form 'Go to location X and get object Y'. (One possibility may be that what is formulated as an apparently single request, schematically *go-get apple*$_{Object}$ *microwave*$_{Location}$, is easier for Kanzi to process than an apparently dual request, schematically *go microwave*$_{Location}$, *get apple*$_{Object}$.) But this difference in response cannot, on the evidence available, be attributed to mastery of sentential recursion.

## 6.5. Conclusion

The task of this chapter has been to explore whether the scenario of Chapter 5 is consistent with relevant facts from biological anthropology, from the study of the brain, and from the study of apes. It seems fair to conclude that the answer is yes. In particular, biological anthropology supplies language-independent reasons why a lowered larynx should have begun to develop in bipedal savannah-dwelling hominids. Without such reasons, the scenario of Chapter 5 (which presupposes that larynx-lowering began before any syntactic elaboration had taken place) would be empirically more precarious.

Are there any facts in these three areas that the scenario of Chapter 5 may help to explain? If so, that will count in its favour. Naturally, no work has been done to address this question directly, because my scenario is so novel. But in two domains the scenario suggests new avenues to explore. The first is aphasia. Will further research support the suggestion made in Section 6.3.1 that brain injury may affect syllable-derived and non-syllable-derived syntactic competence differently? The second is sign language. Will further research support the suggestion made in Section 6.3.4 that sign languages may lack any syntactic motivation for a distinction between sentences and NPs? If the answer to either question is yes, then the scenario of Chapter 5 will turn out to shed light on a topic whose relevance to language evolution is superficially quite tenuous—hence all the more interesting, if it can be established.

# 7  Just How Unique Are We?

## 7.1. A Surprising Outcome

Readers who have found my argument persuasive on the whole may nevertheless feel uneasy about where it has led. Human language turns out (if I am right)
to be a by-product of a change in the anatomy of the vocal tract brought about
by our ancestors' taking to the ground and walking on two legs. The only other
essential ingredient was an expectation that distinct vocalizations should mean
different things. But this picture looks topsy-turvy. Surely brain development
must have more to do with language evolution that I have given it credit for!
And what about the suggestion that the distinction between reference and truth,
as relationships between linguistic expressions and the world, is in turn merely a
by-product of vocal-tract-driven syntax? Surely such bizarre conclusions must
be wrong!

That kind of reaction is understandable, but it does not justify shrugging evidence aside. A proposal may sound bizarre at first, but still be right. In Chapter 2
I suggested that a merit of my proposal is that it makes sense of a range of facts
about language that at first sight have nothing to do with one another. This does
not conclusively prove the proposal correct. But it scores highly, I suggest, in the
only way that any proposal can score highly when the field with which it is concerned is not open to direct experiment: it unifies seemingly unconnected
phenomena.

If this proposal stands the test of further evidence and debate, its implications
for our understanding of what distinguishes humans from other animals are likely
to be considerable. I will sketch some of these implications in Section 7.4, where
I draw attention to one final consideration that favours my scenario. But first,
in what may seem a paradoxical fashion, I will suggest that in two areas (psychological and philosophical) the ramifications of my proposal may not be so dis-
tasteful as they at first seem.

## 7.2. Linguistic and Cognitive Evolution

Cognitive factors—awareness of other minds, the development of conceptual structure, the elaboration of culture and social organization—have played little part in my story. At first sight, that may seem to indicate that I regard them as unimportant. But no. Their low profile indicates only that, according to my argument, there is no need to invoke them to account for those aspects of language evolution that I have addressed.

For the study of the development of human cognition, that should be seen not as a humiliating conclusion but as a liberating one. The issue becomes not how cognitive developments *caused* our large vocabularies or our sentence–NP syntax, but how they *interacted with* them. I have already suggested that one field of interaction lay in vocabulary development: synonymy-avoidance principles may have exerted a pressure for a bigger vocabulary, but it would have been cognitive and social factors that largely determined the directions in which lexical elaboration should proceed. On the other hand, if I am right, cognitive factors do not have to be invoked to explain why our categorization of the world is so relentlessly bipolar and unidimensional: thing versus event, static versus dynamic, noun versus verb. This bipolarity may reflect no more than the strong imprint on semantics of a syntactic mould incorporating a homologue of the bipolar continuum of sonority, from sounds involving most obstruction of the vocal tract (stop consonants) to those involving least (low vowels). So, if the binary strait-jacket is not cognitive in origin, the way is open to explore the possibility of significant differences in how the world is categorized by creatures not constrained by it, such as chimpanzees or elephants or dolphins. (This would not be the same as questioning whether chimpanzees have some notion of predicate–argument structure, for, as I argued in Chapter 4, predicate–argument structure does not necessarily lead to a syntactic bipolarity of the verb–noun kind.) I have no idea what the outcome of such an exploration might be or even how it might be conducted. My concern here is only to illustrate how, perhaps unexpectedly, a vocal-tract-based account of linguistic evolution may suggest new avenues for research in comparative cognition.

## 7.3. The Demotion of Propositional Thought and Knowledge

In the eyes of some religious believers, the possession of souls is a Rubicon that separates humans from other animals. For others, the Rubicon is language—which partly explains the controversy over the ape language experiments. But even many people who reject any such absolute barrier and who regard humans as just another animal species still, I suspect, postulate a barrier of a more subtle kind: access to **knowledge-that**, the sort of knowledge that can be expressed propositionally, as opposed to **knowledge-how**, the compendium of skills that enables a creature to get along more or less successfully in its environment. When a vervet monkey utters the eagle call, that is not a sign that it *knows that* an eagle is present, merely that it *knows how* to respond to an appropriate stimulus—and it is perhaps stretching things to call the vervet's reaction a manifestation of 'knowledge' of any kind. Even when a chimpanzee such as Sherman gives his partner Austin a wrench to open a container where food is to be found, that is not a sign that Sherman *knows that* Austin wants the wrench or that the wrench is the appropriate tool for this container; it is merely (many would say) a sign that Sherman *knows how* to play his part in a complex routine that will lead to a food reward. Knowledge-that implies an ability to discriminate between truth and falsity, and that is an ability that cannot be ascribed to any animals except humans; for only humans can formulate true sentences or propositions, which are the vehicles in which knowledge-that is expressed.

An illustration of this kind of attitude is supplied by the philosopher Michael Dummett (1994). He announces as 'the fundamental axiom of analytical philosophy' the axiom 'that the only route to the analysis of thought goes through the analysis of language' (1994: 127–8). Correspondingly, he urges the importance of 'acknowledging the primacy of the sentence in an account of meaning'—acknowledging, that is, 'the primacy of complete thoughts over their constituent senses', a 'complete thought' being 'that which it makes sense to qualify as true or as false' (1994: 129–30). It follows that animals, because they do not have language and cannot formulate sentences, cannot entertain thoughts and, *a fortiori*, have no access to propositional knowledge. This is a consequence that Dummett is happy to accept. Even when a chimpanzee makes a ladder out of a pile of boxes so as to reach a banana, or when a pony negotiates a cattle grid by lying down and rolling across it, the chimpanzee or the pony is not engaged in thought, only in 'proto-thought' (1994: 122). Similarly, a cat cannot have a concept of a dog, only a 'proto-concept'. So, for Dummett at least, there is still a Rubicon separating animals from humans: because only we use sentences, only we are capable of thought.

But what if syntax had evolved so as not to yield sentences, in the sense of linguistic entities distinct from referring expressions? One of the main themes of this book has been that this outcome is conceivable, and the fact that syntactic evolution has not yielded it needs to be explained. What would Dummett say of a hypothetical world in which this conceivable outcome is actually realized—where, for instance, all languages display Monocategoric syntax rather than syntax-as-it-is? Would he decide that, in that world, humans too are capable only of proto-thoughts? If so, it is clear that the distinction between 'thoughts' and 'proto-thoughts' is merely a reflection of a contingency in syntactic evolution, and the doctrine that only humans can think is emptied of substance. On the other hand, if Dummett insists that even in that world only humans can think, it must be for some reason other than 'the primacy of the sentence'.

Dummett's association of thinking with sentences and with truth and falsity goes along with a view of the relationship between meaning and truth that I sum up in Figure 7.1. It will be seen that reference has a hybrid status: it is part of 'meaning', along with sense, but it is tied to an occasion of use, like truth. A better way of looking at the relationship between language and the world, I suggest, is summed up in Figure 7.2. There, reference is unhooked from sense and linked with truth under the superordinate term 'applicability'. I do not attach any special importance to that term; the important point is that the two kinds of linguistic unit that have special ties to occasions of use (namely, NPs and sentences) are seen as having essentially the same kind of relationship to the world, of which 'having reference' and 'being true' are just subtypes.

At one philosophical level, a readjustment on these lines need not have much impact. Distinct philosophical theories about truth (emphasizing correspondence, coherence, pragmatism, or deflation) would simply re-emerge as theories about

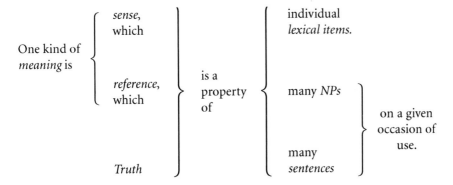

Fig. 7.1.  A conventional view of meaning and truth

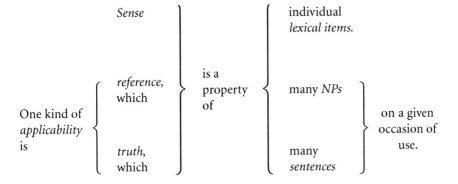

Fig. 7.2.  An alternative view of meaning and truth

applicability.[1] But at another level, I suggest, there would be an impact that would (as in the case of cognition) be liberating rather than destructive. If the truth/ reference distinction is merely a by-product of how vocal-tract changes affected syntactic evolution, then philosophers are spared the task of trying to make sense of it. It will be a parochial linguistic phenomenon, scarcely more relevant to philosophy than (say) the distinction between strong and weak noun declensions in German. And to the extent that animals are capable of solving problems, they are capable of (proto-)thoughts that are applicable to the world, just as true sentences and propositional knowledge are. It is not that their modes of thought are necessarily the same as ours; it is just that sentencehood and truth need no longer be regarded as symptoms of a fundamental divide between human and non-human thinking.

## 7.4. Why Humans?

Two questions that one can pose about the origin of language need to be distinguished:

1. How did language originate?
2. Why was it in humans that language evolved?

The two questions are logically independent; one can envisage having a detailed answer to one without having anything at all to say about the other. Yet enquirers into language origins often seem to take it for granted that an answer to (1) automatically incorporates an answer to (2). That is, questions about the origin of language are interpreted as being self-evidently questions about the origin of language in humans.

If one keeps the distinction between the two questions firmly in mind, however, new problems arise for quite a few current approaches to language evolution. If a factor that is proposed as a fundamental impetus in language evolution turns out to be a characteristic that humans share with some other species (particularly with some other primate species), then the proposal runs into an immediate difficulty: why was it humans, rather than these other animals, that developed language? The more we discover about the cognitive capacities and behavioural sophistication of other animals (particularly other apes), the more insistently this difficulty arises. Toolmaking, social intelligence, and the capacity for deception have all in recent years lost their status as peculiarly human traits; so any scenario for language evolution that places one of these at its centre can offer no immediately obvious answer to question (2). For example, Bickerton's scenario, according to which full language was reached via a marriage between social intelligence and

---

[1] For a collection of papers illustrating recent philosophical theories of truth, see Horwich (1994).

protolanguage, faces the problem that (according to him) neither social intelligence nor protolanguage (at least in its 'latent' form) is peculiar to humans. That is not to say that, in such approaches, no plausible answer to question (2) can ever be found. However, it does mean that any scenario that supplies an answer straightaway, rather than as something that must be grafted on, enjoys a prima-facie advantage.

The scenario that I have presented in this book enjoys just such an advantage, I suggest. At its centre is a human characteristic that really is peculiar to humans, at least among primates: habitual bipedalism. The only other essential ingredient is a synonymy-avoidance bias, which we share with chimpanzees (and perhaps more widely). The idea that something so immense in its effects as human language could have its beginnings in physiological adjustments consequent on bipedalism strikes deeply at the assumption that human uniqueness must be based on something rather grand and profound, such as access to unique kinds of knowledge and self-awareness. But, once we get used to the idea, I think we will come to realize that it is only our pride that is hurt. Certain historical accidents have indeed supplied us with a uniquely sophisticated mechanism for communication and for the mental representation of the world; but, apart from that, we are just one species among many.

# Appendix: Sentences, Statements, and Propositions

In Chapter 3 I was not overly scrupulous about certain distinctions that are familiar to all philosophers and logicians. These are the distinction between sentences and statements and that between sentences and propositions. To announce that I have glossed over these distinctions may seem like a Quixotic admission that my argument is vitiated by vagueness. In fact, however, these distinctions are orthogonal to the issue that concerns us, so to gloss them is a sensible way of avoiding distracting side issues.[1]

The following are distinct English sentences:

(1)   It will rain in Christchurch tomorrow.
(2)   It rained in Christchurch yesterday.

However, in appropriate circumstances both can be used to say the same thing, in some sense. Specifically, if (1) is uttered on 2 January 1997 and (2) is uttered on 4 January 1997, both say the same thing in the sense that both relate to 3 January; and what they say happens, moreover, to be true, since as I write (on 3 January 1997) it is raining. On the other hand, if (1) were uttered on 24 December 1996 it would say something false, since no rain fell in Christchurch on 25 December 1996. So truth and falsity cannot be ascribed to sentences pure and simple, only to sentences on a given occasion of use. Some philosophers have expressed this by saying that truth and falsity do not belong to sentences at all, but rather to the **statements** that sentences express. They would accordingly analyse (1) and (2), uttered on 2 and 4 January 1997 respectively, as expressing the same statement, while (1) uttered on 24 December 1996 expresses a different statement. So one sentence can express many statements and one statement can be expressed by many sentences. The statement relating to 3 January 1997 could, for example, be expressed by French sentences rather than English ones:

(3)   Il pleuvra demain à Christchurch.
(4)   Il a plu hier à Christchurch.

These illustrate the fact that a sentence (as the term is generally used in both linguistics and philosophy) belongs to a particular language, whereas a statement (in the sense introduced here) does not.

The type of sentence to which statements are most directly linked is the declarative type. Other types of sentence are the imperative and (especially relevant here) the simple or

[1] For a philosophical logician's discussion of issues raised in this section, see Strawson (1952).

'yes/no' interrogative. Roughly speaking, declarative sentences are used to make statements, interrogatives to ask questions, and imperatives to issue commands. This association is only rough, however, because, as (5) shows, in order to get someone to do something one may use not only an imperative sentence, as in (5*a*), but also a declarative, as in (5*b*), or an interrogative, as in (5*c*):

(5)  (*a*)  Open the door.
 (*b*)  I would be grateful if you would open the door.
 (*c*)  Would you mind opening the door?

Similarly, an inquiry may be expressed not just by an interrogative but also by a declarative or an imperative:

(6)  (*a*)  What's the boy's name?
 (*b*)  I'd like to know what that boy's name is.
 (*c*)  Tell me what that boy's name is.

The point of mentioning sentence types here is that some but not all philosophers distinguish between sentences and **propositions** in a fashion that renders propositions neutral between sentence types. According to this usage, the declarative sentence (1) expresses the same proposition as the interrogative (7):

(7)  Will it rain in Christchurch tomorrow?

Similarly, the imperative sentence (5*a*) expresses the same proposition as the declarative (8):

(8)  You will open the door.[2]

Correspondingly, some philosophers hold that the entities that can properly be said to be true or false are neither sentences nor statements but propositions. Only when a proposition is expressed in a declarative sentence is its truth asserted, but the proposition underlying an interrogative sentence can be true too, if the right answer to the question is 'Yes'. This usage is reflected in the English term 'propositional calculus' for a branch of formal logic.

The upshot is that there are at least three kinds of linguistic or logical entity, each of which has been held by some philosophers to be the sole proper bearer of the epithets 'true' or 'false':

- sentence (on a given occasion of use);
- statement;
- proposition.

In some philosophical debates the choice between these three possibilities is important. What matters to us, however, is how one might justify discriminating between the way in which any one of these three kinds of entity fits the world and the way in which expressions such as *the President of the United States*, *we*, and *yesterday afternoon* fit the world—the kind of fit that I have called 'referring'. But the sentence–statement–proposition

---

[2] The same point is made, with different terminology, by the moral philosopher R. M. Hare (1952: ch.2).

issue has never (so far as I can discover) been discussed in a way that has any bearing on the truth–reference issue that concerns us. So it is legitimate to ignore the sentence–statement–proposition issue here. In Chapter 3, when labelling the kinds of entity that can be true or false, I in general follow the usage of whatever philosopher I am discussing; but nothing hinges on this.

# References

Abler, William. 1989. On the particulate principle of self-diversifying systems. *Journal of Social and Biological Structures*, 12: 1–13.

Abney, Steven. 1987. The English noun phrase in its sentential aspect. Ph.D. dissertation, MIT.

Abondolo, Daniel. 1987. Hungarian. In Bernard Comrie (ed.), *The World's Major Languages*. Beckenham: Croom Helm, 569–92.

Aiello, Leslie C. 1996a. Hominine preadaptations for language and cognition. In Paul Mellars and Kathleen Gibson (eds.), *Modelling the Early Human Mind*. Cambridge: McDonald Institute Monographs, 89–99.

—— 1996b. Terrestriality, bipedalism and the origin of language. In W. G. Runciman, John Maynard-Smith, and R. I. M. Dunbar (eds.), *Evolution of Social Behaviour Patterns In Primates and Man* (*Proceedings of the British Academy*, 88). Oxford: Oxford University Press, 269–89.

—— and Dean, Christopher. 1990. *An Introduction to Human Evolutionary Anatomy*. London: Academic Press.

—— and Wheeler, Peter. 1995. The expensive-tissue hypothesis: the brain and the digestive system in human and primate evolution. *Current Anthropology*, 36: 199–211.

Aitchison, Jean. 1981. *Language Change: Progress or Decay?* London: Fontana.

—— 1987. *Words in the Mind: An Introduction to the Mental Lexicon*. Oxford: Blackwell.

Anderson, Stephen R. 1992. *A-Morphous Morphology*. Cambridge: Cambridge University Press.

Armstrong, David F., Stokoe, William C., and Wilcox, Sherman E. 1995. *Gesture and the Nature of Language*. Cambridge: Cambridge University Press.

Aronoff, Mark. 1976. *Word Formation in Generative Grammar*. Cambridge, Mass.: MIT Press.

Baker, G. P. , and Hacker, P. M. S. 1984. *Frege: Logical Excavations*. New York: Oxford University Press; Oxford: Blackwell.

Barber, C. L. 1972. *The Story of Language* (rev. edn.). London: Pan.

Batali, John. 1998. Computational simulations of the emergence of grammar. In Hurford *et al.* (1998), 405–26.

Bates, Elizabeth, and MacWhinney, Brian. 1989. Functionalism and the Competition Model. In Brian MacWhinney and Elizabeth Bates (eds.), *The Cross-Linguistic Study of Sentence Processing*. Cambridge: Cambridge University Press, 3–73.

—— Wulfeck, Beverly, and MacWhinney, Brian. 1991. Cross-linguistic research in aphasia: an overview. *Brain and Language*, 41: 123–48.

Bavin, Edith L. 1995. Inflections and lexical organization: some evidence from Warlpiri. In

Hanna Pishwa and Karl Maroldt (eds.), *The Development of Morphological Systematicity: A Cross-Linguistic Perspective.* Tübingen: Gunter Narr, 39–53.

Bennett, Jonathan. 1988. *Events and their Names.* Indianapolis: Hackett.

Bickerton, Derek. 1981. *Roots of Language.* Ann Arbor: Karoma.

—— 1990. *Language and Species.* Chicago: University of Chicago Press.

—— 1995. *Language and Human Behavior.* Seattle: University of Washington Press.

—— 1998. Catastrophic evolution: the case for a single step from protolanguage to full human language. In Hurford *et al.* (1998), 341–58.

Bittner, Dagmar. 1988. Motivationsstrukturen im Flexionsverhalten der neuhochdeutschen Substantive—Vorschlag eines Modells. In Wolfgang U. Wurzel (ed.), *Studien zur Morphologie und Phonologie III* (Linguistische Studien, Reihe A: Arbeitsberichte, 188). Berlin: Akademie der Wissenschaften der DDR, 36–52.

Blevins, Juliette. 1995. The syllable in phonological theory. In John A. Goldsmith (ed.), *The Handbook of Phonological Theory.* Oxford: Blackwell, 206–44.

Borras, F. M., and Christian, R. F. 1959. *Russian Syntax.* Oxford: Clarendon Press.

Bradshaw, John, and Rogers, Lesley. 1992. *The Evolution of Lateral Asymmetries, Language, Tool Use, and Intellect.* San Diego: Academic Press.

Brandon, Robert N., and Hornstein, Norbert. 1986. From icons to symbols: some speculations on the origins of language. *Biology and Philosophy,* 1: 169–89. (Reprinted in Brandon, *Concepts and Methods In Evolutionary Biology.* Cambridge: Cambridge University Press, 1996, 85–105.)

Bréal, Michel. 1897. *Essai de sémantique.* Paris: Hachette.

Broschart, Jürgen. 1997. Why Tongan does it differently: categorial distinctions in a language without nouns and verbs. *Linguistic Typology,* 1: 123–65.

Brown, Roger. 1973. *A First Language: The Early Stages.* Cambridge, Mass.: Harvard University Press.

Bruner, Jerome S., Goodnow, Jacqueline J., and Austin, George A. 1956. *A Study in Thinking.* New York: Wiley.

Burling, Robbins. 1993. Primate calls, human language, and nonverbal communication. *Current Anthropology,* 34: 25–54.

Burr, D. B. 1976. Neandertal vocal tract reconstruction: a critical appraisal. *Journal of Human Evolution,* 5: 285–90.

Bybee, Joan, Perkins, Revere, and Pagliuca, William. 1994. *The Evolution of Grammar: Tense, Aspect and Modality in the Languages of the World.* Chicago: University of Chicago Press.

Byrne, Richard. 1995. *The Thinking Ape: Evolutionary Origins of Intelligence.* Oxford: Oxford University Press.

—— and Whiten, Andrew. 1988 (eds.). *Machiavellian Intelligence: Social Expertise and the Evolution of Intellect in Monkeys, Apes and Humans.* Oxford: Clarendon Press.

Calvin, William H. 1989. *The Cerebral Symphony: Seashore Reflections on the Structure of Consciousness.* New York: Bantam.

—— 1992. Evolving mixed-media messages and grammatical language: secondary uses of the neural sequencing machinery needed for ballistic movements. In Wind *et al.* (1992), 163–79.

—— 1993. The unitary hypothesis: a common neural circuitry for novel manipulations, language, plan-ahead, and throwing? In Gibson and Ingold (1993), 230–50.

Calvin, William H., and Ojemann, George A. 1994. *Conversations with Neil's Brain: The Neural Nature of Thought and Language.* Reading, Mass.: Addison-Wesley.

Cann, Rebecca L. 1995. Mitochondrial DNA and human evolution. In Changeux and Chavaillon (1995), 127–35.

—— Stoneking, Mark, and Wilson, Allan C. 1987. Mitochondrial DNA and human evolution. *Nature*, 325: 31–6.

—— Rickards, Olga, and Lum, J. Koji. 1994. Mitochondrial DNA and human evolution: our one lucky mother. In Nitecki and Nitecki (1994), 135–48.

Caramazza, Alfonso, and Zurif, Edgar B. 1976. Dissociation of algorithmic and heuristic processes in language comprehension: evidence from aphasia. *Brain and Language*, 3: 572–82.

Carré, René, and Mrayati, Mohamed. 1992. Distinctive regions in acoustic tubes: speech production modelling. *Journal d'acoustique*, 5: 141–59.

Carstairs, Andrew. 1983. Paradigm economy. *Journal of Linguistics*, 19: 115–28.

—— 1987. *Allomorphy in Inflexion.* London: Croom Helm.

—— 1988a. Paradigm economy: a reply to Nyman. *Journal of Linguistics*, 24: 489–99.

—— 1988b. Some implications of phonologically conditioned suppletion. In Geert Booij and Jaap van Marle (eds.), *Yearbook of Morphology 1988.* Dordrecht: Foris, 67–94.

Carstairs-McCarthy, Andrew. 1991. Inflection classes: two questions with one answer. In Frans Plank (ed.), *Paradigms: The Economy of Inflection.* Berlin: Mouton de Gruyter, 213–53.

—— 1994. Inflection classes, gender and the Principle of Contrast. *Language*, 70: 737–88.

—— 1996. Review of Armstrong *et al.* (1995). *Lingua*, 99: 135–8.

—— 1997. Review of Ruhlen (1994). *Language*, 73: 611–14.

—— 1998a. How lexical semantics constrains inflectional allomorphy. In Geert Booij and Jaap van Marle (eds.), *Yearbook of Morphology 1997.* Dordrecht: Kluwer, 1–24.

—— 1998b. Synonymy avoidance, phonology, and the origin of syntax. In Hurford *et al.* (1998), 279–96.

Changeux, Jean-Pierre, and Chavaillon, Jean. 1995 (eds.). *Origins of the Human Brain.* Oxford: Clarendon Press.

Cheney, Dorothy L., and Seyfarth, Robert M. 1990. *How Monkeys See the World: Inside the Mind of Another Species.* Chicago: University of Chicago Press.

Chomsky, Noam. 1957. *Syntactic Structures.* The Hague: Mouton.

—— 1965. *Aspects of the Theory of Syntax.* Cambridge, Mass.: MIT Press.

—— 1986a. *Knowledge of Language: Its Nature, Origin and Use.* New York: Praeger.

—— 1986b. *Barriers.* Cambridge, Mass.: MIT Press.

—— 1995. Bare phrase structure. In Gert Webelhuth (ed.), *Government and Binding Theory and the Minimalist Program.* Oxford: Blackwell, 383–439.

Clark, Eve V. 1987. The Principle of Contrast: a constraint on language acquisition. In Brian MacWhinney (ed.), *Mechanisms of Language Acquisition.* Hillsdale, NJ: Erlbaum, 1–33.

——1993. *The Lexicon in Acquisition.* Cambridge: Cambridge University Press.

Clark, John, and Yallop, Colin. 1995. *An Introduction to Phonetics and Phonology* (2nd edn.). Oxford: Blackwell.

Clements, George N., and Keyser, Samuel Jay. 1983. *CV Phonology: A Generative Theory of the Syllable.* Cambridge, Mass.: MIT Press.

Comrie, Bernard. 1981. *The Languages of the Soviet Union.* Cambridge: Cambridge University Press.

—— 1989. *Language Universals and Linguistic Typology* (2nd edn.). Oxford: Blackwell.

Coxon, A. H. 1970. Parmenides. In N. G. L. Hammond and H. H. Scullard (eds.), *Oxford Classical Dictionary* (2nd edn). Oxford: Clarendon Press, 782.

Cruse, D. A. 1986. *Lexical Semantics.* Cambridge: Cambridge University Press.

David, Edward E., and Denes, Peter B. 1972 (eds.). *Human Communication: A Unified View.* New York: McGraw-Hill.

Davidson, Iain, and Noble, William. 1993. Tools and language in human evolution. In Gibson and Ingold (1993), 363–88.

Deacon, Terrence W. 1989. The neural circuitry underlying primate calls and human language. *Human Evolution,* 4: 367–401. (Reprinted in Wind *et al.* (1992), 121–62.)

—— 1992. Brain-language coevolution. In Hawkins and Gell-Mann (1992), 49–83.

—— 1996. Prefrontal cortex and symbol learning: why a brain capable of language evolved only once. In Velichkovsky and Rumbaugh (1996), 103–38.

—— 1997. *The Symbolic Species: The Co-Evolution of Language and the Human Brain.* London: Allen Lane.

Deane, Paul D. 1992. *Grammar in Mind and Brain: Explorations in Cognitive Syntax.* Berlin: Mouton de Gruyter.

De Grolier, Éric. 1983 (ed). *Glossogenetics: The Origin and Evolution of Language.* Chur: Harwood.

Dell, François, and Elmedlaoui, Mohamed. 1985. Syllabic consonants and syllabification in Imdlawn Tashlhiyt Berber. *Journal of African Languages and Linguistics,* 7: 105–30.

—— —— 1988. Syllabic consonants in Berber: some new evidence. *Journal of African Languages and Linguistics,* 10: 1–17.

Dennett, Daniel C. 1995. *Darwin's Dangerous Idea: Evolution and the Meanings of Life.* New York: Simon & Schuster.

Dennis, Maureen, and Whitaker, Harry. 1976. Language acquisition following hemidecortication: linguistic superiority of the left over the right hemisphere. *Brain and Language,* 3: 404–33.

Deuchar, Margaret. 1984. *British Sign Language.* London: Routledge.

DeYoe, E. A., and Van Essen, D. C. 1988. Concurrent processing streams in monkey visual cortex. *Trends in Neurosciences,* 11: 219–26.

Diffloth, Gérard. 1994. *i*: big, *a*: small. In Hinton *et al.* (1994), 107–14.

Dimmendaal, Gerrit J. 1987. Drift and selective mechanisms in morphological changes: the eastern Nilotic case. In Anna Giacalone Ramat, Onofrio Carruba, and Giuliano Bernini (eds.), *Papers from the 7th International Conference on Historical Linguistics.* Amsterdam: Benjamins, 193–210.

Dixon, R. M. W. 1980. *The Languages of Australia.* Cambridge: Cambridge University Press.

DuBrul, E. Lloyd. 1958. *Evolution of the Speech Apparatus.* Springfield, Ill.: Charles C. Thomas.

—— 1976. Biomechanics of speech sounds. In Harnad *et al.* (1976), 631–42.

—— 1977. Origin of the speech apparatus and its reconstruction in fossils. *Brain and Language,* 4: 365–81.

Duchin, Linda E. 1990. The evolution of articulate speech: comparative anatomy of the oral cavity of *Pan* and *Homo. Journal of Human Evolution,* 19: 687–97.

Dummett, Michael. 1981. *Frege: Philosophy of Language* (2nd edn.). Cambridge, Mass.: Harvard University Press.

—— 1994. *Origins of Analytical Philosophy*. Cambridge, Mass.: Harvard University Press.

Dunbar, Robin. 1996. *Grooming, Gossip and the Evolution of Language*. London: Faber & Faber.

—— 1998. Theory of mind and the evolution of language. In Hurford *et al.* (1998), 92–110.

Foley, Robert. 1995. *Humans before Humanity: An Evolutionary Perspective*. Oxford: Blackwell.

Foster, Mary LeCron. 1978. The symbolic structure of primordial language. In S. L. Washburn and Elizabeth R. McCown (eds.), *Human Evolution: Biosocial Perspectives*. Menlo Park, Calif.: Benjamin/Cummings, 77–121.

—— 1983. Solving the insoluble: language genetics today. In De Grolier (1983), 455–80.

—— 1990. Symbolic origins and transitions in the Palaeolithic. In Paul Mellars (ed.), *The Emergence of Modern Humans: An Archaeological Perspective*. Edinburgh: Edinburgh University Press, 517–39.

Fouts, Roger S., and Rigby, Randall L. 1977. Man–chimpanzee communication. In Thomas A. Sebeok (ed.), *How Animals Communicate*. Bloomington, Ind.: Indiana University Press, 1034–54.

Frege, Gottlob. 1980. *Translations from the Philosophical Writings of Gottlob Frege*, ed. Peter Geach and Max Black (3rd edn.). Oxford: Blackwell.

Fromkin, Victoria A. 1973 (ed.). *Speech Errors as Linguistic Evidence*. The Hague: Mouton.

Fry, D. B. 1979. *The Physics of Speech*. Cambridge: Cambridge University Press.

Fudge, Erik. 1969. Syllables. *Journal of Linguistics*, 5: 253–86.

Gardner, Beatrix T., Gardner, R. Allen, and Nichols, Susan G. 1989*a*. The shapes and uses of signs in a cross-fostering laboratory. In Gardner *et al.* (1989*b*), 55–180.

Gardner, R. Allen, Gardner, Beatrix T., and Van Cantfort, Thomas E. 1989*b*. *Teaching Sign Language to Chimpanzees*. Albany, NY: SUNY Press.

Geach, Peter Thomas. 1980. *Reference and Generality: An Examination of Some Medieval and Modern Theories* (3rd edn.). Ithaca, NY: Cornell University Press.

Gibson, Kathleen R. 1993. Tool use, language and social behavior in relationship to information processing capacities. In Gibson and Ingold (1993), 251–69.

—— and Ingold, Tim. 1993. (eds.) *Tools, Language and Cognition in Human Evolution*. Cambridge: Cambridge University Press.

Givón, Talmy. 1995. *Functionalism and Grammar*. Amsterdam: John Benjamins.

Gould, Stephen Jay, and Vrba, Elisabeth S. 1982. Exaptation—a missing term in the science of form. *Paleobiology*, 8: 4–15.

Greenfield, Patricia M. 1991. Language, tools and the brain: the ontogeny and phylogeny of hierarchically organized sequential behavior. *Behavioral and Brain Sciences*, 14: 531–51.

—— and Savage-Rumbaugh, E. Sue. 1990. Grammatical combination in *Pan paniscus*: processes of learning and invention in the evolution and development of language. In Parker and Gibson (1990), 540–78.

—— —— 1991. Imitation, grammatical development, and the invention of protogrammar by an ape. In Krasnegor *et al.* (1991), 235–62.

Grice, Paul. 1989. *Studies in the Way of Words*. Cambridge, Mass.: Harvard University Press.

Grimshaw, Jane. 1990. *Argument Structure*. Cambridge, Mass.: MIT Press.

Haider, Hubert, and Prinzhorn, Martin. 1986 (eds.). *Verb Second Phenomena in Germanic Languages*. Dordrecht: Foris.

Hare, R. M. 1952. *The Language of Morals*. Oxford: Oxford University Press.

Harms, Robert. 1957. The Finnish genitive plural. *Language*, 33: 533–7.

Harnad, Stevan. 1996. The origin of words: a psychophysical hypothesis. In Velichkovsky and Rumbaugh (1996), 27–44.

—— Steklis, Horst D., and Lancaster, Jane. 1976 (eds.). *Origins and Evolution of Language and Speech* (Annals of the New York Academy of Sciences, vol. 280). New York: New York Academy of Sciences.

Harris, John. 1994. *English Sound Structure*. Oxford: Blackwell.

Hauser, Marc D. 1996. *The Evolution of Communication*. Cambridge, Mass.: MIT Press.

—— and Wolfe, Nathan D. 1995. Human language: are nonhuman precursors lacking? *Behavioral and Brain Sciences*, 18: 190–1.

Hawkins, John A. 1992. Innateness and function in language universals. In Hawkins and Gell-Mann (1992), 87–120.

—— 1994. *A Performance Theory of Order and Constituency*. Cambridge: Cambridge University Press.

—— and Gell-Mann, Murray. 1992 (eds.). *The Evolution of Human Languages* (Santa Fe Institute Studies in the Science of Complexity, vol. XI). Redwood City, Calif.: Addison-Wesley.

Head, Lyndsay. 1989. *Making Maori Sentences*. Auckland: Longman Paul.

Hewes, Gordon W. 1973. Primate communication and the gestural origin of language. *Current Anthropology*, 14: 5–24.

—— 1976. The current status of the gestural theory of language origin. In Harnad *et al.* (1976), 482–504.

Hewitt, B. G., and Khiba, Z. K. 1989. *Abkhaz*. London: Routledge.

Hinton, Leanne, Nichols, Johanna, and Ohala, John J. 1994 (eds.). *Sound Symbolism*. Cambridge: Cambridge University Press.

Hockett, Charles F. 1960*a*. The origin of speech. *Scientific American*, 203/3 (September), 88–96.

—— 1960*b*. Logical considerations in the study of animal communication. In W. E. Lanyon and W. N. Tavolga (eds.), *Animal Sounds and Communication*. Washington: American Institute of Biological Sciences, 392–430.

—— and Ascher, Robert. 1964. The human revolution. *Current Anthropology*, 5: 135–47.

Horwich, Paul. 1994 (ed.). *Theories of Truth*. Aldershot: Dartmouth.

Houghton, Philip. 1993. Neandertal supralaryngeal vocal tract. *American Journal of Physical Anthropology*, 90: 139–46.

Hubel, David H. 1988. *Eye, Brain and Vision*. New York: Freeman.

Hurford, James R. 1990. Beyond the roadblock in linguistic evolution studies. *Behavioral and Brain Sciences*, 13: 736–7.

—— Studdert-Kennedy, Michael, and Knight, Chris. 1998 (eds.). *Approaches to the Evolution of Language: Social and Cognitive Bases*. Cambridge: Cambridge University Press.

Hyman, Larry. 1985. A *Theory of Phonological Weight*. Dordrecht: Foris.

Isaacs, Elizabeth, Vargha-Khadem, Faraneh, Carr, Lucinda, Brett, Edward, Adams, Christopher, and Mishkin, Mortimer. 1996. Onset of speech after left hemispherectomy in a nine-year-old boy. Paper delivered at the Conference on the Evolution of Human Language, Edinburgh, 1–4 April 1996.

Jackendoff, Ray. 1977. X̄ *Syntax: A Study of Phrase Structure*. Cambridge, Mass.: MIT Press.

—— 1983. *Semantics and Cognition*. Cambridge, Mass.: MIT Press.

—— 1985. Multiple subcategorization and the θ-criterion: the case of *climb*. *Natural Language and Linguistic Theory*, 3: 271–95.

Jakobson, Roman. 1962. *Selected Writings 1: Phonological Studies*. The Hague: Mouton.

—— and Waugh, Linda R. 1979. *The Sound Shape of Language*. Brighton: Harvester Press.

Jelinek, Eloise, and Demers, Richard A. 1994. Predicates and pronominal arguments in Straits Salish. *Language*, 70: 697–736.

Jerison, Harry J. 1973. *Evolution of the Brain and Intelligence*. New York: Academic Press.

—— 1982. The evolution of biological intelligence. In Robert J. Sternberg (ed.), *Handbook of Human Intelligence*. Cambridge: Cambridge University Press, 723–91.

Karlsson, Fred. 1983. *Finnish Grammar*. Porvoo: Werner Söderström Osakeyhtiö.

Kaye, Jonathan, Lowenstamm, Jean, and Vergnaud, Jean-Roger. 1990. Constituent structure and government in phonology. *Phonology*, 7: 193–231.

Kempson, Ruth. 1977. *Semantic Theory*. Cambridge: Cambridge University Press.

Kenstowicz, Michael. 1994. *Phonology in Generative Grammar*. Oxford: Blackwell.

Kent, R. D. 1983. The segmental organization of speech. In MacNeilage (1983), 57–89.

Kirby, Simon. 1999. *Function, Selection, and Innateness: The Emergence of Language Universals*. Oxford: Oxford University Press.

Klima, Edward S., and Bellugi, Ursula. 1979. *The Signs of Language*. Cambridge, Mass.: Harvard University Press.

Knight, Chris. 1998. Ritual/speech coevolution: a 'selfish gene' solution to the problem of deception. In Hurford *et al.* (1998), 68–91.

—— Power, Camilla, and Watts, Ian. 1995. The human symbolic revolution: a Darwinian account. *Cambridge Archaeological Journal*, 5: 75–114.

Köpcke, Klaus-Michael. 1988. Schemas in German plural formation. *Lingua*, 74: 303–35.

Krantz, Grover S. 1980. Sapienization and speech [with peer commentary and response]. *Current Anthropology*, 21: 773–92.

—— 1988. Laryngeal descent in 40,000 year old fossils. In Landsberg (1988), 173–80.

Krasnegor, Norman A., Rumbaugh, Duane M., Schiefelbusch, Richard L., and Studdert-Kennedy, Michael. 1991 (eds.). *Biological and Behavioral Determinants of Language Development*. Hillsdale, NJ: Erlbaum.

Kuipers, Aerts H. 1960. *Phoneme and Morpheme in Kabardian*. The Hague: Mouton.

Ladefoged, Peter. 1962. *Elements of Acoustic Phonetics*. Chicago: Chicago University Press.

—— 1993. *A Course in Phonetics* (3rd international edn.). Fort Worth, Tex.: Harcourt Brace.

Laitman, Jeffrey T., and Reidenberg, Joy S. 1988. Advances in understanding the relationship between the skull base and the larynx with comments on the origin of speech. *Human Evolution*, 3: 99–109.

—— —— and Gannon, Patrick J. 1992. Fossil skulls and hominid vocal tracts: new approaches to charting the evolution of human speech. In Wind *et al.* (1992), 385–97.

Lakoff, George. 1991. Cognitive versus generative linguistics: how commitments influence results. *Language and Communication*, 11: 53–62.

Landsberg, Marge E. 1988 (ed.). *The Genesis of Language: A Different Judgement of Evidence.* Berlin: Mouton de Gruyter.

Langacker, Ronald W. 1987. *Foundations of Cognitive Grammar,* i: *Theoretical Prerequisites.* Stanford, Calif.: Stanford University Press.

—— 1990. *Concept, Image, and Symbol: The Cognitive Basis of Grammar.* Berlin: Mouton de Gruyter.

—— 1991. *Foundations of Cognitive Grammar,* ii: *Descriptive Application.* Stanford, Calif.: Stanford University Press.

Lass, Roger. 1984. *Phonology: An Introduction to the Basic Concepts.* Cambridge: Cambridge University Press.

—— 1990. How to do things with junk: exaptation in language evolution. *Journal of Linguistics,* 26: 79–102.

Laver, John. 1994. *Principles of Phonetics.* Cambridge: Cambridge University Press.

Leech, Geoffrey, Deuchar, Margaret, and Hoogenraad, Robert. 1982. *English Grammar for Today: A New Introduction.* Basingstoke: Macmillan.

Lenneberg, Eric H. 1967. *Biological Foundations of Language.* New York: John Wiley & Sons.

Levin, Juliette. 1985. A metrical theory of syllabicity. Ph.D. dissertation, MIT.

Li, Charles N. 1976 (ed.). *Subject and Topic.* New York: Academic Press.

—— and Thompson, Sandra A. 1976. Subject and topic: a new typology of language. In Li (1976), 457–89.

Liberman, A. M. 1970. The grammars of speech and language. *Cognitive Psychology,* 1: 301–23.

—— Cooper, F. S., Shankweiler, D. P. , and Studdert-Kennedy, M. 1967. Perception of the speech code. *Psychological Review,* 74: 431–61. (Reprinted in David and Denes (1972), 13–50. Also in Liberman, *Speech: A Special Code.* Cambridge, Mass.: MIT Press, 1996.)

Liddell, Scott K. 1978. Nonmanual signals and relative clauses in American Sign Language. In Siple (1978), 59–90.

—— 1980. *American Sign Language Syntax.* The Hague: Mouton.

Lieberman, Philip. 1984. *The Biology and Evolution of Language.* Cambridge, Mass.: Harvard University Press.

—— 1991. *Uniquely Human: The Evolution of Speech, Thought and Selfless Behavior.* Cambridge, Mass.: Harvard University Press.

—— 1992. On the evolution of human language. In Hawkins and Gell-Mann (1992), 21–47.

—— and Blumstein, Sheila E. 1988. *Speech Physiology, Speech Perception and Acoustic Phonetics.* Cambridge: Cambridge University Press.

—— and Crelin, Edmund S. 1971. On the speech of Neanderthal man. *Linguistic Inquiry,* 2: 203–22.

—— Laitman, Jeffrey T., Reidenberg, Joy S., and Gannon, Patrick J. 1992. The anatomy, physiology, acoustics and perception of speech: essential elements in analysis of the evolution of human speech. *Journal of Human Evolution,* 23: 447–67.

Lightfoot, David. 1991. Subjacency and sex. *Language and Communication,* 11: 67–9.

Lindblom, Björn. 1983. Economy of speech gestures. In MacNeilage (1983), 217–45.

—— MacNeilage, Peter, and Studdert-Kennedy, Michael. 1983. Self-organizing processes and the explanation of phonological universals. *Linguistics,* 21: 181–203.

Linebarger, Marcia C., Schwartz, Myrna F., and Saffran, Eleanor M. 1983. Sensitivity to grammatical structure in so-called agrammatic aphasics. *Cognition*, 13: 361–92.

Locke, John L. 1993. *The Child's Path to Spoken Language*. Cambridge, Mass.: Harvard University Press.

Lyons, John. 1968. *Introduction to Theoretical Linguistics*. Cambridge: Cambridge University Press.

McCloskey, James. 1996. On the scope of verb movement in Irish. *Natural Language and Linguistic Theory*, 14: 47–104.

MacLarnon, Ann. 1993. The vertebral canal. In A. Walker and R. E. Leakey (eds.), *The Nariokotome Homo Erectus Skeleton*. Cambridge, Mass.: Harvard University Press, 359–90.

MacLaughlin, Dawn. 1997. The structure of determiner phrases: evidence from American Sign Language. Ph.D. dissertation, Boston University.

MacNeilage, Peter F. 1983 (ed.). *The Production of Speech*. New York: Springer-Verlag.

—— 1994. Prolegomena to a theory of the sound pattern of the first spoken language. *Phonetica*, 51: 184–94.

—— 1998. The frame/content theory of evolution of speech production. *Behavioral and Brain Sciences*, 21: 499–546.

—— Studdert-Kennedy, Michael G., and Lindblom, Björn. 1984. Functional precursors to language and its lateralization. *American Journal of Physiology*, 246: R912–14.

Maiden, Martin. 1996. The Romance gerund and 'system-dependent naturalness' in morphology. *Transactions of the Philological Society*, 94: 167–201.

Malcolm, Norman. 1958. *Ludwig Wittgenstein: A Memoir*. Oxford: Oxford University Press.

Markman, Ellen M. 1989. *Categorization and Naming in Children: Problems of Induction*. Cambridge, Mass.: MIT Press.

Martinet, André. 1960. *Éléments de linguistique générale*. Paris: Librairie Colin. (English translation: *Elements of General Linguistics*. 1964. London: Faber.)

Mauner, Gail, Fromkin, Victoria A. and Cornell, Thomas L. 1993. Comprehension and acceptability judgements in agrammatism: disruptions in the syntax of referential dependency. *Brain and Language*, 45: 340–70.

Maynard Smith, John, and Szathmáry, Eörs. 1995. *The Major Transitions in Evolution*. Oxford: W. H. Freeman.

Medawar, P. B. 1967. *The Art of the Soluble*. London: Methuen.

Merriman, William E., and Bowman, Laura L. 1989. The mutual exclusivity bias in children's word learning. *Monographs of the Society for Research in Child Development*, serial no. 220, vol. 54, nos. 3–4.

Miles, H. Lyn White. 1990. The cognitive foundations for reference in a signing orangutan. In Parker and Gibson (1990), 511–39.

Miller, Geoffrey, and Todd, Peter. 1998. Evolution of vocabulary size through runaway sexual selection: theory, data and simulations. Paper delivered at the Second International Conference on the Evolution of Language, London, April 1998.

Mithen, Steven. 1996. *The Prehistory of the Mind*. London: Thames & Hudson.

Monk, Ray. 1990. *Ludwig Wittgenstein: The Duty of Genius*. New York: Free Press.

Morgan, Elaine. 1982. *The Aquatic Ape*. London: Souvenir Press.

—— 1989. The Aquatic Ape Theory and the origin of speech. In Wind *et al.* (1989), 199–207.

Myers, Ronald E. 1976. Comparative neurology of vocalization and speech: proof of a dichotomy. In Harnad *et al.* (1976), 745–57.

Nash, David. 1985. *Topics in Warlpiri Grammar*. New York: Garland.

Nearey, T. 1978. *Phonetic Features for Vowels*. Bloomington, Ind.: Indiana University Linguistics Club.

Newman, John D. 1992. The primate isolation call and the evolution and physiological control of human speech. In Wind *et al.* (1992), 301–21.

Newmeyer, Frederick J. 1991. Functional explanation in linguistics and the origins of language [with peer commentary and response]. *Language and Communication*, 11: 3–114.

—— 1995. Conceptual structure and syntax. *Behavioral and Brain Sciences*, 18: 202.

—— 1998. On the supposed 'counterfunctionality' of Universal Grammar: some evolutionary implications. In Hurford *et al.* (1998), 305–19.

Newport, Elissa L., and Supalla, Ted. 1980. Clues from the acquisition of signed and spoken language. In Ursula Bellugi and Michael Studdert-Kennedy (eds.), *Signed and Spoken Language: Biological Constraints on Linguistic Form*. Weinheim: Verlag Chemie, 188–211.

Nitecki, Matthew H., and Nitecki, Doris V. 1994 (eds.). *Origins of Anatomically Modern Humans*. New York: Plenum.

Noble, William, and Davidson, Iain. 1996. *Human Evolution, Language and Mind: A Psychological and Archaeological Inquiry*. Cambridge: Cambridge University Press.

Nyman, Martti. 1987. Is the Paradigm Economy Principle relevant? *Journal of Linguistics*, 23: 251–67.

Paradis, Carole. 1991. *The Special Status of Coronals: Internal and External Evidence*. San Diego: Academic Press.

Parker, Sue Taylor, and Gibson, Kathleen Rita. 1979. A developmental model for the evolution of language and intelligence in early hominids. *Behavioral and Brain Sciences*, 2: 367–81.

—— —— 1990 (eds.). *'Language' and Intelligence in Monkeys and Apes: Comparative Developmental Perspectives*. Cambridge: Cambridge University Press.

Parkinson, G. H. R. 1968 (ed.). *The Theory of Meaning*. Oxford: Oxford University Press.

Patterson, Francine. 1978. The gestures of a gorilla: language acquisition in another pongid. *Brain and Language*, 5: 72–97.

Pepperberg, Irene Maxine. 1990. Conceptual abilities of some nonprimate species, with an emphasis on an African Grey parrot. In Parker and Gibson (1990), 469–507.

Peterson, Philip L. 1997. *Fact Proposition Event*. Dordrecht: Kluwer.

Piattelli-Palmarini, Massimo. 1980 (ed.). *Language and Learning: The Debate between Jean Piaget and Noam Chomsky*. London: Routledge & Kegan Paul.

Pinker, Steven. 1984. *Language Learnability and Language Development*. Cambridge, Mass.: Harvard University Press.

—— 1994. *The Language Instinct*. New York: William Morrow.

—— 1995. Facts about human language relevant to its evolution. In Changeux and Chavaillon (1995), 262–83.

—— and Bloom, Paul. 1990. Natural language and natural selection [with peer commentary and response]. *Behavioral and Brain Sciences*, 13: 707–84.

Poizner, Howard, Klima, Edward S., and Bellugi, Ursula. 1987. *What the Hands Reveal about the Brain*. Cambridge, Mass.: MIT Press.

Power, Camilla, and Aiello, Leslie C. 1997. Female proto-symbolic strategies. In Lori D. Hager (ed.), *Women in Human Evolution*. London: Routledge, 153–71.

Premack, David. 1976. *Intelligence in Ape and Man*. Hillsdale, NJ: Lawrence Erlbaum.

—— 1986. *Gavagai! or the Future History of the Animal Language Controversy*. Cambridge, Mass.: MIT Press.

Prince, Alan, and Smolensky, Paul. 1993. *Optimality Theory: Constraint Interaction in Generative Grammar*. Piscataway, NJ: Rutgers University Center for Cognitive Science.

Prior, Arthur. 1962. *Formal Logic* (2nd edn.). Oxford: Clarendon Press.

Pulleyblank, Edwin G. 1983. The beginnings of duality of patterning in language. In De Grolier (1983), 469–510.

—— 1989. The meaning of duality of patterning and its importance in language evolution. In Wind *et al.* (1989), 53–65.

Quine, Willard Van Orman. 1960. *Word and Object*. Cambridge, Mass.: MIT Press.

Radford, Andrew. 1988. *Transformational Grammar: A First Course*. Cambridge: Cambridge University Press.

Ramsey, F. P. 1925. Universals. *Mind*, 34: 401–17. (Reprinted in Ramsey, *Philosophical Papers*, ed. D. H. Mellor. Cambridge: Cambridge University Press, 1990.)

Reynolds, Peter C. 1983. Ape constructional ability and the origin of linguistic structure. In De Grolier (1983), 185–200.

Rhys Jones, T. J. 1977. *Living Welsh*. London: Hodder & Stoughton.

Richards, Graham. 1987. *Human Evolution: An Introduction for the Behavioural Sciences*. London: Routledge & Kegan Paul.

Riesenfeld, Alphonse. 1969. Head balance and brachycephalization. *Homo*, 20: 81–90.

Rosch, Eleanor, and Mervis, Carolyn B. 1975. Family resemblances: studies in the internal structure of categories. *Cognitive Psychology*, 7: 573–605. (Reprinted in Heimir Geirsson and Michael Losonsky (eds.), *Readings in Language and Mind*. Oxford: Blackwell, 1996.)

Ruhlen, Merritt. 1994. *The Origin of Language: Tracing the Evolution of the Mother Tongue*. New York: John Wiley.

Rumbaugh, Duane M. (ed.). 1977. *Language Learning by a Chimpanzee: The LANA Project*. New York: Academic Press.

—— and Savage-Rumbaugh, E. Sue. 1996. Biobehavioral roots of language: words, apes, and a child. In Velichkovsky and Rumbaugh (1996), 257–74.

Russell, Bertrand. 1905. On denoting. *Mind*, 14: 479–93.

—— 1927. *The Analysis of Matter*. London: Kegan Paul.

Ruwet, Nicolas. 1991. *Syntax and Human Experience*, ed. and translated by John Goldsmith. Chicago: University of Chicago Press.

Ryle, Gilbert. 1960. Letters and syllables in Plato. *Philosophical Review*, 69: 431–51. (Reprinted in Ryle (1971).)

—— 1971. *Collected Papers*, i: *Critical Essays*. London: Hutchinson.

Sampson, Geoffrey. 1980. *Making Sense*. Oxford: Oxford University Press.

—— 1997. *Educating Eve: The 'Language Instinct' Debate*. London: Cassell.

Sapir, Edward. 1921. *Language*. New York: Harcourt Brace.

Sasse, Hans-Jürgen. 1987. The thetic/categorical distinction revisited. *Linguistics*, 25: 511–80.

Sauvageot, Aurélien. 1949. *Esquisse de la langue finnoise*. Paris: Klincksieck.

Savage-Rumbaugh, E. Sue. 1986. *Ape Language: From Conditioned Response to Symbol*. New York: Columbia University Press.

Savage-Rumbaugh, E. Sue, and Lewin, Roger. 1994. *Kanzi: The Ape at the Brink of the Human Mind.* New York: Wiley.

—— and Rumbaugh, Duane M. 1993. The emergence of language. In Gibson and Ingold (1993), 86–108.

—— Murphy, Jeanine, Sevcik, Rose A., Brakke, Karen E., Williams, Shelly L., and Rumbaugh, Duane M. 1993. Language comprehension in ape and child. *Monographs of the Society for Research in Child Development,* serial no. 233, vol. 58, nos. 3–4.

Schepartz, L. A. 1993. Language and modern human origins. *Yearbook of Physical Anthropology,* 36: 91–126.

Selkirk, Elisabeth O. 1982. The syllable. In Harry van der Hulst and Norval Smith (eds.), *The Structure of Phonological Representations* (Part II). Dordrecht: Foris, 337–83.

Shannon, Claude E., and Weaver, Warren. 1949. *The Mathematical Theory of Communication.* Urbana, Ill.: University of Illinois Press.

Simon, Herbert A. 1962. The architecture of complexity. *Proceedings of the American Philosophical Society,* 106: 467–82. (Reprinted in Simon (1996), 183–216.)

—— 1996. *The Sciences of the Artificial* (3rd edn.). Cambridge, Mass.: MIT Press.

Siple, Patricia (ed.). 1978. *Understanding Language through Sign Language Research.* New York: Academic Press.

Sperber, Dan, and Wilson, Deirdre. 1995. *Relevance: Communication and Cognition* (2nd edn.). Oxford: Blackwell.

Steele, Susan, Akmajian, Adrian, Demers, Richard, Jelinek, Eloise, Kitagawa, Chisato, Oehrle, Richard, and Wasow, Thomas. 1981. *An Encyclopedia of AUX: A Study in Cross-linguistic Equivalence.* Cambridge, Mass.: MIT Press.

Steels, Luc. 1998. Synthesizing the origins of language and meaning using coevolution, self-organization and level formation. In Hurford *et al.* (1998), 384–404.

Steklis, Horst D. 1985. Primate communication, comparative neurology, and the origin of language re-examined. *Journal of Human Evolution,* 14: 157–73. (Reprinted in Landsberg (1988), 37–63.)

Stevens, Kenneth N. 1972. The quantal nature of speech: evidence from articulatory-acoustic data. In David and Denes (1972), 51–66.

—— 1989. On the quantal nature of speech. *Journal of Phonetics,* 17: 3–45.

Stopa, Roman. 1972. *Structure of Bushman and its Traces in Indo-European.* Kraków: Polska Akademia Nauk.

Strawson, P. F. 1950. On referring. *Mind,* 54: 320–44. (Reprinted in Parkinson (1968) and in Strawson (1971*b*).)

—— 1952. *Introduction to Logical Theory.* London: Methuen.

—— 1959. *Individuals: An Essay in Descriptive Metaphysics.* London: Methuen.

—— 1971*a*. The asymmetry of subjects and predicates. In Strawson (1971*b*), 96–115.

—— 1971*b*. *Logico-Linguistic Papers.* London: Methuen.

—— 1974. *Subject and Predicate in Logic and Grammar.* London: Methuen.

—— 1994. Individuals. In Guttorm Fløistad (ed.), *Philosophical Problems Today:* vol. i. Dordrecht: Kluwer, 21–44.

Stringer, Chris, and McKie, Robin. 1996. *African Exodus: The Origins of Modern Humanity.* London: Jonathan Cape.

Studdert-Kennedy, Michael. 1998. The particulate origins of language generativity: from syllable to gesture. In Hurford *et al.* (1998), 202–21.

Supalla, Ted, and Newport, Elissa L. 1978. How many seats in a chair? The derivation of nouns and verbs in American Sign Language. In Siple (1978), 91–132.

Swisher, Carl C. III, Rink, W. J., Antón, S. C., Schwarcz, H. P. , Curtis, G. H., Suprijo, A., and Widiasmoro. 1996. Latest *Homo erectus* of Java: potential contemporaneity with *Homo sapiens* in Southeast Asia. *Science*, 274: 187–94.

Talmy, Leonard. 1985. Lexicalization patterns: semantic structure in lexical forms. In Timothy Shopen (ed.), *Language Typology and Syntactic Description*, iii: *Grammatical Categories and the Lexicon.* Cambridge: Cambridge University Press, 57–149.

Tan, Li Hai, and Perfetti, Charles A. 1997. Visual Chinese character recognition: does phonological information mediate access to meaning? *Journal of Memory and Language*, 37: 41–57.

Taylor, John R. 1996. *Possessives in English: An Exploration in Cognitive Grammar.* Oxford: Clarendon Press.

Terrace, Herbert S. 1979. *Nim.* New York: Knopf.

Thieme, Hartmut. 1997. Lower Palaeolithic hunting spears from Germany. *Nature*, 385: 807–10.

Tomlin, Russell. 1986. *Basic Word Order: Functional Principles.* London: Croom Helm.

Trinkaus, Erik, and Shipman, Pat. 1993. *The Neandertals: Changing the Image of Mankind.* New York: Knopf.

Velichkovsky, Boris M., and Rumbaugh, Duane M. 1996 (eds.). *Communicating Meaning: The Evolution and Development of Language.* Mahwah, NJ: Lawrence Erlbaum.

Wallman, Joel. 1992. *Aping Language.* New York: Cambridge University Press.

Waters, Michael R., Forman, Steven L., and Pierson, James M. 1997. Diring Yuriakh: a Lower Paleolithic site in central Siberia. *Science*, 275: 1281–4.

Wehr, Barbara. 1984. *Diskursstrategien im Romanischen.* Tübingen: Narr.

Wilkins, Wendy K., and Wakefield, Jennie. 1995. Brain evolution and neurolinguistic preconditions [with peer commentary and response]. *Behavioral and Brain Sciences*, 18: 161–226.

Wills, Christopher. 1993. *The Runaway Brain: The Evolution of Human Uniqueness.* New York: HarperCollins.

Wind, Jan. 1976. Phylogeny of the human vocal tract. In Harnad *et al.* (1976), 612–30.

—— 1989. The evolutionary history of the human speech organs. In Wind *et al.* (1989), 173–97.

—— Pulleyblank, Edward [*sic*] G., Grolier, Éric de, and Bichakjian, Bernard H. 1989 (eds.). *Studies in Language Origins*, vol. i. Amsterdam: Benjamins.

—— Chiarelli, Brunetto, Bichakjian, Bernard, Nocentini, Alberto, and Jonker, Abraham. 1992 (eds.). *Language Origin: A Multidisciplinary Approach* (NATO Advanced Science Institute Series D, Behavioural and Social Sciences, 61). Dordrecht: Kluwer.

Wittgenstein, Ludwig. 1958. *Philosophical Investigations*, trans. G. E. M. Anscombe (2nd edn.). Oxford: Blackwell.

—— 1961. *Tractatus logico-philosophicus* (the German text of *Logisch-philosophische Abhandlung* with a new translation by D. F. Pears and B. F. McGuinness). London: Routledge & Kegan Paul.

Worden, Robert. 1998. The evolution of language from social intelligence. In Hurford *et al.* (1998), 148–66.

Wulfeck, Beverly B. 1988. Grammaticality judgments and sentence comprehension in agrammatic aphasia. *Journal of Speech and Hearing Research*, 31: 72–81.

Wurzel, Wolfgang Ullrich. 1984. *Flexionsmorphologie und Natürlichkeit*. Berlin: Akademie-Verlag. (English translation: *Inflectional Morphology and Naturalness*. Dordrecht: Kluwer, 1989.)

Wynn, Thomas. 1993. Layers of thinking in tool behavior. In Gibson and Ingold (1993), 389–406.

Zurif, Edgar B. 1995. Brain regions of relevance to syntactic processing. In Lila R. Gleitman and Mark Liberman (eds.), *An Invitation to Cognitive Science*, i: *Language* (2nd edn.). Cambridge, Mass.: MIT Press, 381–97.

# Further Reading

I hope that some readers will have had their appetites whetted for more reading and thinking about language evolution. This applies particularly to readers who may be attracted by my scenario, at least in some degree, but who may nevertheless be cautious about accepting anything so novel before exploring some of the alternatives on offer. So I offer here suggestions for further reading on various relevant topics, to supplement the technical references citied in the text. I also offer a few comments on what I regard as their strengths and weaknesses— that is, apart from the common weakness that none of them, I believe, offers a satisfactory account of the evolution of the sentence-NP distinction in syntax!

## 1. The Structure of Language

General readers and beginning students are well served by the introductory books on language currently available. Pinker's is justly famous, but Aitchison's is equally easy to read and Jackendoff's discusses interesting links between language and other human characteristics, such as musical creativity.

Aitchison, Jean. *The Articulate Mammal: An Introduction to Psycholinguistics* (4th edn.) London: Routledge, 1998.
Jackendoff, Ray. *Patterns in the Mind: Language and Human Nature.* New York: Harvester Wheatsheaf, 1993.
Pinker, Steven. *The Language Instinct.* New York: William Morrow, 1994. (Paperback editions published by Penguin and HarperCollins.)

## 2. Darwinian Evolutionary Theory

A hypothesis such as mine on language evolution cannot be correct unless it is compatible with what is known about evolution in general. I do not discuss this issue at length in the text, but it goes without saying that I think that the two are indeed compatible. Some readers may be uneasy that my scenario seems to present language as arising in humans more by accident than as a response to environmental pressures. Such unease is likely to rest on two mistaken notions: first, that the existence of some environmental pressure guarantees biological change at the level of the species in order to meet it successfully, and, secondly, that all changes at the level of the species occur only in response to clearly identifiable pressures. The following books should help to clear up those misunderstandings. Dawkins, and Williams in *Plan and Purpose in Nature*, offer excellent introductions to evolution for the non-biologist. William's earlier books are somewhat more technical. Dennett shares the same perspective on evolution as the other two, but delves further into philosophical issues and into the evolution of cognitive abilities, including language; he is also a most engaging and entertaining writer.

Dawkins, Richard. *The Blind Watchmaker*. New York: Norton, 1985.
Dennett, Daniel. *Darwin's Dangerous Idea: Evolution and the Meanings of Life*. New York: Simon and Schuster, 1995. (Paperback edition published by Penguin.)
Williams, George C. *Natural Selection: Domains, Levels and Challenges*. New York: Oxford University Press, 1992.
—— *Adaptation and Natural Selection: A Critique of Some Current Evolutionary Thought* (2nd edn.). Princeton: Princeton University Press, 1996.
—— *Plan and Purpose in Nature*. London: Weidenfeld & Nicolson, 1996.

## 3. Human Evolution

Most writers on human evolution are archaeologists or biological anthropologists. That applies to all the authors mentioned here except Donald, who is a psychologist. Of all the items I suggest here, his book is the furthest from mine in its perspective on language.

Donald, Merlin. *Origins of the Modern Mind: Three Stages in the Evolution of Culture and Cognition*. Cambridge, Mass: Harvard University Press, 1991.
Foley, Robert. *Humans before Humanity: An Evolutionary Perspective*. Oxford: Blackwell, 1995.
Mithen, Steven. *The Prehistory of the Mind*. London: Thames & Hudson, 1996.
Stringer, Chris, and McKie, Robin. *African Exodus: The Origins of Modern Humanity*. London: Jonathan Cape, 1996.

## 4. Language and the Brain

The neurophysiology of the brain is a highly technical subject. Nevertheless, Calvin and Ojemann offer an accessible and entertaining introduction for the general reader. Deacon's book is more challenging, but packed with information as well as opinions—some of which, relating to language, I criticize in Chapter 6. The details of the relationship between brain pathologies and linguistic deficiencies, in so far as these are understood, are summarized in introductory texts for students of medicine and speech and language therapy; Caplan's book has the merit of being well informed linguistically as well as neurologically.

Calvin, William, and Ojemann, George A. *Conversations with Neil's Brain: The Neural Nature of Thought and Language*. Reading, Mass.: Addison-Wesley, 1994.

Caplan, David. *Neurolinguistics and Linguistic Aphasiology: An Introduction*. Cambridge: Cambridge University Press, 1987.

Deacon, Terrence. *The Symbolic Species: The Co-Evolution of Language and the Human Brain*. London: Allen Lane, 1997.

## 5. Deaf Sign Language

For readers who know nothing about the characteristics of any deaf sign language, Klima and Bellugi provide perhaps the most attractive introduction, from which one can go on to explore books on more technical aspects (e.g. Poizner *et al.*) or on languages other than ASL (e.g. Kyle and Woll). The case for a gestural origin for human language (criticized in Chapter 4) has been restated recently by Armstrong, Stokoe, and Wilcox.

Armstrong, David F., Stokoe, William C., and Wilcox, Sherman E. *Gesture and the Nature of Language*. Cambridge: Cambridge University Press, 1995.

Klima, Edward S., and Bellugi, Ursula. *The Signs of Language*. Cambridge, Mass.: Harvard University Press, 1979.

Kyle, J. G., and Woll, B. *Sign Language: The Study of Deaf People and their Language*. Cambridge: Cambridge University Press, 1985.

Poizner, Howard, Klima, Edward S., and Bellugi, Ursula. *What the Hands Reveal about the Brain*. Cambridge, Mass.: MIT Press, 1987.

## 6. Language and Other Primates

Many readers will already be aware of the controversy over whether apes, with training, can or cannot acquire a level of competency with sign language that deserves to be compared with what normal humans achieve. Savage-Rumbaugh and Lewin offer a positive answer. Savage-Rumbaugh in *Ape Language* also offers a more detailed account of chimpanzees' signalling abilities using a keyboard of arbitrary symbols rather than manual signs. But more striking than any of these findings, in my view, are the discoveries documented by Cheney and Seyfarth about monkey communication in the wild. Goodall offers an immensely impressive account of the lives of chimpanzees in the wild, though she devotes proportionately less space to vocal communication.

Cheney, Dorothy L, and Seyfarth, Robert M. *How Monkeys See the World: Inside the Mind of Another Species*. Chicago: University of Chicago Press, 1990.

Goodall, Jane. *The Chimpanzees of Gombe: Patterns of Behavior*. Cambridge, Mass.: Harvard University Press, 1986.

Savage-Rumbaugh, E. Sue. *Ape Language: From Conditioned Response to Symbol*. New York: Columbia University Press, 1986.

—— and Lewin, Roger. *Kanzi: The Ape at the Brink of the Human Mind*. New York: Wiley, 1994.

## 7. Language Evolution from a Linguistic Perspective

A paradox, mentioned in Chapter 1, is that, of the specialist disciplines relevant to language evolution, linguistics has contributed least during the twentieth century. That said, there have been notable, though controversial, contributions by the linguists Derek Bickerton and Philip Lieberman, both of whom write in a manner accessible to the general reader. Aitchison and Foley provide the only up-to-date overviews of the field from a linguistic point of view. Jespersen's book is extremely readable and stimulating, though due allowance must be made for its age. Anybody intending to study language evolution seriously needs at an early stage to read Pinker and Bloom's article and the peer commentary on it.

Aitchinson, Jean. *The Seeds of Speech: Language Origin and Evolution.* Cambridge: Cambridge University Press, 1996.

Bickerton, Derek. *Language and Species.* Chicago: University of Chicago Press, 1990.

—— *Language and Human Behavior.* Seattle: University of Washington Press, 1995.

Foley, William A. *Anthropological Linguistics: An Introduction.* Oxford: Blackwell, 1997.

Jespersen, Otto. *Language: Its Nature, Development and Origin.* London: Allen & Unwin, 1922.

Lieberman, Philip. *The Biology and Evolution of Language.* Cambridge, Mass.: Harvard University Press, 1984.

—— *Uniquely Human: The Evolution of Speech, Thought and Selfless Behavior.* Cambridge, Mass: Harvard University Press, 1991.

Pinker, Steven, and Bloom, Paul. "Natural language and natural selection" [with peer commentary and response]. *Behavioral and Brain Sciences*, 13: 707–84.

## 8. Philosophical Implications

Twentieth-century philosophers have taken little interest in language evolution and in the relationship between human language and other animal communication systems. (Exceptions are Jonathan Bennett, cited here, and Daniel Dennett, cited in Section 2 above.) In particular, there has been no discussion at all (so far as I can discover) of the issue raised in Chapter 3: whether the distinction between truth and reference is motivated independently of the distinction between sentences and NPs. The closest approach to this is the discussion by Strawson of the relationship between the grammatical and logical notions of 'subject' and 'predicate'—technical, but accessible to anyone with persistence and little background in philosophy such as one might glean from Bertrand Russell's classic introduction.

Bennett, Jonathan. *Linguistic Behaviour.* Cambridge: Cambridge University Press, 1976.

Russell, Bertrand. *The Problems of Philosophy.* London: Thornton Butterworth, 1912. (Reprinted more recently by Oxford University Press.)

Strawson, P. F. *Logico-Linguistic Papers.* London: Methuen, 1971.

# Name Index

# Subject Index

Abkhaz 74
Acheulean tools, *see* hand-axe
achievement 25, 28
acoustics of speech 126–9, 138–9
action-or-state 86, 87, 163
  *see also* predicate–argument structure
activity 25, 28
adaptation 12, 123–5, 131–2, 182, 184
  language as 80, 173
Afrikaans 120, 122
agrammatism 195
American Sign Language 103, 213–15
ape language experiments 215–25, 228
aphasia, *see* Broca's aphasia; Wernicke's aphasia
Aquatic Ape Theory 183
Arabic 166
archaeological evidence 177–81
argument 99
  *see also* predicate–argument structure
assertion 28–9, 60, 63–5, 83
  in Frege's philosophy 36
  by means of a NP 30, 31–2, 153
  *see also* reference, versus truth
'Asyntactic' communication 15–16, 97
Austin (chimpanzee) 216–17
Australia, earliest population of 177
australopithecines 74, 97, 174, 183
autonomous syntax 78
auxiliary 4, 82–3, 165–9

babbling 137
basicranial flexion 183
Berber 140, 164
bipedalism 182–4, 231
blending of calls 70–1
blurred affix 117
bonobo, *see* Kanzi
brain–language coevolution 203–9
brain size 189–91
  and vocabulary size 11
British Sign Language 103

Broca's aphasia 195–203
Broca's area 187, 209, 210, 212

captions 31–2
categorical statement 26, 95, 172
cell in paradigm 112
Chinese 84, 103, 137, 202
  writing system 14
class-default 116
class-identifier 116
closed call system, *see* openness of call system
coda of syllable 136, 139–43
  in relation to object 169–70
  *see also* margin of syllable
cognitive and social factors in language
    evolution 9–10, 131–2, 171–2, 174, 191–4,
    227, 230–1
  *see also* mental representation
cognitive grammar 90
collocational restriction 122
comment, *see* topic
complement 146
complete expression, *see* expression, in
    Spatiotemporal
completeness 57–60
conceptual structure 78
  *see also* mental representation
content, *see* judgeable content
continuist theory, *see* discontinuist view of
    language evolution
contrast, *see* Principle of Contrast
Cooperative Principle 30
creole language 85
cross-modal association 209

deontic modal 167
determiner phrase 3 n.
Diegueño 214
discontinuist view of language evolution 150,
    153, 180, 205, 208, 210–12
disjunctive categories 108–10, 120

Printed in the United Kingdom
by Lightning Source UK Ltd.
120667UK00001B/452